*For William E. Leuchtenburg*
*our teacher and friend*
*with gratitude and affection*
     *–W.H.C.*
     *–H.S.*

*and for Max*
     *–B.B.*

# Contents

# Preface

More than two decades ago, when we first contemplated putting together a collection of documents and essays on U.S. history since 1945, we agreed that our overriding aim was a book that addressed the *real* concerns and needs of the students we knew and taught, one lively and challenging enough to provoke discussions in the dorm room as well as the classroom. That is still our aim. Of course, much has changed in the intervening years, and this seventh edition addresses new matters of interest and new viewpoints on continuing issues of relevance. As always, we have incorporated the suggestions of students and instructors who used earlier editions of *A History of Our Time*. We are grateful for such advice and hope to continue to receive recommendations for future editions.

As in the earlier editions, this book is structured to give students the opportunity to hear different voices of and about the past, to enable them to compare and contrast, and thus to provide a basis for asking critical questions and arriving at independent judgments on major issues. Consequently, each section of the book contains an introduction and headnotes that place the readings in historical perspective and highlight their relevance, documents that provide first-hand, and personal, analyses of postwar issues, and well-written essays that both convey the drama and "humanness" of history and reveal the diversity of themes and interpretations of the recent past. Much, of necessity, has been left out of this brief collection, and we urge those interested to consult the updated Suggestions for Further Reading.

The recent past is not dead; indeed, much of it is not even past. We firmly believe that the history of the last half-century still strongly influences our lives and that any conscious shaping of the future requires an understanding of this past. To that end, this collection illuminates the major political and social developments and events from the anxieties of the Cold War and McCarthyism to the movements for political and social change in the 1960s, the American involvement in the Vietnam War, and the conservative backlash in the 1970s and 1980s.

In its final two sections, the collection focuses on the United States and the world in the post–Cold War era, and then offers documents that should encourage discussion of some of the significant issues that Americans discuss today: environmental change, globalization, immigration, the meaning of race and ethnicity, the state of marriage, the relationship of science and religion, and the "culture wars."

We hope that this edition of *A History of Our Time* will help readers better understand America's past and also serve as a guide to some of the unresolved questions in American life as we face the challenges of the Twenty-first century.

| | |
|---|---|
| *Durham, N.C.* | *W. H. C.* |
| *Durham, N.H.* | *H. S.* |
| *Philadelphia, P.A.* | *B. B.* |

# A History of Our Time

# Part 1

## AMERICA BECOMES
## A WORLD POWER

On May 14, 1945, *Time* magazine celebrated the Allied victory over Nazi Germany with a cover portraying "the Big Three": a drawing of three smiling soldiers, one from the United States, one from Great Britain, and one from the Soviet Union, each holding his nation's flag. Despite the unity *Time* portrayed, relations among the major World War II Allies were under strain throughout the war. Leaders of the three nations struggled over priorities and strategies in their attempt to defeat the Axis powers. Franklin Roosevelt, the president who had led the United States through the Great Depression and into war (following Japan's attack on Pearl Harbor in December 1941), refused Stalin's repeated requests for American and British troops to open a "second front" that would draw German troops away from their massive invasion of the USSR, joining, instead, the British campaign against the Germans in North Africa. By spring 1943, against all odds, the Soviets had stopped the German invasion—but at the cost of millions and millions of lives. As the end of the war neared, it was ever clearer that the uneasy alliance between the United States and the Soviet Union would not hold.

World War II caused global devastation. At the end of the war, millions lay dead. Cities were turned to rubble—or ash. Factories were destroyed, economies devastated. The old European imperial powers had lost their might, and their former colonies asserted their independence. Of the major wartime combatants, only the United States emerged from the war stronger than when it began. America was physically untouched by the war that had laid waste to nations in Europe, Africa, and Asia. The United States was the most powerful nation in the world. But as America sought to shape the global chaos, the Soviet Union countered American power. The Soviets wanted secure borders and control over those nations closest to Russia; they sought to refashion Eastern Europe in the Soviet image. The United States, in contrast, insisted that the war had been fought for self-determination, territorial integrity, free trade, and traditional Western freedoms. This conflict over priorities and values would come to a head in the immediate postwar years, exacerbated by a dangerous nuclear arms race between the two nations.

The resulting Cold War between the United States and the Soviet Union defined the half-century after World War II. It shaped international relations around the globe, not only in the Soviet Union's geographic proximity, but in Latin America and Asia as well. As former imperial powers lost or ceded control over colonial holdings to nations that became the "Third World," both major powers attempted to wield influence and claim allies. From struggles over the future of Germany and Poland and Greece, to those within China, Korea, and Vietnam, loomed Cold War understandings of a world divided between Soviet and American influence.

The enormous and still-growing literature on the causes and origins of the Cold War presents students with an array of conflicting interpretations. Historians disagree on whether the United States or the Soviet Union was most responsible for the conflict, on whether the Cold War could have been avoided, and on which factors determined the shape it took. What influence, they have asked, did the existence of atomic weaponry have in shaping the Cold War? What roles were played by domestic politics, or by the economic systems and relative economic strengths of the two nations? How did geopolitics, ideology, concerns about national security, and the personalities of national leaders determine the actions of the two superpowers? These debates became even more complicated at the end of the Cold War, when once-secret documents from the Soviet Union, as well as formerly classified U.S. materials, became available to historians.

Part 1 contains material on the Cold War's role in both foreign affairs and domestic life. The material on foreign affairs includes a historian's introduction to the origins of the Cold War, along with documents written in the mid-1940s through the early 1960s that shed light on America's rise to world power and the U.S. policy of "containment" of the Soviet Union. Historian Robert McMahon argues that the Cold War was virtually inescapable, given the vacuum of power left in the wake of World War II and the powerfully conflicting interests of the United States and the Soviet Union. Primary documents shed light on the development of American Cold War policy. Writing from Moscow in early 1946, American diplomat George F. Kennan warned of an expansionist Soviet communist system and proposed policies that might serve to contain it "without recourse to war." The world did come to the brink of nuclear war in October 1962, as the United States squared off against the Soviet Union in the Cuban Missile Crisis. President Kennedy's October 22 speech to the nation makes clear the enormous stakes involved in this confrontation. The Missile Crisis, in fact, was a turning point in the Cold War, as both nations attempted to stabilize relations and move in the direction of limiting the arms race.

Reading these selections, students ought to consider such questions as: Was the Cold War virtually inevitable, as historian Robert McMahon argues? If so, what made it so? If not, how could it have been avoided? Or, at least, how could its pervasive costs have been minimized? In what areas was compromise possible? Would it have made much difference if Roosevelt had lived and remained president until 1949? Or if Stalin had died in 1945? How did the Cold War logic lead to American involvement in the struggles in Korea, and then in Vietnam? Why did the Cuban Missile Crisis serve as a watershed in the ongoing Cold War struggle? And finally, how does the end of the Cold War lead us to understand its origins and its powerful role in international relations from 1945 to 1991?

Worsening relations between the United States and the Soviet Union after World War II shaped not only international relations but also domestic life. Following the end of the war, America's former ally quickly moved to assert control over Eastern Europe. American apprehension grew when, before the end of the decade, the Soviet Union exploded its own atomic bomb. Tension escalated when Chinese communists took control of the Chinese mainland in 1949. American anxieties—reasonable ones in a world just beginning recovery from a worldwide conflagration that had killed millions—affected domestic policy, politics, and even family life.

This section demonstrates the domestic impact of the Cold War with a series of primary documents. The United States had never before maintained a large standing military in peacetime, nor devoted a large percentage of its national budget to military and defense spending. The Cold War seemed to make such growth necessary. But President Eisenhower, in his farewell address to the nation, warned against the growing "military-industrial complex" and its potential threat to the democratic governance of the nation. American fears of nuclear war are captured by a *Good Housekeeping* editorial from the magazine's 1958 Thanksgiving issue that explains what American families could expect following an attack.

The American public was rightly concerned about U.S.-Soviet relations. But Cold War fears left Americans unsure where to draw the line between caution in a volatile world and the sort of paranoia that destroyed innocent lives and curtailed civil liberties and free speech.

Three documents illustrate the techniques and impacts of the postwar Red Scare that came to be known after its most visible practioner: McCarthyism. The first, an excerpt from the House Un-American Activities Committee's (HUAC) 1947 investigation of communism in Hollywood, illustrates the reach of the postwar Red Scare. The second, a revised version of Senator McCarthy's February 1950 speech, in which he falsely insisted that he had a list of 205 card-carrying communists in the State Department, illustrates his "big lie" tactics. Finally, two historians, John Earl Haynes and Harvey Klehr, offer powerful evidence, based on newly available documents, that there were communist spies in the atomic weapons program and U.S. government, and that American government officials had certain knowledge of that fact.

Students should consider how newly opened archives complicate our understanding of Cold War anticommunism and its lessons. Historians have generally seen this movement as an example of national hysteria, in which government officials engaged in a "witch-hunt" or a "search for scapegoats to take the blame" for "America's difficulties in the world," to quote an earlier edition of *A History of Our Time*. Does the proof offered by historians John Earl Haynes and Harvey Klehr challenge that interpretation? How should knowledge that the American government had proof that Soviet spies operated within the United States be combined with our knowledge that McCarthyism and the postwar Red Scare limited vital political debate and destroyed the careers, even lives, of loyal Americans? These questions might lead to others: Why would Hollywood be an obvious target for HUAC or for any group attempting to control the sentiments of the nation? Could leaders with actual knowledge of Soviet espionage have prevented the spread of suspicion throughout the nation, the ruin of innocent lives, the loss of dissenting voices, and the quashing of democratic debate?

Finally, it is worth considering the question in its broadest form: What are the valid limits of ideological dissent in a democracy? As the nation faces new challenges to civil liberties following an undeniably real incident of terrorism, America's domestic Cold War experience is especially worth pondering.

# World War II and the Destruction of the Old Order

*Robert McMahon*

*In this excerpt from* The Cold War: A Very Short Introduction, *diplomatic historian Robert McMahon builds on the long history of debate about the origins of the Cold War. He argues that the Cold War was, if not inevitable, at least close to it—not because of the particular intentions of either the United States or the Soviet Union, but because World War II had devastated a huge portion of the globe. Facing what many at the time understood to be the threat of global anarchy, both emerging "superpowers" sought to impose order and stability. And they did so in accordance with their own understandings of national security, with their own visions of right, of progress, and of the proper future shape of the world. At the same time, their courses were influenced by the specifics of personality and of each nation's history. McMahon's argument that the devastation and disorder caused by World War II is the critical condition for the origins of the Cold War is not only a useful way to begin to understand the four decades of Cold War struggle that reached well beyond the two main antagonists, but also the most important way to begin to understand the postwar era in the United States. Though America emerged from the war with unprecedented and unequaled strength, "lessons" drawn from this war continued to shape the nation's foreign and domestic policies, and the American people felt their lives shaped by the lingering shadow of this terrible conflagration, often in unpredictable ways.*

Explanations for the onset of the Cold War must begin with World War II. A conflict that ranks, by any conceivable measure, as the most destructive in human history, World War II brought unparalleled levels of death, devastation, privation, and disorder.

"The conflagration of 1939–1945 was so wrenching, so total, so profound, that a world was overturned," notes historian Thomas G. Paterson, "not simply a human world of healthy and productive laborers, farmers, merchants, financiers, and intellectuals, not simply a secure world of close-knit families and communities, not simply a military world of Nazi storm troopers and Japanese kamikazes, but all that and more." By unhinging as well "the world of stable politics, inherited wisdom, traditions, institutions, alliances, loyalties, commerce and classes," the war created the conditions that made great power conflict highly likely, if not inevitable.

## A WORLD OVERTURNED

Approximately 60 million people lost their lives as a direct result of the war, fully two-thirds of them noncombatants. The war's losers, the Axis states of Germany, Japan, and Italy, suffered more than 3 million civilian deaths; their conquerors, the Allies, suffered far more: at least 35 million civilian deaths. An astonishing 10 to 20% of the total populations of the Soviet Union, Poland, and Yugoslavia perished, between 4 and 6% of the total populations of Germany, Italy, Austria, Hungary, Japan, and China. If the exact toll of this wrenching global conflagration continues to defy all efforts at statistical precision, the magnitude of the human losses it claimed surely remains as shockingly unfathomable two generations after World War II as it was in the conflict's immediate aftermath. . . .

The vast swath of death and destruction precipitated by the war left not only much of Europe and Asia in ruins but the old international order as well. . . . Indeed, the Eurocentric international system that had dominated world affairs for the past 500 years had, virtually overnight, vanished. Two continent-sized military behemoths—already being dubbed superpowers—had risen in its stead, each intent upon forging a new order consonant with its particular needs and values. As the war moved into its final phase, even the most casual observer of world politics could see that the United States and the Soviet Union held most of the military, economic, and diplomatic cards. On one basic goal, those adversaries-turned-allies were in essential accord: that some semblance of authority and stability needed to be restored with dispatch—and not just to those areas directly affected by the war but to the broader international system as well. The task was as urgent as it was daunting since, as Under Secretary of State Joseph Grew warned in June 1945: "Anarchy may result from the present economic distress and political unrest."

The immediate roots of the Cold War, at least in broad, structural terms, lay in the intersection between a world rendered prostrate by a devastating global conflict and the conflicting recipes for international order that Washington and Moscow sought to impose on that pliable, war-shattered world. Some degree of conflict invariably results whenever a prevailing international order and its accompanying balance of power system are overturned. One would certainly expect no less when the overturning occurs with such shattering suddenness. The tension, suspicion, and rivalry that came to plague US–Soviet relations in the immediate aftermath of war was, in that elemental sense, hardly a surprise. Yet the *degree* and *scope* of the ensuing conflict, and particularly its *duration,* cannot be explained by appeals to structural forces alone. History, after all, offers numerous examples of great powers following the path of compromise and cooperation, opting to act in concert so as to establish a mutually acceptable international order capable of satisfying the most fundamental interests of each. Scholars have employed the term "great power condominium" to describe such systems. Despite the hopes of some leading officials in both the United States and the Soviet Union, however, that would not be the case this time. The reasons why go to the heart of the question of Cold War origins. In brief, it was the divergent aspirations, needs, histories, governing institutions, and ideologies of the United States and the Soviet Union that turned unavoidable tensions into the epic four-decade confrontation that we call the Cold War.

## AMERICAN VISIONS OF POSTWAR ORDER

The United States emerged from the wreckage of World War II with relatively moderate losses. Although some 400,000 of the nation's soldiers and sailors gave their lives in the struggle against the Axis powers, approximately three-quarters of them on the battlefield, it bears emphasizing that those numbers represent less than 1% of the war's overall death toll and less than 2% of the losses suffered by America's Soviet partner. For most US civilians, in stunning contrast to their counterparts across Europe, East Asia, North Africa, and elsewhere, the war meant not suffering and privation but prosperity—even abundance. The nation's gross domestic product doubled between

1941 and 1945, bestowing the wonders of a highly productive, full-employment economy on a citizenry that had become accustomed to the deprivations imposed by a decade-long depression. Real wages rose rapidly and dramatically during the war years, and homefront Americans found themselves awash in a cornucopia of now-affordable consumer goods. "The American people," remarked the director of the Office of War Mobilization and Reconversion, "are in the pleasant predicament of having to learn to live 50 percent better than they have ever lived before."

In March 1945, newly installed President Harry S. Truman was merely stating the self-evident when he commented: "We have emerged from this war the most powerful nation in the world—the most powerful nation, perhaps, in all history." Yet neither the economic benefits conferred on the American people by the war nor the soaring military power, productive strength, and international prestige attained by their nation during the struggle against Axis aggression could lessen the frightening uncertainties of the new world ushered in by the war. The Japanese attack at Pearl Harbor decisively shattered the illusion of invulnerability that Americans had enjoyed ever since the end of the Napoleonic Wars of the early 19th century. The obsession with national security that became so central a motif of US foreign and defence policy throughout the Cold War era can be traced back directly to the myth-puncturing events that culminated with the Japanese strike of 7 December 1941. Not until the terrorist attacks on New York and Washington 60 years later would Americans again experience so direct, and so wholly unanticipated, an assault on their homeland.

Military strategists took several lessons from the bold Japanese strike, each of which carried profound implications for the future. They became convinced, first, that technology, and especially air power, had so contracted the globe that America's vaunted two-ocean barrier no longer afforded sufficient protection from external assault. True security now required a defence that began well beyond the home shores—a defence in depth, in military parlance. That concept led defence officials of the Roosevelt and Truman administrations to advocate the establishment of an integrated, global network of US-controlled air and naval bases, as well as the negotiation of widespread military air transit rights. Together, those would allow the United States to project its power more easily into potential trouble spots and to stifle or deter prospective enemies long before they gained the power to strike at American territory. A sense of how extensive US military base requirements were can be gleaned from a 1946 list of "essential" sites compiled by the State Department; it included, among other locales, Burma, Canada, the Fiji Islands, New Zealand, Cuba, Greenland, Ecuador, French Morocco, Senegal, Iceland, Liberia, Panama, Peru, and the Azores.

Second, and even more broadly, senior American strategists determined that the nation's military power must never again be allowed to atrophy. US military strength, they were agreed, must form a core element of the new world order. The Franklin D. Roosevelt and Harry S. Truman administrations were, accordingly, insistent upon maintaining naval and air forces second to none; a strong military presence in the Pacific; dominance of the Western hemisphere; a central role in the occupations of defeated adversaries Italy, Germany, Austria, and Japan; and a continued monopoly on the atomic bomb. Even before the eruption of the Cold War, US strategic planners were operating from an extraordinarily expansive concept of national security.

That broad vision of the nation's security requirements was reinforced by a third, overarching lesson that US policy-makers drew from the World War II experience: namely, that never again could a hostile state, or coalition of states, be allowed to gain preponderant control over the populations, territories, and resources of Europe and East Asia. The Eurasian heartland, as geopoliticians were fond of labelling it, ranked as the world's greatest strategic-economic prize; its combination of rich natural resources, advanced industrial infrastructure, skilled labour, and sophisticated military facilities made it the fulcrum of world power, as the events of 1940–1 made painfully clear. When the Axis powers seized control over much of Eurasia in the early 1940s, they gained the wherewithal to wage protracted war, subvert the world economy, commit heinous crimes against humanity, and threaten and ultimately attack the Western hemisphere. If such an eventuality came to pass again, US defence officials worried, the international system would once again be badly destabilized, the balance of world power dangerously distorted, and the physical safety of the United States put at grave risk. Moreover, even if a direct attack on the United States could be averted, American leaders would still be forced to prepare for one—and that would mean a radical increase in both military spending and the size of its permanent defence establishment, a reconfiguration of the domestic economy, and the curtailment of cherished economic and political freedoms at home. Axis dominance of Eurasia, in short, or control over Eurasia by any future enemy, would thus also jeopardize the political economy of freedom so crucial to core US beliefs and values. The World War II experience thus offered hard lessons about the critical importance of maintaining a favourable balance of power in Eurasia.

The military-strategic dimensions of world order were, in American thinking, inseparable from the economic dimensions. US planners viewed the establishment of a freer and more open international economic system as equally indispensable to the new order they were determined to construct from the ashes of history's most horrific conflict. Experience had instructed them, Secretary of State Cordell Hull recalled, that free trade stood as an essential prerequisite for peace. The autarky, closed trading blocs, and nationalistic barriers to foreign investment and currency convertibility that had characterized the depression decade just encouraged interstate rivalry and conflict. A more open world, according to the American formula, would be a more prosperous world; and a more prosperous world would, in turn, be a more stable and peaceful world. To achieve those ends, the United States pushed hard in wartime diplomatic councils for a multilateral economic regime of liberalized trade, equal investment opportunities for all nations, stable exchange rates, and full currency convertibility. At the Bretton Woods Conference late in 1944, the United States gained general acceptance of those principles, along with support for the establishment of two key supranational bodies, the International Monetary Fund and the International Bank for Reconstruction and Development (World Bank), charged with helping to stabilize the global economy. That the United States, the world's leading capitalist state and one that was producing an astonishing 50% of the world's goods and services at war's end, would surely benefit from the new, multilateral commercial regime so vigorously endorsed by the Roosevelt and Truman administrations and the US business community was a given. American ideals here were inextricably interwoven with American interests.

In a December 1944 editorial, the *Chicago Tribune* captured the buoyancy and self-confidence of American society when it proudly proclaimed that it was "the good fortune of the world," and not just the United States, that "power and unquestionable intentions" now "went together" in the Great American Republic. Such convictions about the righteous destiny of the United States tapped deep roots within American history and culture. Elites and non-elites alike accepted the notion that it was their country's historic responsibility to bring about a new, more peaceful, prosperous, and stable world. US leaders betrayed few doubts about the ability of their nation to effect so momentous a transition; nor did they acknowledge any potential conflict between the global order they sought to forge and the needs and interests of the rest of humanity. With the hubris of a people who had known few failures, Americans thought that they could, in Dean Acheson's choice words, "grab hold of history and make it conform." Only one significant obstacle loomed. The Soviet Union, cautioned *Life* magazine in July 1945, "is the number one problem for Americans because it is the only country in the world with the dynamic power to challenge our own conceptions of truth, justice, and the good life."

## SOVIET VISIONS OF POSTWAR ORDER

The Soviet blueprint for postwar order was also born of deep-rooted security fears. As in the American case, those fears were refracted through the filters of history, culture, and ideology. Soviet memories of Hitler's surprise attack of June 1941 were just as vivid—and far more terrifying—than were American memories of Pearl Harbor. It could hardly have been otherwise in a land that had endured such staggering losses. Of the 15 Soviet Republics, 9 had been occupied in whole or in part by the Germans. Hardly any Soviet citizens remained untouched personally by what they came to sanctify as The Great Patriotic War. Nearly every family lost a loved one; most sacrificed several. In addition to the millions of human lives cut short by the conflict, 1,700 cities and towns, more than 70,000 villages and hamlets, and 31,000 factories were demolished. Leningrad, the country's most historic city, was decimated in a prolonged siege that alone claimed over a million lives. The German invasion also wreaked havoc with the nation's agricultural base, destroying millions of acres of crops and resulting in the slaughter of tens of millions of cattle, hogs, sheep, goats, and horses.

Searing memories of the German attack and occupation merged with other, longer memories—of the German invasion during World War I, of Allied intervention during the Russian civil war, of Napoleon's attempted conquest of Russia at the beginning of the previous century—to induce in the Soviet leadership a veritable obsession with ensuring the protection of their homeland from future territorial violations. The geographical expanse of the Soviet Union, a nation that covered one-sixth of the earth's land mass and was three times larger than the United States, made the challenge of an adequate national defence especially acute. Its two most economically vital regions, European Russia and Siberia, lay at the country's extremes; and each had in the recent past shown itself highly vulnerable to attack. The former fronted on the infamous Polish corridor, the invasion route through which the troops of Napoleon, the Kaiser, and Hitler had so easily poured in the past. The latter had twice within the last 25 years fallen prey to Japanese aggression; Siberia, moreover, shared a vast land border with China, an unstable neighbour still in the throes of revolutionary upheaval. No friendly neighbours, such as Mexico and Canada, and no two-ocean barriers existed to ease the task of Soviet defence planners.

The overwhelming need to defend the Soviet homeland lay at the heart of all Kremlin designs for the postwar world. Blocking the Polish invasion route, or "gateway," ranked foremost in that regard. Poland, stressed Stalin, was "a matter of life or death" to his country. "In the course of twenty-five years the Germans had twice invaded Russia via Poland," Soviet ruler Joseph Stalin lectured US envoy Harry Hopkins in May 1945. "Neither the British nor the American people had experienced such German invasions which were a horrible thing to endure. . . . It is therefore in Russia's vital interest that Poland should be strong and friendly." Convinced that the Germans would recover quickly and once again pose a threat to the Soviet Union, Stalin considered it mandatory that steps be taken while the world was still malleable to ensure future Soviet security needs. Those required, at a minimum, that acquiescent, pro-Soviet governments be installed in Poland and other key Eastern European states; that Soviet borders be expanded to their fullest pre-revolutionary extent—meaning the permanent annexation of the Baltic states and the eastern part of pre-war Poland; and that Germany be hobbled through a harsh occupation regime, systematic de-industrialization, and extensive reparations obligations. German reparations could also contribute to the massive rebuilding effort facing the Soviet Union as it sought to recover from the ravages of the war.

Yet those plans, based as they were on the age-old formula of security-through-expansion, needed to be balanced against a countervailing desire to maintain the framework of cooperation with the

United States and Great Britain that had evolved, however imperfectly, during the war years. The Kremlin's interest in sustaining the Grand Alliance partnership forged in the heat of total war rested not on sentiment, which had no place in Soviet diplomacy, but on a set of quite practical considerations. First, Soviet rulers recognized that an open break with the West needed to be avoided, at least for the foreseeable future. Given the crippling losses to manpower, resources, and industrial plant inflicted on their nation by the war, a premature conflict with the United States and Great Britain would place the Soviets at a severe disadvantage, a disadvantage made even more palpable after the US demonstration of its atomic capabilities in August 1945. Second, Stalin and his chief lieutenants were hopeful that the United States could be induced to make good on its promise of generous financial support to their reconstruction efforts. A policy of unbridled territorial expansion would likely prove counterproductive, since it could precipitate the very dissolution of the wartime alliance and consequent withholding of economic assistance that they sought to prevent.

Finally, the Soviets were looking to be treated as a respected, responsible great power after being shunned as a pariah state for so long. They craved respect, somewhat paradoxically, from the same capitalist states their ideological convictions taught them to loathe. The Russians wanted not just respect, of course; they insisted upon an equal voice in international councils and acceptance of the legitimacy of their interests. Even more to the point, they sought formal Western recognition of their expanded borders and acceptance of, or at least acquiescence in, their emerging sphere of influence in Eastern Europe. All those considerations served as brakes on any imprudent inclinations to gobble up as much territory as the Red Army's naked power might allow.

The fact that one of history's most brutal, ruthless, and suspicious rulers presided over the Soviet Union's delicate balancing act at this critical juncture adds an unavoidable personal element to the story of Moscow's postwar ambitions. The imperious Stalin completely dominated Soviet policy-making before, during, and after the war, brooking no dissent. In the recollection of Nikita Khrushchev, Stalin's eventual successor, "he spoke and we listened." The former Bolshevik revolutionary "transformed the government he ran and even the country he ruled, during the 1930s, into a gargantuan extension of his own pathologically suspicious personality," suggests historian

John Lewis Gaddis. It was a "supreme act of egoism" that "spawned innumerable tragedies." In the aftermath of World War II, Stalin viewed his Western allies, as he viewed all potential competitors at home and abroad, with the deepest suspicion and mistrust.

Yet Russian foreign policy cannot be understood as the product, pure and simple, of Stalin's brutishness and unquenchable thirst for dominance, as important as those surely were. For all his ruthlessness and paranoia, and for all his cruelty towards his own people, Stalin pursued a generally cautious, circumspect foreign policy, seeking always to balance opportunity with risk. The Russian dictator invariably calculated with great care the prevailing "correlation of forces". He evinced a realist's respect for the superior military and industrial power possessed by the United States and oft-times sought the proverbial half a loaf when pursuit of a full loaf seemed likely to generate resistance. The needs of the Soviet state, which always took precedence for Stalin over the desire to spread communism, dictated a policy that mixed opportunism with caution and an inclination to compromise, not a strategy of aggressive expansion.

The ideology of Marxism-Leninism that undergirded the Soviet state also influenced the outlook and policies of Stalin and his top associates, though in complex, hard-to-pin-down ways. A deep-seated belief in the teachings of Marx and Lenin imparted to them a messianic faith in the future, a reassuring sense of confidence that, whatever travails Moscow might face in the short run, history lay on their side. Stalin and the Kremlin elite assumed conflict between the socialist and capitalist worlds to be inevitable, and they were certain that the forces of proletarian revolution would eventually prevail. They were thus unwilling to press too hard when the correlation of forces seemed so favourable to the West. "Our ideology stands for offensive operations when possible," as Foreign Minister V. M. Molotov put it, "and if not we wait." If ideological certitude at times bred a cautious patience, at other times it distorted reality. Russian leaders failed to comprehend, for example, why so many East Germans and Eastern Europeans saw Red Army forces more as oppressors than liberators; they continued as well to calculate that a war between rival capitalist states was bound to occur and that the capitalist system would before long face another global depression.

Ideology imparted to Soviets and Americans alike a messianic faith in the world-historical roles of their respective nations. On each side of what would soon become the Cold War divide, leaders and ordinary citizens saw their countries acting for much broader purposes than the mere advancement of national interests. Soviets and Americans each, in fact, saw themselves acting out of noble motives—acting to usher humanity into a grand new age of peace, justice, and order. Married to the overwhelming power each nation possessed at a time when much of the world lay prostrate, those mirror-opposite ideological values provided a sure-fire recipe for conflict.

# The Necessity for Containment (1946)

## George F. Kennan

*A diplomat in the U.S. Embassy in Moscow and a leading expert on Soviet affairs, George F. Kennan sent a long, eight-thousand-word, secret telegram to the State Department early in 1946 sketching the roots of Soviet policy and warning of serious difficulties with the Soviet Union in the years ahead. Kennan then recommended a long-term, firm policy of resistance by the United States to Soviet expansionism. Known as the containment policy, it became the basis of President Truman's foreign policy. In reading the excerpts from Kennan's telegram that follow, students should note Kennan's view of the methods the Soviet Union was likely to employ to expand its economic and political influence, the principles of Soviet foreign policy, the U.S. interests involved, what the United States has to fear from the Soviets, and the course of action the United States should take.*

### BASIC FEATURES OF POST WAR SOVIET OUTLOOK, AS PUT FORWARD BY OFFICIAL PROPAGANDA MACHINE, ARE AS FOLLOWS:

(a)  USSR still lives in antagonistic "capitalist encirclement" with which in the long run there can be no permanent peaceful coexistence. As stated by Stalin in 1927 to a delegation of American workers:

> In course of further development of international revolution there will emerge two centers of world significance: a socialist center, drawing to itself the countries which tend toward socialism, and a capitalist center, drawing to itself the countries that incline toward capitalism. Battle between these two centers for command of world economy will decide fate of capitalism and of communism in entire world.

Excerpted from U.S. Department of State, *Foreign Relations of the United States, 1946* (Washington, D.C., 1969), 6:697–99, 701–9.

(b) Capitalist world is beset with internal conflicts, inherent in nature of capitalist society. These conflicts are insoluble by means of peaceful compromise. Greatest of them is that between England and US.

(c) Internal conflicts of capitalism inevitably generate wars. Wars thus generated may be of two kinds: intra-capitalist wars between two capitalist states, and wars of intervention against socialist world. Smart capitalists, vainly seeking escape from inner conflicts of capitalism, incline toward latter.

(d) Intervention against USSR, while it would be disastrous to those who undertook it, would cause renewed delay in progress of Soviet socialism and must therefore be forestalled at all costs.

(e) Conflicts between capitalist states, though likewise fraught with danger for USSR, nevertheless hold out great possibilities for advancement of socialist cause, particularly if USSR remains militarily powerful, ideologically monolithic and faithful to its present brilliant leadership.

. . . So much for premises. To what deductions do they lead from standpoint of Soviet policy? To following:

(a) Everything must be done to advance relative strength of USSR as factor in international society. Conversely, no opportunity must be missed to reduce strength and influence, collectively as well as individually, of capitalist powers.

(b) Soviet efforts, and those of Russia's friends abroad, must be directed toward deepening and exploiting of differences and conflicts between capitalist powers. If these eventually deepen into an "imperialist" war, this war must be turned into revolutionary upheavals within the various capitalist countries.

(c) "Democratic-progressive" elements abroad are to be utilized to maximum to bring pressure to bear on capitalist governments along lines agreeable to Soviet interests.

(d) Relentless battle must be waged against socialist and social-democratic leaders abroad. . . .

## BACKGROUND OF OUTLOOK

Before examining ramifications of this party line in practice there are certain aspects of it to which I wish to draw attention.

First, it does not represent natural outlook of Russian people. . . .

But party line is binding for outlook and conduct of people who make up apparatus of power—party, secret police and Government—and it is exclusively with these that we have to deal.

Second, please note that premises on which this party line is based are for most part simply not true. Experience has shown that peaceful and mutually profitable coexistence of capitalist and socialist states is entirely possible. . . .

Nevertheless, all these theses, however baseless and disproven, are being boldly put forward again today. What does this indicate? It indicates that Soviet party line is not based on any objective analysis of situation beyond Russia's borders: that it has, indeed, little to do with conditions outside of Russia; that it arises mainly from basic inner-Russian necessities which existed before recent war and exist today.

At bottom of Kremlin's neurotic view of world affairs is traditional and instinctive Russian sense of insecurity. Originally, this was insecurity of a peaceful agricultural people trying to live on vast exposed plain in neighborhood of fierce nomadic peoples. To this was added, as Russia came into contact with economically advanced West, fear of more competent, more powerful, more highly organized societies in that area. . . . For this reason they have always feared foreign penetration, feared direct contact between Western world and their own, feared what would happen if Russians learned truth about world without or if foreigners learned truth about world within. And they have learned to seek security only in patient but deadly struggle for total destruction of rival power, never in compacts and compromises with it. . . .

## PROJECTION OF SOVIET OUTLOOK IN PRACTICAL POLICY ON OFFICIAL LEVEL

. . . (a) Internal policy devoted to increasing in every way strength and prestige of Soviet state: intensive military-industrialization; maximum development of armed forces; great displays to impress outsiders; continued secretiveness about internal matters, designed to conceal weaknesses and to keep opponents in dark.

(b) Wherever it is considered timely and promising, efforts will be made to advance official limits of Soviet power. . . .

(c) Russians will participate officially in international organizations where they see opportunity of extending Soviet power or of inhibiting or diluting power of others. . . .

(d) Toward colonial areas and backward or dependent peoples, Soviet policy, even on official plane, will be directed toward weakening of power and influence and contacts of advanced Western nations, on theory that in so far as this policy is successful, there will be created a vacuum which will favor Communist-Soviet penetration. . . .

## BASIC SOVIET POLICIES ON UNOFFICIAL, OR SUBTERRANEAN PLANE . . .

Agencies utilized for promulgation of policies on this plane are following:

1. Inner central core of Communist Parties in other countries . . . tightly coordinated and directed by Moscow. . . .
2. Rank and file of Communist Parties. . . . no longer even taken into confidence about realities of movement. . . .
3. A wide variety of national associations or bodies which can be dominated or influenced. . . . These include: labor unions, youth leagues, women's organizations, racial societies, religious societies, social organizations, cultural groups, liberal magazines, publishing houses, etc.
4. International organizations which can be similarly penetrated through influence over various national components. Labor, youth and women's organizations are prominent among them. . . .

It may be expected that component parts of this far-flung apparatus will be utilized . . . as follows:

(a) To undermine general political and strategic potential of major western powers. Efforts will be made in such countries to disrupt national self confidence, to hamstring measures of national defense, to increase social and industrial unrest, to stimulate all forms of disunity. . . . Here poor will be set against rich, black against white, young against old, newcomers against established residents, etc.

(b) On unofficial plane particularly violent efforts will be made to weaken power and influence of Western Powers of [on] colonial backward, or dependent peoples. On this level, no holds will be barred. . . .

(c) Where individual governments stand in path of Soviet purposes pressure will be brought for their removal from office. . . .

(d)  In foreign countries Communists will, as a rule, work toward destruction of all forms of personal independence, economic, political or moral.  . . .

(e)  Everything possible will be done to set major Western Powers against each other.  . . .

(f)  In general, all Soviet efforts on unofficial international plane will be negative and destructive in character, designed to tear down sources of strength beyond reach of Soviet control. . . . The Soviet regime is a police regime par excellence, reared in the dim half world of Tsarist police intrigue, accustomed to think primarily in terms of police power. This should never be lost sight of in gauging Soviet motives.  . . .

## PRACTICAL DEDUCTIONS FROM STANDPOINT OF US POLICY

In summary, we have here a political force committed fanatically to the belief that with US there can be no permanent *modus vivendi*, that it is desirable and necessary that the internal harmony of our society be disrupted, our traditional way of life be destroyed, the international authority of our state be broken, if Soviet power is to be secure. . . . This is admittedly not a pleasant picture. Problem of how to cope with this force in [*is*] undoubtedly greatest task our diplomacy has ever faced and probably greatest it will ever have to face. . . . I would like to record my conviction that problem is within our power to solve—and that without recourse to any general military conflict. And in support of this conviction there are certain observations of a more encouraging nature I should like to make:

1. Soviet power . . . does not take unnecessary risks. . . . For this reason it can easily withdraw—and usually does—when strong resistance is encountered at any point. Thus, if the adversary has sufficient force and makes clear his readiness to use it, he rarely has to do so. . . .

2. Gauged against Western World as a whole, Soviets are still by far the weaker force. Thus, their success will really depend on degree of cohesion, firmness and vigor which Western World can muster. . . .

3. Success of Soviet system, as form of internal power, is not yet finally proven. . . .

4. All Soviet propaganda beyond Soviet security sphere is basically negative and destructive. It should therefore be relatively easy to combat it by any intelligent and really constructive program.

For these reasons I think we may approach calmly and with good heart problem of how to deal with Russia. . . . [B]y way of conclusion, following comments:

1. Our first step must be to apprehend, and recognize for what it is, the nature of the movement with which we are dealing. . . .
2. We must see that our public is educated to realities of Russian situation. . . .
3. Much depends on health and vigor of our own society. World communism is like malignant parasite which feeds only on diseased tissue. . . .
4. We must formulate and put forward for other nations a much more positive and constructive picture of sort of world we would like to see than we have put forward in past. . . .
5. Finally we must have courage and self-confidence to cling to our own methods and conceptions of human society. After all, the greatest danger that can befall us in coping with this problem of Soviet communism, is that we shall allow ourselves to become like those with whom we are coping.

# The Cuban Missile Crisis: President Kennedy's Address to the Nation (1962)

*John F. Kennedy*

On Monday, October 22, 1962, President John F. Kennedy preempted regularly scheduled television programming to address the nation. The Soviet Union, he announced, had begun the process of installing ballistic missiles in Cuba; these missiles, if launched, could strike any city in the American Southeast.

Cuba's relationship with the United States was long and complicated. In the late nineteenth century, American interests had supported Cubans' efforts to free their country from Spain, and in 1898, U.S. victory in the Spanish-American War resulted in Cuban independence. The United States government, however, maintained the right to interfere in Cuban affairs. When a revolutionary movement brought an unfriendly government into power in 1933, the United States replaced this regime with one more friendly to U.S. interests. Under Fulgencia Batista, Cuba supported American foreign policy, welcomed U.S. investment, and became a mecca for American tourists seeking gambling, nightlife, and prostitution. In the late 1950s, Fidel Castro's rebels overthrew the corrupt regime of Batista. Castro vowed to end American dominance in Cuba. In 1960, he signed a trade treaty with the Soviet Union and seized North American–owned companies. President Eisenhower ended diplomatic relations with Cuba in early 1961, just before John Kennedy became president. Soon thereafter, on April 17, 1961, Kennedy went forward with a plan designed under Eisenhower to use CIA-trained Cuban exiles to invade the island, assuming that they would find broad support. The "Bay of Pigs" invasion failed; soon thereafter the CIA began developing plans for assassinating

*The History Place—Great Speeches Collection* (http://www.historyplace.com/speeches/jfk-cuban.htm).

*Castro; proposals included harpooning Castro while he snorkeled and providing him with poison-laced cigars.*

*The U.S. discovery of Soviet missile sites in Cuba, then, fit not only into the superpowers' Cold War but also into a tense relationship between the United States and Cuba. In days of intense discussion, advisors suggested options ranging from a full invasion of Cuba to secret diplomatic negotiations. Kennedy chose a middle option, publicly calling for Soviet withdrawal and instituting a naval quarantine of the island. The opposing superpowers came to the brink of nuclear war. But following secret negotiations, Soviet leader Nikita Khrushchev withdrew.*

*In reading Kennedy's speech, pay attention to his use of the "lessons" of World War II. Are these appropriate "lessons" on which to build foreign policy? How does Kennedy portray Cuba in this speech? How might you analyze his direct words to the people of Cuba? And why do you think that, in the months following this crisis, the United States and the Soviet Union worked to stabilize their relations?*

*Recordings of President Kennedy's meetings with his advisors during the crisis are available through the George Washington University National Security Archives, on-line at http://www.gwu.edu/~nsarchiv/nsa/cuba_mis_cri/audio.htm.*

Good evening my fellow citizens:

This Government, as promised, has maintained the closest surveillance of the Soviet Military buildup on the island of Cuba. Within the past week, unmistakable evidence has established the fact that a series of offensive missile sites is now in preparation on that imprisoned island. The purpose of these bases can be none other than to provide a nuclear strike capability against the Western Hemisphere.

Upon receiving the first preliminary hard information of this nature last Tuesday morning at 9 a.m., I directed that our surveillance be stepped up. And having now confirmed and completed our evaluation of the evidence and our decision on a course of action, this Government feels obliged to report this new crisis to you in fullest detail.

The characteristics of these new missile sites indicate two distinct types of installations. Several of them include medium range ballistic missiles capable of carrying a nuclear warhead for a distance of more than 1,000 nautical miles. Each of these missiles, in short, is capable of striking Washington, D.C., the Panama Canal, Cape Canaveral, Mexico City, or any other city in the southeastern part of the United States, in Central America, or in the Caribbean area.

Additional sites not yet completed appear to be designed for intermediate range ballistic missiles—capable of traveling more than twice as far—and thus capable of striking most of the major cities in the Western Hemisphere, ranging as far north as Hudson Bay, Canada, and as far south as Lima, Peru. In addition, jet bombers, capable of carrying nuclear weapons, are now being uncrated and assembled in Cuba, while the necessary air bases are being prepared.

This urgent transformation of Cuba into an important strategic base—by the presence of these large, long range, and clearly offensive weapons of sudden mass destruction—constitutes an explicit threat to the peace and security of all the Americas, in flagrant and deliberate defiance of the Rio Pact of 1947, the traditions of this Nation and hemisphere, the joint resolution of the 87th Congress, the Charter of the United Nations, and my own public warnings to the Soviets on September 4 and 13. This action also contradicts the repeated assurances of Soviet spokesmen, both publicly and privately delivered, that the arms buildup in Cuba would retain its original defensive character, and that the Soviet Union had no need or desire to station strategic missiles on the territory of any other nation.

The size of this undertaking makes clear that it has been planned for some months. Yet only last month, after I had made clear the distinction between any introduction of ground-to-ground missiles and the existence of defensive antiaircraft missiles, the Soviet Government publicly stated on September 11, and I quote, "the armaments and military equipment sent to Cuba are designed exclusively for defensive purposes," that, and I quote the Soviet Government, "there is no need for the Soviet Government to shift its weapons . . . for a retaliatory blow to any other country, for instance Cuba," and that, and I quote their government, "the Soviet Union has so powerful rockets to carry these nuclear warheads that there is no need to search for sites for them beyond the boundaries of the Soviet Union." That statement was false.

Only last Thursday, as evidence of this rapid offensive buildup was already in my hand, Soviet Foreign Minister Gromyko told me in my office that he was instructed to make it clear once again, as he said his government had already done, that Soviet assistance to Cuba, and I quote, "pursued solely the purpose of contributing to the the defense capabilities of Cuba," that, and I quote him, "training by Soviet specialists of Cuban nationals in handling defensive armaments was by no means offensive, and if it were otherwise," Mr. Gromyko went on, "the Soviet Government would never become involved in rendering such assistance." That statement also was false.

Neither the United States of America nor the world community of nations can tolerate deliberate deception and offensive threats on the part of any nation, large or small. We no longer live in a world where only the actual firing of weapons represents a sufficient challenge to a nation's security to constitute maximum peril. Nuclear weapons are so destructive and ballistic missiles are so swift, that any substantially increased possibility of their use or any sudden change in their deployment may well be regarded as a definite threat to peace.

For many years both the Soviet Union and the United States, recognizing this fact, have deployed strategic nuclear weapons with great care, never upsetting the precarious status quo which insured that these weapons would not be used in the absence of some vital challenge. Our own strategic missiles have never been transferred to the territory of any other nation under a cloak of secrecy and deception; and our history—unlike that of the Soviets since the end of World War II—demonstrates that we have no desire to dominate or conquer any other nation or impose our system upon its people. Nevertheless, American citizens have become adjusted to living daily on the Bull's-eye of Soviet missiles located inside the U.S.S.R. or in submarines.

In that sense, missiles in Cuba add to an already clear and present danger—although it should be noted the nations of Latin America have never previously been subjected to a potential nuclear threat.

But this secret, swift, and extraordinary buildup of Communist missiles—in an area well known to have a special and historical relationship to the United States and the nations of the Western Hemisphere, in violation of Soviet assurances, and in defiance of American and hemispheric policy—this sudden, clandestine decision to station strategic weapons for the first time outside of Soviet soil—is a deliberately provocative and unjustified change in the status quo which cannot be accepted by this country, if our courage and our commitments are ever to be trusted again by either friend or foe.

The 1930's taught us a clear lesson: aggressive conduct, if allowed to go unchecked and unchallenged ultimately leads to war. This nation is opposed to war. We are also true to our word. Our unswerving objective, therefore, must be to prevent the use of these missiles against this or any other country, and to secure their withdrawal or elimination from the Western Hemisphere.

Our policy has been one of patience and restraint, as befits a peaceful and powerful nation, which leads a worldwide alliance. We have been determined not to be diverted from our central concerns by mere irritants and fanatics. But now further action is required—and it is under way; and these actions may only be the beginning. We will not prematurely or unnecessarily risk the costs of worldwide nuclear war in which even the fruits of victory would be ashes in our mouth—but neither will we shrink from that risk at any time it must be faced.

Acting, therefore, in the defense of our own security and of the entire Western Hemisphere, and under the authority entrusted to me by the Constitution as endorsed by the resolution of the Congress, I have directed that the following initial steps be taken immediately:

- First: To halt this offensive buildup, a strict quarantine on all offensive military equipment under shipment to Cuba is being initiated. All ships of any kind bound for Cuba from whatever nation or port will, if found to contain cargoes of offensive weapons, be turned back. This quarantine will be extended, if needed, to other types of cargo and carriers. We are not at this time, however, denying the necessities of life as the Soviets attempted to do in their Berlin blockade of 1948.

- Second: I have directed the continued and increased close surveillance of Cuba and its military buildup. The foreign ministers of the OAS, in their communique of October 6, rejected secrecy in such matters in this hemisphere. Should these offensive military preparations continue, thus increasing the threat to the hemisphere, further action will be justified. I have directed the Armed Forces to prepare for any eventualities; and I trust that in the interest of both the Cuban people and the Soviet technicians at the sites, the hazards to all concerned in continuing this threat will be recognized.

- Third: It shall be the policy of this Nation to regard any nuclear missile launched from Cuba against any nation in the Western Hemisphere as an attack by the Soviet Union on the United States, requiring a full retaliatory response upon the Soviet Union.

- Fourth: As a necessary military precaution, I have reinforced our base at Guantanamo, evacuated today the dependents of our personnel there, and ordered additional military units to be on a standby alert basis.

- Fifth: We are calling tonight for an immediate meeting of the Organ of Consultation under the Organization of American States, to consider this threat to hemispheric security and to invoke articles 6 and 8 of the Rio Treaty in support of all necessary action. The United Nations Charter allows for regional security arrangements—and the nations of this hemisphere decided long ago against the military presence of outside powers. Our other allies around the world have also been alerted.

- Sixth: Under the Charter of the United Nations, we are asking tonight that an emergency meeting of the Security Council be convoked without delay to take action against this latest Soviet threat to world peace. Our resolution will call for the prompt dismantling and withdrawal of all offensive weapons in Cuba, under the supervision of U.N. observers, before the quarantine can be lifted.

- Seventh and finally: I call upon Chairman Khrushchev to halt and eliminate this clandestine, reckless and provocative threat to world peace and to stable relations between our two nations. I call upon him further to abandon this course of world domination, and to join in an historic effort to end the perilous arms race and to transform the history of man. He has an opportunity now to move the world back from the abyss of destruction—by returning to his government's own words that it had no need to station missiles outside its own territory, and withdrawing these weapons from Cuba—by refraining from any action which will widen or deepen the present crisis—and then by participating in a search for peaceful and permanent solutions.

This Nation is prepared to present its case against the Soviet threat to peace, and our own proposals for a peaceful world, at any time and in any forum—in the OAS, in the United Nations, or in any other meeting that could be useful—without limiting our freedom of action. We have in the past made strenuous efforts to limit the spread of nuclear weapons. We have proposed the elimination of all arms and military bases in a fair and effective disarmament treaty. We are prepared to discuss new proposals for the removal of tensions on both sides—including the possibility of a genuinely independent Cuba, free to determine its own destiny. We have no wish to war with the Soviet Union—for we are a peaceful people who desire to live in peace with all other peoples.

But it is difficult to settle or even discuss these problems in an atmosphere of intimidation. That is why this latest Soviet threat—or any other threat which is made independently or in response to our actions this week—must and will be met with determination. Any hostile move anywhere in the world against the safety and freedom of peoples to whom we are committed—including in particular the brave people of West Berlin—will be met by whatever action is needed.

Finally, I want to say a few words to the captive people of Cuba, to whom this speech is being directly carried by special radio facilities. I speak to you as a friend, as one who knows of your deep attachment to your fatherland, as one who shares your aspirations for liberty and justice for all. And I have watched and the American people have watched with deep sorrow how your nationalist revolution was betrayed—and how your fatherland fell under foreign domination. Now your leaders are no longer Cuban leaders inspired by Cuban ideals. They are puppets and agents of an international conspiracy which has turned Cuba against your friends and neighbors in the Americas—and turned it into the first Latin American country to become a target for nuclear war—the first Latin American country to have these weapons on its soil.

These new weapons are not in your interest. They contribute nothing to your peace and well-being. They can only undermine it. But this country has no wish to cause you to suffer or to impose any system upon you. We know that your lives and land are being used as pawns by those who deny your freedom.

Many times in the past, the Cuban people have risen to throw out tyrants who destroyed their liberty. And I have no doubt that most Cubans today look forward to the time when they will be truly free— free from foreign domination, free to choose their own leaders, free to select their own system, free to own their own land, free to speak and write and worship without fear or degradation. And then shall Cuba be welcomed back to the society of free nations and to the associations of this hemisphere.

My fellow citizens: let no one doubt that this is a difficult and dangerous effort on which we have set out. No one can see precisely what course it will take or what costs or casualties will be incurred. Many months of sacrifice and self-discipline lie ahead—months in which our patience and our will will be tested—months in which many threats and denunciations will keep us aware of our dangers. But the greatest danger of all would be to do nothing.

The path we have chosen for the present is full of hazards, as all paths are—but it is the one most consistent with our character and courage as a nation and our commitments around the world. The cost of freedom is always high—and Americans have always paid it. And one path we shall never choose, and that is the path of surrender or submission.

Our goal is not the victory of might, but the vindication of right— not peace at the expense of freedom, but both peace and freedom, here in this hemisphere, and, we hope, around the world. God willing, that goal will be achieved.

Thank you and good night.

# President Eisenhower's Farewell Address (1961)

## Dwight D. Eisenhower

*As the United States became one of two rival superpowers squared off against one another in a Cold War in the years following World War II, the nation faced difficult questions about how to ensure national security and about where and when it should act to prevent the expansion of what was often portrayed (incorrectly) as monolithic, worldwide communism. The Cold War was, of course, only "cold" in terms of direct confrontation between the United States and the Soviet Union. U.S. Cold War logic, which in simple terms defined a bipolar struggle between the forces of democratic freedom (led by the United States) and the forces of communist repression (led by the Soviet Union), drew the United States into "hot" wars in Korea and then Vietnam, and significantly shaped those conflicts.*

*Dwight D. Eisenhower, the widely admired World War II general who had planned and overseen the Allied invasion of Normandy on D-Day, was elected president in 1952 in great part because Americans had faith in his ability to end the Korean War. "Ike," as most Americans referred to the folksy-seeming president and former five-star general, did not believe the nation should maintain a large standing army in peacetime, in part because he worried that the enormous rate of defense spending would harm national economic growth. Eisenhower instead proposed to manage the Cold War through a policy of "massive retaliation," which he translated as "simply . . . the ability to blow hell out of them in a hurry if they start anything." His military "New Look" shifted focus from a large standing conventional military force to nuclear weaponry and airpower, and to covert operations. Eisenhower hoped to reduce military spending, but the arms race was enormously expensive, and even more so after the Soviets beat America into outer space with the launch of Sputnik in 1957.*

*Public Papers of the Presidents of the United States, Dwight D. Eisenhower,* 1960, pp. 1035–40.

*In 1959 the U.S. federal budget had jumped to $92 billion, with almost half devoted to military costs, including weapons research and development.*

*As President Eisenhower left office in 1961, he warned his fellow citizens that the emerging "military-industrial complex" was a threat to democracy. The conjunction of an "immense military establishment" and an enormous arms industry, he warned, has a "total influence—economic, political, even spiritual—[that] is felt in every city, every statehouse, every office of the federal government." In the twenty-first century, is Eisenhower's concern about the power of an intertwined military-industrial complex still significant?*

My fellow Americans:

Three days from now, after half a century in the service of our country, I shall lay down the responsibilities of office as, in traditional and solemn ceremony, the authority of the Presidency is vested in my successor.

This evening I come to you with a message of leave-taking and farewell, and to share a few final thoughts with you, my countrymen.

Like every other citizen, I wish the new President, and all who will labor with him, Godspeed. I pray that the coming years will be blessed with peace and prosperity for all. . . .

## I.

We now stand ten years past the midpoint of a century that has witnessed four major wars among great nations. Three of these involved our own country. Despite these holocausts America is today the strongest, the most influential and most productive nation in the world. Understandably proud of this pre-eminence, we yet realize that America's leadership and prestige depend, not merely upon our unmatched material progress, riches and military strength, but on how we use our power in the interests of world peace and human betterment.

## II.

Throughout America's adventure in free government, our basic purposes have been to keep the peace; to foster progress in human achievement, and to enhance liberty, dignity and integrity among people and among nations. To strive for less would be unworthy of a free and religious people. Any failure traceable to arrogance, or our lack of comprehension or readiness to sacrifice would inflict upon us grievous hurt both at home and abroad.

Progress toward these noble goals is persistently threatened by the conflict now engulfing the world. It commands our whole attention, absorbs our very beings. We face a hostile ideology—global in scope, atheistic in character, ruthless in purpose, and insidious in method. Unhappily the danger it poses promises to be of indefinite duration. To meet it successfully, there is called for, not so much the emotional and transitory sacrifices of crisis, but rather those which enable us to carry forward steadily, surely, and without complaint the burdens of a prolonged and complex struggle—with liberty the stake. Only thus shall we remain, despite every provocation, on our charted course toward permanent peace and human betterment.

Crises there will continue to be. In meeting them, whether foreign or domestic, great or small, there is a recurring temptation to feel that some spectacular and costly action could become the miraculous solution to all current difficulties. A huge increase in newer elements of our defense; development of unrealistic programs to cure every ill in agriculture; a dramatic expansion in basic and applied research—these and many other possibilities, each possibly promising in itself, may be suggested as the only way to the road we wish to travel.

But each proposal must be weighed in the light of a broader consideration: the need to maintain balance in and among national programs—balance between the private and the public economy, balance between cost and hoped for advantage—balance between the clearly necessary and the comfortably desirable; balance between our essential requirements as a nation and the duties imposed by the nation upon the individual; balance between actions of the moment and the national welfare of the future. Good judgment seeks balance and progress; lack of it eventually finds imbalance and frustration.

The record of many decades stands as proof that our people and their government have, in the main, understood these truths and have responded to them well, in the face of stress and threat. But threats, new in kind or degree, constantly arise. I mention two only.

**III.**

A vital element in keeping the peace is our military establishment. Our arms must be mighty, ready for instant action, so that no potential aggressor may be tempted to risk his own destruction.

Our military organization today bears little relation to that known by any of my predecessors in peacetime, or indeed by the fighting men of World War II or Korea.

Until the latest of our world conflicts, the United States had no armaments industry. American makers of plowshares could, with time and as required, make swords as well. But now we can no longer risk emergency improvisation of national defense; we have been compelled to create a permanent armaments industry of vast proportions. Added to this, three and a half million men and women are directly engaged in the defense establishment. We annually spend on military security more than the net income of all United States corporations.

This conjunction of an immense military establishment and a large arms industry is new in the American experience. The total influence—economic, political, even spiritual—is felt in every city, every State house, every office of the Federal government. We recognize the imperative need for this development. Yet we must not fail to comprehend its grave implications. Our toil, resources and livelihood are all involved; so is the very structure of our society.

In the councils of government, we must guard against the acquisition of unwarranted influence, whether sought or unsought, by the military-industrial complex. The potential for the disastrous rise of misplaced power exists and will persist.

We must never let the weight of this combination endanger our liberties or democratic processes. We should take nothing for granted. Only an alert and knowledgeable citizenry can compel the proper meshing of the huge industrial and military machinery of defense with our peaceful methods and goals, so that security and liberty may prosper together.

Akin to, and largely responsible for the sweeping changes in our industrial-military posture, has been the technological revolution during recent decades.

In this revolution, research has become central; it also becomes more formalized, complex, and costly. A steadily increasing share is conducted for, by, or at the direction of, the Federal government.

Today, the solitary inventor, tinkering in his shop, has been over-shadowed by task forces of scientists in laboratories and testing fields. In the same fashion, the free university, historically the fountainhead of free ideas and scientific discovery, has experienced a revolution in the conduct of research. Partly because of the huge costs involved, a government contract becomes virtually a substitute for intellectual curiosity. For every old blackboard there are now hundreds of new electronic computers.

The prospect of domination of the nation's scholars by Federal employment, project allocations, and the power of money is ever present and is gravely to be regarded. Yet, in holding scientific research and discovery in respect, as we should, we must also be alert to the equal and opposite danger that public policy could itself become the captive of a scientific-technological elite.

It is the task of statesmanship to mold, to balance, and to integrate these and other forces, new and old, within the principles of our democratic system—ever aiming toward the supreme goals of our free society.

**IV.**

Another factor in maintaining balance involves the element of time. As we peer into society's future, we—you and I, and our government—must avoid the impulse to live only for today, plundering, for our own ease and convenience, the precious resources of tomorrow. We cannot mortgage the material assets of our grandchildren without risking the loss also of their political and spiritual heritage. We want democracy to survive for all generations to come, not to become the insolvent phantom of tomorrow. . . .

**VI.**

So—in this my last good night to you as your President—I thank you for the many opportunities you have given me for public service in war and peace. I trust that in that service you find some things worthy; as for the rest of it, I know you will find ways to improve performance in the future.

You and I—my fellow citizens—need to be strong in our faith that all nations, under God, will reach the goal of peace with justice. May we be ever unswerving in devotion to principle, confident but humble with power, diligent in pursuit of the Nation's great goals.

To all the peoples of the world, I once more give expression to America's prayerful and continuing aspiration:

We pray that peoples of all faiths, all races, all nations, may have their great human needs satisfied; that those now denied opportunity shall come to enjoy it to the full; that all who yearn for freedom may experience its spiritual blessings; that those who have freedom will understand, also, its heavy responsibilities; that all who are insensitive to the needs of others will learn charity; that the scourages of poverty, disease and ignorance will be made to disappear from the earth, and that, in the goodness of time, all peoples will come to live together in a peace guaranteed by the binding force of mutual respect and love.

# A Frightening Message for a Thanksgiving Issue (1958)

## Editors of Good Housekeeping

*In the aftermath of World War II, when the United States had sole posses-
sion of atomic weapons, many Americans saw "the bomb" as a guarantee of
national power and security. But almost immediately after the United States
dropped atomic bombs on the Japanese cities of Hiroshima and Nagasaki, others spoke of the immense threat such a weapon posed to the survival of humanity. As Americans learned, in 1949, that the Soviet Union had tested an
atomic bomb, and then a nuclear weapon in 1953, fear of a nuclear exchange
grew. As the editors of the* Bulletin of Atomic Scientists *explained in 1954,
"an untoward event tomorrow may trigger a tense world to erupt in flames of
atomic or thermonuclear warfare . . . [with] 'no place to hide' for the great
masses of civilized mankind."*

*America's civil defense planners attempted to prepare the public for the possibil-
ity of nuclear attack. The Civil Defense Office's 1950 publication, the frighten-
ingly inaccurate Survival Under Atomic Attack, reassured Americans that they
could survive an atomic attack without "protective clothing or special training."
Chances of "making a complete recovery" from exposure to atomic radiation, it
claimed, "are much the same as for every day accidents." And "there is one important thing you can do to lessen your chances of injury by blast: Fall flat on your
face." Children watched Bert the Turtle explain what to do in the event of atomic
war in the animated film* Duck and Cover, *and practiced "duck and cover"
drills in their school classrooms. Increasingly, American magazines carried specu-
lative fiction detailing nuclear holocaust and its aftermath in the United States.
This article, the monthly editorial message in the November (Thanksgiving) issue
of* Good Housekeeping, *portrays an atomic attack on St. Louis, Missouri.
Why does it suggest that atomic attack is virtually inevitable? And why might
this article make the claim that—even faced with such national catastrophe—*

From *Good Housekeeping*, November 1958, p. 61.

*survival depends on the preparations of individuals, not the action of federal or local government agencies?*

This is an article about nuclear warfare and what will happen to you if it comes. Even though the article is printed on this important page, most people won't read it. And that's too bad, because it could save their lives.

Very likely you won't finish this article, because it's about death. You probably don't like to think about death, especially violent death. Hardly anybody does.

You may not read it, because it concerns civil defense. Quite possibly, you think civil defense is a bore, a lot of make-believe. Quite possibly, you think that if a bomb fell, civil defense wouldn't do any good anyway.

But in spite of this, we are publishing the article. Even if only a few people read it, the time may come when it will prove the most important thing they ever read.

The story begins when the first atomic bomb falls in the United States. Let's say it's ten o'clock on a January Tuesday in St. Louis, Missouri.

Workers are at work, children are at school, housewives are at home or at the market. The weather is cold and clear—no rain or snow predicted for the next few days. The winds in the upper air are from the southwest.

At exactly 10 A.M., an atomic bomb explodes a few hundred feet above the heart of the city. There is a searing flash of light; the earth itself shivers; the day seems to darken. In a split second, millions of dollars worth of buildings crumble to the ground; thousands of fires are instantly ignited; and between one breath and the next, a quarter of a million lives are snuffed out. Everybody you know may be dead.

The survivors—and there will be some survivors—open their eyes to a holocaust. Against a scene of incredible destruction and chaos, a scene of smoke and flame and heavy, choking dust, will be the wounded, the disfigured, the terribly burned, and the horribly bleeding. If, by some miracle, a survivor escapes unharmed, he will seem to be the only whole, uninjured person in the world.

*But the bomb has only begun its business.*

As soon as it has exploded, it forms a vast cloud, casting a twilight darkness over the entire city. This cloud gushes upward like a geyser and shapes itself into a giant umbrella, which covers all St. Louis and casts a twilight pall over it.

The cloud is filled with tons and tons of particles—fragments of the bomb, billions of pieces of cement and wood from the exploded buildings, hundreds of thousands of pounds of displaced earth. And the nuclear reaction set off by the explosion *makes all this material radioactive,* each tiny particle giving off deadly rays.

When the cloud has reached an altitude of about 60,000 feet, it begins to move—on this particular Tuesday, in a northeasterly direction. Slowly, inexorably, it stretches out into a long cigar shape, extending its length hour by hour until it reaches for hundreds of miles. *And as it moves, it deposits the radioactive particles, in the form of fallout, over the entire area.*

By 10:30, just thirty minutes after the explosion, the farm land of a wide strip of western Illinois has been rendered deadly for crop and animal and human being.

By noon, Chicago's five million inhabitants are menaced by the creeping black cloud that started in St. Louis.

By sundown, Detroit and Cleveland are under the pall.

In these cities even outside the immediate target, death lies on the streets, filters through the windows, and hangs in the air. You can't see it, but you can see its effects—the bright red burns, the choked breathing, the retching of those who have come in contact with it.

If you happen to live anywhere within a five-hundred-mile radius of St. Louis on this cool, clear, hypothetical January Tuesday, you, too, will be facing death. No one—*but no one*—will be around to help you.

Your only hope of salvation is a *place to go*—a place to gather your family together, protected from the unseen rays; a place where it's safe to drink the water, to eat the food, to touch the objects around you, to breathe.

Once the bomb has exploded, there is no time to prepare such a place. Its walls and ceiling must be one to three feet thick; its windows, if any, must be completely shielded with layer on layer of bricks or sandbags. Even the door must be reinforced with cinder blocks, once you're inside.

Some provision *must* have been made for ventilation. Some provision *should* have been made for sanitation. There must be water, and food, and first-aid equipment. There must be a radio—a *battery* radio.

Even if there were time—and there won't be—to assemble all the supplies, they wouldn't be available. Where would you find 100 sandbags or 20 cinder blocks? How would you know—and in the midst of chaos who would tell you?—which method of ventilating is safe, which suicide?

So, once the bomb falls, you and your family have just one chance of survival—a shelter you have prepared in advance.

The length of time you will have to stay in the shelter will depend on a number of unpredictable factors—the winds, the weather, the exact amount of fallout, and the speed with which the "cleanup" operation progresses. It may be a few days if you're relatively far away from the larger area, or as long as two weeks if you're close by. You will be completely cut off from the world—unable to see even what is going on in the yard next door—except for reports and instructions broadcast over the emergency radio system, Conelrad (640 or 1240 kc.). From this source you will learn the intensity of the fallout in your area (trained and protected crews will measure it periodically during the emergency period) and will get your only news of the world outside. When the streets are once again safe, Conelrad will tell you, and will outline the precautions you should take as you emerge from the shelter.

All this may happen. You have the choice of believing that it can't. But if you recognize the possibility of war between major powers, you must go further and acknowledge that atomic bombs will be dropped. On *us*.

*No one can say where.* Perhaps St. Louis. Perhaps Dallas. Perhaps Boston. Perhaps twenty-five areas at once.

*No one can say when.* Wars are declared suddenly these days. These days they even begin *without* being declared. You *know*—you surely have been reading the newspapers.

This is to remember: if and when a single bomb falls within 200 to 500 miles of you, your survival depends on a shelter—and the shelter depends on you.

# HUAC Investigates Hollywood (1947)

*In the fall of 1947 the House Un-American Activities Committee (HUAC) garnered national attention by investigating the Communist Party's influence within the motion picture industry. Most of the witnesses, like actors Gary Cooper and Ronald Reagan, cooperated with the committee, testifying about communist involvement in the film business and/or assuring HUAC that the movie colony was overwhelmingly anticommunist. A group of screenwriters and directors known as the "Hollywood Ten," however, refused to answer the committee's questions about their political beliefs and activities. Led by John Howard Lawson of the Screen Writers Guild, who had on other occasions openly urged fellow-leftists to present the communist position in their films, the ten current or past Communist Party members sought to turn the table and put HUAC on trial for violating their rights of freedom of speech and association. For not divulging their political affiliations, the Hollywood Ten were found guilty of contempt of Congress and served prison terms. Consequently, the entertainment industry adopted blacklists barring the employment of suspected communists or anyone who failed to cooperate with congressional investigators, and HUAC, looking for bigger game, began investigating espionage by public officials and atomic scientists.*

## RONALD REAGAN, TESTIMONY BEFORE THE HOUSE UN-AMERICAN ACTIVITIES COMMITTEE (1947)

*Staff members present:* Mr. Robert E. Stripling, Chief Investigator; Messrs. Louis Russell, H. A. Smith, and Robert B. Gatson, Investigators; and Mr. Benjamin Mand, Director of Research.

MR. STRIPLING: When and where were you born, Mr. Reagan?

Excerpted from House Committee on Un-American Activities, *Hearings Regarding Communist Infiltration of the Hollywood Motion-Picture Industry,* 80 Congress, 1st Session (Oct. 23, 27, 1947).

MR. REAGAN: Tampico, Illinois, February 6, 1911.

MR. STRIPLING: What is your present occupation?

MR. REAGAN: Motion-picture actor. . . .

MR. STRIPLING: Have you ever held any other position in the Screen Actors Guild?

MR. REAGAN: Yes, sir. Just prior to the war I was a member of the board of directors, and just after the war, prior to my being elected president, I was a member of the board of directors.

MR. STRIPLING: As a member of the board of directors, as president of the Screen Actors Guild, and as an active member, have you at any time observed or noted within the organization a clique of either Communists or Fascists who were attempting to exert influence or pressure on the guild?

MR. REAGAN: Well, sir, my testimony must be very similar to that of Mr. [George] Murphy and Mr. [Robert] Montgomery. There has been a small group within the Screen Actors Guild which has consistently opposed the policy of the guild board and officers of the guild, as evidenced by the vote on various issues. That small clique referred to has been suspected of more or less following the tactics that we associate with the Communist Party.

MR. STRIPLING: Would you refer to them as a disruptive influence within the guild?

MR. REAGAN: I would say that at times they have attempted to be a disruptive influence.

MR. STRIPLING: You have no knowledge yourself as to whether or not any of them are members of the Communist Party?

MR. REAGAN: No, sir, I have no investigative force, or anything, and I do not know.

MR. STRIPLING: Has it ever been reported to you that certain members of the guild were Communists?

MR. REAGAN: Yes, sir, I have heard different discussions and some of them tagged as Communists.

MR. STRIPLING: Would you say that this clique has attempted to dominate the guild?

MR. REAGAN: Well, sir, by attempting to put over their own particular views on various issues, I guess you would have to say that our side was attempting to dominate, too, because we were fighting just as hard to put over our views, and I think we were proven correct by the figures—Mr. Murphy gave the figures—and those figures were always approximately the same, an average of ninety per cent or better of the Screen Actors Guild voted in favor of those matters now guild policy.

MR. STRIPLING: Mr. Reagan, there has been testimony to the effect here that numerous Communist-front organizations have been set up in Hollywood. Have you ever been solicited to join any of those organizations or any organization which you considered to be a Communist-front organization?

MR. REAGAN: Well, sir, I have received literature from an organization called the Committee for a Far-Eastern Democratic Policy. I don't know whether it is Communist or not. I only know that I didn't like their views and as a result I didn't want to have anything to do with them.

MR. STRIPLING: Were you ever solicited to sponsor the Joint Anti-Fascist Refugee Committee?

MR. REAGAN: No, sir, I was never solicited to do that, but I found myself misled into being a sponsor on another occasion for a function that was held under the auspices of the Joint Anti-Fascist Refugee Committee.

MR. STRIPLING: Did you knowingly give your name as a sponsor?

MR. REAGAN: Not knowingly. Could I explain what that occasion was?

MR. STRIPLING: Yes, sir.

MR. REAGAN: I was called several weeks ago. There happened to be a financial drive on to raise money to build a badly needed hospital called the All Nations Hospital. I think the purpose of the building is so obvious by the title that it has the support of most of the people of Los Angeles. Certainly of most of the doctors. Some time ago I was called to the telephone. A woman introduced herself by name. I didn't make any particular note of her name, and I couldn't give it now. She told me that there would be a recital held at which Paul Robeson would sing, and she said that all the money for the tickets would go to the hospital, and asked if she could use my name as one of the sponsors. I hesitated for a moment, because I don't think that Mr. Robeson's and my political views coincide at all, and then I thought I was being a little stupid because, I thought, here is an occasion where Mr. Robeson is perhaps appearing as an artist, and certainly the object, raising money, is above any political consideration: it is a hospital supported by everyone. I have contributed money myself. So I felt a little bit as if I had been stuffy for a minute, and I said, "Certainly, you can use my name." I left town for a couple of weeks, and, when I returned, I was handed a newspaper story that said that this recital was held at the Shrine Auditorium in Los Angeles under the auspices of the Joint Anti-Fascist Refugee Committee. The principal speaker was Emil Lustig [Ludwig?], Robert Burman took up a collection, and remnants of the Abraham Lincoln Brigade were paraded on the platform. I did not, in the newspaper story, see one word about the hospital. I called the newspaper and said I am not accustomed to writing to editors but would like to explain my position, and he laughed and said, "You needn't bother, you are about the fiftieth person that has called with the same idea, including most of the legitimate doctors who had also been listed as sponsors of that affair."

MR. STRIPLING: Would you say from your observation that that is typical of the tactics or strategy of the Communists, to solicit and use the names of prominent people to either raise money or gain support?

MR. REAGAN: I think it is in keeping with their tactics, yes, sir.

MR. STRIPLING: Do you think there is anything democratic about those tactics?

MR. REAGAN: I do not, sir.

MR. STRIPLING: As president of the Screen Actors Guild, you are familiar with the jurisdictional strike which has been going on in Hollywood for some time?

MR. REAGAN: Yes, sir.

MR. STRIPLING: Have you ever had any conferences with any of the labor officials regarding this strike?

MR. REAGAN: Yes, sir.

MR. STRIPLING: Do you know whether the Communists have participated in any way in this strike?

MR. REAGAN: Sir, the first time that this word "Communist" was ever injected into any of the meetings concerning the strike was at a meeting in Chicago with Mr. William Hutchinson, president of the carpenters' union, who were on strike at the time. He asked the Screen Actors Guild to submit terms to Mr. [Richard] Walsh, and he told us to tell Mr. Walsh that, if he would give in on these terms, he in turn would run this Sorrell and the other Commies out—I am quoting him—and break it up. I might add that Mr. Walsh and Mr. Sorrell were running the strike for Mr. Hutchinson in Hollywood.

Mr. Stripling: Mr. Reagan, what is your feeling about what steps should be taken to rid the motion-picture industry of any Communist influences?

Mr. Reagan: Well, sir, ninety-nine per cent of us are pretty well aware of what is going on, and I think, within the bounds of our democratic rights and never once stepping over the rights given us by democracy, we have done a pretty good job in our business of keeping those people's activities curtailed. After all, we must recognize them at present as a political party. On that basis we have exposed their lies when we came across them, we have opposed their propaganda, and I can certainly testify that in the case of the Screen Actors Guild we have been eminently successful in preventing them from, with their usual tactics, trying to run a majority of an organization with a well-organized minority. In opposing those people, the best thing to do is make democracy work. In the Screen Actors Guild we make it work by insuring everyone a vote and by keeping everyone informed. I believe that, as Thomas Jefferson put it, if all the American people know all of the facts they will never make a mistake. Whether the Party should be outlawed, that is a matter for the Government to decide. As a citizen, I would hesitate to see any political party outlawed on the basis of its political ideology. We have spent a hundred and seventy years in this country on the basis that democracy is strong enough to stand up and fight against the inroads of any ideology. However, if it is proven that an organization is an agent of a foreign power, or in any way not a legitimate political party—and I think the Government is capable of proving that—then that is another matter. I happen to be very proud of the industry in which I work; I happen to be very proud of the way in which we conducted the fight. I do not believe the Communists have ever at any time been able to use the motion-picture screen as a sounding board for their philosophy or ideology. . . .

Mr. Chairman: There is one thing that you said that interested me very much. That was the quotation from Jefferson. That is just why this Committee was created by the House of Representatives: to acquaint the American people with the facts. Once the American people are acquainted with the facts there is no question but what the American people will do the kind of a job that they want done: that is, to make America just as pure as we can possibly make it. We want to thank you very much for coming here today.

Mr. Reagan: Sir, I detest, I abhor their philosophy, but I detest more than that their tactics, which are those of the fifth column, and are dishonest, but at the same time I never as a citizen want to see our country become urged, by either fear or resentment of this group, that we ever compromise with any of our democratic principles through that fear or resentment. I still think that democracy can do it.

## JOHN HOWARD LAWSON, TESTIMONY BEFORE THE HOUSE UN-AMERICAN ACTIVITIES COMMITTEE (1947)

STRIPLING: What is your occupation, Mr. Lawson?

LAWSON: I am a writer.

STRIPLING: How long have you been a writer?

LAWSON: All my life—at least thirty-five years—my adult life.

STRIPLING: Are you a member of the Screen Writers Guild?

LAWSON: The raising of any question here in regard to membership, political beliefs, or affiliation—

STRIPLING: Mr. Chairman—

LAWSON: Is absolutely beyond the powers of this committee.

STRIPLING: Mr. Chairman—

LAWSON: But—

(The chairman pounding gavel.)

LAWSON: It is a matter of public record that I am a member of the Screen Writers Guild.

STRIPLING: I ask—

[Applause.]

CHAIRMAN: I want to caution the people in the audience: You are the guests of this committee and you will have to maintain order at all times. I do not care for any applause or any demonstrations of one kind or another.

STRIPLING: Now, Mr. Chairman, I am also going to request that you instruct the witness to be responsive to the questions.

CHAIRMAN: I think the witness will be more responsive to the questions.

LAWSON: Mr. Chairman, you permitted—

CHAIRMAN (ponding gavel): Never mind—

LAWSON (continuing): Witnesses in this room to make answers of three or four or five hundred words to questions here.

CHAIRMAN: Mr. Lawson, you will please be responsive to these questions and not continue to try to disrupt these hearings.

LAWSON: I am not on trial here, Mr. Chairman. This committee is on trial here before the American people. Let us get that straight. . . .

STRIPLING: Have you ever held any office in the guild?

LAWSON: The question of whether I have held office is also a question which is beyond the purview of this committee.

(The chairman pounding gavel.)

LAWSON: It is an invasion of the right of association under the Bill of Rights of this country.

CHAIRMAN: Please be responsive to the question. . . .

LAWSON: I wish to frame my own answers to your questions, Mr. Chairman, and I intend to do so.

CHAIRMAN: And you will be responsive to the questions or you will be excused from the witness stand.

STRIPLING: I repeat the question, Mr. Lawson:

Have you ever held any position in the Screen Writers Guild?

LAWSON: I stated that it is outside the purview of the rights of this committee to inquire into any form of association—

CHAIRMAN: The Chair will determine what is in the purview of this committee.

LAWSON: My rights as an American citizen are no less than the responsibilities of this committee of Congress.

CHAIRMAN: Now, you are just making a big scene for yourself and getting all "het up." [Laughter.]

Be responsive to the questioning, just the same as all the witnesses have. You are no different from the rest. . . .

LAWSON: It is absolutely beyond the power of this committee to inquire into my association in any organization.

CHAIRMAN: Mr. Lawson, you will have to stop or you will leave the witness stand. And you will leave the witness stand because you are in contempt. That is why you will leave the witness stand. And if you are just trying to force me to put you in contempt, you won't have to try much harder. You know what has happened to a lot of people that have been in contempt of this committee this year, don't you?

LAWSON: I am glad you have made it perfectly clear that you are going to threaten and intimidate the witnesses, Mr. Chairman.

(The chairman pounding gavel.)

LAWSON: I am an American and I am not at all easy to intimidate, and don't think I am.

(The chairman pounding gavel.) . . .

STRIPLING: Mr. Lawson, are you now, or have you ever been a member of the Communist Party of the United States?

Lawson: In framing my answer to that question I must emphasize the points that I have raised before. The question of communism is in no way related to this inquiry, which is an attempt to get control of the screen and to invade the basic rights of American citizens in all fields.

McDOWELL: Now, I must object—

STRIPLING: Mr. Chairman—

(The chairman pounding gavel.)

LAWSON: The question here relates not only to the question of my membership in any political organization, but this committee is attempting to establish the right—

(The chairman pounding gavel.)

LAWSON (continuing): Which has been historically denied to any committee of this sort, to invade the rights and privileges and immunity of American citizens, whether they be Protestant, Methodist, Jewish, or Catholic, whether they be Republicans or Democrats or anything else.

CHAIRMAN (pounding gavel): Mr. Lawson, just quiet down again.

Mr. Lawson, the most pertinent question that we can ask is whether or not you have ever been a member of the Communist Party. Now, do you care to answer that question?

LAWSON: You are using the old technique, which was used in Hitler's Germany in order to create a scare here—. . .

STRIPLING: Mr. Chairman, the witness is not answering the question. . . .

CHAIRMAN (pounding gavel): We are going to get the answer to that question if we have to stay here for a week.

Are you a member of the Communist Party, or have you ever been a member of the Communist Party? . . .

LAWSON: I am framing my answer in the only way in which any American citizen can frame his answer to a question which absolutely invades his rights.

CHAIRMAN: Then you refuse to answer that question; is that correct?

LAWSON: I have told you that I will offer my beliefs, affiliations, and everything else to the American public, and they will know where I stand.

CHAIRMAN (pounding gavel): Excuse the witness—

LAWSON: As they do from what I have written.

CHAIRMAN (pounding gavel): Stand away from the stand—

LAWSON: I have written Americanism for many years, and I shall continue to fight for the Bill of Rights, which you are trying to destroy.

CHAIRMAN: Officers, take this man away from the stand—

[Applause and boos.]

# The Internal Communist Menace (1950)

## Joseph R. McCarthy

*Strong anti-communist sentiments had emerged in America well before Senator Joseph R. McCarthy began his flamboyant and destructive actions, but McCarthy did more to foster a second "Red Scare," turning the fear of international communism into a national hysteria, than any other individual in the United States. His name still stirs violent emotions in those who lived through that turbulent period. The words McCarthyism and McCarthyite have become a part of our language.*

*McCarthy had floundered through four years in the Senate and was desperately searching for a winning reelection issue when he appeared before the Ohio County Women's Republican Club in Wheeling, West Virginia, on February 9, 1950. Following the lead of other Republican politicians, and adding his own hyperbole, McCarthy blamed American reverses in the world not on the Soviet Union but on Democratic traitors. He claimed to have a list of 205 communist spies in Truman's State Department. When later challenged to produce the evidence for his charges, McCarthy changed his accusation to "bad risks" and lowered the number to fifty-seven. The excerpt below is from the revised speech that McCarthy introduced into the Congressional Record on February 20, 1950.*

*In fact, McCarthy had no list at all. But that did not matter. In an atmosphere charged by the Truman administration's own campaign against subversion, by the communist victory in China and the successful explosion of an A-bomb by the Soviet Union, by the Hiss-Chambers confrontations, and very soon by the arrest of the Rosenbergs as atomic spies and the outbreak of war in Korea, Joe McCarthy had an issue that dominated news headlines and the Republican party had a potent weapon to pummel Democrats.*

From the *Congressional Record*, 81 Congress, 2d Session, pp. 1954–57.

Five years after a world war has been won, men's hearts should anticipate a long peace, and men's minds should be free from the heavy weight that comes with war. But this is not such a period—for this is not a period of peace. This is a time of the "cold war." This is a time when all the world is split into two vast, increasingly hostile armed camps—a time of a great armaments race. . . .

Today we are engaged in a final, all-out battle between communistic atheism and Christianity. The modern champions of communism have selected this as the time. And, ladies and gentlemen, the chips are down—they are truly down. . . .

Six years ago, at the time of the first conference to map out the peace—Dumbarton Oaks—there was within the Soviet orbit 180,000,000 people. Lined up on the antitotalitarian side there were in the world at that time roughly 1,625,000,000 people. Today, only 6 years later, there are 800,000,000 people under the absolute domination of Soviet Russia—an increase of over 400 percent. On our side, the figure has shrunk to around 500,000,000. In other words, in less than 6 years the odds have changed from 9 to 1 in our favor to 8 to 5 against us. This indicates the swiftness of the tempo of Communist victories and American defeats in the cold war. As one of our outstanding historical figures once said, "When a great democracy is destroyed, it will not be because of enemies from without, but rather because of enemies from within." . . .

The reason why we find ourselves in a position of impotency is not because our only powerful potential enemy has sent men to invade our shores, but rather because of the traitorous actions of those who have been treated so well by this Nation. It has not been the less fortunate or members of minority groups who have been selling this Nation out, but rather those who have had all the benefits that the wealthiest nation on earth has had to offer—the finest homes, the finest college education, and the finest jobs in Government we can give.

This is glaringly true in the State Department. There the bright young men who are born with silver spoons in their mouths are the ones who have been the worst. . . . In my opinion the State Department, which is one of the most important government departments, is thoroughly infested with Communists.

I have in my hand 57 cases of individuals who would appear to be either card carrying members or certainly loyal to the Communist Party, but who nevertheless are still helping to shape our foreign Policy. . . .

I know that you are saying to yourself, "Well, why doesn't the Congress do something about it?" Actually, ladies and gentlemen, one of the important reasons for the graft, the corruption, the dishonesty, the disloyalty, the treason in high Government positions—one of the most important reasons why this continues is a lack of moral uprising on the part of the 140,000,000 American people. In the light of history, however, this is not hard to explain.

It is the result of an emotional hang-over and a temporary moral lapse which follows every war. It is the apathy to evil which people who have been subjected to the tremendous evils of war feel. As the people of the world see mass murder, the destruction of defenseless and innocent people, and all of the crime and lack of morals which go with war, they become numb and apathetic. It has always been thus after war.

However, the morals of our people have not been destroyed. They still exist. This cloak of numbness and apathy has only needed a spark to rekindle them. Happily, this spark has finally been supplied.

As you know, very recently the Secretary of State proclaimed his loyalty to a man guilty of what has always been considered as the most abominable of all crimes—of being a traitor to the people who gave him a position of great trust. The Secretary of State in attempting to justify his continued devotion to the man who sold out the Christian world to the atheistic world, referred to Christ's Sermon on the Mount as a justification and reason therefore, and the reaction of the American people to this would have made the heart of Abraham Lincoln happy.

When this pompous diplomat in striped pants, with a phony British accent, proclaimed to the American people that Christ on the Mount endorsed communism, high treason, and betrayal of a sacred trust, the blasphemy was so great that it awakened the dormant indignation of the American people.

He has lighted the spark which is resulting in a moral uprising and will end only when the whole sorry mess of twisted, warped thinkers are swept from the national scene so that we may have a new birth of national honesty and decency in government.

# The Venona Project and Atomic Espionage

*John Earl Haynes and Harvey Klehr*

*Historians' interpretations of the past are shaped by the sources available to them. For that reason, writing about the Cold War has been an especial challenge for historians. Before 1991 and the end of the Cold War, most records of the Soviet Union, for obvious reasons, were not available to U.S. historians. But neither were many of the records of the U.S. government. For reasons of national security, large numbers of important U.S. documents were classified and kept secret from researchers and the American public alike.*

*Among those classified documents were almost three thousand telegraphic cables between Soviet officials about Soviet spies in the United States. These cables, decrypted in the years following World War II in a project code-named Venona, were among the most closely guarded secrets of the American Cold War until 1995, when the National Security Agency, acting as part of a Clinton administration initiative, began to open these files to historians.*

*These cables, when read in conjunction with FBI files, congressional hearings, and documents from Soviet archives, proved something long disputed by many historians: There were a large number of spies within the United States passing information to the Soviet Union.*

*Historians John Earl Haynes and Harvey Klehr are careful to distinguish their history of espionage from McCarthyism and its effects. They see McCarthy as a demagogue and a liar and McCarthyism as a partisan attack by conservative Republicans on the loyalty of the Truman and Roosevelt administrations. But they also make a strong claim: Our understanding of Cold War anticommunism and the domestic Red Scare has been fundamentally warped. The Venona Project, they argue, proves that there was a "fifth column" work-*

*ing inside the United States during the Cold War. Thus, the anticommunist
actions of the U.S. government—such as President Truman's executive order
that denied government employment to anyone judged a security risk—were
not paranoid repressions of basic freedoms but reasonable attempts to counter
a very real threat.*

*How might the existence of such documents change our interpretations of
the Cold War and domestic anticommunism? Was the U.S. government justified in keeping these materials secret at the time?*

The Venona Project began because Carter Clarke did not trust Joseph
Stalin. Colonel Clarke was chief of the U.S. Army's Special Branch, part
of the War Department's Military Intelligence Division, and in 1943
its officers heard vague rumors of secret German-Soviet peace negotiations. With the vivid example of the August 1939 Nazi-Soviet Pact in
mind, Clarke feared that a separate peace between Moscow and Berlin
would allow Nazi Germany to concentrate its formidable war machine
against the United States and Great Britain. Clarke thought he had a
way to find out whether such negotiations were under way.

Clarke's Special Branch supervised the Signal Intelligence Service,
the Army's elite group of code-breakers and the predecessor of the
National Security Agency. In February 1943 Clarke ordered the service to establish a small program to examine ciphered Soviet diplomatic cablegrams. Since the beginning of World War II in 1939, the
federal government had collected copies of international cables leaving and entering the United States. If the cipher used in the Soviet cables could be broken, Clarke believed, the private exchanges between
Soviet diplomats in the United States and their superiors in Moscow
would show whether Stalin was seriously pursuing a separate peace.

The coded Soviet cables, however, proved to be far more difficult
to read than Clarke had expected. American code-breakers discovered that the Soviet Union was using a complex two-part ciphering
system involving a "one-time pad" code that in theory was unbreakable. The Venona code-breakers, however, combined acute intellectual analysis with painstaking examination of thousands of coded
telegraphic cables to spot a Soviet procedural error that opened the
cipher to attack. But by the time they had rendered the first messages
into readable text in 1946, the war was over and Clarke's initial goal
was moot. Nor did the messages show evidence of a Soviet quest for a
separate peace. What they did demonstrate, however, stunned American officials. Messages thought to be between Soviet diplomats at the

Soviet consulate in New York and the People's Commissariat of Foreign Affairs in Moscow turned out to be cables between professional intelligence field officers and Gen. Pavel Fitin, head of the foreign intelligence directorate of the KGB in Moscow. Espionage, not diplomacy, was the subject of these cables. One of the first cables rendered into coherent text was a 1944 message from KGB officers in New York showing that the Soviet Union had infiltrated America's most secret enterprise, the atomic bomb project.

By 1948 the accumulating evidence from other decoded Venona cables showed that the Soviets had recruited spies in virtually every major American government agency of military or diplomatic importance. American authorities learned that since 1942 the United States had been the target of a Soviet espionage onslaught involving dozens of professional Soviet intelligence officers and hundreds of Americans, many of whom were members of the American Communist Party (CPUSA). The deciphered cables of the Venona Project identify 349 citizens, immigrants, and permanent residents of the United States who had had a covert relationship with Soviet intelligence agencies. Further, American cryptanalysts in the Venona Project deciphered only a fraction of the Soviet intelligence traffic, so it was only logical to conclude that many additional agents were discussed in the thousands of unread messages. . . .

## AMERICANS' UNDERSTANDING OF SOVIET AND COMMUNIST ESPIONAGE

During the early Cold War, in the late 1940s and early 1950s, every few months newspaper headlines trumpeted the exposure of yet another network of Communists who had infiltrated an American laboratory, labor union, or government agency. Americans worried that a Communist fifth column, more loyal to the Soviet Union than to the United States, had moved into their institutions. By the mid-1950s, following the trials and convictions for espionage-related crimes of Alger Hiss, a senior diplomat, and Julius and Ethel Rosenberg for atomic spying, there was a widespread public consensus on three points: that Soviet espionage was serious, that American Communists assisted the Soviets, and that several senior government officials had betrayed the United States. The deciphered Venona messages provide a solid factual basis for this consensus. But the government did not release the Venona decryptions to the public, and it successfully disguised the source of its information about Soviet espionage. This decision denied the public the incontestable evidence afforded by the messages of the Soviet Union's own spies. . . . There were sensible reasons for the decision to keep Venona a highly compartmentalized secret within the government. In retrospect, however, the negative consequences of this policy are glaring. Had Venona been made public, it is unlikely there would have been a forty-year campaign to prove that the Rosenbergs were innocent. The Venona messages clearly display Julius Rosenberg's role as the leader of a productive ring of Soviet spies. Nor would there have been any basis for doubting his involvement in atomic espionage, because the deciphered messages document his recruitment of his brother-in-law, David Greenglass, as a spy. It is also unlikely, had the messages been made public or even circulated more widely within the government than they did, that Ethel Rosenberg would have been executed. The Venona messages do not throw her guilt in doubt; indeed, they confirm that she was a participant in her husband's espionage and in the recruitment of her brother for atomic espionage. But they suggest that she was essentially an accessory to her husband's activity, having knowledge of it and assisting him but not acting as a principal. Had they been introduced at the Rosenberg trial, the Venona messages would have confirmed Ethel's guilt but also reduced the importance of her role. . . .

There were broader consequences, as well, of the decision to keep Venona secret. The overlapping issues of Communists in government, Soviet espionage, and the loyalty of American Communists quickly became a partisan battleground. Led by Republican senator Joseph McCarthy of Wisconsin, some conservatives and partisan Republicans launched a comprehensive attack on the loyalties of the Roosevelt and Truman administrations. Some painted the entire New Deal as a disguised Communist plot and depicted Dean Acheson, Truman's secretary of state, and George C. Marshall, the Army chief of staff under Roosevelt and secretary of state and secretary of defense under Truman, as participants, in Senator McCarthy's words, in "a conspiracy on a scale so immense as to dwarf any previous such venture in the history of man. A conspiracy of infamy so black that, when it is finally exposed, its principals shall be forever deserving of the maledictions of all honest men." There is no basis in Venona for implicating Acheson or Marshall in a Communist conspiracy, but because the deciphered Venona messages were classified and unknown to the public, demagogues such as McCarthy had the opportunity to mix together accurate information about betrayal by men such as Harry White and Alger Hiss with falsehood about Acheson and Marshall that served partisan political goals.

A number of liberals and radicals pointed to the excesses of McCarthy's charges as justification for rejecting the allegations altogether. Anticommunism further lost credibility in the late 1960s, when critics of U.S. involvement in the Vietnam War blamed it for America's ill-fated participation. By the 1980s many commentators, and perhaps most academic historians, had concluded that Soviet espionage had been minor, that few American Communists had assisted the Soviets, and that no high officials had betrayed the United States. Many history texts depicted America in the late 1940s and 1950s as a "nightmare in red" during which Americans were "sweatdrenched in fear" of a figment of their own paranoid imaginations. As for American Communists, they were widely portrayed as having no connection with espionage. One influential book asserted emphatically, "There is no documentation in the public record of a direct connection between the American Communist Party and espionage during the entire postwar period.". . .

Unfortunately, the success of government secrecy in this case has seriously distorted our understanding of post-World War II history. Hundreds of books and thousands of essays on McCarthyism, the federal loyalty security program, Soviet espionage, American communism, and the early Cold War have perpetuated many myths that have given Americans a warped view of the nation's history in the 1930s, 1940s, and 1950s. The information that these messages reveal substantially revises the basis for understanding the early history of the Cold War and of America's concern with Soviet espionage and Communist subversion. . . .

## GIVING STALIN THE BOMB

Even before the 1995 release of the Venona cables, several books reported rumors that deciphered Soviet cables had played a critical role in uncovering atomic spies. Not only were the rumors true, but the decryptions exposed several theretofore-unknown Soviet agents responsible for the remarkable success of the USSR's atomic bomb program.

## Klaus Fuchs and Harry Gold

The British began their atomic bomb program before the United States, and the Soviets quickly developed a key source within the project. One of the scientists enlisted to work on the British bomb project was a naturalized British subject and brilliant young physicist named Klaus Fuchs. A refugee from Nazi Germany, Fuchs had also been a member of the German Communist party. After he joined the British atomic project in 1941, Fuchs contacted a refugee German Communist leader, Jürgen Kuczynski, and offered to spy for the Soviets. Kuczynski put Fuchs in touch with a contact at the Soviet embassy, and Fuchs was soon reporting the secrets of the British bomb project to the GRU through Ursula Kuczynski (Jürgen's sister). After America entered the war, the British threw their resources into the U.S. bomb program, whose immense industrial capacities would be more likely to develop a practical atomic weapon swiftly.

Fuchs arrived in the United States in late 1943, part of a contingent of fifteen British scientists augmenting the Manhattan Project. (By this point the KGB had also taken over control of Fuchs from the GRU.) Initially he worked with a Manhattan Project team at Columbia University, which was experimenting with uranium separation through gaseous diffusion. . . .

After his work on gaseous diffusion, Fuchs was transferred in August 1944 to Los Alamos, the top-secret heart of the U.S. atomic bomb project, to join its theoretical division. He continued working at Los Alamos until mid-1946, when he returned to England as one of the leaders of the once-again-independent British atomic bomb program. He also continued his work as a spy for the Soviet Union.

In late 1948 the FBI turned over to its British counterparts the Venona decryptions and the supporting evidence that Fuchs was a Soviet agent. The British were convinced. In December officers of MI5 began to question Fuchs. Under interrogation, he collapsed quickly and began his confession of January 24, 1950, which led to his trial and conviction on charges of espionage. Released in 1959 after serving nine years of a fourteen-year sentence, Fuchs moved to Communist East Germany, where he became director of a nuclear research institute.

Because he did confess, the Venona cables serve primarily to confirm and enrich the story Fuchs told. They also corroborate the confession of Harry Gold, the American who was the chief link between

Fuchs and the KGB. Gold first appears in the Venona cables in 1944 in connection with his work as the liaison with Fuchs. As noted earlier, Gold had been working as an industrial spy for the Soviets for nine years. On the basis of information from Fuchs's confession and on decrypted Venona cables, the FBI confronted Gold in 1950 and found ample evidence in his house of his long work as a Soviet agent. Like Fuchs, Gold easily broke and confessed. He received a thirty-year sentence for his crimes and served sixteen years before receiving a parole in 1966. . . .

### Greenglass and the Rosenbergs

Harry Gold's confession did more than corroborate Klaus Fuchs's story. Although most of his trips to New Mexico had been to get material from Fuchs, on one trip he picked up documents from another Soviet source at Los Alamos, whom he described, in the words of his FBI interrogators, as "a soldier, non-commissioned, married, no children (name not recalled.)" Gold's description quickly led the FBI to Sgt. David Greenglass, a machinist working at one of Los Alamos's secret laboratories. Greenglass confessed to espionage and also implicated his wife, Ruth, and his brother-in-law, Julius Rosenberg. Ruth Greenglass also confessed, corroborating David's testimony that Julius Rosenberg had recruited David as a Soviet source. Under further interrogation, the Greenglasses implicated David's sister Ethel (Julius's wife) in espionage. Simultaneously the FBI was comparing the decrypted Venona cables containing their cover names with the confessions of Fuchs, Gold, and the Greenglasses and with the results of their investigative work. Fuchs, it had been determined earlier, had the cover names Rest and Charles, while Harry Gold was known as Goose and Arnold in the Venona traffic. By the latter half of June, the FBI and the NSA had identified the cover names Antenna and Liberal as Julius Rosenberg, Caliber as David Greenglass, and Osa as Ruth Greenglass.

David and Ruth Greenglass were both fervent Communists who had joined the Young Communist League as teenagers. David had ambitions to become a scientist, but the need for a job forced him to drop out of Brooklyn Polytechnic Institute after only one semester. Just a few months after his marriage in late 1942 he was drafted. After he entered the army, the young soldier's letters to his bride mixed declarations of love and longing with equally ardent profession of loyalty to Marxism-Leninism. One letter declared, "Victory shall be ours and the future is socialism's. Another looked to the end of the war when "we will be together to build—under social- ism—our future." In yet another David wrote of his proselytizing for communism among his fellow soldiers: "Darling, we who under- stand can bring understanding to others because we are in love and have our Marxist outlook." And in a June 1944 letter he reconciled his Communist faith with the violence of the Soviet regime: "Dar- ling, I have been reading a lot of books on the Soviet Union. Dear, I can see how farsighted and intelligent those leaders are. They are really geniuses, everyone of them . . . I have come to a stronger and more resolute faith in and belief in the principles of Socialism and Communism. I believe that every time the Soviet Government used force they did so with pain in their hearts and the belief that what they were doing was to produce good for the greatest num- ber. . . . More power to the Soviet Union and a fruitful and abun- dant life for their peoples."

At the time David Greenglass wrote this last letter, he was a skilled machinist in an Army ordnance unit that was preparing to go over- seas. But he was unexpectedly transferred to work on a secret project. By August he was in Los Alamos and assigned to work in a facility that made models of the high-technology bomb parts being tested by vari- ous scientific teams; specifically he worked on models of the implo- sion detonators being developed for the plutonium bomb.

Through phone calls and letters David let Ruth know something about what he was working on. She, in turn, informed David's older sister, Ethel Rosenberg, and her husband, Julius. Although they did not know the details, both of the Greenglasses were aware that Julius was involved in secret work with concealed Communist engineers who worked in defense plants. Julius immediately understood the importance of the project on which David was working. He quickly reported this to the KGB. A September 1944 cable from the New York KGB states: "Liberal Rosenberg recommended the wife of his wife's brother, Ruth Greenglass, with a safe flat in view. She is 21 years old, a Townswoman [U.S. citizen], Gymnast [Young Commu- nist]. Liberal and wife recommend her as an intelligent and clever girl. . . . Ruth learned that her husband was called up by the army but he was not sent to the front. He is a mechanical engineer and is now working at the Enormous [atomic bomb project] plant in Santa Fe, New Mexico."

The Rosenbergs suggested to the Greenglasses that David should put the knowledge he was gaining in the service of the Soviet Union. David worked under secure conditions at Los Alamos, so in the initial approach guarded language was used in phone calls and letters. Nevertheless, in early November 1944 David wrote a letter to Ruth in which he said plainly that he would "most certainly will be glad to be part of the community project that Julius and his friends have in mind" [sic].

Shortly afterward, David got five days of leave, and Ruth prepared to visit him in Santa Fe, the city nearest to the secret Los Alamos facility. She testified that she had dinner with the Rosenbergs just before she left. Julius and Ethel both pushed her to press David to take part in Julius's plan for espionage. According to those who believe the Rosenbergs to be innocent, Ruth's testimony was phony and there had been no such discussion. Among the Venona cables, however, there is a KGB message dated November 14, 1944, and devoted entirely to the work of Julius Rosenberg. Among other matters, it reported that Ruth Greenglass had agreed to assist in "drawing in" David, and that Julius would brief her before she left for New Mexico.

As for Ethel's role, the same September KGB cable that first noted the contact with Ruth Greenglass stated that Ethel had recommended recruitment of her sister-in-law. Both Greenglasses later testified that Ethel was fully aware of Julius's espionage work and assisted him by typing some material. The only other deciphered reference to Ethel in the Venona cables came in November 1944, when the New York KGB responded to a Moscow headquarters inquiry about her: "Information on Liberal's wife. Surname that of her husband, first name Ethel, 29 years old. Married five years. Finished secondary school. A fellow-countryman [CPUSA member] since 1938. Sufficiently well developed politically. Knows about her husband's work and the role of Meter [Joel Barr] and Nil unidentified agent. In view of delicate health does not work. Is characterized positively and as a devoted person."

A December 13 KGB cable stated that the New York office had decided to designate Julius Rosenberg as the liaison with the Greenglasses rather than to shift them to another KGB link. A few days later, on December 16, a triumphant New York KGB reported that Ruth had returned from Sante Fe with the news that David had agreed to become a Soviet source and that he anticipated additional leave and would be visiting New York soon. The cable noted that

Julius Rosenberg felt technically inadequate to ask the right scientific questions and wanted assistance in debriefing David during his visit. Finally, in a January 1945 Venona cable, the New York KGB reported that while David Greenglass had been on leave in New York, his recruitment had been completed and arrangements for delivery of material made. He had also given an initial report on his implosion detonator work. All this information matches the later testimony of both David and Ruth Greenglass.

The Venona cables greatly assisted the FBI's investigation by providing a documentary basis against which interrogators could check Fuchs's, Gold's, and Greenglass's confessions and the statements made by others. It provided leads for follow-up questions and the tracking down of additional witnesses. Because of the policy decision not to reveal the Venona secret, prosecutors could not use cables as evidence in court. Nonetheless, they provided the FBI and other Justice Department officials with the sure knowledge that they were prosecuting the right people.

Initially, the FBI's investigation gave promise of being a classic case of "rolling up" a network link by link. First Fuchs was identified, and he confessed. His confession led to Gold, Gold's confession led to David Greenglass. Greenglass then confessed, followed swiftly by his wife Ruth. But there it ended. The next link in the chain was Julius Rosenberg, and he refused to admit anything. So did Ethel.

The government charged Julius and Ethel Rosenberg with espionage. They were swiftly convicted, even without use of the deciphered Venona cables. The eyewitness testimony of David and Ruth Greenglass, the eyewitness testimony of Max Elitcher, the corroborative testimony of Harry Gold, and an impressive array of supporting evidence led to a quick conviction. David Greenglass was sentenced to fifteen years in prison. In view of her cooperation and that of her husband, Ruth Greenglass escaped prosecution. Morton Sobell was tried with the Rosenbergs and also refused to confess, but Elitcher's testimony and his flight to Mexico led to Sobell's conviction and to a term of thirty years.

The stonewalling by the Rosenbergs and Sobell took its toll, however, on the ability of the government to prosecute additional members of the Rosenberg network. William Perl was convicted, but only of perjury rather than of espionage. Barr and Sarant secretly fled to the USSR and avoided arrest. Others suffered nothing more than exclusion from employment by the government or by firms doing defense work.

The government asked for and got the death penalty for the Rosenbergs, and they were executed on June 19, 1953. It appears that government authorities, hoping to use the death sentences as leverage to obtain their confessions and roll up other parts of the Soviet espionage apparatus, did not expect to carry out the executions. But the Rosenbergs were Communist true believers and refused to confess.

The deciphered KGB messages of the Venona Project do more than confirm the participation of Fuchs, Greenglass, and Rosenberg in Soviet atomic espionage. They also show that the Soviet Union's intelligence services had at least three additional sources within the Manhattan Project.

# Part 2

## THE POLITICS AND CULTURE OF THE AFFLUENT SOCIETY

The 1950s and 1960s are generally seen as very different eras in American history. In our stereotypes of decades, the fifties are the era of conformity, of complacent affluence, a time in which the American people turned away from the challenges of the world, moved to the suburbs, bought refrigerators and televisions and cars with massive tailfins.

There is some truth to this stereotype. Under the leadership of President Eisenhower, the first Republican to be elected in twenty years, the nation seemed remarkable for its stability. While not extending New Deal social welfare programs, neither did the Eisenhower administration attempt to reverse them. Rather, his was an administration of consolidation. Following the Great Depression and World War II, as well as the uncertainty of the immediate postwar years, the 1950s did seem an era of peace, prosperity, and stability—despite the Korean War, the continuing Cold War, McCarthyism, and the growth of a movement for African American civil rights. The 1950s were an age of economic prosperity for most Americans. The percentage of young people attending high school jumped dramatically, as did the number attending college. In a time of low unemployment, rising real wages, and readily available consumer goods, a majority of Americans came to see themselves as middle class. Culturally, as well as politically, the fifties were a time of consolidation.

The sixties, in contrast, are our decade of "great dreams." They are perhaps our most controversial decade, as America's politicians and public figures continue to find the roots of all that is good—or bad—about America in the decade of the sixties. When we talk about "The Sixties," we often mean the latter half of the decade. But the activism and grand visions of the sixties are equally present in the early years. Led by Presidents John F. Kennedy and Lyndon B. Johnson, the nation set forth to alleviate racial discrimination, to combat poverty, and to create a new and improved society. "We can do better," Kennedy had said in 1960. "We will do better," Johnson promised in 1964. In so many ways, the "Fifties" and the "Sixties" seem radically different, one given to complacency, quietude, and stability, the other to activism, challenge, and change.

In fact, the two eras have much in common. The struggles that brought reform in the 1960s were already emerging throughout the "quiet years" of the 1950s. Moreover, the policies and governmental programs of the 1960s built upon the strong foundation of the New Deal; they show continuity as well as new visions. Fundamentally, though, the fifties and the sixties were joined by an underlying set of beliefs, one that historians have attempted to capture in phrases such as "the politics of affluence," or "the liberal consensus." The politics and culture of postwar America were shaped by the belief that improvement is always possible within a fundamentally sound economic and social system, that right-minded and intelligent people can create a healthy, viable social system, that moderation is preferable to extremism, and that an economy committed to growth will provide the basis for eliminating social problems while assuring prosperity for the growing middle class.

In the following mix of historical documents and historians' analysis, this section traces the development of a culture and politics of affluence from the immediate postwar years through the 1960s' Great Society. Thomas Hine, an author who has written extensively on American culture and consumption, discusses the creation of a new suburban middle class in the postwar era. The limits of suburban opportunity are made clear in a 1957 *Time* magazine article about a black family's move into the "white" neighborhood of Levittown, Pennsylvania. Two documents—the 1962 Port Huron Statement, which was the founding manifesto of the New Left group Students for a Democratic Society, and the 1960 Sharon Statement, written by the young conservatives who founded Young Americans for Freedom—demonstrate that young Americans, on both the political/cultural Left and the Right, saw the possibility of transforming their nation.

Speeches by President John F. Kennedy and Lyndon B. Johnson— Kennedy's Inaugural Address and Johnson's "Great Society" speech— offer a glimpse of the "politics of affluence" in our national life.

Animated by grand visions and a sense of possibility perhaps hard to imagine today, these speeches also show important changes in focus and approach from the Kennedy to the Johnson presidency. Finally, historian Bruce Schulman discusses the development of American liberalism and evaluates Lyndon Johnson's Great Society.

Many questions are raised by these selections. Why do we tend to think of the 1950s and 1960s as radically different from one another? To what extent are leaders—Eisenhower, Kennedy, Johnson—responsible for the major changes in American life chronicled here? Do their policies owe more to the ongoing Cold War or to the unprecedented affluence of most Americans? What role does a broader set of cultural changes play in shaping the political possibilities of the 1960s? Looking back to the 1960s, how would you evaluate the Great Society? Would such an ambitious program be possible today?

# The Luckiest Generation

*Thomas Hine*

*America's economic growth was striking during the postwar era. And such growth meant that families' real incomes grew—in 1953, up approximately 50 percent over the pre-Depression boom year of 1929 (in constant dollars). Most strikingly, the modest affluence this brought to the American people was more equitably distributed than any time before or since. Industrial wages increasingly propelled workers into an economic middle class. More and more young Americans were able to complete high school or even attend college. The affluence of the postwar era fundamentally changed America's class structure.*

*This growing middle class moved, by the millions, to the suburbs. In many images, from then and now, these postwar suburbs appear as sites of stifling conformity. But Thomas Hine portrays the new postwar suburbs as more akin to the frontier. In the suburbs, Americans from widely diverse social backgrounds came together and had to figure out how to live in this new space. The cultures they created often emphasized conformity—but a conformity quite different from the rigid traditions and hierarchies of urban ethnic neighborhoods, small towns, or rural communities in which many of these new suburban residents had been raised. In the suburbs, people looked to the advice of national experts on everything from child raising to recipes. According to Hine, the suburbs fostered the creation of a new, national, middle-class culture that was open to a broader range of Americans than ever before.*

*Keep Hine's argument in mind as you look at two sections that follow this piece—the chart portraying sales of consumer goods and the letters responding to news that a black family had moved into a formerly all-white Pennsylvania suburb. How do these documents support or challenge his analysis?*

"Never before," *Life* exclaimed in a 1954 article, "so much for so few. The article was accompanied by photographs of such novel phenomena as crowded student parking lots at a high school. It told of young men just out of college or the service who had their pick of excellent, high-paying jobs that would more than fulfill their parents' dreams for them.

"Never before" was virtually the slogan of the age. Never before had there been a car like this one or a floor wax like that one. The Populuxe generation heard of precedent being shattered several times each day.

Still, *Life* was onto something very important, and statistics bear it out. Americans who were born during the Depression came of age at a time when a number of economic and demographic factors converged in an extremely favorable way. There was more wealth to go around and a decline in the number of people to share it. Nothing like it had ever happened before, and nothing like it has happened since. . . .

The postwar period brought a much more equitable distribution of income than ever before. The increase in real income went almost entirely to the middle class. The absolute number of high-income people, which *Fortune* defined as those making more than $7,500 annually in 1953 dollars, more than doubled from 1929, but their share of the nation's total income declined sharply. The biggest increase came in the number of families in the $4,000–$7,000 salary range, which was understood to be solidly middle class. There were 5.5 million families in this category in 1929, 17.9 million in 1953. They accounted for 35 percent of the nation's population; they earned 42 percent of its income. These were the candidates for suburbia, the cream of the American market. . . .

The new world without sidewalks was, at once, an exciting and perplexing place. It was a world of the young, a place apart from mothers and uncles and familiar neighbors. You were new, and so were all your neighbors. And in many suburbs the chances were that neither you nor they would be in the neighborhood very long. Nationwide, one American in five moved every year. . . .

The mobility of these trend-setting suburbanites probably contributed to the increasing uniformity of suburbs from coast to coast as new styles, products and trends hit the housing market. Such standardization had its value for the highly mobile segment of the suburban population. If your company moved you from Cherry Hill, New Jersey, to Anaheim, California, the vegetation would be different, but you could probably move into much the same house. Your furniture would fit, and it would be blessedly familiar besides. . . .

This itinerant young suburban market was far from a majority of the American people, but it was considered the cream of the market and it set the tone for the rest. The look and accessories of casual suburban living moved quickly into older urban row-house neighborhoods, and suburbanites set the goals to strive for. In some part of his being, every American wanted a Cadillac. And even though television and magazines united the country as never before, the amount of contact Americans had with other people was steadily diminishing as they drove to where they were going and stayed away from the crowds and jostling of the cities. . . .

The new suburbanites were attractive consumers, and almost everything they encountered in the popular media treated them as consumers. Moreover, because they were usually far from their families and others who would traditionally set standards for them, they were considered to be a very malleable market. They were very receptive to newness, they believed that things were improving. They watched a lot of television and read a lot of magazines, from which they were believed to be taking ideas about how they should live. In short, they were ideal targets for advertising.

One indication that this was true could be seen in the way people ate. In the early 1950s, a very unusual thing happened. Americans increased the percentage of their income they were willing to spend on food. No industry marketed more aggressively or came up with a larger array of new, more profitable products. Food was more than mere nourishment; it was convenience, modernity and a fulfillment of parental obligations. A bit of the increased expenditure came from moving up in status—eating high on the hog—but most came in manufactured food, such as canned goods, frozen foods, boxed mixes, prepared snacks. . . .

Recipes found on the backs of cans and boxes became increasingly influential during this period. Typically there were directions for the preparation of the product and suggestions about how to use the product to make a fancier "company" dish. Just as basic automobiles were made more exciting by the addition of tailfins and chrome, so were ordinary sweet potatoes dressed up by the addition of Campfire marshmallows and Dole crushed pineapple. Just as buyers of automobiles and other products knew that styling was a bit fraudulent, eaters seemed to enjoy the revelation that the apple pie was really made out of Ritz crackers and the snack at the party was just plain old Wheat Chex putting on airs. . . .

Even as Americans became more and more widely dispersed geographically, they became more and more a single nation, all making the same recipes found on the backs of boxes. Betty Crocker represented a new kind of authority, acting *in loco parentis.*

Authorities and experts seemed everywhere in the popular media, in editorial copy, advertising and often both. They served as national parents, telling young people separated from their families and thrown into unfamiliar contexts how to deal with their problems, raise their children, take care of their house and yard, dress, entertain and enjoy themselves.

Folk wisdom, the sort of thing your family might tell you, was called into serious question by the rapidly changing circumstances of modern life. Parents wondering about what to do about their children were more likely to consult—and believe—Dr. Spock's child-rearing manual than their own parents, who had been through it all before. . . .

Anyone who paid attention to all the experts and all the advertising, and tried to behave accordingly, would probably have gone mad from trying to reconcile the many contradictions routinely set forth in the popular magazines.

Men were to be consummate breadwinners, protectors of their family, who journeyed to work each day to do their part for the most productive and robust economy the world had ever seen. They were told that they must be close to their families and to their houses. *Life* discovered in suburbia "the new domesticated male" and noted that he typically had three children at the age his father was when he married. Men were believed to be taking an ever larger share in the tasks of keeping a household together, and these chores seemed to become more important as home and family were increasingly depicted as the only respectable obsessions. Lawns had to be attended to. Men were emissaries of modern styles from their workplaces to their homes, and they should assist their wives in deciding how to decorate those homes. And the man was expected to be a do-it-yourselfer, getting special rewards from solving the crises of the homeowner while steadily improving his investment. He was the support on which the household rested, and the stability of his family's life was a very important goal. Yet he was also married to his employer and expected to uproot his family and take it off to distant places to serve the company. He was, at once, more domesticated and more career-oriented than his father, and he did not have the support of old friends and nearby family to help him through difficult times.

He was likely to be the first member of his family to be doing well economically, and he was part of a generation of pioneers in the new kind of suburbia that was emerging. Still, he was constantly being reassured that his kind of life was normal. He was not defeated by these contradictions. He consistently told pollsters that he was happy, that his chief regret was that he did not have more education, that he expected to do better next year and that his children would do even better than he did.

While women were rarely assumed to have a productive place in the economy, they were taken very seriously as consumers and indeed were often depicted as the chief decision makers in regard to what their families would purchase. They were marrying younger than their mothers had, and their husbands were younger too. That made more children, indeed a lot of children all at once, nearly inevitable.

The physical nature of most suburbs, with their lack of public facilities and public transportation, increased the demands on mothers, even those of older, theoreticaly more self-sufficient children. They organized their children's social life and their educational and athletic achievement. One of the most prevalent commercial images of Mom was behind the wheel of a station wagon, sitting at a curbside while pigtailed Susie and freckled-faced Tommy come running to be picked up from ballet lessons or Little League. . . .

Around the house, Mom was said to be an engineer, someone who keeps a technologically and organizationally complex institution running smoothly. In advertising at least, she did not have to exert herself very much. If anyone was depicted on her hands and knees scrubbing a floor it was someone from her parents' generation, before the availability of modern cleansers and labor-saving appliances. Women in magazines were always stylishly and impractically dressed. In advertising, they sometimes wore a glove to press the button of the latest household machine. More often than you would expect, they were shown striking poses in the kitchen while wearing a tiara. Somebody must have liked this, because the image persisted for many years. . . .

The polls generally found women slightly less happy than their husbands, although far more satisfied than not. They expressed extreme displeasure with housework perhaps because the media were leading them to believe that they would not have to do any. They said they wanted more excitement in their lives. And by 1959 teenage girls were saying that they planned to have a career outside of the home.

It was difficult to live up to the image of the new suburban man and woman found in mass magazines, television and advertising.

On top of this was tremendous criticism that emanated from intellectuals and was often disseminated through these very same outlets. Chief among these critiques were that suburbanites were abject conformists without any minds of their own. They were dupes whose culture had been sugar-coated by hucksters, and they chose to live in what Lewis Mumford called "the proliferating nonentity" of suburbia. Their environment was not paradise, as everyone knew, nor was it countryside or the relatively more privileged suburbs known to previous generations, something that commentators spent quite a lot of time deploring.

There was a distinct class bias in most of what was written about suburbia and suburbanites during this time. For most intellectuals, it represented not a triumph of democracy but a proof of Robert Maynard Hutchins' formulation that the industrial revolution made it possible for a moron to be successful. There arose a successful minor genre of trouble-in-the-suburbs literature, with such titles as *The Crack in the Picture Window,* the story of John and Mary Drone and the way in which development living drives them crazy, without their knowing it. One of the most extreme was *The Split Level Trap,* based on the experiences of a psychiatrist in a northern New Jersey suburb. Things were so bad out there, he wrote, that the phenomenon should be renamed. He proposed Disturbia.

One of the problems that commentators seemed to have had was that they had far higher expectations for suburbia than the residents themselves had. Suburbia was where new houses were, where there were yards and barbecues. Buyers of development houses knew they were not getting a carefully landscaped, picturesque environment. The neighbors of sociologist Herbert Gans, who in 1958 was one of the first people to move into the third Levittown, now Willingboro, New Jersey, told him they hardly thought about a new community or a new environment when they were making their decisions. They were there because Levittown offered the most house for the money. In a few cases where chunks of whole urban neighborhoods moved en masse to a particular suburb or when an industrial plant relocated, people were able to simply transplant the society with which they were comfortable. Many people changed the way they lived upon moving to suburbia, but that was a by-product, not a goal.

Some of the anti-suburban commentary of the period seems fired by anger at many new suburbanites betraying their working-class backgrounds by voting for Eisenhower. Later it became clear that they had not all metamorphosed into Republicans, but rather that they voted for someone who represented the same kind of security and stability they looked for in their neighborhoods and within their families.

Even the reputation for conformity has probably been overstated. One of the hallmarks of suburbia was, in fact, a lack of the standards and expectations one would find in an ethnic neighborhood of a large city or in a small town. The suburbs were inhabited by people who didn't know one another, let alone their neighbors' parents, who had never lived in such a place before and weren't quite sure of how to do it. And like most people in such a novel situation, they suspected that other people really knew how to behave. They might criticize how their neighbors were bringing up their children, but they looked to their neighbors for signals on how to behave.

In the 1950s and early 1960s, most suburban places had not been around long enough to have become communities, a situation that was exacerbated by the extreme mobility of their residents. They felt anxiety about how to fit into a society whose shape and rules were more or less indeterminate. Far from being conformist. many suburbs were highly tolerant, more tolerant than the communities from which most of their residents had moved. In both city and small town. worry over what the neighbors would think kept people in line. In the suburbs, one had little idea of what the neighbors were doing inside their houses and was reluctant to disapprove.

Yet there were new situations to confront, new etiquette to be formulated in order to keep things humming in at least apparent harmony. Sometimes the atmosphere of mutual unfamiliarity led to the kind of social horror story Gans came across in Levittown, New Jersey. A couple newly arrived from New York invited some neighbors for a cocktail party. The hostess wore Capri pants for the occasion. Early arrivals, who saw the hostess through the window, noticed her unfamiliar outfit and concluded that she was in her pajamas. Had they shown up on the wrong night? What sort of a woman wears her pajamas in front of company? They went back home and telephoned other neighbors who were going to the party and spread doubt throughout the neighborhood. Despite grave doubts and much social discomfort, the party finally took place. Eventually, the hostess heard about what happened and the Capri pants were put in the closet and left there. Such incidents were common and disconcerting. New people and new situations bring new hazards.

# Trends in Postwar American Culture and Society

*Roland Marchand*

*Historian Roland Marchand created the following table to demonstrate some of the trends in U.S. postwar culture. At first glance, it is an odd and idiosyncratic list, encompassing everything from the Gross National Product to the percentage of men who disapprove of women wearing shorts in public. But he used it to support his argument that a more homogenous popular culture than anything Americans had ever known emerged in the postwar period and the homogeneity often appeared as a "decline of class and regional differences in clothing and recreation." What can you learn by looking at the statistics? How do they support or challenge the argument made by Thomas Hine in "The Luckiest Generation"?*

From Roland Marchand, "Visions of Classlessness, Quests for Dominion: American Popular Culture, 1945–1960," from Robert H. Bremner and Gary W. Reichard, eds., *Reshaping America: Society and Institutions, 1945–1960.* Copyright © 1982, Ohio State University Press. Reprinted by permission of Betsy Marchand, Trustee, Marchand Family Trust.

| Phenomenon | Period Spanned by Data | Initial Measurement | Second Measurement | Unit of Measure | Source of Data | Average Rate of Change per Year |
|---|---|---|---|---|---|---|
| 1. Persons arrested under age 18 | 1946–60 | 38 | 527 | Thousands of individuals | e | +91.9% |
| 2. Construction contracts awarded for religious buildings | 1947–60 | 118 | 789 | Millions of $ | b | +43.7% |
| 3. Value of television[a] advertising[a] | 1951–60 | 332 | 1,590 | Millions of $ | e | +42.1% |
| 4. Residential use of electrical energy | 1946–60 | 42,919 | 196,269 | Millions of kilowatt-hours | e | +25.5% |
| 5. Potato chips produced | 1947–58 | 155.9 | 424.6 | Millions of lbs. | a | +15.7% |
| 6. Phonograph records | 1954–58 | 80.2 | 136.2 | Value in millions of $ | a | +17.5% |
| 7. Expenditures on participant amusements (golf, bowling, skating etc.) | 1946–60 | 379 | 1,161 | Millions of $ | b | +14.7% |
| 8. Kitchen and other household appliances | 1946–60 | 1,900 | 5,000 | Value in millions of constant $ | b | +11.6% |
| 9. Total corporate assets (per tax returns) | 1946–60 | 454,705 | 1,136,668 | Millions of $ | e | +10.7% |
| 10. Total advertising expenditures | 1951–60 | 6,426 | 11,932 | Value in millions of $ | e | +9.5% |
| 11. Miles of travel by motor vehicles | 1946–60 | 340,880 | 718,485 | Millions of miles | e | +7.9% |
| 12. Gross National Product | 1946–60 | 312.6 | 487.7 | Billions of constant 1958 $ | b | +4.0% |
| 13. Consumer Price Index (all items) | 1946–60 | 58.5 | 88.7 | 1967 CPI=100 | e | +3.7% |
| 14. Personal expenditures on spectator sports | 1946–60 | 200 | 290 | Millions of $ | b | +3.2% |

| | | | | | | |
|---|---|---|---|---|---|---|
| 15. Average weekly hours of workers in manufacturing | 1946–60 | 40.3 | 39.7 | Weekly hours | e | – 0.1% |
| 16. Percentage of females not in labor force | 1946–60 | 69.1 | 62.2 | % of all females | e | – 0.7% |
| 17. Production of men's and boys' work shirts | 1946–60 | 98.5 | 78.3 | Value of production in millions of $ | a | – 1.5% |
| 18. Foreign-born as percentage of total U.S. population | 1940–60 | 8.8 | 5.4 | % of population | c | – 1.9% |
| 19. Circulation of *Narod Polski* (Chicago Polish language weekly and semi-monthly—Catholic and Labor) | 1940–60 | 120 | 64.4 | Circulation in thousands | d | – 2.3% |
| 20. Personal expenditures on motion picture admissions | 1946–60 | 1,692 | 951 | Millions of $ | b | – 3.1% |
| 21. Disapproval of women wearing shorts on the street | 1951–55 | 69 | 55 | % of men polled | f | – 5.1% |

SOURCES:

a. U.S., Bureau of the Census, *United States Census of Manufactures*, 1958, Vol. 2, Part I.

b. U.S., Office of Business Economics, *The National Income and Product Accounts of the Unites States, 1929–65.*

c. U.S., Bureau of Labor Statistics, Report No. 238-5, *Survey of Consumer Expenditures*, 1960–61.

d. N. W. Ayer & Son, *N. W. Ayer & Son's Directory, Newspapers and Periodicals*, 1946 and 1960.

e. U.S., Bureau of the Census, *Historical Statistics of the United States* (Washington, D.C., 1975) 2 Vols.

f. George Horace Gallup, *The Gallup Poll: Public Opinion 1935–1971*, 3 vols. (New York, 1972), Vol. 2.

# The Myers Move to Levittown

*In late 1956, anticipating the birth of their third child, Daisy and William Myers began looking for a larger house. The Myers were in most ways a typical American family. William Myers was a World War II veteran. After the war he'd received a college degree from Hampton University, and by the mid-1950s, he earned a good salary as a laboratory technician. Like the majority of American women with small children at that time, Daisy Myers was a "housewife." Along with the other new suburbanites Thomas Hine described in the previous article, the Myers were benefiting from postwar American prosperity. But unlike those other Americans, the Myers were black.*

*As Levittown residents learned about the sale of a house to a black family, they debated what that would mean. Some were supportive, others not. About six hundred residents met to discuss the issue and signed a petition protesting the racial integration of their "closed community." Some chose violence instead. Hundreds of protesters surrounded the Myers' home, shouting and throwing rocks. Cars drove by festooned with Confederate flags; "Old Man River" blasted from a neighboring house at all hours of the day and night. Pennsylvania's governor, seeing the situation spiraling out of control, sent in the state police to restore order. The Myers continued to live in Levittown.*

*During the 1950s, more than two million African Americans left the rural South. Very, very few of them moved to the suburbs. They were not legally excluded. The Supreme Court had ruled in 1948 that "restrictive covenants" (agreements that prevented homeowners from selling to members of another race or religion) could not be enforced against the will of the buyer and seller, but nothing prevented sellers from choosing not to sell to members of another race or religion. And the Federal Housing Authority, which financed mortgages for a large percentage of new houses in the 1950s, generally refused to approve loans to purchase houses in racially mixed neighborhoods.*

*The following letters—written to Pennsylvania governor George M. Leader about his decision to intervene in Levittown—suggest how controversial racial integration was in this northern community. How does the Myers' story compli-*

Letters from Manuscript Group 207: George M. Leader Papers, Subject File, "State Police Action at Levittown," Pennsylvania State Archives. For on-line materials, see http://www.docheritage.state.pa.us.

*cate Thomas Hine's analysis? Does the fact that African Americans were often denied entry to the new suburbs invalidate his claim about the inclusiveness of the new national culture? Why or why not? What does the hostile reaction of some Levittown residents indicate about the state of race relations in America? And what should we make of the fact that Levittown is not a southern suburb but a northern one, not far from Philadelphia? What is the relationship between race and the opportunities of the postwar culture of abundance? Could African Americans join the growing American middle class?*

2139 Allen Street<br>
Allentown, Pennsylvania<br>
August 19, 1957

Governor George M. Leader
Governor of Pennsylvania
Harrisburg, Pennsylvania

My dear Governor:

I want to congratulate you for having taken prompt action in helping to stop the disgraceful action of mobs against the citizen who wanted to move into his home in Levittown. Pennsylvania has a noble history in this respect, as a center for the Underground Railway, as the home of Thaddeus Stevens and it is shameful that a handful of people are attempting to mar it. I urge you to take the strongest action possible against those who would stir up racial antagonisms in this way.

Sincerely yours,

Richard W. Reichard

Aug. 20, 1957

Gov. Leader,

Dear Sir,

I think your handling of the Levittown situation is brutal, and does not show good judgement on the part of one who is suppose to be Governor of our state.

If you had ever lived near those savages, then you would know why people object to their moving into Levittown.

Pardon me for not signing my name for it has reached the point where people like I are not free to express our opinions, thanks to people like you.

See you at the Polls.

# The Port Huron Statement (1962)

## Students for a Democratic Society

*To young Americans in the early 1960s, everything seemed possible. A youthful, activist president had come into office promising that "we can do better." Black students throughout the South had demonstrated through sit-ins and kneel-ins that people willing to act on their convictions could help to turn society around. Inspired by these examples and given hope by the new leadership in Washington, young white reformers came together to draw up a manifesto for social change. Those who formed Students for a Democratic Society (SDS) were deeply critical of the complacency and indifference of their society. They hoped to marshall the resources of technology, the university, corporations, and government to eliminate poverty and racism. Hence, their agenda of reform. What remains most impressive from the Port Huron Statement, however, is its moderation, its faith that change can take place within the system, its conviction that social democracy could be achieved quickly and effectively, without revolution. The Port Huron Statement speaks eloquently to the idealism of a generation of student activists. Just as eloquently, it testifies to their innocence.*

### INTRODUCTION: AGENDA FOR A GENERATION

We are people of this generation, bred in at least modest comfort, housed now in universities, looking uncomfortably to the world we inherit.

When we were kids the United States was the wealthiest and strongest country in the world; the only one with the atom bomb, the least scarred by modern war, an initiator of the United Nations that we thought would distribute Western influence throughout the world. Freedom and equality for each individual, government of, by, and for the people—these American values we found good, prin-

Excerpted from Tom Hayden et al., Port Huron Statement, mimeographed (n.p., Students for a Democratic Society, 1962).

ciples by which we could live as men. Many of us began maturing in complacency.

As we grew, however, our comfort was penetrated by events too troubling to dismiss. First, the permeating and victimizing fact of human degradation, symbolized by the Southern struggle against racial bigotry, compelled most of us from silence to activism. Second, the enclosing fact of the Cold War, symbolized by the presence of the Bomb, brought awareness that we ourselves, and our friends, and millions of abstract "others" we knew more directly because of our common peril, might die at any time. We might deliberately ignore, or avoid, or fail to feel all other human problems, but not these two, for these were too immediate and crushing in their impact, too challenging in the demand that we as individuals take the responsibility for encounter and resolution.

While these and other problems either directly oppressed us or rankled our consciences and became our own subjective concerns, we began to see complicated and disturbing paradoxes in our surrounding America. The declaration "all men are created equal . . . " rang hollow before the facts of Negro life in the South and the big cities of the North. The proclaimed peaceful intentions of the United States contradicted its economic and military investments in the Cold War status quo. . . .

Our work is guided by the sense that we may be the last generation in the experiment with living. But we are a minority—the vast majority of our people regard the temporary equilibriums of our society and world as eternally-functional parts. In this is perhaps the outstanding paradox: we ourselves are imbued with urgency, yet the message of our society is that there is no viable alternative to the present. Beneath the reassuring tones of the politicians, beneath the common opinion that America will "muddle through," beneath the stagnation of those who have closed their minds to the future, is the pervading feeling that there simply are no alternatives, that our times have witnessed the exhaustion not only of Utopias, but of any new departures as well. . . .

Some would have us believe that Americans feel contentment amidst prosperity—but might it not better be called a glaze above deeply-felt anxieties about their role in the new world? And if these anxieties produce a developed indifference to human affairs, do they not as well produce a yearning to believe there *is* an alternative to the present, that something *can* be done to change circumstances in the school, the workplaces, the bureaucracies, the government? It is to this latter yearning, at once the spark and engine of change, that we direct our present appeal. The search for truly democratic alternatives to the present, and a commitment to social experimentation with them, is a worthy and fulfilling human enterprise, one which moves us and, we hope, others today. On such a basis do we offer this document of our convictions and analysis: as an effort in understanding and changing the conditions of humanity in the late twentieth century, an effort rooted in the ancient, still unfulfilled conception of man attaining determining influence over his circumstances of life. . . .

## THE STUDENTS

If student movements for change are still rareties on the campus scene, what is commonplace there? The real campus, the familiar campus, is a place of private people, engaged in their notorious "inner emigration." It is a place of commitment to business-as-usual, getting ahead, playing it cool. It is a place of mass affirmation of the Twist, but mass reluctance toward the controversial public stance. Rules are accepted as "inevitable," bureaucracy as "just circumstances," irrelevance as "scholarship," selflessness as "martyrdom," politics as "just another way to make people, and an unprofitable one, too." . . .

Tragically, the university could serve as a significant source of social criticism and an initiator of new modes and molders of attitudes. But the actual intellectual effect of the college experience is hardly distinguishable from that of any other communications channel— say, a television set—passing on the stock truths of the day. Students leave college somewhat more "tolerant" than when they arrived, but basically unchallenged in their values and political orientations. With administrators ordering the institution, and faculty the curriculum, the student learns by his isolation to accept elite rule within the university, which prepares him to accept later forms of minority control. The real function of the educational system—as opposed to its more rhetorical function of "searching for truth"—is to impart the key information and styles that will help the student get by, modestly but comfortably, in the big society beyond.

## THE SOCIETY BEYOND

Look beyond the campus, to America itself. That student life is more intellectual, and perhaps more comfortable, does not obscure the fact that the fundamental qualities of life on the campus reflect the habits of society at large. The fraternity president is seen at the junior manager levels; the sorority queen has gone to Grosse Pointe; the serious poet burns for a place, any place, to work; the once-serious and never-serious poets work at the advertising agencies. The desperation of people threatened by forces about which they know little and of which they can say less; the cheerful emptiness of people "giving up" all hope of changing things; the faceless ones polled by Gallup who listed "international affairs" fourteenth on their list of "problems" but who also expected thermonuclear war in the next few years; in these and other forms, Americans are in withdrawal from public life, from any collective effort at directing their own affairs. . . .

The very isolation of the individual—from power and community and ability to aspire—means the rise of a democracy without publics. With the great mass of people structurally remote and psychologically hesitant with respect to democratic institutions, those institutions themselves attenuate and become, in the fashion of the vicious circle, progressively less accessible to those few who aspire to serious participation in social affairs. The vital democratic connection between community and leadership, between the mass and the several elites, has been so wrenched and perverted that disastrous policies go unchallenged time and again.

## POLITICS WITHOUT PUBLICS

The American political system is not the democratic model of which its glorifiers speak. In actuality it frustrates democracy by confusing the individual citizen, paralyzing policy discussion, and consolidating the irresponsible power of military and business interests. . . .

A most alarming fact is that few, if any, politicians are calling for changes in these conditions. Only a handful even are calling on the President to "live up to" platform pledges; no one is demanding structural changes, such as the shuttling of Southern Democrats out of the Democratic Party. Rather than protesting the state of politics, most politicians are reinforcing and aggravating that state. . . .

## THE ECONOMY

We live amidst a national celebration of economic prosperity while poverty and deprivation remain an unbreakable way of life for millions in the "affluent society," including many of our own generation. We hear glib references to the "welfare state," "free enterprise," and "shareholder's democracy" while military defense is the main item of "public" spending and obvious oligopoly and other forms of minority rule defy real individual initiative or popular control. Work, too, is often unfulfilling and victimizing, accepted as a channel to status or plenty, if not a way to pay the bills, rarely as a means of understanding and controlling self and events. In work and leisure the individual is regulated as part of the system, a consuming unit, bombarded by hard-sell, soft-sell, lies and semitrue appeals to his basest drives. He is always told that he is a "free" man because of "free enterprise." . . .

### The Military-Industrial Complex

The most spectacular and important creation of the authoritarian and oligopolistic structure of economic decision-making in America is the institution called "the military-industrial complex" by former President Eisenhower—the powerful congruence of interest and structure among military and business elites which affects so much of our development and destiny. Not only is ours the first generation to live with the possibility of world-wide cataclysm—it is the first to experience the actual social preparation for cataclysm, the general militarization of American society. . . .

Since our childhood these two trends—the rise of the military and the installation of a defense-based economy—have grown fantastically. The Department of Defense, ironically the world's largest single organization, is worth $160 billion, owns 32 million acres of America and employs half the 7.5 million persons directly dependent on the military for subsistence, has an $11 billion payroll which is larger than the net annual income of all American corporations. Defense spending in the Eisenhower era totaled $350 billions and President Kennedy entered office pledged to go even beyond the present defense allocation of 60 cents from every public dollar spent. Except for a war-induced boom immediately after "our side" bombed Hiroshima, American economic prosperity has coincided with a growing dependence on military outlay—from 1911 to 1959 America's Gross

National Product of $5.25 trillion included $700 billion in goods and services purchased for the defense effort, about one-seventh of the accumulated GNP. . . .

## TOWARD AMERICAN DEMOCRACY

Every effort to end the Cold War and expand the process of world industrialization is an effort hostile to people and institutions whose interests lie in perpetuation of the East-West military threat and the postponement of change in the "have not" nations of the world. Every such effort, too, is bound to establish greater democracy in America. The major goals of a domestic effort would be:

1. America must abolish its political party stalemate. . . .
2. Mechanisms of voluntary association must be created through which political information can be imparted and political participation encouraged. . . .
3. Institutions and practices which stifle dissent should be abolished, and the promotion of peaceful dissent should be actively promoted.
4. Corporations must be made publicly responsible. . . .
5. The allocation of resources must be based on social needs. A truly "public sector" must be established, and its nature debated and planned. . . .
6. America should concentrate on its genuine social priorities: abolish squalor, terminate neglect, and establish an environment for people to live in with dignity and creativeness. . . .

# The Sharon Statement (1960)

## Young Americans for Freedom

*When we talk about the 1960s as an era of radicalism, as a time when young people rejected the status quo and attempted to transform American life and politics, we are almost always talking about the Left and groups such as Students for a Democratic Society. But in the 1960s, the sense of possibility that motivated young people to seek fundamental changes in American society was by no means restricted to the Left. Beginning at the dawn of the decade, conservative youth also rejected the domestic policies of what was called the "liberal consensus," a dominant political understanding that combined relatively modest government-sponsored social programs with a faith in capitalism and economic individualism. Unlike their peers in the New Left, however, conservative youth did not reject the two-party political system, but instead attempted to capture the Republican Party and move it dramatically to the right.*

*Young Americans for Freedom was the most important organization for conservative youth in the 1960s. The organization was founded in September 1960, at the Sharon, Connecticut, family estate of conservative columnist and* National Review *editor William F. Buckley. Like the authors of the Port Huron Statement, which was written two years later, the ninety young men and women who gathered for the Sharon Conference believed that the United States was at a critical turning point in its history. Their "Sharon Statement" was a statement of principles for a time of "moral and political crises." It affirmed what the authors called "eternal truths" derived from the individual's right to use his "God-given free will," central to which was an unrestricted free market economy. The Sharon Statement also offered a justification for States' Rights and called for victory over—not coexistence with—communism.*

*In the mid-1960s, the YAF had roughly the same membership as the historically much-better-known SDS, and wielded greater political power. YAF played a critical role in securing the 1964 Republican presidential nomination for the "true conservative" Goldwater over more moderate Republican candidates such as Nelson Rockefeller. Though Goldwater was defeated, YAF saw victory in its ability to shift the party to the right. At the same time, it had to contend with new supporters drawn not by what it defined as "traditional" conservative principles but by a States' Rights platform that defined racial segregation and discrimination as local issues beyond the purview of the federal government. In the latter half of the decade, YAF splintered and lost visibility, but it served as a training ground for leaders who claimed political power in the 1980s.*

In this time of moral and political crises, it is the responsibility of the youth of America to affirm certain eternal truths.

We, as young conservatives, believe:

That foremost among the transcendent values is the individual's use of his God-given free will, whence derives his right to be free from the restrictions of arbitrary force;

That liberty is indivisible, and that political freedom cannot long exist without economic freedom;

That the purpose of government is to protect those freedoms through the preservation of internal order, the provision of national defense, and the administration of justice;

That when government ventures beyond these rightful functions, it accumulates power, which tends to diminish order and liberty;

That the Constitution of the United States is the best arrangement yet devised for empowering government to fulfill its proper role, while restraining it from the concentration and abuse of power;

That the genius of the Constitution—the division of powers—is summed up in the clause that reserves primacy to the several states, or to the people, in those spheres not specifically delegated to the Federal government;

That the market economy, allocating resources by the free play of supply and demand, is the single economic system compatible with the requirements of personal freedom and constitutional government, and that it is at the same time the most productive supplier of human needs;

That when government interferes with the work of the market economy, it tends to reduce the moral and physical strength of the nation; that when it takes from one man to bestow on another, it diminishes the incentive of the first, the integrity of the second, and the moral autonomy of both;

That we will be free only so long as the national sovereignty of the United States is secure; that history shows periods of freedom are rare, and can exist only when free citizens concertedly defend their rights against all enemies;

That the forces of international Communism are, at present, the greatest single threat to these liberties;

That the United States should stress victory over, rather than coexistence with, this menace; and

That American foreign policy must be judged by this criterion: does it serve the just interests of the United States?

# Inaugural Address (1961)

## John F. Kennedy

*Bareheaded and coatless in the bitter cold of a bright January day, John F. Kennedy, the youngest man ever elected president of the United States, placed his hand on the Bible and swore the oath of office. In his inaugural address, Kennedy offered a grand vision. We remember the inspirational words, "ask not what your country can do for you—ask what you can do for your country." What is too often lost in our collective memories, shaped as they are by the tragedy of a young man cut down before his time, is what he asked us to do for our country. "Pay any price, bear any burden, meet any hardship . . .": Kennedy was summoning Americans to a global mission. His words rang out in warning to America's foes abroad. It was a moment, as Robert Frost wrote in his inaugural poem, "Of young ambition eager to be tried. . . . In any game the nations want to play."*

*How does this speech express the sense of possibility we associate with Kennedy's presidency? Does it matter that his call for Americans to "bear any burden" was in relation to the Cold War and not a summons to confront America's domestic problems of poverty and racial discrimination? Does Kennedy's address fit best here, in the section on "The Politics and Culture of the Affluent Society," or with the documents in "America Becomes a World Power"?*

VICE PRESIDENT JOHNSON, MR. SPEAKER, MR. CHIEF JUSTICE, PRESIDENT EISENHOWER, VICE PRESIDENT NIXON, PRESIDENT TRUMAN, REVEREND CLERGY, FELLOW CITIZENS:

We observe today not a victory of party but a celebration of freedom—symbolizing an end as well as a beginning—signifying renewal as well as change. For I have sworn before you and Almighty God the same solemn oath our forbears prescribed nearly a century and three-quarters ago.

The world is very different now. For man holds in his mortal hands the power to abolish all forms of human poverty and all forms of human life. And yet the same revolutionary beliefs for which our forebears fought are still at issue around the globe—the belief that the rights of man come not from the generosity of the state but from the hand of God.

We dare not forget today that we are the heirs of that first revolution. Let the word go forth from this time and place, to friend and foe alike, that the torch has been passed to a new generation of Americans—born in this century, tempered by war, disciplined by a hard and bitter peace, proud of our ancient heritage—and unwilling to witness or permit the slow undoing of those human rights to which this nation has always been committed, and to which we are committed today at home and around the world.

Let every nation know, whether it wishes us well or ill, that we shall pay any price, bear any burden, meet any hardship, support any friend, oppose any foe to assure the survival and the success of liberty.

This much we pledge—and more.

To those old allies whose cultural and spiritual origins we share, we pledge the loyalty of faithful friends. United there is little we cannot do in a host of cooperative ventures. Divided there is little we can do—for we dare not meet a powerful challenge at odds and split asunder.

To those new states whom we welcome to the ranks of the free, we pledge our word that one form of colonial control shall not have passed away merely to be replaced by a far more iron tyranny. We shall not always expect to find them supporting our view. But we shall always hope to find them strongly supporting their own freedom—and to remember that, in the past, those who foolishly sought power by riding the back of the tiger ended up inside.

To those people in the huts and villages of half the globe struggling to break the bonds of mass misery, we pledge our best efforts to help them help themselves, for whatever period is required—not because the communists may be doing it, not because we seek their votes, but because it is right. If a free society cannot help the many who are poor, it cannot save the few who are rich.

To our sister republics south of our border, we offer a special pledge—to convert our good words into good deeds—in a new alliance for progress—to assist free men and free governments in casting off the chains of poverty. But this peaceful revolution of hope cannot become the prey of hostile powers. Let all our neighbors know that we shall join with them to oppose aggression or subversion anywhere in the Americas. And let every other power know that this Hemisphere intends to remain the master of its own house.

To that world assembly of sovereign states, the United Nations, our last best hope in an age where the instruments of war have far outpaced the instruments of peace, we renew our pledge of support—to prevent it from becoming merely a forum for invective—to strengthen its shield of the new and the weak—and to enlarge the area in which its writ may run.

Finally, to those nations who would make themselves our adversary, we offer not a pledge but a request: that both sides begin anew the quest for peace, before the dark powers of destruction unleashed by science engulf all humanity in planned or accidental self-destruction.

We dare not tempt them with weakness. For only when our arms are sufficient beyond doubt can we be certain beyond doubt that they will never be employed.

But neither can two great and powerful groups of nations take comfort from our present course—both sides overburdened by the cost of modern weapons, both rightly alarmed by the steady spread of the deadly atom, yet both racing to alter that uncertain balance of terror that stays the hand of mankind's final war.

So let us begin anew—remembering on both sides that civility is not a sign of weakness, and sincerity is always subject to proof. Let us never negotiate out of fear. But let us never fear to negotiate.

Let both sides explore what problems unite us instead of belaboring those problems which divide us.

Let both sides, for the first time, formulate serious and precise proposals for the inspection and control of arms—and bring the absolute power to destroy other nations under the absolute control of all nations.

Let both sides seek to invoke the wonders of science instead of its terrors. Together let us explore the stars, conquer the deserts, eradicate disease, tap the ocean depths and encourage the arts and commerce.

Let both sides unite to heed in all corners of the earth the command of Isaiah—to "undo the heavy burdens . . . (and) let the oppressed go free."

And if a beachhead of cooperation may push back the jungle of suspicion, let both sides join in creating a new endeavor, not a new balance of power, but a new world of law, where the strong are just and the weak secure and the peace preserved.

All this will not be finished in the first one hundred days. Nor will it be finished in the first one thousand days, nor in the life of this

Administration, nor even perhaps in our lifetime on this planet. But let us begin.

In your hands, my fellow citizens, more than mine, will rest the final success or failure of our course. Since this country was founded, each generation of Americans has been summoned to give testimony to its national loyalty. The graves of young Americans who answered the call to service surround the globe.

Now the trumpet summons us again—not as a call to bear arms, though arms we need—not as a call to battle, though embattled we are—but a call to bear the burden of a long twilight struggle, year in and year out, "rejoicing in hope, patient in tribulation"—a struggle against the common enemies of man: tyranny, poverty, disease and war itself.

Can we forge against these enemies a grand and global alliance, North and South, East and West, that can assure a more fruitful life for all mankind? Will you join in that historic effort?

In the long history of the world, only a few generations have been granted the role of defending freedom in its hour of maximum danger. I do not shrink from this responsibility—I welcome it. I do not believe that any of us would exchange places with any other people or any other generation. The energy, the faith, the devotion which we bring to this endeavor will light our country and all who serve it—and the glow from that fire can truly light the world.

And so, my fellow Americans: ask not what your country can do for you—ask what you can do for your country.

My fellow citizens of the world: ask not what America will do for you, but what together we can do for the freedom of man.

Finally, whether you are citizens of America or citizens of the world, ask of us here the same high standards of strength and sacrifice which we ask of you. With a good conscience our only sure reward, with history the final judge of our deeds, let us go forth to lead the land we love, asking His blessing and His help, but knowing that here on earth God's work must truly be our own.

# "The Great Society": Remarks at the University of Michigan (1964)

## Lyndon B. Johnson

*On May 22, 1964, President Lyndon Johnson gave the commencement address at the University of Michigan. Before the audience of young men and women and their families, he unveiled his vision of a "Great Society." Though much less well known than John F. Kennedy's Inaugural Address, Johnson's Great Society speech marks a major turning point in American government and politics. Johnson's legislative agenda (as documented in the next article) was extraordinarily ambitious and would reshape the role of American government. But the larger ideas about the role of government Johnson sets forth here are also significant. Compare this speech to Kennedy's Inaugural Address. How do their visions of the nation's purpose differ?*

I have come today from the turmoil of your Capital to the tranquility of your campus to speak about the future of our country. The purpose of protecting the life of our Nation and preserving the liberty of our citizens is to pursue the happiness of our people. Our success in that pursuit is the test of our success as a nation. For a century we labored to settle and to subdue a continent. For half a century, we called upon unbounded invention and untiring industry to create an order of plenty for all our people. The challenge of the next half century is whether we have the wisdom to use that wealth to enrich and elevate our national life, and to advance the quality of our American civilization.

Your imagination, your initiative, and your indignation will determine whether we build a society where progress is the servant of our needs, or a society where old values and new visions are buried under unbridled growth. For in your time we have the opportunity to

*Public Papers of the Presidents of the United States, Lyndon B. Johnson, 1963–64,* pp. 704–7.

move not only toward the rich society and the powerful society, but upward to the Great Society. The Great Society rests on abundance and liberty for all. It demands an end to poverty and racial injustice, to which we are totally committed in our time. But that is just the beginning. The Great Society is a place where every child can find knowledge to enrich his mind and to enlarge his talents. It is a place where leisure is a welcome chance to build and reflect, not a feared cause of boredom and restlessness. It is a place where the city of man serves not only the needs of the body and the demands of commerce, but the desire for beauty and the hunger for community.

It is a place where man can renew contact with nature. It is a place which honors creation for its own sake and for what it adds to the understanding of the race. It is a place where men are more concerned with the quality of their goals than the quantity of their goods. But most of all, the Great Society is not a safe harbor, a resting place, a final objective, a finished work. It is a challenge constantly renewed, beckoning us toward a destiny where the meaning of our lives matches the marvelous products of our labor.

So I want to talk to you today about three places where we begin to build the Great Society—in our cities, in our countryside, and in our classrooms. Many of you will live to see the day, perhaps 50 years from now, when there will be 400 million Americans; four-fifths of them in urban areas. In the remainder of this century urban population will double, city land will double, and we will have to build homes, highways and facilities equal to all those built since this country was first settled. So in the next 40 years we must rebuild the entire urban United States.

Aristotle said, "Men come together in cities in order to live, but they remain together in order to live the good life."

It is harder and harder to live the good life in American cities today. The catalogue of ills is long: There is the decay of the centers and the despoiling of the suburbs. There is not enough housing for our people or transportation for our traffic. Open land is vanishing and old landmarks are violated. Worst of all, expansion is eroding the precious and time-honored values of community with neighbors and communion with nature. The loss of these values breeds loneliness and boredom and indifference. Our society will never be great until our cities are great. Today the frontier of imagination and innovation is inside those cities, and not beyond their borders. New experiments are already going on. It will be the task of your generation to make the American city a place where future generations will come, not only to live but to live the good life.

I understand that if I stay here tonight I would see that Michigan students are really doing their best to live the good life. This is the place where the Peace Corps was started. It is inspiring to see how all of you, while you are in this country, are trying so hard to live at the level of the people.

A second place where we begin to build the Great Society is in our countryside. We have always prided ourselves on being not only America the strong and America the free, but America the beautiful. Today that beauty is in danger. The water we drink, the food we eat, the very air that we breathe, are threatened with pollution. Our parks are overcrowded. Our seashores overburdened. Green fields and dense forests are disappearing.

A few years ago we were greatly concerned about the Ugly American. Today we must act to prevent an Ugly America.

For once the battle is lost, once our natural splendor is destroyed, it can never be recaptured. And once man can no longer walk with beauty or wonder at nature, his spirit will wither and his sustenance be wasted.

A third place to build the Great Society is in the classrooms of America. There your children's lives will be shaped. Our society will not be great until every young mind is set free to scan the farthest reaches of thought and imagination. We are still far from that goal. Today, eight million adult Americans, more than the entire population of Michigan, have not finished five years of school. Nearly 20 million have not finished 8 years of school. Nearly 54 million, more than one-quarter of all America, have not even finished high school.

Each year more than 100,000 high school graduates, with proven ability, do not enter college because they cannot afford it. And if we cannot educate today's youth, what will we do in 1970 when elementary school enrollment will be 5 million greater than 1960? And high school enrollment will rise by 5 million. College enrollment will increase by more than 3 million. In many places, classrooms are overcrowded and curricula are outdated. Most of our qualified teachers are underpaid, and many of our paid teachers are unqualified. So we must give every child a place to sit and a teacher to learn from. Poverty must not be a bar to learning, and learning must offer an escape from poverty.

But more classrooms and more teachers are not enough. We must seek an educational system which grows in excellence as it grows in size. This means better training for our teachers. It means preparing youth to enjoy their hours of leisure as well as their hours of labor. It means exploring new techniques of teaching, to find new ways to stimulate the love of learning and the capacity for creation.

These are three of the central issues of the Great Society. While our government has many programs directed at those issues, I do not pretend that we have the full answer to those problems. But I do promise this: We are going to assemble the best thought and the broadest knowledge from all over the world to find those answers for America. I intend to establish working groups to prepare a series of White House conferences and meetings on the cities, on natural beauty, on the quality of education, and on other emerging challenges. And from these meetings and from this inspiration and from these studies we will begin to set our course toward the Great Society.

The solution to these problems does not rest on a massive program in Washington, nor can it rely solely on the strained resources of local authority. They require us to create new concepts of cooperation, a creative federalism, between the national Capitol and the leaders of local communities.

Woodrow Wilson once wrote: "Every man sent out from this university should be a man of his nation as well as a man of his time."

Within your lifetime powerful forces, already loosed, will take us toward a way of life beyond the realm of our experience, almost beyond the bounds of our imagination. For better or for worse, your generation has been appointed by history to deal with those problems and to lead America toward a new age. You have the chance never before afforded to any people in any age. You can help build a society where the demands of morality, and the needs of the spirit, can be realized in the life of the Nation. So will you join in the battle to give every citizen the full equality which God enjoins and the law requires, whatever his belief, or race, or the color of his skin? Will you join in the battle to give every citizen an escape from the crushing weight of poverty? Will you join in the battle to make it possible for all nations to live in enduring peace as neighbors and not as mortal enemies? Will you join in the battle to build the Great Society, to prove that our material progress is only the foundation on which we will build a richer life of mind and spirit?

There are those timid souls who say this battle cannot be won, that we are condemned to a soulless wealth. I do not agree. We have the power to shape the civilization that we want. But we need your will, your labor, your hearts, if we are to build that kind of society.

Those who came to this land sought to build more than just a new country. They sought a free world.

So I have come here today to your campus to say that you can make their vision our reality. Let us from this moment begin our work so that in the future men will look back and say: It was then, after a long and weary way, that man turned the exploits of his genius to the full enrichment of his life.

Thank you. Goodbye.

# Lyndon B. Johnson and American Liberalism

*Bruce J. Schulman*

*Elevated to the presidency in late 1963 by the assassination of John Kennedy, Lyndon Johnson faced a difficult task. Stepping into the shoes of the nation's slain leader, a man very different from himself, required enormous political savvy. But Johnson turned the challenge to his advantage. As he later explained, his goal was to take a "dead man's program and turn it into a martyr's cause."*

*Johnson was elected to the presidency in 1964 with 61 percent of the popular vote. He used this mandate to further his ambitious legislative agenda, which he called the Great Society. In the following excerpts from his book,* Lyndon B. Johnson and American Liberalism, *historian Bruce Schulman analyzes the Great Society and explains the development of 1960s liberalism. In this portrait of a larger-than-life political figure waging legislative war on the ills of American society, Schulman assesses the successes and failures of the Great Society and, by extension, of American political liberalism in the 1960s.*

In the early years of the twentieth century, T[eddy] R[oosevelt], [Woodrow] Wilson, and the Progressives had initiated a transformation of American liberalism, changing the very meaning of the term. *Liberalism* derived, of course, from a passion for liberty, a concern for freedom. Nineteenth-century liberalism, what historians now term *classical liberalism,* embraced a largely negative view of freedom. Freedom, in this sense, meant only absence of restraint, the ability to do as one pleased without undue encumbrance or regulation. Classical liberals saw government as the gravest threat to freedom and believed that the government that governs least governs best.

The complexity of modern life and the forces unleashed by the industrial revolution called into question this negative definition of liberty. Small, limited government conferred only the most tenuous sort of freedom when it afforded citizens no protection against contaminated meat, adulterated drugs, unsafe factories, and price-gouging monopolists. Encountering these new realities, modern liberals recognized that real freedom required the active protection of an interventionist government. "In the present day," Theodore Roosevelt had explained, "the limitation of governmental power means the enslavement of the people." He and his fellow Progressives envisioned a larger role for government as a referee or police officer, ensuring that the economy and society operated freely and fairly.

Franklin Roosevelt inherited and extended this positive view of freedom. He cemented the alliance between liberalism and activist government that his forebear first forged. When FDR laid out what he described as the four basic freedoms in 1941, he included not only traditional liberties like freedom of speech and freedom of religion, but also freedom from want and freedom from fear. These last freedoms represented guaranteed security against economic depression and foreign aggression, freedoms that only an energetic, vigilant big government could assure. . . .

[In the post–World War II era,] liberalism itself evolved, breaking its New Deal template in three crucial respects. First, postwar liberals developed a new attitude toward business and the economy. Economic policy had always been redistributive—taking advantages from one segment of the population and conferring them on another. . . . New Deal liberals had believed that government needed to restrain the worst excesses of big business, guarantee workers a fair shake, and ensure a minimum American standard of living for the poorest citizens. . . .

The wartime experience seemed to prove the efficacy of a new type of liberal economic policy—a way to improve the lives of ordinary Americans without offending business, to feed the hungry and shelter the homeless without asking the well-off to sacrifice.

This new liberal tool was called Keynesian economics, named for its originator, the British economist John Maynard Keynes. For American liberals after World War II, Keynes's most useful insight was that government could use fiscal policy, its powers of taxing and spending, to stimulate the economy. Washington policymakers learned from Keynes that they could heat up a slowing economy and prevent future depressions. But American Keynesians were not content with averting future downturns; they wanted to use Keynesian economics to ensure continued and continuous economic growth, to make the economic pie bigger and bigger. There would be more for everyone, rich and poor, labor and business. . . .

Second, American liberals developed a new view of the political process after World War II, a new vision of democracy. Public policy had become so complicated and distant that individuals had little knowledge of and less input into the nation's most important decisions. . . . In the 1950s political theorists believed that when the people did mobilize and masses of citizens involved themselves in the political process, they tended to act on vague, irrational principles and emotions, not on informed, sober reflection. The rise of Nazism in Germany had proved that mass participation did not necessarily mean increased democracy. In this setting postwar liberals championed pluralist politics, a view of American democracy as a process of bargaining among groups. . . .

Third, and most important, postwar liberals focused their energies on the struggle against international communism. . . . In fact, the cold war struggle against communism underlay all of these changes in liberal outlook. Constant economic growth distinguished American capitalism from Soviet communism, with its commitment to class conflict. . . . Pluralist politics allowed Americans to contrast American democracy with Soviet dictatorship, to champion pragmatic problem solving over crusading ideology. . . .

## LYNDON JOHNSON AND 1960S LIBERALISM

[Following Kennedy's assassination,] Johnson assumed the Kennedy mantle, declaring himself the "dutiful executor" of his predecessor's legacy. He shouldered a heavy burden, for the shock of the assassination instantly elevated Kennedy, an uncertain leader only beginning to establish himself, into an unparalleled martyr, the symbol of all that was grand in the nation. Only 49.7 percent of the electorate had cast their ballots for JFK in 1960, but after the assassination, 65 percent claimed that they had voted for him. Even opponents of the slain president, a national poll revealed, overwhelmingly mourned his death as "the loss of someone close and dear."

Five days after the assassination, Johnson made his first presidential address to the American people. Significantly, he made the speech not from the Oval Office of the White House, but before a joint session of Congress, in the place where he had started his career. Johnson began by expressing the collective grief of the nation but did not content himself with honoring the fallen hero. Committing himself to vigorous action on behalf of the Kennedy agenda, Johnson promised to complete the slain leader's work, and he made it clear that the most immediate tasks were on Capitol Hill. He asked for enactment of the Kennedy tax bill and most emphatically for civil rights legislation: "We have talked long enough in this country about equal rights. We have talked for one hundred years or more. It is time now to write the next chapter, and to write it in the books of law."

President Johnson had reassured the American people with his promise to "continue"; he accepted his duty as custodian of the Kennedy legacy. But he made it clear that his would be no caretaker administration. When one adviser warned him against risking too much prestige and power to implement Kennedy's legislative program, LBJ paused, raised his eyebrows, and replied, "Well, then what the hell's the presidency for?"

Johnson immediately went on what his exhausted assistants called the "two-shift day." Rising at six-thirty, LBJ would work furiously until about two o'clock, when he left the Oval Office and took a walk or a swim. Then he would change into his pajamas for a catnap, usually on the long couch in the private sitting room adjoining his office. At four, he was showered and dressed, ready for a "new day's work." The second shift would end after midnight, sometimes lasting until two in the morning if affairs were especially pressing. . . .

Johnson immediately began placing his own distinctive, earthy stamp on the White House. When special assistant Jack Valenti cluttered up the president's schedule with "brief visits" from prominent citizens, Johnson warned him that there was no such thing as a brief visit. "Hell," LBJ complained, "by the time a man scratches his ass, clears his throat, and tells me how smart he is, we've already wasted fifteen minutes." Occasionally, Johnson would interrupt a high-level meeting for a swimming break; he would lead the assembled staff (and sometimes reporters or guests) down to the White House pool, strip naked, and dive in. He expected others to do the same. When using the bathroom, when showering in the morning, when receiving a massage at night—at all of those intimate and possibly embarrassing moments—he expected staff members to follow him into bedroom and bathroom and continue their conversations as if still in an office. . . .

Even as he stamped the White House as his own, Johnson carefully honored the Kennedy legacy. In contrast to his disconcertingly familiar behavior with his own aides, he remained deeply respectful of JFK's cabinet and top officials. He needed Kennedy's aides, needed the image of continuity; and with very few exceptions, Kennedy's appointees stayed on and served the new president. . . .

With the White House geared up for two shifts and the Kennedy men on board, LBJ prepared to revive the stalled Kennedy agenda. In many ways, the moment perfectly suited Johnson's talents. The shocked and sorrowful country cried out for unity and healing, and Lyndon Johnson had spent his whole life fashioning consensus, bringing bitter rivals to compromise through sheer force of will. The liberal agenda had been formulated; it just needed congressional approval. The assassination placed LBJ—an unparalleled legislative tactician and savvy horse trader—in the White House and allowed him to use the president's tragic death to ram through Johnson's legislative program. Few legislators dared oppose the last, best hope of the martyred Kennedy, especially with Lyndon Johnson twisting their arms. Moreover, 1964 was a time of relative quiet in foreign policy. Despite two small-scale crises in Latin America and the deteriorating situation in Vietnam, Johnson was able to hold the line on international affairs—to continue the Kennedy foreign policies while devoting himself to domestic politics. His first State of the Union Address, delivered on January 8, 1964, dealt almost exclusively with problems and prospects at home—the first State of the Union to do so since the beginning of the cold war.

In that speech, Johnson asked the Congress to "carry forward the plans and programs of John Fitzgerald Kennedy." But it was left to Lyndon Johnson to formulate those plans and to execute them. "Everything I had ever learned in the history books taught me that martyrs have to die for causes," LBJ recalled later. "John Kennedy had died. But his 'cause' was not really clear. That was my job. I had to take the dead man's program and turn it into a martyr's cause. . . ."

No president matched Johnson's skills as chief legislator. Despite the far-reaching and controversial nature of his program, LBJ won congressional approval for 58 percent of his proposals in 1964, 69 percent in 1965, and 56 percent in 1966, compared, for example, with 37 percent for Eisenhower in 1957 and just 27 percent for JFK in 1963. In the early days of LBJ's presidency, Republicans complained about the "Xerox Congress" or the "three-B Congress—bullied, badgered, and brainwashed," but they found themselves powerless against Johnson's legislative juggernaut. When the "Great 89th," the Congress which LBJ swept into office with his 1964 landslide, completed its work in the autumn of 1966, it left behind the most productive law-making record in American history. Lawrence O'Brien, LBJ's chief congressional liaison, and domestic policy chief Joseph Califano proudly produced a summary of the legislative achievements.

The list was staggering. For LBJ not only secured the civil rights, health, education, and welfare measures commonly associated with the Great Society, but a host of other reforms. Less noted than Medicare or the war on poverty, many of these proved to have broader and more durable effects. The Immigration Act of 1965 eliminated the odious quota system which first became law amidst an outburst of racist nativism in the 1920s. The national origins system, as it was called, had severely limited immigration from eastern and southern Europe and all but banned arrivals from Asia. Declaring the limits "incompatible with our basic American tradition," Johnson outlawed ethnic quotas and opened the doors to a steady stream of arrivals from Asia. The act made possible the large migrations of Koreans, Filipinos, Japanese, and Vietnamese to the United States that have contributed so much to the nation's economic and cultural life and so dramatically transformed the nation's western states.

Johnson pressed for restrictions on government wiretapping and surveillance and signed an act granting scholars, investigators, and private citizens access to government files. Although he privately taped many of his own phone conversations and allowed the FBI to continue electronic eavesdropping, Johnson ordered other government agencies to halt bugging and urged the Congress to limit the practice.

LBJ also stepped up government regulation of the environment. He signed major federal initiatives restricting water and air pollution, initiated with Lady Bird's help a national highway beautification program, and added more land to the national wildlife refuges, wilderness, and national park systems than any president of the era. At the end of his administration, the chairman of the National Geographic Society called LBJ "our greatest conservation president."

Johnson had spent a lifetime working to pass laws; for him, the major struggle of political life, the principal task of presidential liberalism, was obtaining congressional approval for a broad-scale liberal program. No other president—not JFK, not even FDR, had done that so well. With a stroke of a pen, he set aside land as wilderness, opened the nation's doors to Asian immigrants, or increased the minimum wage. But, in most cases, signing a law was not enough to produce effective action. Making law was only the first step in making policy—programs needed to be implemented and administered as well as enacted by the Congress. Johnson thought that if he could just plant the seeds for his Great Society, it would slowly but surely grow into a vast, powerful, impregnable oak. But he proved better at planting than at watering and nurturing. As one Johnson-watcher put it, "Pass the bill now, worry about its effects and implementation later—this was the White House strategy. . . . The standard of success was the passage of the law—and not only within the administration, but in the press and among the public. By this standard, the Great Society was on its way to becoming the most successful domestic program in history."

## THE NOT-SO-GREAT SOCIETY: IMPLEMENTING LBJ'S PROGRAM

Unfortunately, the very compromises and concessions needed to prevail on Capitol Hill hampered the programs after they won legislative approval. For example, Title I of the Elementary and Secondary Education Act, the marrow of LBJ's education program, allocated one billion federal dollars in compensatory education funds for poor students. Before Title I, local communities had always controlled and financed education in the United States. Local control not only created vast inequities between wealthier and poorer neighborhoods, but perpetuated them, since without good schools, residents of poor areas were unlikely to break free of poverty.

The Johnson administration designed Title I to end this depressing cycle of ignorance and want. The law's rationale was simple: children from poor families lacked the advantages of their better-off classmates and tended to fall behind academically. Schools could compensate for this problem by devoting more attention and resources to the poor than to the nonpoor; needy students would improve in the classroom and stay in school longer. Better education would eventually translate into higher incomes and break the cycle of poverty.

To pass the bill, however, the Johnson administration needed the support of local school districts, of the educational establishment in place. So the ESEA granted local districts the primary responsibility for conceiving and implementing the compensatory program. In the Senate hearings on the bill, LBJ's nemesis, Robert Kennedy, challenged this provision. He asked whether local schools bore responsibility for the educational deficiencies of the poor in the first place—whether it made sense to trust the very people who created the inequities with the funds to remedy them. LBJ's commissioner of education admitted the potential problem but pledged that local school officials would change their attitudes and work for reform.

Robert Kennedy's fears proved justified. The government allocated money to a district based on the number of poor students enrolled in it, but the districts selected which schools, students, and programs received the funds. Most districts pocketed the money and continued business-as-usual. Fresno, California, used its Title I allocation to buy an educational TV system for all students; Camden, New Jersey, subsidized physical education classes for pupils regardless of income. In fact, a 1977 study revealed that few Title I dollars actually benefited poor students; most of the funds supported programs for the middle class and well-to-do. As historian Allen Matusow explained, "President Johnson always believed that Title I was an anti-poverty program. The local school districts made sure it was not."

Similarly, Johnson compromised on Medicare to win the acquiescence of doctors, on the highway beautification bill to conciliate business interests, and on the food stamp program to satisfy southern planters. By amending Great Society bills, Johnson won over stubborn lawmakers, but in the process he diluted his programs and complicated their execution.

If LBJ had dedicated his insatiable energies to implementing the Great Society, he might have overcome weaknesses in the statutes. But Johnson displayed little interest in administrating the agencies he created. This oversight surprised many of LBJ's closest confidants. As a young congressman, Johnson had seen executive branch officials sabotage FDR's initiatives by delaying and obfuscating the president's orders. In fact, one of LBJ's favorite political stories, an anecdote he repeated over and over again to impress on his staff the need for implementing his directives, concerned a visit to a tiny east Texas town during World War II. Purchasing some gasoline, LBJ handed over the Office of Price Administration (OPA) coupons needed to purchase gasoline under wartime rationing rules. The puzzled attendant looked cockeyed at Johnson and then realized where the strange coupons had come from. "Oh, the O, P and A," he exclaimed. "Well, we didn't put that in down here." Johnson understood that laws alone accomplished little good "if you didn't put 'em in," but he found implementing them easier said than done.

Johnson stinted on administration in part because he concentrated on legislative battles and because the war in Vietnam increasingly dominated his attention. But to a large extent, the problem was built into the nature of the presidency. Executive branch officials, from the lowliest bureaucrat to the president himself, papered over the problems and failures of their agencies. They believed that once Congress heard about miscues or failures, it would cut a program, rather than applaud an honest assessment and let the administration try again. "Of course, I understand the difficulties of bureaucracy," LBJ told an aide when informed of deficiencies in one Great Society program. "But what you don't understand is that the President's real trouble is with the Congress, not the bureaucracy. . . . If we went around beating our breasts and admitting difficulties in our programs, then the Congress would immediately slash all our funds for next year and then where would we be? Better to send in the reports as they are, even knowing the situation is more complicated than it appears, and then work from within to make things better and correct the problems." Constantly jockeying with Congress, LBJ mainly ignored the challenges of "putting in" the Great Society programs.

No component of the Great Society aroused higher expectations in the Congress and the country than the war on poverty; none occasioned so much controversy and disappointment when it was put into effect. In 1964, the newly created Office of Economic Opportunity (OEO) led to a multipronged attack on poverty. Head Start, an early education program for preschoolers, began in 1965. Its objective was to prepare underprivileged children for first grade, equipping them with basic academic and social skills, so that they would perform better in the early grades and be more likely to remain in school. Head Start ultimately proved a modest success, although during the Johnson years, it registered few results. . . .

The most celebrated and controversial skirmish of the war on poverty involved the Community Action Program (CAP). Attacking

persistent urban poverty head on, CAP encouraged poor neighborhoods to form their own community action agencies. These agencies
would mobilize all parts of the community "to promote fundamental
change in the interests of the poor." As OEO chief Sargent Shriver
testified before the Congress, the War on Poverty aimed not only at
individuals: "It embraces entire neighborhoods, communities, cities,
and states. It is an attempt to change institutions as well as people. It
must deal with the culture of poverty as well as the individual victims."

Shriver's remarks revealed a new understanding of poverty, especially of the hard-core poor in inner cities, that was taking shape in
the Johnson administration during the mid-1960s. Policymakers gradually developed a conception of a "culture of poverty" in the nation's
slum communities. Adherents of this view no longer conceived of the
urban poor as "rich people without money," essentially like everyone
else but lacking resources, skills, and job opportunities. Instead they
argued that the hard-core poor possessed a distinctive cultural pro-
file, a way of life passed on from generation to generation, characterized by unstable families, high rates of illegitimacy, low levels of
voting and political participation, poor self-esteem, and traumatic
childhood experiences. For some liberal policymakers, like LBJ himself, the new concept of a culture of poverty barely altered their outlook; it merely offered an additional rationale for concerted federal
effort to ameliorate conditions in the nation's inner cities. For other,
more radical observers, it proved that traditional transfer programs
must give way to community action projects that actively empowered
the poor and involved them in managing their own communities.

The CAP staff contained many people of that more aggressive
stripe—young idealists committed as much to stirring up the poor
as to helping them. Initially, LBJ paid them little attention. Johnson
gave Sargent Shriver one, and only one, piece of advice: "Keep out
crooks, communists, and cocksuckers."

Allowed so much free rein, the Community Action Program not
only financed neighborhood development projects, but also insisted
on including the poor in designing and running local programs.
Convinced that the urban poor needed power as well as resources to
transform their communities, CAP administrators wanted the needy
to form, in the words of the program's Community Action workbook,
"autonomous and self-managed organizations which are competent to exert political influence on behalf of their own self-interest."
Unlike federal aid to education, which granted power and money to

local school boards, community action would circumvent municipal officials and local elites, directly empowering and funding the poor to rebuild their own neighborhoods. For that reason, inserted into the Economic Opportunity Act was the so-called maximum feasible participation doctrine, a clause requiring that community action agencies be developed, conducted, and administered with the maximum feasible participation of residents of the area—including the poor.

The "maximum feasible participation" directive set up an irreconcilable conflict between national and local authorities. The federalist character of the American political system—the strange division of powers among federal, state, and local governments—has always offered local actors an unusually large bag of tricks for frustrating national policy. This obstructionism was peculiarly in evidence during the War on Poverty. City governments resented the strictures and proceeded to ignore them. They designed community action projects without representatives of the impoverished communities, with little attention to the special needs of blighted neighborhoods. But the OEO meant business: it rejected these plans, held up the funds, and sent city leaders back to the drawing board. It forced them to include minorities and poor people on the boards of their community agencies and to devise projects more responsive to the problems of slum neighborhoods. The conflicts took LBJ and his top aides by surprise. Neither the Congress nor the president seemed to understand the full implications of the maximum feasible participation clause. Congress, which approved the doctrine, certainly opposed any such disruptive influences on local power structures. And President Johnson acceded to it because he feared southern whites might otherwise freeze blacks out of the program. Johnson never envisioned that the overwhelmingly Democratic mayors of northern cities would rage against a program funneling federal dollars into their towns.

The Community Action Program quickly became a political liability. Bowing to the complaints from mayors and other local officials, the Johnson administration retreated. Shriver reined in the idealists on his staff and community action agencies returned to the control of city officials concerned mainly with white middle-class constituencies. When the program came up for renewal in 1967, its ambitious agenda had vanished. Sniffing the pork barrel, ravenous mayors had become its biggest supporters.

Certainly, LBJ bore a great deal of responsibility for CAP's failure; he did not run a tight ship. But the gravest problem of CAP and of the

Great Society in general was what one administration official called "a tendency to oversell and underperform." Johnson launched new programs with extravagant claims, but he put up neither the monetary muscle not the clear administrative strategy to put them through.

Domestic policy chief Joseph Califano reflected on the administrative failures of the Great Society in similar terms: "Johnson's extravagant rhetoric announcing new programs belied the modest funds he requested to being them." Johnson thus alienated both conservatives who "believed that he was hiding his real intentions just to get a foot in the door" and liberals who thought "he wasn't asking for enough to smash the door open."

## ASSESSING THE GREAT SOCIETY

Since the 1960s, many voices have debated the success of the Great Society and the reasons for its shortcomings. For thirty years, Johnson's program has remained the standard of liberal public policy in the United States, in both indictments and defenses of modern American liberalism.

Johnson himself took pride in his record. In his memoirs, Johnson pointed to the steep drop in the number of people living below the official poverty line during his term in office, a drop caused by the expanding wartime economy as well as the social programs of the Great Society. "We started something in motion with the attack on poverty," LBJ insisted. "Its effects were felt in education, law, medicine, and social welfare, in business and industry, in civil and philanthropic life, and in religion. . . . Of course, we had not lifted everyone out of poverty," Johnson conceded. "There would be setbacks and frustrations and disappointments ahead. But no one would ever again be able to ignore the poverty in our midst, and I believe that is enough to assure the final outcome and to change the way of life for millions of our fellow human beings."

Johnson's poverty warriors shared their chief's assessment. Joseph Califano claimed that Johnson "converted the hopes and aspirations of all kinds of Americans into a political force that brought out much of the good in each of us. . . . Whatever historians of the Great Society say twenty years later, they must admit that we tried, and I believe they will conclude that America is a better place because we did." Other liberals agreed that the Great Society moved the nation in the right direction but complained that Johnson did not move fast or far enough, did not give programs enough time, and did not allocate enough money.

Conservatives, on the other hand, viewed the Great Society as big government run amok—too much intervention, too much waste, and too much bureaucratic red tape. Writing in 1968, conservative commentator Ernest Van Den Haag denounced the "welfare mess" as a "wasteful hodgepodge" of programs which only trapped and humiliated the poor. During the 1970s and 1980s, this conservative critique of the Great Society gained political force. Nearly two decades after LBJ launched his program, Ronald Reagan used the Great Society as a whipping boy for his resurgent conservative platform. The first annual report of Reagan's Council of Economic Advisers, published in January 1982, listed "reducing the role of the Federal Government in all its dimensions" as Reagan's top priority and blamed all the nation's woes on government "meddling." The report rejected "paternalism" in welfare policies, suggesting that antipoverty programs only aggravated the distress of the needy and trapped them in a cycle of poverty and dependence.

Indeed, Reaganite calls for dismantling the welfare system rested on arguments that Great Society programs had actually harmed the impoverished—encouraging illegitimacy, welfare dependence, and hopelessness. "With the coming of the Great Society," President Reagan declared in 1982, "government began eating away at the underpinnings of the private enterprise system. The big taxers and big spenders in the Congress had started a binge that would slowly change the nature of our society and, even worse, it threatened the character of our people. . . . By the time the full weight of Great Society programs was felt, economic progress for America's poor had come to a tragic halt."

During the 1960s, however, the principal critique of the Great Society came not from conservatives, but from radicals, from the student New Left, the Black Power movement, and various social protest groups. Ultimately, Johnsonian liberalism proved too timid to challenge the powers that be. Johnson could not, would not, see that the interests of rich and poor, business and labor, must sometimes collide; he could not win everyone's cooperation without compromising the effectiveness of his programs.

In 1971, in retirement at the LBJ ranch, Johnson reflected bitterly on the fate of his beloved Great Society. "I figured when my legislative program passed the Congress," he told Doris Kearns, "that the Great Society had the chance to grow into a beautiful woman. And I figured her growth and development would be as natural and inevitable as any small child's. . . . And when she grew up, I figured she'd be so big and beautiful that the American people couldn't help but fall in love with her, and once they did, they'd want to keep her around forever, making her a permanent part of American life, more permanent even than the New Deal." Instead, he saw his successor Richard Nixon starving his program to death: "She's getting thinner and uglier all the time; now her bones are beginning to stick out and her wrinkles are beginning to show. Soon she'll be so ugly that the American people will refuse to look at her; they'll stick her in a closet to hide her away and there she'll die. And when she dies, I, too, will die."

Poignant words, but deceptive ones, for it was Lyndon Johnson himself, more than his aides or opponents or successors, who neglected the Great Society and stunted its growth. Early in his presidency, LBJ made two political mistakes, two fateful errors that ultimately stifled his beloved "child." First, he underestimated the expense of the two-front war in Vietnam. Deciding that he had no choice but to escalate the war in Southeast Asia, Johnson determined to pursue the war and the Great Society simultaneously. Strongly in his mind remained the examples of Woodrow Wilson and FDR who had abandoned domestic reform to lead the nation into war. Johnson believed he could protect the Great Society only by downplaying the expense of his two-front war; he covered up the costs of the Asian struggle, economized on every domestic program, and delayed a tax increase as long as possible. This strategy failed. Eventually, he had to scale back the Great Society to fight the war that took up more and more of his time and energy. "That bitch of a war," Johnson later admitted, "killed the lady I really loved—the Great Society."

Second, he did not anticipate the insidious political current that would further undermine LBJ's liberal program—racial backlash. Even though Great Society programs mainly benefited middle-class whites—aid to education, Medicare, farm subsidies, expanded Social Security—Johnson spoke repeatedly and passionately about eradicating poverty. The special attention to the poor, combined with the ongoing civil rights revolution, convinced many Americans that Johnson and his fellow liberals lavished too many benefits on African Americans and other racial minorities. This perception stirred up simmering racial antagonisms, a backlash against civil rights and the poverty war which stoked white discontent against liberal government. As one of Johnson's cabinet members warned in 1966, "Many people think the Great Society programs are mainly designed to help the very poor and they don't believe that this Administration has much interest in the middle-class, middle income family. There must be a way to make these people see that every American has an enormous stake in what we're doing."

Johnson feared the white backlash; he worried particularly about losing the backbone of the liberal coalition, the blue-collar, white ethnics of the northeast and midwest who had provided electoral support for every Democratic president since FDR. The Civil Rights Act of 1964 had already sacrificed the votes of white southerners. Now the heart of the New Deal coalition complained about Johnson's poverty program and the intensifying demands of African Americans for power and equality. These constituencies had supported the early civil rights movement—what they saw as largely southern battles for legal equality. When African Americans turned their eyes toward informal discrimination in northern cities and the federal courts began to order the integration of schools in the North, however, the fears and hatreds of people who had voted for FDR, JFK, and LBJ exploded. Liberalism's electoral base began melting in the heat and fury of those racial confrontations.

# Part 3

## CIVIL RIGHTS AND RACIAL JUSTICE

No domestic development has been more important to postwar American society than the struggle for racial equality. That struggle had a long history. During the three-quarters of a century after the end of Reconstruction, little had occurred to improve the status of African Americans. The vast majority of blacks lived in the South, were denied the right to vote, suffered the overt and covert consequences of segregation, experienced dire poverty, and were subject—at virtually every moment—to the threat of physical intimidation and violence. Yet throughout that time, African Americans had fought back, using their own institutions, resources, and energies to build the best schools, churches, and homes that they could for their children and themselves.

The modern civil rights struggle received its major impetus from three sources: the New Deal, World War II, and the long and finally successful campaign of the National Association for the Advancement of Colored People (NAACP) to overturn the legal sanction for segregation, accomplished in 1954 with the Supreme Court's unanimous ruling in *Brown v. Board of Education* that segregation was inherently unconstitutional.

During the 1930s and 1940s, hundreds of thousands of African Americans left the rural South to migrate to cities within the South, and, especially during World War II, began to take new jobs in the North and West. The number of blacks in labor unions doubled, some economic improvements occurred, and in the North especially, there was the opportunity for some political participation. Eleanor Roosevelt had encouraged her husband, Franklin, to do more to address problems of racial oppression, and in coalition with similar-minded allies in the New Deal, had succeeded in making some differences in administration attitudes toward civil rights. On the other hand, throughout the New Deal and World War II, policies of indifference, hostility, and racism continued largely to predominate. During the war, African American soldiers were not allowed to fight beside white soldiers, black blood supplies were segregated from white blood supplies, and black soldiers in Jim Crow southern training camps were subject to brutal white racism. Together, the New Deal and World War II brought some progress, yet in a context of continued and pervasive discrimination. The combination spurred black anger and frustration, helping to galvanize a new mood of protest. NAACP memberships shot up 1,000 percent during World War II, the black press insistently waged a "Double V" campaign—victory against Nazism abroad *and* racism at home—and a new awareness developed of the linkage between the struggle of African Americans for freedom in the United States, and of colored peoples around the globe for freedom from colonialism.

In the face of ever growing black militancy, liberal Democrats and Republicans began to pay more attention to the issue of civil rights. President Harry Truman established a civil rights commission, which called for desegregation of the armed services and greater protection of voting rights; President Dwight Eisenhower proceeded to desegregate Washington, D.C., in response to the *Brown* decision; and the State Department started to use black entertainers—Louis Armstrong and Dizzy Gillespie—as "cultural" ambassadors for the United States abroad. But in general, support was more rhetorical than substantive. Eisenhower refused to endorse the *Brown* decision or promote compliance with it in southern states; the Congress responded slowly and hesitantly to civil rights initiatives; and the State Department had to be dragged into supporting self-determination in Africa. And throughout much of the white South, resolve grew. Integration would not be forced upon southern states by an interventionist federal government.

By the 1960s, it was evident that only when blacks forced white institutions into action could any substantive change be anticipated. The mass of Montgomery blacks had to boycott the city's buses for 381 days in 1955–56 before that city—and the courts—finally agreed to desegregate public transportation there; in 1960, four black college students in Greensboro, North Carolina, had to "sit-in" at a local Woolworth's—and galvanize thousands of others in support— before local merchants agreed to provide the same equal service at the lunch counter that they provided at other counters. By now, it was clear that black Americans would not tolerate any further delay. Within two months of the Greensboro sit-ins, similar demonstrations had erupted in fifty-four cities in nine different states. The Civil Rights movement headed by Martin Luther King, Jr., and the Student Non-Violent Coordinating Committee (SNCC) had taken off. There would be no turning back.

Spurred by the example of the African American Civil Rights movement, and in reaction to long histories of oppression and discrimination of their own, Mexican Americans and Native Americans also engaged in struggles for social justice. The movements that developed were not wholly new; members of both groups had fought for their rights over the preceding decades. But the mass movements that emerged in the late 1960s and early 1970s were very much influenced by the trajectory of the African American movement, and shaped by the increasing polarization of American life.

There are two general interpretations of developments in race relations since World War II. One emphasizes the importance of external and impersonal factors such as migration, economic progress, shifts in governmental policies, and the emergence of an environment more conducive toward racial justice. Clearly, these preconditions are important to social change. Here, however, while portraying some of the external factors, we focus more on the second interpretation, that which emphasizes the collective demands of African Americans themselves for change. Facing massive resistance in the South, governmental reluctance to take action, and the ambivalence of many northern whites, many black Americans chose to follow the axiom of the black abolitionist Frederick Douglass: "Power concedes nothing without demand. It never has and it never will."

The selections included here provide a framework for thinking about the origins, development, and tactics of these movements for civil rights and racial justice. Excerpts from the Supreme Court's 1954 *Brown v. Board of Education* ruling demonstrate what sort of reasoning led portions of the U.S. government to change position on issues of race. "The Southern Manifesto," adopted by 101 members of Congress in response to the *Brown* decision, illustrates how southern opponents of integration argued—and understood—their position. Historian William Chafe explores the principles and beliefs that supported Martin Luther King, Jr., in his struggles for racial justice, and Anne Moody's account of a lunch counter sit-in reminds us how much of the movement's power lay in the bravery and commitment of countless individuals, most of whose names will never be known. The development of demands for "Black Power" rather than civil rights is represented by the 1966 platform statement of the Black Panther Party. This document should be contrasted with Bayard Rustin's 1965 argument in favor of a black-white progressive alliance.

The final section of Part 3 turns from the African American movement to other movements for racial justice. Historian F. Arturo Rosales analyzes the development of *El Movimiento* through the story of the 1968 East Los Angeles high school "blow out." And in a 1969 proclamation, "Indians of All Tribes" announce the occupation of Alcatraz Island, an action that helped to launch a mass movement for "Red Power."

Given the continuity of race as a shaping force in America, students may wish to think through a series of questions on the civil rights struggle and movements for racial justice. Why did this movement emerge to such prominence only in the 1950s and 1960s? In which ways did the Civil Rights movement succeed, and in which ways did it fail? What are the legacies of the turn toward cultural nationalism in Black Power, Brown Power, and Red Power movements? How important are the very different specific histories of Native Americans, African Americans, and Mexican Americans or Chicanos in shaping their ongoing movements? What are the relative merits of coalition (either Rustin's vision of a black-white coalition or a coalition of what came to be called collectively "people of color") versus strategies of separatism and self-help?

# Brown v. Board of Education (1954)

## Supreme Court of the United States

*In the years following World War II, racially segregated schools were the norm in the United States. In much of the nation the segregation was de facto, the result of residential segregation and economic inequality that was created, in large part, by racial prejudice and discrimination. But in twenty states—most of them in the South—school segregation was de jure, or by law. Although the National Association for the Advancement of Colored People (NAACP) had used the courts to challenge "Jim Crow" laws since the 1930s, arguing that legal segregation violated the "equal protection" clause of the Fourteenth Amendment, the challenges foundered upon the precedent created by* Plessy v. Ferguson. *This 1896 Supreme Court decision established a doctrine of "separate but equal": segregation of public facilities by race was not in violation of the Fourteenth Amendment so long as the facilities were equal in quality. In fact, the public schools designated for "Negroes" were rarely equal to those for whites. In the most extreme cases, they lacked everything from textbooks to indoor plumbing. But the NAACP was not seeking better enforcement of the "separate but equal" principle; instead it sought the "right" cases with which to challenge school segregation in the Supreme Court.*

*Such a case emerged in Topeka, Kansas, in 1951. Oliver Brown, father of a third grader named Linda, sought the help of the NAACP to challenge the restriction that forced his small daughter to travel a great distance to a "black" elementary school even though the "white" school was within walking distance of her home. The U.S. District Court heard Oliver Brown's case against the Topeka Board of Education in June 1951. NAACP lawyers argued that segregated schools were inherently unequal; the Board of Education lawyers argued that segregated schools prepared students for life in a segregated society. While the District Court agreed with the NAACP expert witnesses that segregation had a detrimental effect on black children, it was*

From *Brown v. Board of Education*, 347 U.S. 483 (1954).

*not willing to overturn* Plessy. *The NAACP and Oliver Brown appealed to the Supreme Court.*

*The case that came before the Supreme Court in December 1952 as* Brown v. Board of Education *was actually a combination of appeals, with school desegregation cases from Delaware, South Carolina, and Virginia joining the one from Kansas. Almost a year and one-half passed between oral arguments and the Supreme Court ruling, in part because Chief Justice Warren wanted nothing less than a unanimous decision in such a highly charged case.*

*In reading this document, pay attention to the logic employed in rejecting the doctrine of "separate but equal" for education. Why, nine years after the end of World War II and in the midst of the Cold War, might Chief Justice Warren focus on "the importance of education to our democratic society"?*

MR. CHIEF JUSTICE WARREN delivered the opinion of the Court.

These cases come to us from the States of Kansas, South Carolina, Virginia and Delaware. They are premised on different facts and different local conditions, but a common legal question justifies their consideration together in this consolidated opinion.

In each of the cases, minors of the Negro race, through their legal representatives, seek the aid of the courts in obtaining admission to the public schools of their community on a nonsegregated basis. In each instance, they had been denied admission to schools attended by white children under laws requiring or permitting segregation according to race. This segregation was alleged to deprive the plaintiffs of the equal protection of the laws under the Fourteenth Amendment. In each of the cases other than the Delaware case, a three-judge federal district court denied relief to the plaintiffs on the so-called "separate but equal" doctrine announced by this Court in *Plessy v. Ferguson,* 163 U.S. 537 [1896]. Under that doctrine, equality of treatment is accorded when the races are provided substantially equal facilities, even though these facilities be separate. In the Delaware case, the Supreme Court of Delaware adhered to that doctrine, but ordered that the plaintiffs be admitted to the white schools because of their superiority to the Negro schools.

The plaintiffs contend that segregated public schools are not "equal" and cannot be made "equal" and that hence they are deprived of the equal protection of the laws. Because of the obvious importance of the question presented, the Court took jurisdiction. Argument was heard in the 1952 Term, and reargument was heard this Term on certain questions propounded by the Court.

Reargument was largely devoted to the circumstances surrounding the adoption of the Fourteenth Amendment in 1868. It covered exhaustively consideration of the Amendment in Congress, ratification by the states, then existing practices in racial segregation, and the views of proponents and opponents of the Amendment. This discussion and our own investigation convince us that, although these sources cast some light, it is not enough to resolve the problem with which we are faced. At best, they are inconclusive. The most avid proponents of the post-War Amendments undoubtedly intended them to remove all legal distinctions among "all persons born or naturalized in the United States." Their opponents, just as certainly, were antagonistic to both the letter and the spirit of the Amendments and wished them to have the most limited effect. What others in Congress and the state legislatures had in mind cannot be determined with any degree of certainty.

An additional reason for the inconclusive nature of the Amendment's history, with respect to segregated schools, is the status of public education at that time. In the South, the movement toward free common schools, supported by general taxation, had not yet taken hold. Education of white children was largely in the hands of private groups. Education of Negroes was almost nonexistent, and practically all of the race were illiterate. In fact, any education of Negroes was forbidden by law in some states. Today, in contrast, many Negroes have achieved outstanding success in the arts and sciences as well as in the business and professional world. It is true that public school education at the time of the Amendment had advanced further in the North, but the effect of the Amendment on Northern States was generally ignored in the congressional debates. Even in the North, the conditions of public education did not approximate those existing today. The curriculum was usually rudimentary; ungraded schools were common in rural areas; the school term was but three months a year in many states; and compulsory school attendance was virtually unknown. As a consequence, it is not surprising that there should be so little in the history of the Fourteenth Amendment relating to its intended effect on public education. . . .

In approaching this problem, we cannot turn the clock back to 1868 when the Amendment was adopted, or even to 1896 when *Plessy v. Ferguson* was written. We must consider public education in the light of its full development and its present place in American life throughout the Nation. Only in this way can it be determined if segregation in public schools deprives these plaintiffs of the equal protection of the laws.

Today, education is perhaps the most important function of state and local governments. Compulsory school attendance laws and the great expenditures for education both demonstrate our recognition of the importance of education to our democratic society. It is required in the performance of our most basic public responsibilities, even service in the armed forces. It is the very foundation of good citizenship. Today it is a principal instrument in awakening the child to cultural values, in preparing him for later professional training, and in helping him to adjust normally to his environment. In these days, it is doubtful that any child may reasonably be expected to succeed in life if he is denied the opportunity of an education. Such an opportunity where the state has undertaken to provide it, is a right which must be made available to all on equal terms.

We come then to the question presented: Does segregation of children in public schools solely on the basis of race, even though the physical facilities and other "tangible" factors may be equal, deprive the children of the minority group of equal educational opportunities? We believe that it does. . . .

To separate them from others of similar age and qualifications solely because of their race generates a feeling of inferiority as to their status in the community that may affect their hearts and minds in a way unlikely ever to be undone. The effect of this separation on their educational opportunities was well stated by a finding in the Kansas case by a court which nevertheless felt compelled to rule against the Negro plaintiffs:

> Segregation of white and colored children in public schools has a detrimental effect upon the colored children. The impact is greater when it has the sanction of the law; for the policy of separating the races is usually interpreted as denoting the inferiority of the negro group. A sense of inferiority affects the motivation of a child to learn. Segregation with the sanction of law, therefore, has a tendency to [retard] the educational and mental development of negro children and to deprive them of some of the benefits they would receive in a racial[ly] integrated school system.

Whatever may have been the extent of psychological knowledge at the time of *Plessy v. Ferguson*, this finding is amply supported by modern authority. Any language in *Plessy v. Ferguson* contrary to this finding is rejected.

We conclude that in the field of public education the doctrine of "separate but equal" has no place. Separate educational facilities are inherently unequal. Therefore, we hold that the plaintiffs and others similarly situated for whom the actions have been brought are, by reason of the segregation complained of, deprived of the equal protection of the laws guaranteed by the Fourteenth Amendment. . . .

# Declaration of Constitutional Principles: The Southern Manifesto (1956)

*Signed by 101 members of the U.S. Congress*

*Even though the experience of World War II had done much to draw the distinct regions of the United States into a more powerful national culture, most white southerners still saw the South as a distinct region, with habits and customs that "outsiders" could not understand. Chief among these "customs" was racial segregation. For white southerners, steeped in a culture of racism and still suspicious of "Yankees" almost one hundred years after the end of the "War between the States," it was relatively easy to see the* Brown *decision and all subsequent federal actions related to it as illegitimate interference in problems that northern judges and politicians could not possibly understand. White supremacy was couched in constitutional arguments about States' Rights and the limits of federal power, and much of the white South began a campaign of massive resistance to Court-ordered integration.*

*Communities throughout the South responded differently to the integration order, and much depended upon local leadership, both white and black. In many places nothing changed; in others black schoolchildren faced jeering mobs, racist taunting, and even violence. Polls showed that 80 percent of white southerners opposed school integration. In a vacuum of leadership from President Eisenhower, congressional Democrats from the eleven southern states mobilized, issuing "The Southern Manifesto," which was signed by 101 senators and representatives.*

*While this section focuses on the actions of African Americans in demanding change, it is also important to understand the arena of national politics in which those attempting to change the nation's laws had to maneuver. How*

From the *Congressional Record,* 84th Congress, 2d Session, March 12, 1956, pp. 4460–61, 4515–16.

*does the existence of the "solid South," both Democratic and anti-integration, limit political options on the national level?*

The unwarranted decision of the Supreme Court in the public school cases is now bearing the fruit always produced when men substitute naked power for established law.

The Founding Fathers gave us a Constitution of checks and balances because they realized the inescapable lesson of history that no man or group of men can be safely entrusted with unlimited power. They framed this Constitution with its provisions for change by amendment in order to secure the fundamentals of government against the dangers of temporary popular passion or the personal predilections of public office holders.

We regard the decision of the Supreme Court in the school cases as a clear abuse of judicial power. It climaxes a trend in the federal judiciary undertaking to legislate, in derogation of the authority of Congress, and to encroach upon the reserved rights of the States and the people.

The original Constitution does not mention education. Neither does the Fourteenth Amendment nor any other Amendment. The debates preceding the submission of the Fourteenth Amendment clearly show that there was no intent that it should affect the systems of education maintained by the States.

The very Congress which proposed the Amendment subsequently provided for segregated schools in the District of Columbia.


## ESTABLISHED SEGREGATED SCHOOLS

When the Amendment was adopted in 1868, there were 37 States of the Union. Every one of the 26 States that had any substantial racial differences among its people either approved the operation of segregated schools already in existence or subsequently established such schools by action of the same lawmaking body which considered the Fourteenth Amendment.

As admitted by the Supreme Court in the public school case (*Brown v. Board of Education*), the doctrine of separate but equal schools "apparently originated in *Roberts v. City of Boston* . . . (1849), upholding school segregation against attack as being violative of a State constitutional guarantee of equality." This constitutional doctrine began in the North—not in the South, and it was followed not only in Massachusetts, but in Connecticut, New York, Illinois, Indiana, Michigan, Minnesota, New Jersey, Ohio, Pennsylvania and other northern States until they, exercising their rights as States through the constitutional process of local self-government, changed their school systems.

In the case of *Plessy v. Ferguson* in 1896 the Supreme Court expressly declared that under the Fourteenth Amendment no person was denied any of his rights if the States provided separate but equal public facilities. This decision has been followed in many other cases. It is notable that the Supreme Court, speaking through Chief Justice Taft, a former President of the United States, unanimously declared in 1927 in *Lum v. Rice* that the "separate but equal" principle is " . . . within the discretion of the State in regulating its public schools and does not conflict with the Fourteenth Amendment."

This interpretation, restated time and again, became a part of the life of the people of many of the States and confirmed their habits, customs, traditions and way of life. It is founded on elemental humanity and common sense, for parents should not be deprived by government of the right to direct the lives and education of their own children.

## NO LEGAL BASIS

Though there has been no constitutional amendment or Act of Congress changing this established legal principle, almost a century old, the Supreme Court of the United States, with no legal basis for such action, undertook to exercise their naked judicial power and substituted their personal political and social ideas for the established law of the land.

This unwarranted exercise of power by the Court, contrary to the Constitution, is creating chaos and confusion in the States principally affected. It is destroying the amicable relations between the white and Negro races that have been created through 90 years of patient effort by the good people of both races. It has planted hatred and suspicion where there has been heretofore friendship and understanding.

Without regard to the consent of the governed, outside agitators are threatening immediate and revolutionary changes in our public school system. If done, this is certain to destroy the system of public education in some of the States.

With the gravest concern for the explosive and dangerous condition created by this decision and inflamed by outside meddlers:

We reaffirm our reliance on the Constitution as the fundamental law of the land.

We decry the Supreme Court's encroachments on rights reserved to the States and to the people, contrary to established law and to the Constitution.

## COMMEND MOTIVES

We commend the motives of those States which have declared the intention to resist forced integration by any lawful means.

We appeal to the States and people who are not directly affected by these decisions to consider the constitutional principles involved against the time when they too, on issues vital to them, may be the victims of judicial encroachment.

Even though we constitute a minority in the present Congress, we have full faith that a majority of the American people believe in the dual system of government which has enabled us to achieve our greatness and will in time demand that the reserved rights of the States and of the people be made secure against judicial usurpation.

We pledge ourselves to use all lawful means to bring about a reversal of this decision which is contrary to the Constitution and to prevent the use of force in its implementation.

In this trying period, as we all seek to right this wrong, we appeal to our people not to be provoked by the agitators and troublemakers invading our States and to scrupulously refrain from disorder and lawless acts.

# A Lunch-Counter Sit-In in Jackson, Mississippi (1968)

*Anne Moody*

*The leadership of Martin Luther King, Jr., was critically important to the Civil Rights movement. His eloquence mobilized support throughout the nation and the principles of nonviolence he espoused shaped the movement for almost a decade. Yet the struggle for civil rights was fought, most importantly, at the grassroots level—by the thousands of people who boycotted the buses in Montgomery, who marched in Selma or Chicago, who registered voters in Mississippi and picketed stores and sat-in at lunch counters.*

*Anne Moody was one of these people. A young woman from a poor sharecropper family in rural Mississippi, Moody became involved in the Civil Rights movement when she attended Tougaloo College. Here, she describes sitting-in at a Woolworth's lunch counter in Jackson, Mississippi, in 1963. This brief, matter-of-fact account captures many of the key elements of the movement in the South: the role of local police and of the media; the complex relations with supportive whites; the purposeful contrast between the respectability of the African Americans who asked to be served and the vulgarity of the white mobs who attacked them. It also shows the bravery of those who, like Anne Moody, risked their lives in the movement.*

I had become very friendly with my social science professor, John Salter, who was in charge of NAACP activities on campus. All during the year, while the NAACP conducted a boycott of the downtown stores in Jackson, I had been one of Salter's most faithful canvassers and church speakers. During the last week of school, he told me that sit-in demonstrations were about to start in Jackson and that he wanted me to be the spokesman for a team that would sit-in at Woolworth's lunch counter. The two other demonstrators would be classmates of mine, Memphis and Pearlena. Pearlena was a dedicated NAACP worker, but Memphis had not been very involved in the Movement on campus. It seemed that the organization had had a rough time finding students who were in a position to go to jail. I had nothing to lose one way or the other. Around ten o'clock the morning of the demonstrations, NAACP headquarters alerted the news services. As a result, the police department was also informed, but neither the policemen nor the newsmen knew exactly where or when the demonstrations would start. They stationed themselves along Capitol Street and waited.

To divert attention from the sit-in at Woolworth's, the picketing started at J. C. Penney's a good fifteen minutes before. The pickets were allowed to walk up and down in front of the store three or four times before they were arrested. At exactly 11 A.M., Pearlena, Memphis, and I entered Woolworth's from the rear entrance. We separated as soon as we stepped into the store, and made small purchases from various counters. Pearlena had given Memphis her watch. He was to let us know when it was 11:14. At 11:14 we were to join him near the lunch counter and at exactly 11:15 we were to take seats at it.

Seconds before 11:15 we were occupying three seats at the previously segregated Woolworth's lunch counter. In the beginning the waitresses seemed to ignore us, as if they really didn't know what was going on. Our waitress walked past us a couple of times before she noticed we had started to write our own orders down and realized we wanted service. She asked us what we wanted. We began to read to her from our order slips. She told us that we would be served at the back counter, which was for Negroes."We would like to be served here," I said.

The waitress started to repeat what she had said, then stopped in the middle of the sentence. She turned the lights out behind the counter, and she and the other waitresses almost ran to the back of the store, deserting all their white customers. I guess they thought that violence would start immediately after the whites at the counter realized what was going on. There were five or six other people at the counter. A couple of them just got up and walked away. A girl sitting next to me finished her banana split before leaving. A middle-aged white woman who had not yet been served rose from her seat and came over to us. "I'd like to stay here with you," she said, "but my husband is waiting."

The newsmen came in just as she was leaving. They must have discovered what was going on shortly after some of the people began to leave the store. One of the newsmen ran behind the woman who spoke to us and asked her to identify herself. She refused to give her name, but said she was a native of Vicksburg and a former resident of California. When asked why she had said what she had said to us, she replied, "I am in sympathy with the Negro movement." By this time a crowd of cameramen and reporters had gathered around us taking pictures and asking questions, such as Where were we from? Why did we sit-in? What organization sponsored it? Were we students? From what school? How were we classified?

I told them that we were all students at Tougaloo College, that we were represented by no particular organization, and that we planned to stay there even after the store closed. "All we want is service," was my reply to one of them. After they had finished probing for about twenty minutes, they were almost ready to leave.

At noon, students from a nearby white high school started pouring in to Woolworth's. When they first saw us they were sort of surprised. They didn't know how to react. A few started to heckle and the newsmen became interested again. Then the white students started chanting all kinds of anti-Negro slogans. We were called a little bit of everything. The rest of the seats except the three we were occupying had been roped off to prevent others from sitting down. A couple of the boys took one end of the rope and made it into a hangman's noose. Several attempts were made to put it around our necks. The crowds grew as more students and adults came in for lunch.

We kept our eyes straight forward and did not look at the crowd except for occasional glances to see what was going on. All of a sudden I saw a face I remembered—the drunkard from the bus station sit-in. My eyes lingered on him just long enough for us to recognize each other. Today he was drunk too, so I don't think he remembered where he had seen me before. He took out a knife, opened it, put it in his pocket, and then began to pace the floor. At this point, I told Memphis and Pearlena what was going on. Memphis suggested that we pray. We bowed our heads, and all hell broke loose. A man rushed forward, threw Memphis from his seat, and slapped my face. Then another man who worked in the store threw me against an adjoining counter.

Down on my knees on the floor, I saw Memphis lying near the lunch counter with blood running out of the corners of his mouth. As he tried to protect his face, the man who'd thrown him down kept kicking him against the head. If he had worn hard-soled shoes instead of sneakers, the first kick probably would have killed Memphis. Finally a man dressed in plain clothes identified himself as a police officer and arrested Memphis and his attacker. Pearlena had been thrown to the floor. She and I got back on our stools after Memphis was arrested. There were some white Tougaloo teachers in the crowd. They asked Pearlena and me if we wanted to leave. They said that things were getting too rough. We didn't know what to do. While we were trying to make up our minds, we were joined by Joan Trumpauer. Now there were three of us and we were integrated. The crowd began to chant, "Communists, Communists, Communists." Some old man in the crowd ordered the students to take us off the stools.

"Which one should I get first?" a big husky boy said.

"That white nigger," the old man said.

The boy lifted Joan from the counter by her waist and carried her out of the store. Simultaneously, I was snatched from my stool by two high school students. I was dragged about thirty feet towards the door by my hair when someone made them turn me loose. As I was getting up off the floor, I saw Joan coming back inside. We started back to the center of the counter to join Pearlena. Lois Chaffee, a white Tougaloo faculty member, was now sitting next to her. So Joan and I just climbed across the rope at the front end of the counter and sat down. There were now four of us, two whites and two Negroes, all women. The mob started smearing us with ketchup, mustard, sugar, pies, and everything on the counter. Soon Joan and I were joined by John Salter, but the moment he sat down he was hit on the jaw with what appeared to be brass knuckles. Blood gushed from his face and someone threw salt into the open wound. Ed King, Tougaloo's chaplain, rushed to him.

At the other end of the counter, Lois and Pearlena were joined by George Raymond, a CORE field worker and a student from Jackson State College. Then a Negro high school boy sat down next to me. The mob took spray paint from the counter and sprayed it on the new demonstrators. The high school student had on a white shirt; the word "nigger" was written on his back with red spray paint.

We sat there for three hours taking a beating when the manager decided to close the store because the mob had begun to go wild with stuff from other counters. He begged and begged everyone to leave. But even after fifteen minutes of begging, no one budged. They would not leave until we did. Then Dr. Beittel, the president of Tougaloo College, came running in. He said he had just heard what was happening.

About ninety policemen were standing outside the store; they had been watching the whole thing through the windows, but had not come in to stop the mob or do anything. President Beittel went outside and asked Captain Ray to come and escort us out. The captain refused, stating the manager had to invite him in before he could enter the premises, so Dr. Beittel himself brought us out. He had told the police that they had better protect us after we were outside the store. When we got outside, the policemen formed a single line that blocked the mob from us. However, they were allowed to throw at us everything they had collected. Within ten minutes, we were picked up by Reverend King in his station wagon and taken to the NAACP headquarters on Lynch Street.

After the sit-in, all I could think of was how sick Mississippi whites were. They believed so much in the segregated Southern way of life, they would kill to preserve it. I sat there in the NAACP office and thought of how many times they had killed when this way of life was threatened. I knew that the killing had just begun. "Many more will die before it is over with," I thought. Before the sit-in, I had always hated the whites in Mississippi. Now I knew it was impossible for me to hate sickness. The whites had a disease, an incurable disease in its final stage. What were our chances against such a disease? I thought of the students, the young Negroes who had just begun to protest, as young interns. When these young interns got older, I thought, they would be the best doctors in the world for social problems.

# Dr. Martin Luther King, Jr.: A Voice of Radical Courage and Love

*William H. Chafe*

*In the years after the Montgomery bus boycott of 1955–56, Martin Luther King, Jr., came to be a symbol of the Civil Rights movement. As King was the first to admit, he was a product of the Civil Rights movement, not its creator. The bus boycott itself reflected a powerful indigenous movement in Montgomery, led by people like Rosa Parks of the NAACP, E. D. Nixon of the all-black Brotherhood of Sleeping Car Porters Union, and Jo Ann Robinson of the Women's Political Council (a black version of the all-white Montgomery League of Women Voters). But when these people determined to call for a bus boycott after Rosa Parks was arrested for refusing to give up her bus seat to a white passenger, Martin Luther King, Jr., a relatively new pastor in town, became the spokesperson of the movement.*

*In the ensuing years, King became a charismatic embodiment of the philosophy of nonviolent protest. Preaching a doctrine of redemption as well as protest, he led demonstrations throughout the South and helped found the Southern Christian Leadership Conference. King walked a tightrope, seeking both to maintain communication with white political powers, like President Kennedy, and to sustain among his black followers a willingness to endure brutality when they engaged in protests demanding equal access to public accommodations and the right to vote.*

*King became best known for the Birmingham demonstrations of 1963 when black people, including young children, were greeted by police commissioner Bull Connor's fire hoses and snarling police dogs. When King himself was arrested, he took advantage of his time in jail to address a powerful letter to white preachers who urged that he embrace patience rather than protest. In his response, King declared that the greatest enemies of black civil rights were not Ku Klux Klanners but moderates who preferred order to justice. In the ensuing years, King continued to "speak truth to power," even taking on the president of the United States when he attacked the Vietnam War as unjust.*

*In the decades after King's assassination in Memphis, Tennessee, in April
1968, many American politicians celebrated King as a moderate and applauded
his pleas for racial reconciliation. In doing so, they obscured the true radicalism
of King's legacy. In the following editorial, historian William Chafe explores
the larger dimensions of King's message. Why do you think politicians have
described King in more conservative terms? Was King really a radical? What
would he be saying about race—and politics—in today's world?*

*And he set his face
To go to Jerusalem*
—Luke, Chapter 9

In August 1963, Dr. Martin Luther King, Jr., gave his famous "I Have
a Dream" speech at the March on Washington. In the decades since,
it has become customary for politicians and commentators to celebrate King's commitment to the American Dream, his belief in equal
opportunity, and his hope that one day, the children of black and
white families might be judged "not by the color of their skin" but by
"the content of their character."

Yet these assessments are one-dimensional and fail to do justice
to the struggle of Dr. King's religious journey, the complexity of his
political convictions, and the radical courage of his commitment
to social justice. Only when we understand the full range of King's
vision of equality can we appreciate his true legacy—a transforming
belief in what a truly beloved community might look like in America.

The first point to note is the overwhelming power of King's religious faith. Because King was a new arrival in Montgomery, Alabama,
in 1955 and had almost no enemies, local leaders asked him to take
leadership of the mass boycott that followed the 1955 arrest of Mrs.
Rosa Parks for refusing to give up her seat on a public bus to a white
person. Drawing on his study of Mahatma Gandhi, King immediately
articulated the signature theme of the movement. How could African Americans justify breaking the law and engaging in civil disobedience, he asked? Because, like Jesus, they would use nonviolence and
love to redeem and make whole a divided nation.

But King's faith soon became searingly personal. Nightly phone
calls threatened death to his family. Unable to sleep, tormented by
visions of his little girl suffering, King broke down one night in his
kitchen. As David Garrow writes in his biography of King, at that
moment King heard an inner voice saying, "Stand up for justice, stand
up for truth . . . . [It was] the voice of Jesus saying still to fight on.

He promised never to leave me, never to leave me alone." From that point forward, the voice in the kitchen was King's personal anchor of faith, the message that enabled him to overcome the most dire threats. What had once been an intellectual creed had now become a personal, deep, and overpowering faith.

The second point to recognize is the tension King insisted upon between his embrace of the New Testament's gospel of unconditional love and the Old Testament's prophetic insistence on righteous justice. "It is not enough for us to talk about love," he told movement supporters. "There is another side called justice. . . . Standing beside love is always justice. Not only are we using the tools of persuasion—we've got to use the tools of coercion."

It was King's harnessing of love and justice that led him to write his "Letter from a Birmingham Jail" to the moderate white clergymen who attacked the movement's demonstrations in Birmingham in 1963—which put thousands of blacks in jail—as too radical. To those who pleaded for patience and a reduction of tension, King wrote: "non-violent direct action *seeks* to create . . . a crisis and foster such tension that a community which has constantly refused to negotiate is forced to confront the issue." "I confess that I am not afraid of the word 'tension'," King went on, declaring that "the Negro's great stumbling block in his stride toward freedom is not . . . the Ku Klux Klanner, but the white moderate, who is more devoted to 'order' than to justice; who prefers the negative peace which is the absence of tension to a positive peace which is the presence of justice." In words that would ring forever, King insisted that if America wanted the healing balm of love, it also needed to live with the scorching intensity of militant protest.

The third and final point is the degree to which King insisted that racial justice also required economic justice. "We are engaged in a social revolution," he insisted "[that seeks] basic structural changes in the architecture of American society." Long before sociologists started talking about the "declining significance of race," King focused on the connection between racism and poverty. "The evils of racism, economic exploitation and militarism are all tied together," he said, "and you can't really get rid of one without getting rid of the others." The only answer, he said, was "a radical redistribution of economic and political power."

All these themes came together in the last months of King's life. Preoccupied with death, he talked constantly, his wife Coretta said, "about the fact that he didn't expect to live a long life." "A profound sadness" had settled on King, one of his associates said. But there was also the voice in the kitchen that gave him the courage to continue standing up for justice and love.

By 1968, King was committed to the Poor People's Campaign, the embodiment of his understanding of the ties between racism and poverty. He knew this was an even harder message for America to hear than the insistence on an end to Jim Crow. Yet he persisted, in the face of government wiretaps and a scurrilous letter, written in FBI headquarters, threatening to expose his sexual infidelities and inviting him to commit suicide.

And so he "set his face" toward Memphis—as Jesus had set his face toward Jerusalem—to seek justice for the sanitation workers on strike there, even though he knew the city was a powder keg. He acknowledged that "I don't know what will happen now, we've got some difficult days ahead." But he would not be dissuaded from the course he had set, or his insistence on nonviolence. "It doesn't really matter with me now," he declared the night before his assassination, "because I've been to the mountaintop  . . .  and I've seen the promised land. I may not get there with you. But I want you to know tonight, that we, as a people, will get to the promised land."

As we remember King's life and his famous speech during the March on Washington, let us honor the depth of his faith, his vision, and his courage—not the antiseptic version that has become part of our official culture, but the rich and radical legacy of his struggle for freedom.

# From Protest to Politics (1965)

## Bayard Rustin

*A longtime advocate of nonviolent protest, Bayard Rustin took part in a 1947 effort to desegregate interstate bus facilities in the South, became a principal advisor to Martin Luther King, Jr., during the Montgomery bus boycott, and played a major role in organizing the 1963 March on Washington. By the mid-1960s, however, his path had diverged sharply from that of the more militant black protest leaders. He believed that the realization of true equality for African Americans depended on their remaining part of the broad liberal coalition that had given Lyndon Johnson his landslide victory in 1964. And he feared that black campaigns of disruptive civil disobedience and militant criticism of white leaders would only alienate necessary allies in the labor movement, Congress, and the White House. In the following selection, a 1965 plea for African Americans to turn from protest to politics, Rustin prophesied that despite civil rights victories, the plight of many African Americans would worsen unless a black-and-white progressive force transformed the nation's most fundamental social, economic, and political institutions.*

The decade spanned by the 1954 Supreme Court decision on school desegregation and the Civil Rights Act of 1964 will undoubtedly be recorded as the period in which the legal foundations of racism in America were destroyed. To be sure, pockets of resistance remain; but it would be hard to quarrel with the assertion that the elaborate legal structure of segregation and discrimination, particularly in relation to public accommodations, has virtually collapsed. On the other hand, without making light of the human sacrifices involved in the direct-action tactics (sit-ins, freedom rides, and the rest) that were so instrumental to this achievement, we must recognize that in desegregating public accommodations, we affected institutions which are relatively peripheral both to the American socioeconomic order and to the fundamental conditions of life of the Negro people. In a highly industrialized, twentieth-century civilization we hit Jim Crow precisely where it was most anachronistic, dispensable, and vulnerable—in hotels, lunch counters, terminals, libraries, swimming pools, and the like. For in these forms, Jim Crow does impede the flow of commerce in the broadest sense: it is a nuisance in a society on the move (and on the make). Not surprisingly, therefore, it was the most mobility-conscious and relatively liberated groups in the Negro community—lower-middle-class college students—who launched the attack that brought down this imposing but hollow structure.

The term "classical" appears especially apt for this phase of the civil rights movement. But in the few years that have passed since the first flush of sit-ins, several developments have taken place that have complicated matters enormously. One is the shifting focus of the movement in the South, symbolized by Birmingham; another is the spread of the revolution to the North; and the third, common to the other two, is the expansion of the movement's base in the Negro community. To attempt to disentangle these three strands is to do violence to reality. David Danzig's perceptive article, "The Meaning of Negro Strategy," correctly saw in the Birmingham events the victory of the concept of collective struggle over individual achievement as the road to Negro freedom. And Birmingham remains the unmatched symbol of grass-roots protest involving all strata of the black community. It was also in this most industrialized of Southern cities that the single-issue demands of the movement's classical stage gave way to the "package deal." No longer were Negroes satisfied with integrating lunch counters. They now sought advances in employment, housing, school integration, police protection, and so forth.

Thus, the movement in the South began to attack areas of discrimination which were not so remote from the Northern experience as were Jim Crow lunch counters. At the same time, the interrelationship of these apparently distinct areas became increasingly evident. What is the value of winning access to public accommodations for those who lack money to use them? The minute the movement faced this question, it was compelled to expand its vision beyond race relations to economic relations, including the role of education in modern society. And what also became clear is that all these interrelated problems, by their very nature, are not soluble by private, voluntary efforts but require government action—or politics. Already Southern demonstrators had recognized that the most effective way to strike at the police brutality they suffered from was by getting rid of the local sheriff—and that meant political action, which in turn meant, and still means, political action within the Democratic party where the only meaningful primary contests in the South are fought.

And so, in Mississippi, thanks largely to the leadership of Bob Moses, a turn toward political action has been taken. More than voter registration is involved here. A conscious bid for political power is being made, and in the course of that effort a tactical shift is being effected: direct-action techniques are being subordinated to a strategy calling for the building of community institutions or power bases. Clearly, the implications of this shift reach far beyond Mississippi. What began as a protest movement is being challenged to translate itself into a political movement. Is this the right course? And if it is, can the transformation be accomplished?

The very decade which has witnessed the decline of legal Jim Crow has also seen the rise of de facto segregation in our most fundamental socioeconomic institutions. More Negroes are unemployed today than in 1954, and the unemployment gap between the races is wider. The median income of Negroes has dropped from 57 percent to 54 percent of that of whites. A higher percentage of Negro workers is now concentrated in jobs vulnerable to automation than was the case ten years ago. More Negroes attend de facto segregated schools today than when the Supreme Court handed down its famous decision; while school integration proceeds at a snail's pace in the South, the number of Northern schools with an excessive proportion of minority youth proliferates. And behind this is the continuing growth of racial slums, spreading over our central cities and trapping Negro youth in a milieu which, whatever its legal definition, sows an unimaginable demoralization. Again, legal niceties aside, a resident of a racial ghetto lives in segregated housing, and more Negroes fall into this category than ever before.

These are the facts of life which generate frustration in the Negro community and challenge the civil rights movement. At issue, after all, is not *civil rights*, strictly speaking, but social and economic conditions. Last summer's riots were not race riots; they were outbursts of class aggression in a society where class and color definitions are converging disastrously. How can the (perhaps misnamed) civil rights movement deal with this problem?

Before trying to answer, let me first insist that the task of the movement is vastly complicated by the failure of many whites of good will to understand the nature of our problem. There is a widespread assumption that the removal of artificial racial barriers should result in the automatic integration of the Negro into all aspects of American life. This myth is fostered by facile analogies with the experience of various ethnic immigrant groups, particularly the Jews. But the analogies with the Jews do not hold for three simple but profound reasons. First, Jews have a long history as a literate people, a resource which has afforded them opportunities to advance in the academic and professional worlds, to achieve intellectual status even in the midst of economic hardship, and to evolve sustaining value systems in the context of ghetto life. Negroes, for the greater part of their presence in this country, were forbidden by law to read or write. Second, Jews have a long history of family stability, the importance of which in terms of aspiration and self-image is obvious. The Negro family structure was totally destroyed by slavery and with it the possibility of cultural transmission (the right of Negroes to marry and rear children is barely a century old). Third, Jews are white and have the *option* of relinquishing their cultural-religious identity, intermarrying, passing, etc. Negroes, or at least the overwhelming majority of them, do not have this option. There is also a fourth vulgar reason. If the Jewish and Negro communities are not comparable in terms of education, family structure, and color, it is also true that their respective economic roles bear little resemblance.

This matter of economic role brings us to the greater problem— the fact that we are moving into an era in which the natural functioning of the market does not by itself ensure every man with will and ambition a place in the productive process. The immigrant who came to this country during the late nineteenth and early twentieth centuries entered a society which was expanding territorially and economically. It was then possible to start at the bottom, as an unskilled or semiskilled worker, and move up the ladder, acquiring new skills along the way. Especially was this true when industrial unionism was burgeoning, giving new dignity and higher wages to organized workers. Today the situation has changed. We are not expanding territorially, the western frontier is settled, labor organizing has leveled off, our rate of economic growth has been stagnant for a decade. And we are in the midst of a technological revolution which is altering the fundamental structure of the labor force, destroying unskilled and semiskilled jobs—jobs in which Negroes are disproportionately concentrated.

Whatever the pace of this technological revolution may be, the *direction* is clear: the lower rungs of the economic ladder are being lopped off. This means that an individual will no longer be able to start at the bottom and work his way up; he will have to start in the middle or on top, and hold on tight. It will not even be enough to have certain specific skills, for many skilled jobs are also vulnerable to automation. A broad educational background, permitting vocational adaptability and flexibility, seems more imperative than ever. We live in a society where, as Secretary of Labor Willard Wirtz puts it, machines have the equivalent of a high school diploma. Yet the average educational attainment of American Negroes is 8.2 years.

Negroes, of course, are not the only people being affected by these developments. It is reported that there are now 50 percent fewer unskilled and semiskilled jobs than there are high school dropouts. Almost one-third of the 26 million young people entering the labor market in the 1960s will be dropouts. But the percentage of Negro dropouts nationally is 57 percent, and in New York City, among Negroes 25 years of age or over, it is 68 percent. They are without a future.

To what extent can the kind of self-help campaign recently prescribed by Eric Hoffer in the *New York Times Magazine* cope with such a situation? I would advise those who think that self-help is the answer to familiarize themselves with the long history of such efforts in the Negro community, and to consider why so many foundered on the shoals of ghetto life. It goes without saying that any effort to combat demoralization and apathy is desirable, but we must understand that demoralization in the Negro community is largely a common sense response to an objective reality. Negro youths have no need of statistics to perceive, fairly accurately, what their odds are in American society. Indeed, from the point of view of motivation, some of the healthiest Negro youngsters I know are juvenile delinquents: vigorously pursuing the American Dream of material acquisition and status, yet finding the conventional means of attaining it blocked off, they do not yield to defeatism but resort to illegal (and often ingenious) methods. They are not alien to American culture: They are, in Gunnar Myrdal's phrase, "exaggerated Americans." To want a Cadillac is not un-American; to push a cart in the garment center is. If Negroes are to be persuaded that the conventional path (school, work, etc.) is superior, we had better provide evidence which is now sorely lacking. It is a double cruelty to harangue Negro youth about education and training when we do not know what jobs will be available for them. When a Negro youth can reasonably foresee a future free of slums, when the prospect of gainful employment is realistic, we will see motivation and self-help in abundant enough quantities. Meanwhile, there is an ironic similarity between the self-help advocated by many liberals and the doctrines of the Black Muslims. Professional sociologists, psychiatrists, and social workers have expressed amazement at the Muslims' success in transforming prostitutes and dope addicts into respectable citizens. But every prostitute the Muslims convert to a model of Calvinist virtue is replaced in the ghetto with two more. Dedicated as they are to the maintenance of the ghetto, the Muslims are powerless to affect substantial moral reform. So too with every other group or program which is not aimed at the destruction of slums, their causes and effects. Self-help efforts, directly or indirectly, must be geared to mobilizing people into power units capable of effecting social change. That is, their goal must be genuine self-help, not merely self-improvement. Obviously, where self-improvement activities succeed in imparting to their participants a feeling of some control over their environment, those involved may find their appetites for change whetted; they may move into the political arena.

Let me sum up what I have thus far been trying to say: the civil rights movement is evolving from a protest movement into a full-fledged *social movement*—an evolution calling its very name into question. It is now concerned not merely with removing the barriers to full *opportunity* but with achieving the fact of *equality*. From sit-ins and freedom rides we have gone into rent strikes, boycotts, community organization, and political action. As a consequence of this natural evolution, the Negro today finds himself stymied by obstacles of far greater magnitude than the legal barriers he was attacking before: automation, urban decay, de facto school segregation. These are problems which, while conditioned by Jim Crow, do not vanish upon its demise. They are more deeply rooted in our socioeconomic order; they are the result of the total society's failure to meet not only the Negro's needs, but human needs generally.

These propositions have won increasing recognition and acceptance, but with a curious twist. They have formed the common premise of two apparently contradictory lines of thought which simultaneously nourish and antagonize each other. On the one hand, there is the reasoning of the *New York Times* moderate who says that the problems are so enormous and complicated that Negro militancy is a futile irritation, and that the need is for "intelligent moderation." Thus, during the first New York school boycott, the *Times* editorialized that Negro demands, while abstractly just, would necessitate massive reforms, the funds for which could not realistically be anticipated; therefore the just demands were also foolish demands and would only antagonize white people. Moderates of this stripe are often correct in perceiving the difficulty or impossibility of racial progress in the context of present social and economic policies. But they accept the context as fixed. They ignore (or perhaps see all too well) the potentialities inherent in linking Negro demands to broader pressures for radical revision of existing policies. They apparently see nothing strange in the fact that in the last twenty-five years we have spent nearly a trillion dollars fighting or preparing for wars, yet throw up our hands before the need for overhauling our schools, clearing the slums, and really abolishing poverty. My quarrel with these moderates is that they do not even envision radical changes; their admonitions of moderation are, for all practical purposes, admonitions to the Negro to adjust to the status quo, and are therefore immoral.

The more effectively the moderates argue their case, the more they convince Negroes that American society will not or cannot be reorganized for full racial equality. Michael Harrington has said that a successful war on poverty might well require the expenditure of $100 billion. Where, the Negro wonders, are the forces now in motion to compel such a commitment? If the voices of the moderates were raised in an insistence upon a reallocation of national resources at levels that could not be confused with tokenism (that is, if the moderates stopped being moderates), Negroes would have greater grounds for hope. Meanwhile, the Negro movement cannot escape a sense of isolation.

It is precisely this sense of isolation that gives rise to the second line of thought I want to examine—the tendency within the civil rights movement which, despite its militancy, pursues what I call a "no-win" policy. Sharing with many moderates a recognition of the magnitude of the obstacles to freedom, spokesmen for this tendency survey the American scene and find no forces prepared to move toward radical solutions. From this they conclude that the only viable strategy is shock; above all, the hypocrisy of white liberals must be exposed. These spokesmen are often described as the radicals of the movement, but they are really its moralists. They seek to change white hearts—by traumatizing them. Frequently abetted by white self-flagellants, they may gleefully applaud (though not really agreeing with) Malcolm X because, while they admit he has no program, they think he can frighten white people into doing the right thing. To believe this, of course, you must be convinced, even if unconsciously, that at the core of the white man's heart lies a buried affection for Negroes—a proposition one may be permitted to doubt. But in any case, hearts are not relevant to the issue; neither racial affinities nor racial hostilities are rooted there. It is institutions—social, political, and economic institutions—which are the ultimate molders of collective sentiments. Let these institutions be reconstructed *today*, and let the ineluctable gradualism of history govern the formation of a new psychology.

My quarrel with the "no-win" tendency in the civil rights movement (and the reason I have so designated it) parallels my quarrel with the moderates outside the movement. As the latter lack the vision or will for fundamental change, the former lack a realistic strategy for achieving it. For such a strategy they substitute militancy. But militancy is a matter of posture and volume and not of effect.

I believe that the Negro's struggle for equality in America is essentially revolutionary. While most Negroes—in their hearts—unquestionably seek only to enjoy the fruits of American society as it now exists, their quest cannot *objectively* be satisfied within the framework of existing political and economic relations. The young Negro who would demonstrate his way into the labor market may be motivated by a thoroughly bourgeois ambition and thoroughly "capitalist" considerations, but he will end up having to favor a great expansion of the public sector of the economy. At any rate, that is the position the movement will be forced to take as it looks at the number of jobs being generated by the private economy, and if it is to remain true to the masses of Negroes. . . .

It will be—it has been—argued that these by-products of the Negro struggle are not revolutionary. But the term revolutionary, as I am using it, does not connote violence; it refers to the qualitative transformation of fundamental institutions, more or less rapidly, to the point where the social and economic structure which they comprised can no longer be said to be the same. The Negro struggle has hardly run its course; and it will not stop moving until it has been utterly defeated or won substantial equality. But I fail to see how the movement can be victorious in the absence of radical programs for full employment, abolition of slums, the reconstruction of our educational system, new definitions of work and leisure. Adding up the cost of such programs, we can only conclude that we are talking about a refashioning of our political economy. It has been estimated, for example, that the price of replacing New York City's slums with public housing would be $17 billion. Again, a multibillion dollar federal public works program, dwarfing the currently proposed $2 billion program, is required to reabsorb unskilled and semiskilled workers into the labor market—and this must be done if Negro workers in these categories are to be employed. "Preferential treatment" cannot help them.

I am not trying here to delineate a total program, only to suggest the scope of economic reforms which are most immediately related to the plight of the Negro community. One could speculate on their political implications—whether, for example, they do not indicate the obsolescence of state government and the superiority of regional structures as viable units of planning. Such speculations aside, it is clear that Negro needs cannot be satisfied unless we go beyond what has so far been placed on the agenda. How are these radical objectives to be achieved? The answer is simple, deceptively so: *through political power.* . . . Neither that [the civil rights] movement nor the country's twenty million black people can win political power alone. We need allies. The future of the Negro struggle depends on whether the contradictions of this society can be resolved by a coalition of progressive forces which becomes the *effective* political majority in the United States. I speak of the coalition which staged the March on Washington, passed the Civil Rights Act, and laid the basis for the Johnson landslide—Negroes, trade unionists, liberals, and religious groups. . . .

The task of molding a political movement out of the March on Washington coalition is not simple, but no alternatives have been advanced. We need to choose our allies on the basis of common political objectives. It has become fashionable in some no-win Negro circles to decry the white liberal as the main enemy (his hypocrisy is what sustains racism); by virtue of this reverse recitation of the reactionary's litany (liberalism leads to socialism, which leads to Communism) the Negro is left in majestic isolation, except for a tiny band of fervent white initiates. But the objective fact is that *Eastland* and *Goldwater* are the main enemies—they and the opponents of civil rights, of the war on poverty, of Medicare, of social security, of federal aid to education, of unions, and so forth. The labor movement, despite its obvious faults, has been the largest single organized force in this country pushing for progressive social legislation. And where the Negro-labor-liberal axis is weak, as in the farm belt, it was the religious groups that were most influential in rallying support for the Civil Rights Bill.

The durability of the coalition was interestingly tested during the election. I do not believe that the Johnson landslide proved the "white backlash" to be a myth. It proved, rather, that economic interests are more fundamental than prejudice: the backlashers decided that loss of social security was, after all, too high a price to pay for a slap at the Negro. This lesson was a valuable first step in re-educating such people, and it must be kept alive, for the civil rights movement will be advanced only to the degree that social and economic welfare gets to be inextricably entangled with civil rights. . . .

The role of the civil rights movement in the reorganization of American political life is programmatic as well as strategic. We are challenged now to broaden our social vision, to develop functional programs with concrete objectives. We need to propose alternatives to technological unemployment, urban decay, and the rest. We need to be calling for public works and training, for national economic planning, for federal aid to education, for attractive public housing—all this on a sufficiently massive scale to make a difference. We need to protest the notion that our integration into American life, so long delayed, must now proceed in an atmosphere of competitive scarcity instead of in the security of abundance which technology makes possible. We cannot claim to have answers to all the complex problems of modern society. That is too much to ask of a movement still battling barbarism in Mississippi. But we can agitate the right questions by probing at the contradictions which still stand in the way of the "Great Society." The questions having been asked, motion must begin in the larger society, for there is a limit to what Negroes can do alone.

# What We Want, What We Believe (1966)

## Black Panther Party

*The Civil Rights movement began in the 1950s with goals of integration and assimilation. Its most visible leader, Martin Luther King, Jr., called upon doctrines of brotherly love and adopted tactics of nonviolent protest. It was not long, however, before other voices challenged that vision. Nation of Islam spokesman Malcolm X espoused black nationalism and racial separatism, urging African Americans to take control of their communities and to fight white racism "by any means necessary." After his assassination in 1965 Malcolm X came to symbolize militant defiance and racial pride, inspiring those who would move from demands for civil rights to demands for Black Power.*

*By mid-1965, many of the young people who filled the ranks of major civil rights organizations such as CORE (Congress of Racial Equality) and SNCC (Student Nonviolent Coordinating Committee) had become frustrated with the slow pace of change and angered by the white violence they faced. Both SNCC and CORE had decisively rejected the goal of integration and the tactic of non-violence by mid-decade, but the turning point came in Greenwood, Mississippi, in 1966. Stokely Carmichael, the fiery young head of SNCC, fresh from his twenty-seventh jailing, shouted to the angry crowd of SNCC and CORE workers waiting for his release: "We been saying freedom for six years and we ain't got nothin'. What we gonna start saying now is Black Power!"*

*Black Power meant different things to different people, but one of the groups that developed the philosophy the most fully was the Black Panther Party. Organized in Oakland, California, in 1966 by Bobby Seale and Huey P. Newton, the Black Panthers constructed an ideology rooted in self-defense against racist aggression and police brutality. The media-savvy Panthers appeared in public dressed in berets and leather jackets, brandishing an impressive array of*

Black Panther Party Platform and Program, October 1966.

*weaponry. Claiming that African Americans constituted an oppressed colony within a white oppressor nation, they attempted to create a militant, community-based organization to address the problems of urban blacks outside the South.*

*Compare the claims of the Civil Rights movement to the Black Panthers' statement below, and then compare both to the previous article by Bayard Rustin. How do you explain the differences in their viewpoints? Why might different segments of the black population find different approaches compelling? How might you account for the shift from integrationist to separatist sentiments in the African American community in the mid-1960s?*

1. We want freedom. We want power to determine the destiny of our Black Community.

We believe that black people will not be free until we are able to determine our destiny.

2. We want full employment for our people.

We believe that the federal government is responsible and obligated to give every man employment or a guaranteed income. We believe that if the white American businessmen will not give full employment, then the means of production should be taken from the businessmen and placed in the community so that the people of the community can organize and employ all of its people and give a high standard of living.

3. We want an end to the robbery by the CAPITALIST of our Black Community.

We believe that this racist government has robbed us and now we are demanding the overdue debt of forty acres and two mules. Forty acres and two mules was promised 100 years ago as restitution for slave labor and mass murder of black people. We will accept the payment in currency which will be distributed to our many communities. The Germans are now aiding the Jews in Israel for the genocide of the Jewish people. The Germans murdered six million Jews. The American racist has taken part in the slaughter of over fifty million black people; therefore, we feel that this is a modest demand that we make.

4. We want decent housing, fit for shelter of human beings.

We believe that if the white landlords will not give decent housing to our black community, then the housing and the land should be made into cooperatives so that our community, with government-aid, can build and make decent housing for its people.

5. We want education for our people that exposes the true nature of this decadent American society. We want education that teaches us our true history and our role in the present-day society.

We believe in an educational system that will give to our people a knowledge of self. If a man does not have knowledge of himself and his position in society and the world, then he has little chance to relate to anything else.

6. We want all black men to be exempt from military service.

We believe that black people should not be forced to fight in the military service to defend a racist government that does not protect us. We will not fight and kill other people of color in the world who, like black people, are being victimized by the white racist government of America. We will protect ourselves from the force and violence of the racist police and the racist military, by whatever means necessary.

7. We want an immediate end to POLICE BRUTALITY and MURDER of black people.

We believe we can end police brutality in our black community by organizing black self-defense groups that are dedicated to defending our black community from racist police oppression and brutality. The Second Amendment to the Constitution of the United States gives a right to bear arms. We therefore believe that all black people should arm themselves for self-defense.

8. We want freedom for all black men held in federal, state, county and city prisons and jails.

We believe that all black people should be released from the many jails and prisons because they have not received a fair and impartial trial.

9. We want all black people when brought to trial to be tried in court by a jury of their peer group or people from their black communities, as defined by the Constitution of the United States.

We believe that the courts should follow the United States Constitution so that black people will receive fair trials. The 14th Amendment of the U.S. Constitution gives a man a right to be tried by his peer group. A peer is a person from a similar economic, social, religious, geographical, environmental, historical, and racial background. To do this the court will be forced to select a jury from the black community from which the black defendant came. We have been, and are being tried by all-white juries that have no understanding of the "average reasoning man" of the black community.

10. We want land, bread, housing, education, clothing, justice, and peace. And as our major political objective, a United Nations–supervised plebiscite to be held throughout the black colony in which only black colonial subjects will be allowed to participate, for the purpose of determining the will of black people as to their national destiny.

When, in the course of human events, it becomes necessary for one people to dissolve the political bands which have connected them with another, and to assume, among the powers of the earth, the separate and equal station to which the laws of nature and nature's God entitle them, a decent respect to the opinions of mankind requires that they should declare the causes which impel them to the separation.

We hold these truths to be self-evident, that all men are created equal; that they are endowed by their Creator with certain unalienable rights; that among these are life, liberty, and the pursuit of happiness. That, to secure these rights, governments are instituted among men, deriving their just powers from the consent of the governed; that, whenever any form of government becomes destructive of these ends, it is the right of the people to alter or to abolish it, and to institute a new government, laying its foundation on such principles, and organizing its powers in such form, as to them shall seem most likely to effect their safety and happiness. Prudence, indeed, will dictate that governments long established should not be changed for light and transient causes; and, accordingly, all experience hath shown, that mankind are more disposed to suffer, while evils are sufferable, than to right themselves by abolishing the forms to which they are accustomed. But, when a long train of abuses and usurpations, pursuing invariably the same object, evinces a design to reduce them under absolute despotism, it is their right, it is their duty, to throw off such government, and to provide new guards for their future security.

# Chicano!

*F. Arturo Rosales*

El Movimiento, *the Chicano movement that emerged in the mid-1960s, sought social justice for Mexican Americans. In that way it was similar to the African American Civil Rights movement. From its beginnings, however,* el Movimiento *was heavily influenced by ideas of cultural nationalism. The major statement produced by the movement,* El Plan Espiritual de Aztlán, *condemned the "brutal 'Gringo' invasion of our territories" and declared "the Independence of our Mestizo Nation."*

*Increasingly, young Mexican American activists claimed for themselves the term* Chicano, *barrio slang associated with pachucos, the hip, rebellious, and sometimes criminal young men who symbolized a world that "respectable" Mexican Americans adamantly rejected. The most militant of these young people rejected a Mexican-American, hyphenated identity. As they explained in* El Plan de Aztlán, *the Mexican American "lacks respect for his culture and ethnic heritage . . . [and] seeks assimilation as a way out of his 'degraded' social status." In contrast, they believed, their own* chicanismo, *or ethnic pride, made meaningful political action possible. Chicano activists did not seek assimilation; they sought the liberation of "la Raza."*

*Historian F. Arturo Rosales chronicles an early event in the development of the Chicano movement, the East Los Angeles high school walkout of 1968. His story of the birth of "Brown Power" demonstrates once again the importance of grassroots protest in bringing about social change. But he, more than any of the other authors in this section, focuses on the large-scale structural factors underlying the movements for racial equality.*

At the end of the 1950s Mexican American attempts to end the educational neglect affecting their people seemed to be making headway.

From F. Arturo Rosales, *Chicano!* (Arte Publico Press, 1997). Excerpts of the work by F. Arturo Rosales are reprinted with permission from the publisher of *Chicano! The History of the Mexican American Civil Rights Movement* (Houston: Arte Publico Press–University of Houston, 1997).

No Mexicans were segregated by *de jure* methods anywhere in the country—not even in Texas, where as recently as the previous decade school authorities had segregation codes for Mexican children. Certainly by the 1960s more U.S. Mexicans than ever were entering the work force with a high school education or were attending college. Despite these advances, the perception of inadequate education served as one of the most crucial forces motivating the 1960s Chicano Movement. Why was this so at this time when conditions were seemingly improving?

In large cities like Los Angeles, an underlying and partial explanation for this is that whites and a small number of minority families had abandoned the inner cities for the suburbs (white flight), leaving minorities behind. Except in border communities or in towns with large, long-standing Mexican populations such as Santa Fe, San Antonio or Tucson, Mexicans lived in mixed neighborhoods in the larger southwestern cities. In the 1950s this ethnic heterogeneity started changing and, by the 1960s the shift resulted in the division of metropolitan areas—with whites living in more affluent peripheries and the minorities in the central cities. Black ghettos and Mexican barrios were now islands in a complex of freeways, tacky industrial parks, auto repair shops, sporting complexes, small office buildings and expanded airport areas. The large Asian communities that are in inner cities now had not yet emerged except in California. And even there, they were not as large as today.

In cities like Los Angeles, Denver, Phoenix, San Jose and Houston, large-scale de facto school segregation of Mexicans and Blacks took hold as never before. Before, their populations were rarely large enough to dominate elementary, middle-, and high-school enrollments, as they did by the 1960s and thereafter. Moreover, with white flight, educational funding was diverted to institutions in the suburbs at the expense of urban core schools, which by now were stigmatized as minority institutions.

In addition, the creation of new and better-paying jobs took place mainly in the suburbs, a factor compounding the inner-city woes. With whites gone, law-enforcement attitudes toward inner-city residents became uniformly less tolerant and, too often, police and media overreacted to minority crime. All in all, tension and resentment were on the rise. Their increasing ghettoization made Chicanos feel betrayed by the American Dream. The optimism that in the U.S. anything was possible, proclaimed so often by the Mexican American generation, came into question. This generation had chased an all-American status, but the real white society, it seemed, had left them behind in the barrios, perceiving them simply as "Mexicans." As a result, like Blacks, many Mexicans gave up on the dream and became more conscious of their own lost identity. Thus, as Chicano intellectuals reconciled themselves to remaining Mexican, they formulated a catharsis to build a positive self-image. But where to start? In their haste to Americanize, their predecessors (Mexican Americans) had seemingly misplaced Mexican identity—not just the leaders and intellectuals but regular folks who did not speak Spanish to their kids and had named them Brenda and Mark, a sign that they wanted their children to Americanize.

It is no small wonder that an impassioned searching for roots—in *lo mexicano*—dominated the beginning of the Chicano Movement. Incipient issues discussed by fledgling Chicanos revolved around cultural nationalism. Mainly Chicanos in institutions of higher education, with access to information about the state of their communities, were stimulated to treat these themes. Then, the degree to which they influenced the folks back in the community was in proportion to the distance of barrios from their universities.

## NASCENT YOUTH RUMBLINGS

The first major rumblings of the Chicano youth movement were heard in California in 1967. . . . That year at California college campuses, a social revolution of sorts affected the first large contingent of Chicano Movement participants. Throughout the decade of the 1960s, more Mexican Americans attended college than ever before; they formed part of the college-age population created by the baby boom. A sheer weight of numbers put them on campus. In addition, the Educational Opportunity Programs (EOP), funded by President Johnson's War on Poverty, recruited thousands of Mexican Americans throughout the Southwest, but more so in California. Arizona State University did not make EOP available until 1969, for example. The Vietnam-era GI Bill, instituted in 1966, also brought many Chicanos to campuses. A large number of new student organizations started appearing in the mid-1960s, with an orientation only slightly different from that of the 1940s Mexican American Movement. But the Mexican American student enrollment grew at the precise moment when colleges were radicalizing. . . .

Young *Chicanismo* showed the most vital signs of growth in Southern California. At the end of 1967, thirty-five Mexican American student organizations existed with almost two thousand members. The following year, according to Professor Juan Gómez-Quiñones, thousands more participated as the organizations multiplied to about fifty. By 1968 they were making a greater commitment to confrontationist strategy—white radicals and Black civil rights activists were in the throes of adopting these tactics as well. . . .

## LOS ANGELES WALKOUTS: SHOCK WAVES THROUGH THE COMMUNITY

The key event that ushered in the *movimiento* in Los Angeles, and to a great degree elsewhere, was the East Los Angeles high-school walkout. But this action cannot be separated from the student movement. Because college organizations joined a combination of nonstudent activists to organize the protest, it is likely that college student mobilization served as a necessary precursor to the events.

On March 1, 1968, three hundred high-school students walked out of their Friday morning classes upon discovering that Wilson High School Principal Donald Skinner had canceled production of "Barefoot in the Park" because it "was an inappropriate play to be showing the student body." The cancellation was only a surface reason for the walkout. Underneath, discontent and anger stemming from more profound issues had been brewing in the predominantly Mexican American school. This resentment became evident at other schools as well. On Monday, Lincoln High students walked out. On Tuesday, two thousand students evacuated Garfield High School, another predominantly Mexican American high school. By Wednesday, the walkouts, or blowouts, as the students called them, had extended to Roosevelt High School. Some forty-five hundred students marched out of classes that day. In the ensuing two days, thousands of Mexican American students reported to school only to trek out the front doors once inside the buildings. By Friday, more than fifteen thousand students had left their classes throughout the Los Angeles area.

Chicano youths used the walkouts to dramatize what they considered the abysmally poor educational conditions affecting their schools. But the walkout organizers were not the first Mexican Americans to take a critical view of the educational system. It had certainly been a major issue among Mexican American civil rights leaders for at least four decades. In this case, however, the planners were all young people, many not yet out of their teens; none was over thirty, except Lincoln High School teacher Sal Castro. In themselves, the events were significant because they affected so many schools, students, teachers, and parents. But more crucial was that the publicity created by the walkouts reminded the Mexican-origin community throughout the U.S. to examine educational conditions in their own communities. The sight of high-school kids on picket lines, carrying placards emblazoned with "Chicano Power!" "¡Viva la Raza!" and "Viva la Revolución," prompted a *Los Angeles Times* reporter to dub the walkouts as "The Birth of Brown Power"—this was an accurate prognosis.

The genesis of these events is found at Camp Hess Kramer, a four-hundred-acre spread in the rolling hills just east of Malibu. Significantly, here too were the elements that linked previous Mexican American politics and their ideological orientation to Los Angeles *Chicanismo*. In April 1966 in an effort to tackle Mexican American youth issues such as gangs, school dropout rates, and access to college education, the Los Angeles County Human Relations Council invited adults in community leadership positions to meet with about two hundred teenagers from various backgrounds in roundtable discussions.

The next year, many of the same young people attended a follow-up meeting at the camp. As one of them, David Sánchez, began to stand out, adult camp organizers decided to mentor his progress. Since age fifteen, Sánchez had worked as a youth counselor for the Social Training Center at the Episcopalian Church of the Epiphany under Father John Luce. The Episcopal priest introduced Sánchez to one of Los Angeles's busiest political activists of the time, Richard Alatorre, then a staff member of the Los Angeles Community Services Program, an associate of the NAACP Legal Defense Fund and a Democratic Party activist. Alatorre's connections earned Sánchez a place on the Mayor's Youth Council, which elected him chairman. . . .

By his own admission, Sánchez was clean-cut and not a *cholo* (street tough). When he was chairperson, no inkling existed as to the future of this precocious teenager, except that he might be headed for a successful college career. But most young, Mexican American males growing up in East Los Angeles, regardless of their orientation eventually butted heads with policemen. At one point, Sánchez had been "slapped around by the police," an experience that convinced him that police brutality was a community problem. When he tried to bring up the issue to the youth council, it was ignored because the adult politicians did not wish to air the problem.

In Los Angeles, most Mexican boys his age worked in grocery stores, movie theaters, and car-washes to make spending money. Richard Alatorre, however, obtained for Sánchez a winter job with the Boy's Club while Father Luce used him as youth counselor in the summer under the auspices of Volunteers In Service to America (VISTA). In the summer of 1967, at age seventeen, Sánchez wrote a successful proposal to the Southern California Council of Churches for funding to start the Piranya coffee house—envisioned as a teenager hangout to keep them out of trouble. The grant provided rent and other expenses for one year, enough time for a social revolution to emerge. Sánchez recruited Vickie Castro, Ralph Ramírez and other friends from Camp Hess Kramer, and they formed the Young Citizens for Community Action (YCCA). The Piranya became the headquarters of the YCCA. This upward-bound, clean-cut youthful group became the foundation of one of the most militant, sometimes violence-prone, Chicano organizations in the country: the Brown Berets.

Initially the group worked within the system, but the social ferment which characterized East Los Angeles during this time radicalized the YCCA. Eleazar Risco, for example, a Cuban acculturated to Mexicans (he spoke Spanish with a Mexican accent), began publishing *La Raza*, a tabloid specializing in exposing police brutality and educational inadequacies, issues that resonated among East Los Angeles Mexican Americans.

The crudely printed, passionately written, if not-too-well-researched, *La Raza*, which Risco regularly left at the Piranya clubhouse, excited the young patrons who read not only about police brutality, but also blistering attacks on the school system. This latter issue was close to a group more interested in college than gang life . . . .

But *La Raza* also appealed to the *cholo* (street tough) element of East Los Angeles. Risco and his helpers shaped the tabloid's content to appeal to this marginalized element, chronicling *la vida loca* (the crazy life), as life in LA's mean streets was known. Police bashing was particularly attractive to this group. To their delight, the first issue of *La Raza* led off with a banner headline attacking Los Angeles Police Department (LAPD) Chief Thomas Redding, "*Jefe Placa, tu abuela en mole*" (Fuzz Chief, your grandmother in chili sauce)." But the LAPD and the Sheriff's Department, noting the critical police stance of persons connected with Father Luce's operation, harassed Piranya club members by enforcing a curfew law for teenagers. David Sánchez's sister, for instance, was detained because she was in the coffee house after 10 P.M. The group decided to protest. For many YCCA members who picketed the sheriff's substation located across the street, it was their first militant act. Not all of the coffee house members agreed with the gradual radicalization of the group, however, and many walked out as a consequence.

About this time, Carlos Montes, who also played a crucial role in the rise of the Brown Berets, entered the scene. As a student at East Los Angeles City College, he had obtained a job as a teen post director for the Lincoln Heights area. This was a federal program sponsored by Father Luce's center and the CSO that Tony Ríos, César Chávez's former boss, ran out of Los Angeles. The YCCA members spent a great deal of time at the Church of the Epiphany, and soon Montes blended in with them. At Father Luce's center, Montes also met the passionate Risco, who produced *La Raza* in the church basement.

While it is difficult to trace the idea of the walkouts to any one group or individual, it is certain that Camp Hess Kramer veterans, some who became Brown Berets, were the core planners. But certainly many activists participated from other groups. . . . They devoted numerous hours to discussing educational inadequacies and how they could be changed. Perhaps influenced by the Black cultural movement, they all agreed that education of Mexican Americans lacked cultural relevancy.

Soon the planners favored the idea of a walkout as a means of dramatizing their issues. They then printed propaganda broadsides designed to persuade students to abandon their classes. Their activities became so overt that weeks before the strike, students, teachers, and administrators knew about the impending walkout. In fact, one month before the incident, teachers openly debated the issue and started taking sides. Meanwhile, Chicano newspapers *La Raza, Inside Eastside* and *The Chicano Student* helped fuel the passions of students and boycott supporters by spreading an "awareness" among students and non-students alike. A few days before the walkouts, for example, *La Raza* blasted the shortcomings of the school system and encouraged students to leave their classes. . . .

The college students and Brown Berets must have possessed a precise rationale as to why the walkouts were necessary. But only a few of the ten thousand high-school students who participated in the boycott were as politicized; they did not have the same ideological motives for their action. As John Ortiz, one of the college leaders, indicated,

> It was happening at Berkeley. . . the media reported strikes occurring throughout the country. So many kids got caught in the climate of protest, they were products of their time. Others felt it was the right thing to do. And others because they wanted to "party."

This motivation would be true in other Chicano student activities, whatever their character. But in the same statement, Ortiz explains the outcome for the uncommitted who just followed the crowd:

> But one thing is for sure; as the strike intensified and people were getting arrested, the students became politically aware. The events politicized the students. And that's why they walked out of their classes!

Mexican American teachers antagonistic to the protest came under much criticism. . . . But such tension reflected a general split in the Los Angeles Mexican community, a fissure symbolized to some degree by those who used the term *Chicano* as a self-identifier and those who did not.

The rift over involvement in the movement existed within families as well. Joe Razo, co-editor of *La Raza,* recalled an incident during the walkouts:

> I saw a man over in one of the East L.A. parks slapping his daughter around because she had walked out . . . she was crying but still arguing with him about the necessity for fighting for some of her rights and for changing the curriculum. . . . I still remember this vividly. . . . It was a family that at least a man had the interest enough to get involved with his kid. . . . there were going to be a lot of long discussions in that family . . . as to why she walked out of school. . . . It was not a matter "of it's nice and sunny, I think I'll go to the park." They were political. They really knew what they were fighting for.

# Proclamation (1969)

## Indians of All Tribes

*In November 1969, a small group of activists from the American Indian Movement (AIM) occupied Alcatraz Island, the former site of Alcatraz prison in San Francisco Bay. By the end of the month almost four hundred Native Americans had taken up residency on Alcatraz. In their "Proclamation," the occupiers, calling themselves "Indians of All Tribes," claimed Alcatraz for all American Indians and offered to sell it back to the government for twenty-four dollars' worth of glass beads and some red cloth—a reference to the legendary "sale" of Manhattan Island to European settlers almost three centuries before. The Proclamation's initial pointed sarcasm gives way in the second half of the document to thoughtful proposals for establishing a variety of Indian institutes on Alcatraz Island. The government adopted a hands-off policy and attempted to outwait the activists. Finally, in June 1971, U.S. marshals and FBI agents removed the remaining fifteen occupiers from Alcatraz.*

*The occupation of Alcatraz was a major watershed in the development of American Indian activism. Before Alcatraz, protest tended to be tribally based and concerned with specific, local issues. Alcatraz signaled the consolidation of a "pan-Indian" approach to activism, as members of different tribes and nations placed their "Indian" identity over significant differences in cultural practices and beliefs, tribal organization, and geography. Though the Alcatraz occupation did not succeed in reclaiming Alcatraz Island for native peoples, it drew national attention to the broken promises and flawed policies of the federal government and inspired participants and supporters to a revitalized sense of purpose.*

*The movement that consolidated in the wake of the Alcatraz occupation was clearly influenced by the African American movements that preceded it; that is evident even in the use of the slogan, "Red Power." But it is useful to consider the similarities and differences between the two movements. How does this "Proclamation" by Indians of All Tribes differ from the Black Panthers' Platform? How much do the different histories of African Americans and Native Americans shape their respective movements, and how much are they shaped by the era in which they both emerged?*

159

**PROCLAMATION:**

To the Great White Father and All His People:

We, the native Americans, re-claim the land known as Alcatraz Island in the name of all American Indians by right of discovery.

We wish to be fair and honorable in our dealings with the Caucasian inhabitants of this land, and hereby offer the following treaty:

We will purchase said Alcatraz Island for twenty-four dollars ($24) in glass beads and red cloth, a precedent set by the white man's purchase of a similar island about 300 years ago. We know that $24 in trade goods for these 16 acres is more than was paid when Manhattan Island was sold, but we know that land values have risen over the years. Our offer of $1.24 per acre is greater than the 47 cents per acre the white men are now paying the California Indians for their land.

We will give to the inhabitants of this island a portion of that land for their own, to be held in trust by the American Indian Government—for as long as the sun shall rise and the rivers go down to the sea—to be administered by the Bureau of Caucasian Affairs (BCA). We will further guide the inhabitants in the proper way of living. We will offer them our religion, our education, our life-ways, in order to help them achieve our level of civilization and thus raise them and all their white brothers up from their savage and unhappy state. We offer this treaty in good faith and wish to be fair and honorable in our dealings with all white men.

We feel that this so-called Alcatraz Island is more than suitable for an Indian Reservation, as determined by the white man's own standards. By this we mean that this place resembles most Indian reservations, in that:

1. It is isolated from modern facilities, and without adequate means of transportation.
2. It has no fresh running water.
3. It has inadequate sanitation facilities.
4. There are no oil or mineral rights.
5. There is no industry so unemployment is great.
6. There are no health care facilities.
7. The soil is rocky and non-productive; and the land does not support game.
8. There are no educational facilities.
9. The population has always exceeded the land base.
10. The population has always been held as prisoners and kept dependent upon others.

Further, it would be fitting and symbolic that ships from all over the world, entering the Golden Gate, would first see Indian land, and thus be reminded of the true history of this nation. This tiny island would be a symbol of the great lands once ruled by free and noble Indians.

## USE TO BE MADE OF ALCATRAZ ISLAND

What use will be made of this land?

Since the San Francisco Indian Center burned down, there is no place for Indians to assemble and carry on our tribal life here in the white man's city. Therefore, we plan to develop on this island several Indian institutes:

1. A Center for Native American Studies will be developed which will train our young people in the best of our native cultural arts and sciences, as well as educate them to the skills and knowledge relevant to improve the lives and spirits of all Indian peoples. Attached to this center will be traveling universities, managed by Indians, which will go to the Indian Reservations in order to learn the traditional values from the people, which are now absent in the Caucasian higher educational system.

2. An American Indian Spiritual center will be developed which will practice our ancient tribal religious ceremonies and medicine. Our cultural arts will be featured and our young people trained in music, dance, and medicine.

3. An Indian center of Ecology will be built which will train and support our young people in scientific research and practice in order to restore our lands and waters to their pure and natural state. We will seek to de-pollute the air and the water of the Bay Area. We will seek to restore fish and animal life, and to revitalize sea life which has been threatened by the white man's way. Facilities will be developed to desalt sea water for human use.

4. A Great Indian Training School will be developed to teach our peoples how to make a living in the world, improve our standards of living, and end hunger and unemployment among all our peoples. This training school will include a center for Indian arts and crafts, and an Indian Restaurant serving native foods and training Indians in culinary arts. This center will display Indian arts and offer the Indian

foods of all tribes to the public, so they all may know of the beauty and spirit of the traditional Indian ways.

5. Some of the present buildings will be taken over to develop an American Indian Museum, which will depict our native foods and other cultural contributions we have given to all the world. Another part of the Museum will present some of the things the white man has given to the Indians, in return for the land and the life he took: disease, alcohol, poverty, and cultural decimation (as symbolized by old tin cans, barbed wire, rubber tires, plastic containers, etc.). Part of the museum will remain a dungeon, to symbolize both Indian captives who were incarcerated for challenging white authority, and those who were imprisoned on reservations. The Museum will show the noble and the tragic events of Indian history, including the broken treaties, the documentary of the Trail of Tears, the Massacre of Wounded Knee, as well as the victory over Yellow-Hair Custer and his army.

In the name of all Indians, therefore, we re-claim this island for Indian nations, for all these reasons. We feel this claim is just and proper, and that this land should rightfully be granted to us for as long as the rivers shall run and the sun shall shine.

SIGNED,
INDIANS OF ALL TRIBES
November 1969
San Francisco, California

# Part 4

## STRUGGLES OVER GENDER AND SEXUAL LIBERATION

In a manner similar to the impact of race, gender has served as a primary determinant of power and opportunity in America. To this day, whether one is born male or female has as much to do with shaping one's life possibilities as almost any other factor. It determines the clothes we wear, the emotions we are taught to cultivate, the jobs we are told we should aspire to, the power we exercise—even our sense of who we are and what we are about. Through most of American history, cultural norms prescribed that women should be the tenders of the hearth, rearers of children, and the moral, spiritual guardians of the family. Men, by contrast, were to be assertive, dominant, in control, the major source of power, influence, and income.

These norms were often in tension with the ways Americans lived. Men and women worked out various sorts of relationships in their married lives, and women played many different roles outside the home. Despite pressure for a "family wage" paid to working men, many poor and working-class women worked outside their homes or took in work to supplement the family income. And America's public life was sustained by the volunteer labor of middle- and upper-class women who did not hold paid employment. But the ideal was powerful, and both women *and* men were judged by how well they conformed to it. When a married woman sought paid employment, it was commonly seen as a negative reflection on her husband, who could not sufficiently provide for her—or as a repudiation of her "natural" role of wife and mother.

World War II played a pivotal role in generating the conditions for significant change in women's roles, just as it created new opportunities for African Americans. Given the urgency of defeating fascism, the government and all its propaganda mechanisms suddenly sanctioned work for women, including wives and mothers. Millions of women took jobs, and under the press of military necessity, older definitions of women's "proper" place were set aside, at least for the moment. On the other hand—as with African Americans—discrimination continued. Woman were paid less than men, they were barred from executive positions, and despite wartime necessity, the government failed to provide or support day care centers in numbers adequate to meet the needs of working parents.

After the war, a kind of cultural schizophrenia occurred. On the one hand, many of the advances that had occurred were reversed. What Betty Friedan labeled the "Feminine Mystique" became once more a pervasive cultural force, pushing women to return to the home and aspire to fulfillment through suburban domesticity. "The independent woman is a contradiction in terms," declared one bestselling treatise. On the other hand, employment figures for women continued to increase—especially after an initial dip immediately after the war; in addition, more and more middle-class and married women were taking jobs in order to make it possible for families to aspire to better lives.

At least partly because of such changes, a revitalized feminism became possible in the late 1960s, exposing the contradiction between traditional definitions of women's place and the new frequency with which women were assuming active economic, political, and social roles outside the home. Questioning most of the traditional definitions of masculinity and femininity, the women's liberation movement became one of the most significant forces of social change in the 1960s and 1970s.

As with the Civil Rights movement, the revival of social protest reflected a combination of external and impersonal changes—such as those triggered by World War II—and the emergence of new insurgent voices among women themselves. At the same time, the women's movement was never as unified as the early Civil Rights movement, neither in goals, tactics, or leadership, nor in its definition of what was wrong with American society.

The first section of Part 4 focuses on the women's movement. In the following pages, historian Jane Sherron De Hart analyzes some of the origins of the "second wave" of U.S. feminism in the 1960s and '70s, emphasizing its diversity. Three documents illustrate the broad range of 1960s and early 1970s feminism: "New York Radical Women" critiqued the "Degrading Mindless-Boob-Girlie Symbol" of the Miss

America Pageant in language that seems quite distant from the careful arguments of the National Organization for Women. And Chicana activist Enriqueta Longeaux Vasquez expressed the doubts of many black and Chicana women about the women's liberation movement in a piece titled "¡Soy Chicana Primero!"

While black and Chicana women critiqued the assumptions of what many saw as a white, middle-class movement insensitive to their concerns and experiences, a great many other women simply rejected feminism altogether. Feminism seemed a threat to their ways of life, especially in its varied critiques of traditional gender roles. The Equal Rights Amendment became a rallying point for antifeminists, including many women, under the leadership of conservative spokeswoman Phyllis Schlafly. In her 1972 article, "What's Wrong with 'Equal Rights' for Women," she argued that feminism was antifamily, and that the ERA would destroy the privileges and preferential rights enjoyed by American women. This argument seemed convincing to many, especially in light of the highly visible, radical critiques of the family offered by some feminists at the time and in the context of social changes exemplified by the Supreme Court's 1973 *Roe v. Wade* decision (included here), which guaranteed women's right to choice in the matter of reproductive freedom.

Closely associated with the movements for women's liberation, in the minds of feminists and antifeminists alike, were issues of sexual behavior and sexuality. A powerful statement from the time, Martha Shelley's 1970 article "Gay Is Good" illustrates the ways in which Gay Liberation embodied a larger critique of American society and of traditional gender roles. Finally, historian Beth Bailey writes about the origins of sexual revolution(s), emphasizing, like De Hart on the women's movement, the diversity of what was often seen as a single "movement."

Among the questions raised by these readings are: Why did it take until the middle of the 1960s for a women's liberation movement to develop? Given the diversity in women's experience evident here, was there any way for a women's movement to encompass that diversity and meet all needs? How closely related are issues of gender equality and sexual liberation? Why, as so many Americans rejected—and continue to reject—feminism, have American women's lives and opportunities changed so dramatically since the 1950s?

# The Creation of a Feminist Consciousness

*Jane Sherron De Hart*

*The mainstream African American Civil Rights movement began as a call for equality and full access to American society. By the late 1960s, many African Americans called instead for Black Power, and the Chicano and American Indian movements similarly embraced cultural nationalism, rejecting the culture of the dominant white society.*

*The women's movement that emerged in the 1960s in many ways mirrors that divide. Some women sought equal rights in the existing society; others sought the radical transformation of American life. There was little unity in the feminism of the 1960s and 1970s.*

*Historian Jane Sherron De Hart traces some of the major origins of 1960s and '70s feminism, showing its variety and its resilience. Analyzing two broadly defined groups, one seeking "women's rights" and the other seeking "women's liberation," she provides the context for reading two historical documents that follow: the National Organization for Women's "Statement of Purpose" and New York Radical Women's "No More Miss America."*

## THE CREATION OF A FEMINIST CONSCIOUSNESS

Mainstream feminism emerged as a mass movement in the 1960s as different groups and a new generation acquired a feminist consciousness. In the vanguard were educated, middle-class women whose diverse experiences had sharpened their sensitivity to the fundamental inequality between the sexes at a time when America had been thrust into the throes of self-examination by a movement for racial equality. Some were young veterans of the civil rights movement and the New Left, steeped in a commitment to equality and the techniques of protest. Others were young professionals increasingly aware of their secondary status. Still others were older women who in their long careers as professionals or as activists had used organizations such as the American Civil Liberties Union (ACLU), the Young Women's Christian Association (YWCA) and the United Auto Workers (UAW) to fight sex-based discrimination. Included, too, were those whose outwardly conformist lives belied an intense awareness of the malaise of domesticity and the untenably narrow boundaries of their prescribed roles. To explore how they came self-consciously to appraise women's condition as one demanding collective action is to explore the process of radicalization that helped to create a new feminist movement.

In its early state, a major component of that movement consisted of two different groups—women's rights advocates and women's liberationists. Although the differences between the two groups began to blur as the movement matured, initial distinctions were sharp. Women's rights advocates were likely to have been older, to have had professional training or work experience, to have been more inclined to form or join organized feminist groups. Reform oriented, these organizations used traditional pressure group tactics to achieve changes in laws and public policy that would guarantee women equal rights. Emphasis on "rights" meant extending to women in life outside the home the same "rights" men had, granting them the same options, privileges, and responsibilities that men enjoyed. There was little suggestion initially of personal or cultural transformation.

Women's liberationists were younger women, less highly educated, whose ideology and political style, shaped in the dissent and violence of the 1960s, led them to look at women's predicament differently. Instead of relying upon traditional organizational structure and lobbying techniques, they developed a new style of politics. Instead of limiting their goals to changes in public policy, they embraced a transformation in private, domestic life as well. They sought liberation from ways of thinking and behaving that they believed stunted or distorted women's growth and kept them subordinate to men. Through the extension of their own personal liberation they hoped to remake the male world, changing it as they had changed themselves. For women's liberationists as for women's rights advocates, however, the first step toward becoming feminists demanded a clear statement of women's position in society, one that called attention to the gap between the egalitarian ideal and the actual position of women in American culture. There also had to be a call to action from women themselves, *for* women, *with* women, *through* women. Redefining themselves, they had to make being a woman a political fact; and, as they did so, they had to live with the radical implications of what could only be called a rebirth.

### The Making of Liberal Feminists: Women's Rights Advocates

For some women, the process of radicalization began with the appointment of a Presidential Commission on the Status of Women in 1961. Presidents, Democrat and Republican, customarily discharged their political debt to female members of the electorate, especially to those who had loyally served the party, by appointing a few token women, usually party stalwarts, to highly visible posts. John Kennedy was no exception. He was, however, convinced by Esther Peterson, the highest-ranking woman in his administration, that the vast majority of women would be better served if he also appointed a commission charged with investigating obstacles to the full participation of women in society.

[The commission] report, *American Women* (1963), was conservative in tone, acknowledging the importance of women's traditional roles within the home and the progress they had made in a "free democratic society." Acknowledging also that women were an underutilized resource that the nation could ill afford to ignore, the report provided extensive documentation of discriminatory practices in government, education, and employment, along with substantial recommendations for change. Governors, replicating Kennedy's move, appointed state commissions on the status of women. . . .

Aroused by growing evidence of "the enormity of our problem," members of state commissions gathered in Washington in 1966 for the Third National Conference of the Commissions on the Status of Women. They encountered a situation that transformed at least some of those present into activists in a new movement for women's equality. The catalyst proved to be a struggle involving Representative Martha Griffiths and the Equal Employment Opportunity Commission (EEOC), the federal agency in charge of implementing the Civil Rights Act of 1964.

Despite the fact that the law proscribed discrimination on the basis of sex as well as race, the commission refused to take seriously the problem of sexual discrimination. The first executive director of EEOC, believing that "sex" had been injected into the bill by opponents seeking to block its passage, regarded the sex provision as a "fluke" best ignored. Representative Griffiths from Michigan thought otherwise.

Griffiths's concern was shared by a group of women working within EEOC. Echoing an argument made the year before by a black trade unionist in the Women's Bureau, they insisted that the agency could be made to take gender-related discrimination more seriously if women had a civil rights organization as adept at applying pressure on their behalf as was the National Association for the Advancement of Colored People (NAACP) on behalf of blacks. Initially the idea was rejected. Conference participants most upset by EEOC's inaction decided instead to propose a resolution urging the agency to treat sexual discrimination with the same seriousness it applied to racial discrimination. When the resolution was ruled inappropriate by conference leaders, they were forced to reconsider. After a whispered conversation over lunch they concluded the time for discussion of the status of women was over. It was time for action. Before the day was out twenty-eight women had paid five dollars each to join the National Organization for Women (NOW), including author Betty Friedan, who happened to be in Washington at the time of the conference. . . .

The formation of NOW signaled a feminist resurgence. The three hundred men and women who gathered in October for the organizational meeting of NOW included mainly professionals, some of them veterans of commissions on the status of women as well as a few feminist union activists, notably Dorothy Haener. Adopting bylaws and a statement of purpose, they elected officers, naming Friedan president. Her conviction that intelligent women needed purposeful, generative work of their own was reflected in NOW's statement of purpose, which attacked "the traditional assumption that a woman has to choose between marriage and motherhood on the one hand and serious participation in industry or the professions on the other." . . .

Not content simply to call for change, NOW leaders, following the lead of equality advocates within the labor movement, worked to make it happen. Using persuasion, pressure, and even litigation, they, with other newly formed women's rights groups such as the Women's Equity Action League (WEAL), launched a massive attack on sex discrimination. By the end of the 1960s NOW members had filed legal suits against newspapers listing jobs under the headings "Help Wanted: Male" and "Help Wanted: Female," successfully arguing that such headings discouraged women from applying for jobs they were perfectly capable of doing. Building on efforts begun in the Kennedy administration such as the passage of the Equal Pay Act, they pressured the federal government to intensify its commitment to equal opportunity. They urged congressmen and labor leaders to persuade the Department of Labor to include women in its guidelines designed to encourage the hiring and promotion of blacks in firms holding contracts with the federal government. They persuaded the Federal Communications Commission to open up new opportunities for women in broadcasting. Tackling the campus as well as the marketplace, WEAL filed suit against more than three hundred colleges and universities, ultimately securing millions of dollars in salary raises for women faculty members who had been victims of discrimination. To ensure that women receive the same pay men received for doing the same work, these new feminists lobbied for passage of a new Equal Employment Opportunity Act that would enable EEOC to fight discrimination more effectively.

NOW also scrutinized the discriminatory practices of financial institutions, persuading them to issue credit to single women and to married women in their own—not their husband's—name. WEAL, in turn, filed charges against banks and other lending institutions that refused to grant mortgages to single women, or in the case of married couples, refused to take into account the wife's earnings in evaluating the couple's eligibility for a mortgage. Colleges and universities that discriminated against female students in their sports programs came under fire, as did fellowship programs that failed to give adequate consideration to female applicants. . . .

### The Making of Radical Feminists: Women's Liberationists

The process of radicalization that transformed some individuals into liberal feminists occurred simultaneously—but in different fashion and with somewhat different results—among a younger generation of women who were also predominantly white and middle class. Many of them veterans of either the civil rights movement or of the New

Left, these were the activists who would initially become identified as women's liberationists. Differing in perspective as well as style, they would ultimately push many of their older counterparts beyond the demand for equal rights to recognition that true emancipation would require a far-reaching transformation of society and culture.

The experiences awakening in this 1960s generation a feminist consciousness have been superbly described by Sara Evans in her book, *Personal Politics.* "Freedom, equality, love and hope," the possibility of new human relationships, the importance of participatory democracy—letting the people decide—were, as Evans points out, part of an egalitarian ideology shared by both the southern-based Student Nonviolent Coordinating Committee (SNCC) in its struggle for racial equality and the Students for a Democratic Society (SDS) in its efforts to mobilize an interracial organization of the urban poor in northern ghettos. Membership in both organizations—"the movement"—thus reinforced commitment to these ideals among the women who joined. In order to translate ideals into reality, however, young, college-age women who had left the shelter of middle-class families for the hard and dangerous work of transforming society found themselves doing things that they would never have thought possible. Amidst the racial strife of the South, they joined picket lines, created freedom schools, and canvassed for voter registration among blacks, often enduring arrest and jailing. SDS women from affluent suburbs entered decaying tenements and were surrounded by the grim realities of the ghetto. They trudged door-to-door in an effort to reach women whose struggle to survive made many understandably suspicious of intruding strangers. In the process, not only did these young activists achieve a heightened sense of self-worth and autonomy, they also learned the skills of movement building and the nuts and bolts of organizing.

Particularly important was the problem of getting people, long passive, to act on their own behalf. SDS women began by encouraging ghetto women to come together to talk about their problems. This sharing of experiences, they believed, would lead these women to recognize not only that their problems were common but that solutions required changes in the system. In the process of organizing, the organizers also learned. They began to understand the meaning of oppression and the valor required of those who fought it. They found new role models, Evans suggests, in extraordinary southern black women whose courage seemed never to waver in the face of violence and in those welfare mothers of the North who confronted the welfare bureaucrat and slum lord after years of passivity.

But if being in the movement brought a new understanding of equality, it also brought new problems. Men who were committed to equality for one group were not necessarily committed to equality for another group. Women in SNCC, as in SDS, found themselves frequently relegated to domestic chores and treated as sex objects, denied most leadership positions, and refused a key voice in the formulation of policy. Moreover, the sexual freedom that had been theirs as part of the cultural revolution taking place in the 1960s soon began to feel more like sexual exploitation as they saw their role in the movement spelled out in the draft resister's slogan: "Girls Say Yes to Guys Who Say No." Efforts to change the situation were firmly rebuffed. When SNCC leader Stokely Carmichael joked that the only "position for women in SNCC is prone," he encapsulated views which, while not his own, reflected all too accurately the feelings of males in the New Left as well as many in SNCC.

By 1967 the tensions had become so intense that white women left the movement to organize on behalf of their own "liberation." Black women, whose own tradition of feminism was venerable, stayed. Fully aware of the double jeopardy involved in being both black and female, many would embrace varieties of feminism that reflected their own problems and priorities. In the meantime, however, racial equality remained their top concern.

The women who left did not leave empty-handed. As radicals, they were impatient with liberalism, critical of capitalism, and profoundly suspicious of authority. Accustomed to challenging prevailing ideas and practices, they had acquired a language of protest, an organizing tactic, and a deep-seated conviction that the personal was political. How that legacy would shape this burgeoning new feminist movement became evident as small women's liberation groups began springing up spontaneously in major cities and university communities across the nation.

# Statement of Purpose (1966)

## The National Organization for Women

*In the previous article, historian Jane Sherron De Hart describes the origins of the National Organization for Women (NOW). Reprinted here is the "Statement of Purpose" this group created on October 29, 1966, at its first national conference. As De Hart explains, members of NOW sought "women's rights" as opposed to "women's liberation." Their goals were practical; their methods fit comfortably within the contemporary American political system. While NOW members certainly were less provocative than the women's liberationists (as demonstrated in the document that follows), it is well worth analyzing the way they made their case. When reading this statement, pay attention to the specific ways that NOW justifies its claims for women's rights. What are they, and how effective might each be in 1966 America? What, according to this statement, are the sources of discrimination against women, and what are their proposed solutions? Why do they use the term "silken curtain"? Finally, compare this document to the New York Radical Women's "No More Miss America." What, if anything, do these two groups have in common?*

We, men and women who hereby constitute ourselves as the National Organization for Women, believe that the time has come for a new movement toward true equality for all women in America, and toward a fully equal partnership of the sexes, as part of the world-wide revolution of human rights now taking place within and beyond our national borders.

The purpose of NOW is to take action to bring women into full participation in the mainstream of American society now, exercising all the privileges and responsibilities thereof in truly equal partnership with men.

We believe the time has come to move beyond the abstract argument, discussion and symposia over the status and special nature of women

National Organization for Women, with permission, http://www.now.org/history/purpos66.html.

which has raged in America in recent years; the time has come to confront, with concrete action, the conditions that now prevent women from enjoying the equality of opportunity and freedom of choice which is their right, as individual Americans, and as human beings.

NOW is dedicated to the proposition that women, first and foremost, are human beings, who, like all other people in our society, must have the chance to develop their fullest human potential. We believe that women can achieve such equality only by accepting to the full the challenges and responsibilities they share with all other people in our society, as part of the decision-making mainstream of American political, economic and social life.

We organize to initiate or support action, nationally, or in any part of this nation, by individuals or organizations, to break through the silken curtain of prejudice and discrimination against women in government, industry, the professions, the churches, the political parties, the judiciary, the labor unions, in education, science, medicine, law, religion and every other field of importance in American society.

Enormous changes taking place in our society make it both possible and urgently necessary to advance the unfinished revolution of women toward true equality, now. With a life span lengthened to nearly 75 years it is no longer either necessary or possible for women to devote the greater part of their lives to child-rearing; yet childbearing and rearing which continues to be a most important part of most women's lives—still is used to justify barring women from equal professional and economic participation and advance.

Today's technology has reduced most of the productive chores which women once performed in the home and in mass-production industries based upon routine unskilled labor. This same technology has virtually eliminated the quality of muscular strength as a criterion for filling most jobs, while intensifying American industry's need for creative intelligence. In view of this new industrial revolution created by automation in the mid-twentieth century, women can and must participate in old and new fields of society in full equality—or become permanent outsiders.

Despite all the talk about the status of American women in recent years, the actual position of women in the United States has declined, and is declining, to an alarming degree throughout the 1950's and 60's. Although 46.4% of all American women between the ages of 18 and 65 now work outside the home, the overwhelming majority—75%—are in routine clerical, sales, or factory jobs, or they are household workers, cleaning women, hospital attendants. About two-thirds of Negro women workers are in the lowest paid service occupations. Working women are becoming increasingly—not less—concentrated on the bottom of the job ladder. As a consequence full-time women workers today earn on the average only 60% of what men earn, and that wage gap has been increasing over the past twenty-five years in every major industry group. In 1964, of all women with a yearly income, 89% earned under $5,000 a year; half of all full-time year round women workers earned less than $3,690; only 1.4% of full-time year round women workers had an annual income of $10,000 or more.

Further, with higher education increasingly essential in today's society, too few women are entering and finishing college or going on to graduate or professional school. Today, women earn only one in three of the B.A.'s and M.A.'s granted, and one in ten of the Ph.D.'s.

In all the professions considered of importance to society, and in the executive ranks of industry and government, women are losing ground. Where they are present it is only a token handful. Women comprise less than 1% of federal judges; less than 4% of all lawyers; 7% of doctors. Yet women represent 51% of the U.S. population. And, increasingly, men are replacing women in the top positions in secondary and elementary schools, in social work, and in libraries—once thought to be women's fields.

Official pronouncements of the advance in the status of women hide not only the reality of this dangerous decline, but the fact that nothing is being done to stop it. The excellent reports of the President's Commission on the Status of Women and of the State Commissions have not been fully implemented. Such Commissions have power only to advise. They have no power to enforce their recommendation; nor have they the freedom to organize American women and men to press for action on them. The reports of these commissions have, however, created a basis upon which it is now possible to build. Discrimination in employment on the basis of sex is now prohibited by federal law, in Title VII of the Civil Rights Act of 1964. But although nearly one-third of the cases brought before the Equal Employment Opportunity Commission during the first year dealt with sex discrimination and the proportion is increasing dramatically, the Commission has not made clear its intention to enforce the law with the same seriousness on behalf of women as of other victims of discrimination. Many of these cases were Negro women, who are the victims of double discrimination of race and sex. Until now, too few women's organizations and official spokesmen have been willing to speak out against these dangers facing women. Too many women have been restrained by the fear of being called "feminist." There is no civil rights movement to speak for women, as there has been for Negroes and other victims of discrimination. The National Organization for Women must therefore begin to speak.

WE BELIEVE that the power of American law, and the protection guaranteed by the U.S. Constitution to the civil rights of all individuals, must be effectively applied and enforced to isolate and remove patterns of sex discrimination, to ensure equality of opportunity in employment and education, and equality of civil and political rights and responsibilities on behalf of women, as well as for Negroes and other deprived groups.

We realize that women's problems are linked to many broader questions of social justice; their solution will require concerted action by many groups. Therefore, convinced that human rights for all are indivisible, we expect to give active support to the common cause of equal rights for all those who suffer discrimination and deprivation, and we call upon other organizations committed to such goals to support our efforts toward equality for women.

WE DO NOT ACCEPT the token appointment of a few women to high-level positions in government and industry as a substitute for serious continuing effort to recruit and advance women according to their individual abilities. To this end, we urge American government and industry to mobilize the same resources of ingenuity and command with which they have solved problems of far greater difficulty than those now impeding the progress of women.

WE BELIEVE that this nation has a capacity at least as great as other nations, to innovate new social institutions which will enable women to enjoy the true equality of opportunity and responsibility in society, without conflict with their responsibilities as mothers and homemakers. In such innovations, America does not lead the Western world, but lags by decades behind many European countries. We do not accept the traditional assumption that a woman has to choose between marriage and motherhood, on the one hand, and serious participation in industry or the professions on the other. We question the present expectation that all normal women will retire from job or profession for 10 or 15 years, to devote their full time to raising children, only to reenter the job market at a relatively minor level.

This, in itself, is a deterrent to the aspirations of women, to their acceptance into management or professional training courses, and to the very possibility of equality of opportunity or real choice, for all but a few women. Above all, we reject the assumption that these problems are the unique responsibility of each individual woman, rather than a basic social dilemma which society must solve. True equality of opportunity and freedom of choice for women requires such practical, and possible innovations as a nationwide network of child-care centers, which will make it unnecessary for women to retire completely from society until their children are grown, and national programs to provide retraining for women who have chosen to care for their children full-time.

WE BELIEVE that it is as essential for every girl to be educated to her full potential of human ability as it is for every boy—with the knowledge that such education is the key to effective participation in today's economy and that, for a girl as for a boy, education can only be serious where there is expectation that it will be used in society. We believe that American educators are capable of devising means of imparting such expectations to girl students. Moreover, we consider the decline in the proportion of women receiving higher and professional education to be evidence of discrimination. This discrimination may take the form of quotas against the admission of women to colleges, and professional schools; lack of encouragement by parents, counselors and educators; denial of loans or fellowships; or the traditional or arbitrary procedures in graduate and professional training geared in terms of men, which inadvertently discriminate against women. We believe that the same serious attention must be given to high school dropouts who are girls as to boys.

WE REJECT the current assumptions that a man must carry the sole burden of supporting himself, his wife, and family, and that a woman is automatically entitled to lifelong support by a man upon her marriage, or that marriage, home and family are primarily woman's world and responsibility—hers, to dominate—his to support. We believe that a true partnership between the sexes demands a different concept of marriage, an equitable sharing of the responsibilities of home and children and of the economic burdens of their support. We believe that proper recognition should be given to the economic and social value of homemaking and child-care. To these ends, we will seek to open a reexamination of laws and mores governing marriage and divorce, for we believe that the current state of "half-equity" between the sexes discriminates against both men and women, and is the cause of much unnecessary hostility between the sexes.

WE BELIEVE that women must now exercise their political rights and responsibilities as American citizens. They must refuse to be segregated on the basis of sex into separate-and-not-equal ladies' auxiliaries in the political parties, and they must demand representation according to their numbers in the regularly constituted party committees—at local, state, and national levels—and in the informal power structure, participating fully in the selection of candidates and political decision-making, and running for office themselves.

IN THE INTERESTS OF THE HUMAN DIGNITY OF WOMEN, we will protest, and endeavor to change, the false image of women now prevalent in the mass media, and in the texts, ceremonies, laws, and practices of our major social institutions. Such images perpetuate contempt for women by society and by women for themselves. We are similarly opposed to all policies and practices—in church, state, college, factory, or office—which, in the guise of protectiveness, not only deny opportunities but also foster in women self-denigration, dependence, and evasion of responsibility, undermine their confidence in their own abilities and foster contempt for women.

NOW WILL HOLD ITSELF INDEPENDENT OF ANY POLITICAL PARTY in order to mobilize the political power of all women and men intent on our goals. We will strive to ensure that no party, candidate, president, senator, governor, congressman, or any public official who betrays or ignores the principle of full equality between the sexes is elected or appointed to office. If it is necessary to mobilize the votes of men and women who believe in our cause, in order to win for women the final right to be fully free and equal human beings, we so commit ourselves.

WE BELIEVE THAT women will do most to create a new image of women by acting now, and by speaking out in behalf of their own equality, freedom, and human dignity—not in pleas for special privilege, nor in enmity toward men, who are also victims of the current, half-equality between the sexes—but in an active, self-respecting partnership with men. By so doing, women will develop confidence in their own ability to determine actively, in partnership with men, the conditions of their life, their choices, their future and their society.

# No More Miss America (1968)

*Robin Morgan and New York Radical Women*

On September 7, 1968, Miss Kansas (Debra Dene Barnes) walked down the runway in swimsuit and high heels. She was crowned America's beauty queen as Bert Parks sang, "There she is, Miss America." Outside, about two hundred women picketed. They crowned a sheep Miss America (just as the Yippies had nominated a pig for president at Democratic National Convention protests in Chicago the previous month). They threw what they called "instruments of torture"—high heels, girdles, bras, false eyelashes, and curlers—into a large "Freedom Trashcan." Women carried signs: "Miss America Sells It," and "Miss America Is a Big Falsie."

The protesters had originally intended to burn the contents of the Freedom Trashcan. Atlantic City Police, however, were concerned that the wooden boardwalk might catch fire. No bras were burned that day, but shortly thereafter the mainstream press began to refer to bra-burnings when describing the movement for women's liberation. In part, the idea that women were burning their bras connected their protests to the draft card burnings by young men. It also added a titillating element to news stories about the women's liberation movement. By reducing the demands of radical women from social justice to sexual freedom alone, such accounts marginalized and trivialized their message.

In "No More Miss America," the organizers of the protest explained their goals. Why, when women faced so many obstacles in contemporary American society, did they choose to protest a beauty pageant? Why might that be an effective strategy? After the protest, some participants felt that they had made a mistake by seeming to target the contestants. "Miss America and all beautiful women came off as our enemies instead of as our sisters who suffer with us," one wrote. This document begins by inviting a broad range of women's groups to join the protest. Is this statement (and the protest that followed) truly inclusive? How well did the Radical Women reach out to their "sisters"?

On September 7th in Atlantic City, the Annual Miss America Pageant will again crown "your ideal." But this year, reality will liberate the contest auction-block in the guise of "genyooine" de-plasticized, breathing women. Women's Liberation Groups, black women, high-school and college women, women's peace groups, women's welfare and social-work groups, women's job-equality groups, pro–birth control and pro-abortion groups—women of every political persuasion—all are invited to join us in a day-long boardwalk-theater event, starting at 1:00 P.M. on the Boardwalk in front of Atlantic City's Convention Hall. We will protest the image of Miss America, an image that oppresses women in every area in which it purports to represent us. There will be: Picket Lines; Guerrilla Theater; Leafleting; Lobbying Visits to the contestants urging our sisters to reject the Pageant Farce and join us; a huge Freedom Trash Can (into which we will throw bras, girdles, curlers, false eyelashes, wigs, and representative issues of *Cosmopolitan, Ladies' Home Journal, Family Circle,* etc.—bring any such woman-garbage you have around the house); we will also announce a Boycott of all those commercial products related to the Pageant, and the day will end with a Women's Liberation rally at midnight when Miss America is crowned on live television. Lots of other surprises are being planned (come and add your own!) but we do not plan heavy disruptive tactics and so do not expect a bad police scene. It should be a groovy day on the Boardwalk in the sun with our sisters. In case of arrests, however, we plan to reject all male authority and demand to be busted by policewomen only. (In Atlantic City, women cops are not permitted to make arrests—dig that!)

Male chauvinist-reactionaries on this issue had best stay away, nor are male liberals welcome in the demonstrations. But sympathetic men can donate money as well as cars and drivers.

Male reporters will be refused interviews. We reject patronizing reportage. *Only newswomen will be recognized.*


**THE TEN POINTS**

We Protest:

1. *The Degrading Mindless-Boob-Girlie Symbol.* The Pageant contestants epitomize the roles we are all forced to play as women. The parade down the runway blares the metaphor of the 4-H Club county fair, where the nervous animals are judged for teeth, fleece, etc., and where the best

"specimen" gets the blue ribbon. So are women in our society forced daily to compete for male approval, enslaved by ludicrous "beauty" standards we ourselves are conditioned to take seriously.

2. *Racism with Roses.* Since its inception in 1921, the Pageant has not had one Black finalist, and this has not been for a lack of test-case contestants. There has never been a Puerto Rican, Alaskan, Hawaiian, or Mexican-American winner. Nor has there ever been a *true* Miss America—an American Indian.

3. *Miss America as Military Death Mascot.* The highlight of her reign each year is a cheerleader-tour of American troops abroad—last year she went to Vietnam to pep-talk our husbands, fathers, sons, and boyfriends into dying and killing with a better spirit. She personifies the "unstained patriotic American womanhood our boys are fighting for." The Living Bra and the Dead Soldier. We refuse to be used as Mascots for Murder.

4. *The Consumer Con-Game.* Miss America is a walking commercial for the Pageant's sponsors. Wind her up and she plugs your product on promotion tours and TV—all in an "honest, objective" endorsement. What a shill.

5. *Competition Rigged and Unrigged.* We deplore the encouragement of an American myth that oppresses men as well as women: the win-or-you're-worthless competitive disease. The "beauty contest" creates only one winner to be "used" and forty-nine losers who are "useless."

6. *The Woman as Pop Culture Obsolescent Theme.* Spindle, mutilate, and then discard tomorrow. What is so ignored as last year's Miss America? This only reflects the gospel of our society, according to Saint Male: women must be young, juicy, malleable—hence age discrimination and the cult of youth. And we women are brainwashed into believing this ourselves!

7. *The Unbeatable Madonna-Whore Combination.* Miss America and Playboy's centerfold are sisters over the skin. To win approval, we must be both sexy and wholesome, delicate but able to cope, demure yet titillatingly bitchy. Deviation of any sort brings, we are told, disaster: "You won't get a man!!"

8. *The Irrelevant Crown on the Throne of Mediocrity.* Miss America represents what women are supposed to be: unoffensive, bland, apolitical. If you are tall, short, over or under what weight The Man prescribes you should be, forget it. Personality, articulateness, intelligence, commitment—unwise. Conformity is the key to the crown—and, by extension, to success in our society.

9. *Miss America as Dream Equivalent To—?* In this reputedly democratic society, where every little boy supposedly can grow up to be President, what can every little girl hope to grow to be? Miss America. That's where it's at. Real power to control our own lives is restricted to men, while women get patronizing pseudo-power, an ermine cloak and a bunch of flowers; men are judged by their actions, women by their appearance.

10. *Miss America as Big Sister Watching You.* The Pageant exercises Thought Control, attempts to scar the Image onto our minds, to further make women oppressed and men oppressors; to enslave us all the more in high-heeled, low-status roles; to inculcate false values in young girls; to use women as beasts of buying; to seduce us to prostitute ourselves before our own oppression.

NO MORE MISS AMERICA

# ¡Soy Chicana Primero! (1971)

## Enriqueta Longeaux Vasquez

When the contemporary "second wave" feminist movement began, many of its proponents argued that women shared "bonds of sisterhood" across race and class lines. This position presumed that the common experience of being born female in a patriarchal social structure transcended in importance and impact the very dissimilar experiences that divided women of different classes and races or ethnicities. All too often, however, it was the experience of white, college-educated women that was being used as a basis for generalization. Controversy over this issue became a critical dividing point in the feminist movement. Was gender in fact a more important source of opposition than class or race? Did the mainstream feminist movement deny the validity of the experiences of women of color, working-class women, or lesbians?

Women of color, especially, faced hard questions. Were women who embraced feminism betraying their brothers in the Black Power or Chicano movements, as some male leaders charged? Was feminism simply a divisive force within the larger and more important struggle for racial justice? Were the sources of women's oppression only external (white supremacy; capitalism), or did they exist within African American and Chicano/a culture as well?

Like African American women, Chicanas struggled with these questions. The cultural nationalism of the early Chicano movement glorified the traditional, family-oriented, and subordinate woman as a cornerstone of Chicanismo, and that made the issue of feminism particularly difficult. Was it sexist oppression, or was it a central part of the culture around which the movement was built? Feminism did grow strong within el movimiento, as Chicanas debated these issues and wrote platform statements of their own. But not all women declared themselves feminists first. In the following article, Enriqueta Longeaux Vasquez makes a powerful claim: "¡Soy Chicana Primero!" but at the same time gives voice to the ambivalence and confusion many women felt in this tumultuous

From *El Cuaderno*, Vol. 1, No. 2, 1971: pp. 17–22. Copyright © 1997. From *Chicana Feminist Thought*, edited by Alma M. Garcia. Reproduced by permission of Routledge, Inc., part of the Taylor & Francis group.

*and difficult time. How does Vasquez answer the question above? How does her vision of "la familia de la Raza" differ from the goals of white radical and liberal feminists that appear in earlier documents in this section?*

The Chicana today is becoming very serious and observant. On one hand she watches and evaluates the white women's liberation movement and on the other hand she hears the echoes of the "Chicano" movement, "Viva La Raza," the radical raps and rhetoric. For some it becomes fashionable, while for many of us it becomes survival itself. Some of our own Chicanas may be attracted to the white woman's liberation movement, but we really don't feel comfortable there. We want to be a Chicana *primero,* we want to walk hand in hand with the Chicano brothers, with our children, our *viejitos* [elders], our Familia de La Raza.

Then too we hear the whisper that if you are a radical Chicana you lose some of your femininity as a woman. And we question this as we look at the world struggles and know that this accusation as to femininity doesn't make sense. After all, we have seen the Vietnamese woman fight for survival with a gun in one hand and a child sucking on her breast on the other arm. She is certainly feminine. Our own people that fought in the revolution [Mexican Revolution of 1910] were brave and beautiful, even more human because of the struggles we fought for.

So we begin to see what our people are up against as we take very seriously our responsibility to our people, and to our children; as we sense the raging battle for cultural survival. We know that this means we have hardships to endure and we wish to strengthen our endurance in order that we may further strengthen the endurance of our coming generations. Nuestros hijos [our children] that are here and those that are yet to come. Our people would often say when they saw a strong spirited woman, *vienen de buen barro* (she comes from a good clay). Thus we now must make our children strong with the realization that they too, "vienen de buen barro."

When we discuss the Chicana, we have to be informed and know how to relate to the white women's liberation movement in order to come up with some of our own answers. This requires a basic analysis, not just a lot of static. Looking at the issues of the women's lib movement it is easy to relate to the struggle itself as a struggle. We can understand this because the Raza people are no newcomers to struggles, we can sympathize with many basic struggles. However, it is not our business as Chicanas to identify with the white women's liberation movement as a home base for working for our people. We couldn't lead our people there, could we? Remember Raza is our home ground and family and we have strong basic issues and grievances as *a people*. In looking at women's lib we see issues that are relevant to that materialistic, competitive society of the Gringo. This society is only able to function through the sharpening of wits and development of the human instinct of rivalry. For this same dominant society and mentality to arrive at a point where there is now a white women's liberation movement is *dangerous* and *cruel* in that social structure has reached the point of fracture and competition of the male and female. This competitive thought pattern can lead to the conclusion that the man is the enemy and thus create conflict of the sexes.

Now we, Raza, are a colonized people (we have been a colony of New Spain, we have been Mexico, and have only a veneer of U.S. of A. rule—since 1848, just 100 years) and an oppressed people. We must have a clearer vision of our plight and certainly we can not blame our men for oppression of the woman. Our men are not the power structure that oppresses us as a whole. We know who stole our lands: we know who discriminates against us; we know who came in (our parents still remember), threw out our Spanish books and brought in new, fresh-written history books and we know who wrote those books for us to read. In other words, we know where we hurt and why. And even more important, we can not afford to fight within and among ourselves anymore, much less male pitted against female.

When our man is beaten down by society, in employment, housing or whatever, he should no longer come home and beat his wife and family; and when the woman doesn't have all she needs at home or she perhaps has a family to raise alone, she should not turn around and hate her husband or men for it. Both the man and the woman have to realize where we hurt, we have to figure out why we hurt and why these things are happening to us. And more important, through all of these sufferings and tests we have to receive and share strength from each other and together fight the social system that is destroying us and our families, that is eating away at us, little by little. And we have to build a social system of our own.

One of the greatest strengths of Raza is that of our understanding and obedience to nature and its balance and creation. This same awareness makes us realize that there can't be total fulfillment without the other. Life requires both in order for it to go on, to reproduce.

This same basic need of each other is the total fulfillment of beauty in its most creative form. Now the reason that we discuss this is that we must also think of life generally, without the BAD and TABOO connotation that has been placed on our basic human functions. We can not allow negative attitudes in regard to our physical capacities, because when we allow this kind of control on ourselves, we are allowing ourselves to be castrated, controlled, and destroyed at our very basic, essential level. This can affect generations to come.

In working for our people, a woman becomes more and more capable; this Raza woman gains confidence, pride and strength and this strength is both personal and as a people. She gains independence, security, and more human strength because she is working in a familiar area, one in which she puts her *corazón* [heart] and love. When a man sees this kind of spirit and strength, the Chicana may be misunderstood as having lost her femininity. A man may misinterpret this and feel it as a threat. But he, too, must stop and evaluate this. He should not react against her because this is a great source of strength for him, for her, for our children, for the Familia de La Raza. This is the kind of spirit and strength that builds and holds firm La Familia de La Raza. This is love, my Raza; we can not compete with "el barro" that has held us firm for so long. This is total *respect* and equality in loving ourselves, our men, our elders, our children. It is this force that has allowed us to endure through the centuries and it is the strength that carries on the struggle of our people, the demand for justice.

With this kind of strength, how can we possibly question the femininity of the Chicana? Femininity is something more than the outer shell . . . stereotyping of women seems like a materialistic attitude. That kind of judgment should not be placed on our women.

Many Raza women relate to the earth [*La Tierra*]—we have worked in the fields, as migrants and campesinos. We are not afraid of the sweet smell of sweat from our bodies . . . our mother wearing coveralls with knee patches, thinning beets . . . who would dare to say this woman is not feminine?

The Chicana must not choose white woman's liberation. . . . To be a Chicana PRIMERO (first), to stand by her people, will make her stronger for the struggle and endurance of her people. The Raza movement needs "La Chicana" very, very much. Today we face a time of commitment, LA FAMILIA DE LA RAZA needs her for the building of our *nación* de Aztlán [our nation of Aztlán].

# What's Wrong with "Equal Rights" for Women? (1972)

## Phyllis Schlafly

*By an overwhelming margin, Congress passed the Equal Rights Amendment (ERA) in early 1972 and submitted it to the states for ratification. Within a year thirty states had voted in support of adding the amendment to the Constitution. Then Phyllis Schlafly organized a "STOP ERA" campaign. Schlafly, mother of six children, believed that feminism was antifamily, antimarriage, and antichildren. But she was not simply a housewife who reacted against a threat to her chosen way of life. Schlafly was a lawyer with degrees from Harvard and Washington Universities who had risen to prominence in conservative circles after writing the bestselling book,* A Choice Not an Echo, *in support of Barry Goldwater's 1964 presidential candidacy.*

*To fight the ERA, Schlafly put together a coalition of fundamentalist and orthodox religious leaders, conservative businessmen, radical right groups, and a growing number of women who considered themselves antifeminist. Believing that the women's movement had gone too far, these women saw feminism as an enemy responsible for fostering sexual permissiveness, homosexuality, abortion, moral relativism, and what they called "secular humanism." They feared that the ERA would destroy the "special place" of women in the home, force them to fight in combat, and mandate unisex toilets. Because of their efforts, the deadline for ratifying the ERA passed in June 1982 with the amendment still three states short of adoption.*

*In "What's Wrong with 'Equal Rights' for Women?" Schlafly sets forth her case against the Equal Rights Amendment and the feminist movement. To whom might such an argument appeal, and why? Think about Jane Sherron De Hart's analysis and the radical feminist statement, "No More Miss America," as you read Schlafly's argument. Could feminists have attracted conservative women to their cause by using less inflammatory language and*

From *Phyllis Schlafly Report* 5, no. 7 (February 1972). Reprinted by permission of the author.

*showing more sensitivity to differences among American women, or were the interests and goals of the two groups just too different?*

Of all the classes of people who ever lived, the American woman is the most privileged. We have the most rights and rewards, and the fewest duties. Our unique status is the result of a fortunate combination of circumstances.

1. We have the immense good fortune to live in a civilization which respects the family as the basic unit of society. This respect is part and parcel of our laws and our customs. It is based on the fact of life—which no legislation or agitation can erase—that women have babies and men don't.

If you don't like this fundamental difference, you will have to take up your complaint with God because He created us this way. The fact that women, not men, have babies is not the fault of selfish and domineering men, or of the establishment, or of any clique of conspirators who want to oppress women. It's simply the way God made us.

Our Judeo-Christian civilization has developed the law and custom that, since women must bear the physical consequences of the sex act, men must be required to bear the *other* consequences and pay in other ways. These laws and customs decree that a man must carry his share by physical protection and financial support of his children and of the woman who bears his children, and also by a code of behavior which benefits and protects both the woman and the children.

## THE GREATEST ACHIEVEMENT OF WOMEN'S RIGHTS

This is accomplished by the institution of the family. Our respect for the family as the basic unit of society, which is ingrained in the laws and customs of our Judeo-Christian civilization, is the greatest single achievement in the entire history of women's rights. It assures a woman the most precious and important right of all—the right to keep her own baby and to be supported and protected in the enjoyment of watching her baby grow and develop.

The institution of the family is advantageous for women for many reasons. After all, what do we want out of life? To love and be loved? Mankind has not discovered a better nest for a lifetime of reciprocal love. A sense of achievement? A man may search 30 to 40 years for accomplishment in his profession. A woman can enjoy real achievement when she is young—by having a baby. She can have the satisfaction of doing a job well—and being recognized for it.

Do we want financial security? We are fortunate to have the great legacy of Moses, the Ten Commandments, especially this one: "Honor thy father and thy mother that thy days may be long upon the land." Children are a woman's best social security—her best guarantee of social benefits such as old age pension, unemployment compensation, workman's compensation, and sick leave. The family gives a woman the physical, financial, and emotional security of the home—for all her life.

## THE FINANCIAL BENEFITS OF CHIVALRY

2. The second reason why American women are a privileged group is that we are the beneficiaries of a tradition of special respect for women which dates from the Christian Age of Chivalry. The honor and respect paid to Mary, the Mother of Christ, resulted in all women, in effect, being put on a pedestal.

This respect for women is not just the lip service that politicians pay to "God, Motherhood, and the Flag." It is not—as some youthful agitators seem to think—just a matter of opening doors for women, seeing that they are seated first, carrying their bundles, and helping them in and out of automobiles. Such good manners are merely the superficial evidences of a total attitude toward women which expresses itself in many more tangible ways, such as money.

In other civilizations, such as the African and the American Indian, the men strut around wearing feathers and beads and hunting and fishing (great sport for men!), while the women do all the hard, tiresome drudgery including the tilling of the soil (if any is done), the hewing of wood, the making of fires, the carrying of water, as well as the cooking, sewing and caring for babies.

This is not the American way because we were lucky enough to inherit the traditions of the Age of Chivalry. In America, a man's first significant purchase is a diamond for his bride, and the largest financial investment of his life is a home for her to live in. American husbands work hours of overtime to buy a fur piece or other finery to keep their wives in fashion, and to pay premiums on their life insurance policies to provide for her comfort when she is a widow (benefits in which he can never share).

In the states which follow the English common law, a wife has a dower right in her husband's real estate which he cannot take away from her during life or by his will. A man cannot dispose of his real estate without his wife's signature. Any sale is subject to her 1/3 interest. Women fare even better in the states which follow the Spanish and French community-property laws, such as California, Arizona, Texas and Louisiana. The basic philosophy of the Spanish/French law is that a wife's work in the home is just as valuable as a husband's work at his job. Therefore, in community-property states, a wife owns one-half of all the property and income her husband earns during their marriage, and he cannot take it away from her.

In Illinois, as a result of agitation by "equal rights" fanatics, the real-estate dower laws were repealed as of January 1, 1972. This means that in Illinois a husband can now sell the family home, spend the money on his girl friend or gamble it away, and his faithful wife of 30 years can no longer stop him. "Equal rights" fanatics have also deprived women in Illinois and in some other states of most of their basic common-law rights to recover damages for breach of promise to marry, seduction, criminal conversation, and alienation of affections.

**THE REAL LIBERATION OF WOMEN**

3. The third reason why American women are so well off is that the great American free enterprise system has produced remarkable inventors who have lifted the backbreaking "women's work" from our shoulders.

In other countries and in other eras, it was truly said that "Man may work from sun to sun, but woman's work is never done." Other women have labored every waking hour—preparing food on wood-burning stoves, making flour, baking bread in stone ovens, spinning yarn, making clothes, making soap, doing the laundry by hand, heating irons, making candles for light and fires for warmth, and trying to nurse their babies through illnesses without medical care.

The real liberation of women from the backbreaking drudgery of centuries is the American free enterprise system which stimulated inventive geniuses to pursue their talents—and we all reap the profits.

The great heroes of women's liberation are not the straggly-haired women on television talk shows and picket lines, but Thomas Edison who brought the miracle of electricity to our homes to give light and to run all those labor-saving devices—the equivalent, perhaps, of a half-dozen household servants for every middle-class American woman. Or Elias Howe who gave us the sewing machine which resulted in such an abundance of readymade clothing. Or Clarence Birdseye who invented the process for freezing foods. Or Henry Ford, who mass-produced the automobile so that it is within the price-range of every American, man or woman.

A major occupation of women in other countries is doing their daily shopping for food, which requires carrying their own containers and standing in line at dozens of small shops. They buy only small portions because they can't carry very much and have no refrigerator or freezer to keep a surplus anyway. Our American free enterprise system has given us the gigantic food and packaging industry and beautiful supermarkets, which provide an endless variety of foods, prepackaged for easy carrying and a minimum of waiting. In America, women have the freedom from the slavery of standing in line for daily food.

Thus, household duties have been reduced to only a few hours a day, leaving the American woman with plenty of time to moonlight. She can take a full or part-time paying job, or she can indulge to her heart's content in a tremendous selection of interesting educational or cultural or homemaking activities.

## THE FRAUD OF THE EQUAL RIGHTS AMENDMENT

In the last couple of years, a noisy movement has sprung up agitating for "women's rights." Suddenly, everywhere we are afflicted with aggressive females on television talk shows yapping about how mistreated American women are, suggesting that marriage has put us in some kind of "slavery," that housework is menial and degrading, and—perish the thought—that women are discriminated against. New "women's liberation" organizations are popping up, agitating and demonstrating, serving demands on public officials, getting wide press coverage always, and purporting to speak for some 100,000,000 American women.

It's time to set the record straight. The claim that American women are downtrodden and unfairly treated is the fraud of the century. The truth is that American women never had it so good. Why should we lower ourselves to "equal rights" when we already have the status of special privilege?

The proposed Equal Rights Amendment states: "Equality of rights under the law shall not be denied or abridged by the United States or by any state on account of sex." So what's wrong with that? Well, here are a few examples of what's wrong with it.

This Amendment will absolutely and positively make women subject to the draft. Why any woman would support such a ridiculous and un-American proposal as this is beyond comprehension. Why any Congressman who had any regard for his wife, sister, or daughter would support such a proposition is just as hard to understand. Foxholes are bad enough for men, but they certainly are *not* the place for women—and we should reject any proposal which would put them there in the name of "equal rights."

It is amusing to watch the semantic chicanery of the advocates of the Equal Rights Amendment when confronted with this issue of the draft. They evade, they sidestep, they try to muddy up the issue, but they cannot deny that the Equal Rights Amendment will positively make women subject to the draft. Congresswoman Margaret Heckler's answer to this question was, Don't worry, it will take two years for the Equal Rights Amendment to go into effect, and we can rely on President Nixon to end the Vietnam War before then!

Literature distributed by Equal Rights Amendment supporters confirms that "under the Amendment a draft law which applied to men would apply also to women." The Equal Rights literature argues that this would be good for women so they can achieve their "equal rights" in securing veterans' benefits.

Another bad effect of the Equal Rights Amendment is that it will abolish a woman's right to child support and alimony, and substitute what the women's libbers think is a more "equal" policy, that "such decisions should be within the discretion of the Court and should be made on the economic situation and need of the parties in the case."

Under present American laws, the man is *always* required to support his wife and each child he caused to be brought into the world. Why should women abandon these good laws—by trading them for something so nebulous and uncertain as the "discretion of the Court"?

The law now requires a husband to support his wife as best as his financial situation permits, but a wife is not required to support her husband (unless he is about to become a public charge). A husband cannot demand that his wife go to work to help pay for family expenses. He has the duty of financial support under our laws and customs. Why should we abandon these mandatory wife-support and child-support laws so that a wife would have an "equal" obligation to take a job?

By law and custom in America, in case of divorce, the mother always is given custody of her children unless there is overwhelming evidence of mistreatment, neglect or bad character. This is our special privilege because of the high rank that is placed on motherhood in our society. Do women really want to give up this special privilege and lower themselves to "equal rights," so that the mother gets one child and the father gets the other? I think not. . . .

## WHAT "WOMEN'S LIB" REALLY MEANS

Many women are under the mistaken impression that "women's lib" means more job employment opportunities for women, equal pay for equal work, appointments of women to high positions, admitting more women to medical schools, and other desirable objectives which all women favor. We all support these purposes, as well as any necessary legislation which would bring them about.

But all this is only a sweet syrup which covers the deadly poison masquerading as "women's lib." The women's libbers are radicals who are waging a total assault on the family, on marriage, and on children. Don't take my word for it—read their own literature and prove to yourself what these characters are trying to do.

The most pretentious of the women's liberation magazines is called *Ms.*, and subtitled "The New Magazine for Women," with Gloria Steinem listed as president and secretary.

Reading the Spring 1972 issue of *Ms.* gives a good understanding of women's lib, and the people who promote it. It is anti-family, anti-children, and pro-abortion. It is a series of sharp-tongued, highpitched whining complaints by unmarried women. They view the home as a prison, and the wife and mother as a slave. To these women's libbers, marriage means dirty dishes and dirty laundry. One article lauds a woman's refusal to carry up the family laundry as "an act of extreme courage." Another tells how satisfying it is to be a lesbian.

The women's libbers don't understand that most women want to be wife, mother and homemaker—and are happy in that role. The women's libbers actively resent the mother who stays at home with her children and likes it that way. The principal purpose of *Ms.*'s shrill tirade is to sow seeds of discontent among happy, married women so that *all* women can be unhappy in some new sisterhood of frustrated togetherness.

Obviously intrigued by the 170 clauses of exemptions from marital duties given to Jackie Kennedy, and the special burdens imposed on Aristotle Onassis, in the pre-marriage contract they signed, *Ms.* recommends two women's lib marriage contracts. The "utopian marriage contract" has a clause on "sexual rights and freedoms" which approves "arrangements such as having Tuesdays off from one another," and the husband giving "his consent to abortion in advance."

The "Shulmans' marriage agreement" includes such petty provisions as "wife strips beds, husband remakes them," and "Husband does dishes on Tuesday, Thursday and Sunday. Wife does Monday, Wednesday and Saturday, Friday is split . . . " If the baby cries in the night, the chore of "handling" the baby is assigned as follows: "Husband does Tuesday, Thursday and Sunday. Wife does Monday, Wednesday and Saturday, Friday is split . . . " Presumably, if the baby cries for his mother on Tuesday night, he would be informed that the marriage contract prohibits her from answering.

Of course, it is possible, in such a loveless home, that the baby would never call for his mother at all.

Who put up the money to launch this 130-page slick-paper assault on the family and motherhood? A count of the advertisements in *Ms.* shows that the principal financial backer is the liquor industry. There are 26 liquor ads in this one initial issue. Of these, 13 are expensive full-page color ads, as opposed to only 18 full-page ads from all other sources combined, most of which are in the cheaper black-and-white.

Another women's lib magazine, called *Women,* tells the American woman that she is a prisoner in the "solitary confinement" and "isolation" of marriage. The magazine promises that it will provide women with "escape from isolation . . . release from boredom," and that it will "break the barriers . . . that separate wife, mistress and secretary . . . heterosexual women and homosexual women."

These women's libbers do, indeed, intend to "break the barriers" of the Ten Commandments, and the sanctity of the family. It hasn't occurred to them that a woman's best "escape from isolation and boredom" is—not a magazine subscription to boost her "stifled ego"—but a husband and children who love her.

The first issue of *Women* contains 68 pages of such proposals as "The BITCH Manifesto," which promotes the line that "Bitch is Beautiful and that we have nothing to lose. Nothing whatsoever." Another article promotes an organization called W.I.T.C.H. (Women's International Terrorist Conspiracy from Hell), "an action arm of Women's Liberation."

In intellectual circles, a New York University professor named Warren T. Farrell has provided the rationale for why men should support women's lib. When his speech to the American Political Science Association Convention is stripped of its egghead verbiage, his argument is that men should eagerly look forward to the day when they can enjoy free sex and not have to pay for it. The husband will no longer be "saddled with the tremendous guilt feelings" when he leaves his wife with nothing after she has given him her best years. If a husband loses his job, he will no longer feel compelled to take any job to support his family. A husband can go "out with the boys" to have a drink without feeling guilty. Alimony will be eliminated.

## WOMEN'S LIBBERS DO *NOT* SPEAK FOR US

The "women's lib" movement is *not* an honest effort to secure better jobs for women who want or need to work outside the home. This is just the superficial sweet-talk to win broad support for a radical "movement." Women's lib is a total assault on the role of the American woman as wife and mother, and on the family as the basic unit of society.

Women's libbers are trying to make wives and mothers unhappy with their career, make them feel that they are "second-class citizens" and "abject slaves." Women's libbers are promoting free sex instead of the "slavery" of marriage. They are promoting Federal "day-care centers" for babies instead of homes. They are promoting abortions instead of families.

Why should we trade in our special privileges and honored status for the alleged advantage of working in an office or assembly line? Most women would rather cuddle a baby than a typewriter or factory machine. Most women find that it is easier to get along with a husband than a foreman or office manager. Offices and factories require many more menial and repetitive chores than washing dishes and ironing shirts.

Women's libbers do *not* speak for the majority of American women. American women do *not* want to be liberated from husbands and children. We do *not* want to trade our birthright of the special privileges of American women—for the mess of pottage called the Equal Rights Amendment.

Modern technology and opportunity have not discovered any nobler or more satisfying or more creative career for a woman than marriage and motherhood. The wonderful advantage that American women have is that we can have all the rewards of that number-one career, and still moonlight with a second one to suit our intellectual, cultural, or financial tastes or needs.

And why should the men acquiesce in a system which gives preferential rights and lighter duties to women? In return, the men get the pearl of great price: a happy home, a faithful wife, and children they adore.

If the women's libbers want to reject marriage and motherhood, it's a free country and that is their choice. But let's not permit these women's libbers to get away with pretending to speak for the rest of us. Let's not permit this tiny minority to degrade the role that most women prefer. Let's not let these women's libbers deprive wives and mothers of the rights we now possess.

Tell your Senators NOW that you want them to vote NO on the Equal Rights Amendment. Tell your television and radio stations that you want equal time to present the case FOR marriage and motherhood.

# Roe v. Wade (1973)

## Justice Harry A. Blackmun

*Few Supreme Court decisions have provoked more emotional response or societal polarization than that which ensued after the judges handed down their 7–2 ruling in* Roe v. Wade *(1973). The decision held that women had an absolute right to choose an abortion through the first trimester (months one through three) of their pregnancies. Pointing out that state laws prohibiting abortions were a relatively late creation (in the second half of the nineteenth century), the majority opinion, written by Nixon appointee Justice Harry Blackmun, concluded that there was no evidence that the founders of the country meant to include unborn fetuses in their constitutional definition of "personhood." Whether or not human life began at conception or at some undefined later point, the majority reasoned, was a religious question, not a legal certitude. In that circumstance, the judges decided, a woman's right to privacy in controlling her own reproductive life took priority, at least until the health and viability of the fetus gave the state a legitimate right to intervene. The dissenting judges, on the other hand, argued that such reasoning valued "the convenience, whim or caprice of the putative mother more than the life or potential life of the fetus."*

*In the years since 1973, disputes over this decision have animated profound—and intense—political debate. The Roman Catholic Church hierarchy has adamantly opposed the pro-choice position (although many Roman Catholic parishioners disagree with the church); antifeminists and the "new right" have used a "pro-life" position to rally support for their political agenda. The Supreme Court itself has modified its position several times, permitting a series of state regulations to limit the right to abortion; yet in the first years of the new millennium, the core of the* Roe v. Wade *decision remained intact. The brief decision that follows concisely summarizes the issues, even as it raises far more questions than it answers.*

MR. JUSTICE [HARRY A.] BLACKMUN DELIVERED THE OPINION OF THE COURT. . . .

We forthwith acknowledge our awareness of the sensitive and emotional nature of the abortion controversy, of the vigorous opposing views, even among physicians, and of the deep and seemingly absolute convictions that the subject inspires. One's philosophy, one's experiences, one's exposure to the raw edges of human existence, one's religious training, one's attitudes toward life and family and their values, and the moral standards one establishes and seeks to observe, are all likely to influence and to color one's thinking and conclusions about abortion. . . .

The Texas statutes that concern us here are Arts. 1191–1194 and 1196 of the State's Penal Code. These make it a crime to "procure an abortion," as therein defined, or to attempt one, except with respect to "an abortion procured or attempted by medical advice for the purpose of saving the life of the mother." Similar statutes are in existence in a majority of the States. . . .

Jane Roe, a single woman who was residing in Dallas County, Texas, instituted this federal action in March 1970 against the District Attorney of the county. She sought a declaratory judgment that the Texas criminal abortion statutes were unconstitutional on their face, and an injunction restraining the defendant from enforcing the statutes.

Roe alleged that she was unmarried and pregnant; that she wished to terminate her pregnancy by an abortion "performed by a competent, licensed physician, under safe, clinical conditions"; that she was unable to get a "legal" abortion in Texas because her life did not appear to be threatened by the continuation of her pregnancy; and that she could not afford to travel to another jurisdiction in order to secure a legal abortion under safe conditions. She claimed that the Texas statutes were unconstitutionally vague and that they abridged her right of personal privacy, protected by the First, Fourth, Fifth, Ninth, and Fourteenth Amendments. By an amendment to her complaint Roe purported to sue "on behalf of herself and all other women" similarly situated. . . .

The principal thrust of appellant's attack on the Texas statutes is that they improperly invade a right, said to be possessed by the pregnant woman, to choose to terminate her pregnancy. Appellant would discover this right in the concept of personal "liberty" embodied in the Fourteenth Amendment's Due Process Clause; or in personal, marital, familial, and sexual privacy said to be protected by the Bill of Rights . . . or among those rights reserved to the people by the Ninth Amendment, . . .

It perhaps is not generally appreciated that the restrictive criminal abortion laws in effect in a majority of States today are of relatively recent vintage. Those laws, generally proscribing abortion or its attempt at any time during pregnancy except when necessary to preserve the pregnant woman's life, are not of ancient or even of common-law origin. Instead, they derive from statutory changes effected, for the most part, in the latter half of the nineteenth century. . . . It is undisputed that at common law, abortion performed *before* "quickening"—the first recognizable movement of the fetus *in utero,* appearing usually from the sixteenth to the eighteenth week of pregnancy—was not an indictable offense. . . . In this country, the law in effect in all but a few States until mid-nineteenth century was the pre-existing English common law. . . .

Gradually, in the middle and late nineteenth century the quickening distinction disappeared from the statutory law of most States and the degree of the offense and the penalties were increased. By the end of the 1950s, a large majority of the jurisdictions banned abortion, however and whenever performed, unless done to save or preserve the life of the mother. . . .

It is thus apparent that at common law, at the time of the adoption of our Constitution, and throughout the major portion of the nineteenth century, abortion was viewed with less disfavor than under most American statutes currently in effect. Phrasing it another way, a woman enjoyed a substantially broader right to terminate a pregnancy than she does in most States today. At least with respect to the early stage of pregnancy, and very possibly without such a limitation, the opportunity to make this choice was present in this country well into the nineteenth century. Even later, the law continued for some time to treat less punitively an abortion procured in early pregnancy. . . .

The Constitution does not explicitly mention any right of privacy. In a line of decisions, however, . . . the Court has recognized that a right of personal privacy, or a guarantee of certain areas or zones of privacy, does exist under the Constitution. . . . This right of privacy, whether it be founded in the Fourteenth Amendment's concept of personal liberty and restrictions upon state action, as we feel it is, or, as the District Court determined, in the Ninth Amendment's reservation of rights to the people, is broad enough to encompass a woman's decision whether or not to terminate her pregnancy. . . .

We . . . conclude that the right of personal privacy includes the abortion decision, but that this right is not unqualified and must be considered against important state interest in regulation. . . .

In view of all this, we do not agree that, by adopting one theory of life, Texas may override the rights of the pregnant woman that are at stake. We repeat, however, that the State does have an important and legitimate interest in preserving and protecting the health of the pregnant woman, whether she be a resident of the State or a nonresident who seeks medical consultation and treatment there, and that it has still *another* important and legitimate interest in protecting the potentiality of human life. These interests are separate and distinct. Each grows in substantiality as the woman approaches term and, at a point during pregnancy, each becomes "compelling."

With respect to the State's important and legitimate interest in the health of the mother, the "compelling" point, in the light of present medical knowledge, is at approximately the end of the first trimester. This is so because of the now-established medical fact . . . that until the end of the first trimester mortality in abortion may be less than mortality in normal childbirth. It follows that, from and after this point, a State may regulate the abortion procedure to the extent that the regulation reasonably relates to the preservation and protection of maternal health. . . .

This means, on the other hand, that, for the period of pregnancy prior to this "compelling" point, the attending physician, in consultation with his patient, is free to determine, without regulation by the State, that, in his medical judgment, the patient's pregnancy should be terminated. If that decision is reached, the judgment may be effectuated by an abortion free of interference by the State.

With respect to the State's important and legitimate interest in potential life, the "compelling" point is at viability. This is so because the fetus then presumably has the capability of meaningful life outside the mother's womb. State regulation protective of fetal life after viability thus has both logical and biological justifications. If the State is interested in protecting fetal life after viability, it may go so far as to proscribe abortion during that period, except when it is necessary to preserve the life or health of the mother.

Measured against these standards, Art. 1196 of the Texas Penal Code, in restricting legal abortions to those "procured or attempted by medical advice for the purpose of saving the life of the mother," sweeps too broadly. The statute makes no distinction between abortions performed early in pregnancy and those performed later, and it limits to a single reason, "saving" the mother's life, the legal justification for the procedure. The statute, therefore, cannot survive the constitutional attack made upon it here.

# Gay Is Good (1970)

## Martha Shelley

*The Gay Liberation movement had its symbolic beginning on June 27, 1969, when New York police raided the Stonewall Inn, a gay bar in Greenwich Village. The New York State Liquor Authority regulation that no bar could have more than three homosexual patrons at a given time gave police the authority to raid bars frequented by homosexuals, and patrons of these bars risked arrest. This time, however, the police met unexpected resistance. As the* Village Voice *described the scene in language that suggests the prejudices of the time, "Limp wrists were forgotten. Beer cans and bottles were heaved at the windows and a rain of coins descended on the cops. . . . " The next day, the slogan "Gay Power" appeared on walls throughout the neighborhood, and that night gay men and women filled the streets, chanting "Gay Power."*

*Well before Stonewall, gay men and lesbians had created vibrant, if often secret, communities. "Homophile" organizations worked to end discrimination against homosexuals—but kept membership lists confidential. Though the Kinsey Report had suggested that approximately 10 percent of American men were homosexual, there were very few openly gay men and women in the United States. Even the suspicion of homosexuality carried the risk of expulsion from university, loss of job, and social ostracism. While gay men and lesbians arguably had much to gain by "coming out of the closet," they also had much to lose. Building a social movement in this situation was a challenge: unlike black Americans or women, who were (usually) easily identified as such whether or not they wished to be, gay men and lesbians had to choose to be so identified.*

*The Gay Liberation movement that emerged in the summer of 1969, though not the first movement for the rights of homosexuals, was fundamentally a creation of the 1960s. It grew in part from the social changes that contemporaries called "the sexual revolution," and was shaped by struggles and victories of the Civil Rights and Black Power movements and by the tactics of protest developed in the latter half of the 1960s. Unlike the homophile movement, which sought assimilation and "tolerance," the Gay Liberation movement proclaimed "Gay Power" and sought the transformation of society. By 1973 there were almost eight hundred openly gay organizations in the United States. Martha Shelley wrote the following article for the underground paper The* Rat *in 1970. The title came from an editor at the paper; she said later that she would have made a stronger, angrier, statement in her title. Notice how fundamental the critique of "traditional" gender roles is to Shelley's call to revolution. How does the concept of "liberation" link the radical social movements of the 1960s and early 1970s?*

Look out, straights. Here comes the Gay Liberation Front, springing up like warts all over the bland face of Amerika, causing shudders of indigestion in the delicately balanced bowels of the movement. Here come the gays, marching with six-foot banners to Washington and embarrassing the liberals, taking over Mayor Alioto's office, staining the good names of War Resister's League and Women's Liberation by refusing to pass for straight anymore.

We've got chapters in New York, San Francisco, San Jose, Los Angeles, Minneapolis, Philadelphia, Wisconsin, Detroit, and I hear maybe even in Dallas. We're gonna make our own revolution because we're sick of revolutionary posters which depict straight he-man types and earth mothers, with guns and babies. We're sick of the Panthers lumping us together with the capitalists in their term of universal contempt—"faggot."

And I am personally sick of liberals who say they don't care who sleeps with whom, it's what you do outside of bed that counts. This is what homosexuals have been trying to get straights to understand for years. Well, it's too late for liberalism. Because what I do outside of bed may have nothing to do with what I do inside—but my consciousness is branded, is permeated with homosexuality. For years I have been branded with your label for me. The result is that when I am among gays or in bed with another woman, I am a person, not a lesbian. When I am observable to the straight world, I become gay. You are my litmus paper.

We want something more now, something more than the tolerance you never gave us. But to understand that, you must understand who we are.

We are the extrusions of your unconscious mind—your worst fears made flesh. From the beautiful boys at Cherry Grove to the aging queers in the uptown bars, the taxi-driving dykes to the lesbian fashion models, the hookers (male and female) on 42nd Street, the leather lovers . . . and the very ordinary very un-lurid gays . . . we are the sort of people everyone was taught to despise—and now we are shaking off the chains of self-hatred and marching on your citadels of repression.

Liberalism isn't good enough for us. And we are just beginning to discover it. Your friendly smile of acceptance—from the safe position of heterosexuality—isn't enough. As long as you cherish that secret belief that you are a little better because you sleep with the opposite sex, you are still asleep in your cradle and we will be the nightmare that awakens you.

We are women and men who, from the time of our earliest memories, have been in revolt against the sex-role structure and nuclear family structure. The roles we have played amongst ourselves, the self-deceit, the compromises and the subterfuges—these have never totally obscured the fact that we exist outside the traditional structure—and our existence threatens it.

Understand this—that the worst part of being a homosexual is having to keep it secret. Not the occasional murders by police or teenage queer-beaters, not the loss of jobs or expulsion from schools or dishonorable discharges—but the daily knowledge that what you are is so awful that it cannot be revealed. The violence against us is sporadic. Most of us are not affected. But the internal violence of being made to carry—or choosing to carry—the load of your straight society's unconscious guilt—this is what tears us apart, what makes us want to stand up in the offices, in the factories and schools and shout out our true identities.

We were rebels from our earliest days—somewhere, maybe just about the time we started to go to school, we rejected straight society—unconsciously. Then, later, society rejected us, as we came into full bloom. The homosexuals who hide, who play it straight or pretend that the issue of homosexuality is unimportant, are only hiding the truth from themselves. They are trying to become part of a society that they rejected instinctively when they were five years old, to pretend that it is the result of heredity, or a bad mother, or anything but a gut reaction of nausea against the roles forced on us.

If you are homosexual, and you get tired of waiting around for the liberals to repeal the sodomy laws, and begin to dig yourself—and get angry—you are on your way to being a radical. Get in touch with the reasons that made you reject straight society as a kid (remembering my own revulsion against the vacant women drifting in and out of supermarkets, vowing never to live like them) and realize that you were right. Straight roles stink.

And you straights—look down the street, at the person whose sex is not readily apparent. Are you uneasy? Or are you made more uneasy by the stereotype gay, the flaming faggot or diesel dyke? Or most uneasy by the friend you thought was straight—and isn't? We want you to be uneasy, be a little less comfortable in your straight roles. And to make you uneasy, we behave outrageously—even though we pay a heavy price for it—and our outrageous behavior comes out of our rage.

But what is strange to you is natural to us. Let me illustrate. The Gay Liberation Front (GLF) "liberates" a gay bar for the evening. We come in. The people already there are seated quietly at the bar. Two or three couples are dancing. It's a down place. And the GLF takes over. Men dance with men, women with women, men with women, everyone in circles. No roles. You ever see that at a straight party? Not men with men—this is particularly verboten. No, and you're not likely to, while the gays in the movement are still passing for straight in order to keep up the good names of their organizations or to keep up the pretense that they are acceptable—and to have to get out of the organization they worked so hard for.

True, some gays play the same role games among themselves that straights do. Isn't every minority group fucked over by the values of the majority culture? But the really important thing about being gay is that you are forced to notice how much sex role differentiation is pure artifice, is nothing but a game.

Once I dressed up for an American Civil Liberties Union benefit. I wore a black lace dress, heels, elaborate hairdo and makeup. And felt like—a drag queen. Not like a woman—I am a woman every day of my life—but like the ultimate in artifice, a woman posing as a drag queen.

The roles are beginning to wear thin. The makeup is cracking. The roles—breadwinner, little wife, screaming fag, bulldyke, James Bond—are the cardboard characters we are always trying to fit into, as if being human and spontaneous were so horrible that we each have to pick on a character out of a third rate novel and try to cut ourselves down to its size. And you cut off your homosexuality—and we cut off our heterosexuality.

Back to the main difference between us. We gays are separate from you—we are alien. You have managed to drive your own homosexuality down under the skin of your mind—and to drive us down and out into the gutter of self-contempt. We, ever since we became aware of being gay, have each day been forced to internalize the labels: "I am a pervert, a dyke, a fag, etc." And the days pass, until we look at you out of our homosexual bodies, bodies that have become synonymous and consubstantial with homosexuality, bodies that are no longer bodies but labels; and sometimes we wish we were like you, sometimes we wonder how you can stand yourselves.

It's difficult for me to understand how you can dig each other as human beings—in a man-woman relationship—how you can relate to each other in spite of your sex roles. It must be awfully difficult to talk to each other, when the woman is trained to repress what the man is trained to express, and vice-versa. Do straight men and women talk to each other? Or does the man talk and the woman nod approvingly? Is love possible between heterosexuals; or is it all a case of women posing as nymphs, earth mothers, sex objects, what-have-you, and men writing the poetry of romantic illusions to these walking stereotypes?

I tell you, the function of a homosexual is to make you uneasy.

And now I will tell you what we want, we radical homosexuals: not for you to tolerate us, or to accept us, but to understand us. And this you can do only by becoming one of us. We want to reach the homosexuals entombed in you, to liberate our brothers and sisters, locked in the prisons of your skulls.

We want you to understand what it is to be our kind of outcast— but also to understand our kind of love, to hunger for your own sex. Because unless you understand this, you will continue to look at us with uncomprehending eyes, fake liberal smiles; you will be incapable of loving us.

We will never go straight until you go gay. As long as you divide yourselves, we will be divided from you—separated by a mirror trick of your mind. We will no longer allow you to drop us—or the homosexuals in yourselves—into the reject bin; labelled sick, childish or perverted. And because we will not wait, your awakening may be a rude and bloody one. It's your choice. You will never be rid of us, because we reproduce ourselves out of your bodies—and out of your minds. We are one with you.

# Sexual Revolution(s)

## Beth Bailey

*It is hard for contemporary college students to imagine what life was like for students in the early 1960s. Women were subject to rigid curfew systems called parietals—but men weren't. Despite the existence of The Pill, very few doctors would prescribe it to unmarried girls or women. Abortion was illegal. A woman who had "premarital" sex was, in the eyes of much of American society, "ruined." Homosexual sex was grounds for expulsion. A great deal has changed. Is that evidence of a revolution?*

*In "Sexual Revolution(s)," historian Beth Bailey argues that the answer to that question depends upon how one defines "revolution." She argues that there was no single sexual revolution, but rather a set of complicated and contradictory movements that people at the time called "the" sexual revolution. Do you agree with her argument that the most modest strand of the "revolution" was probably the most revolutionary? After reading both this article and the previous pieces on women's liberation, why do you think that so many Americans conflated women's liberation and sexual revolution? What, if anything, do the two broad movements have in common? And after reading the previous document, "Gay Is Good," consider whether the Gay Liberation movement that began in 1969 owed more to the movements for women's liberation or to the sexual revolution of the 1960s.*

In 1957 America's favorite TV couple, the safely married Ricky and Lucy Ricardo, slept in twin beds. Having beds at all was probably progressive—as late as 1962 June and Ward Cleaver did not even have a bedroom. Elvis's pelvis was censored in each of his three appearances on the "Ed Sullivan Show" in 1956, leaving his oddly disembodied upper torso and head thrashing about on the TV screen. But the sensuality in his eyes, his lips, his lyrics was unmistakable, and his genitals were all the more important in their absence. There was, likewise, no mistaking Mick Jagger's meaning when he grimaced ostentatiously and sang "Let's spend some *time* together" on "Ed Sullivan" in 1967. Much of the audience knew that the line was really "Let's spend the night together," and the rest quickly got the idea. The viewing public could see absence and hear silence—and therein lay the seeds of the sexual revolution.

What we call the sexual revolution grew from these tensions between public and private—not only from tensions manifest in public culture, but also from tensions between private behaviors and the public rules and ideologies that were meant to govern behavior. By the 1950s the gulf between private acts and public norms was often quite wide—and the distance was crucial. People had sex outside of marriage, but very, very few acknowledged that publicly. A woman who married the only man with whom she had had premarital sex still worried years later: "I was afraid someone might have learned that we had intercourse before marriage and I'd be disgraced." The consequences, however, were not just psychological. Young women (and sometimes men) discovered to be having premarital sex were routinely expelled from school or college; gay men risked jail for engaging in consensual sex. There were real penalties for sexual misconduct, and while many deviated from the sexual orthodoxy of the day, all but a few did so furtively, careful not to get "caught."

Few episodes demonstrate the tensions between the public and private dimensions of sexuality in midcentury America better than the furor that surrounded the publication of the studies of sexual behavior collectively referred to as the "Kinsey Reports." . . .

Much of the reaction to Kinsey hinge[d] on the distance between the "overt" and the "covert." People were shocked to learn how many men and women were doing what they were not supposed to be doing. Kinsey found that 50 percent of the women in his sample had had premarital sex (even though between 80 percent and 89 percent of his sample disapproved of premarital sex on "moral grounds"), that 61 percent of college-educated men and 84 percent of men who had completed only high school had had premarital sex, that over one-third of the married women in the sample had "engaged in petting" with more than ten different men, that approximately half of the married couples had engaged in "oral stimulation" of both male and female genitalia, and that at least 37 percent of American men had had "some homosexual experience" during their lifetimes. . . .

208 STRUGGLES OVER GENDER AND SEXUAL LIBERATION

Looking back to the century's midpoint, it is clear that the coherence of (to use Kinsey's terms) covert and overt sexual cultures was strained beyond repair. The sexual revolution of the 1960s emerged from these tensions, and to that extent it was not revolutionary, but evolutionary. As much as anything else, we see the overt coming to terms with the covert. But the revision of revolution to evolution would miss a crucial point. It is not historians who have labeled these changes "the sexual revolution"—it was people at the time, those who participated and those who watched. And they called it that before much of what we would see as revolutionary really emerged—before gay liberation and the women's movement and Alex Comfort's *The Joy of Sex* (1972) and "promiscuity" and singles' bars. The term was in general use by 1963—earlier than one might expect.

To make any sense of the sexual revolution, we have to pay attention to the label people gave it. Revolutions, for good or ill, are moments of danger. It matters that a metaphor of revolution gave structure to the myriad of changes taking place in American society. The changes in sexual mores and behaviors could as easily have been cast as evolutionary—but they were not.

Looking back, the question of whether or not the sexual revolution was revolutionary is not easy to answer; it partly depends on one's political (defined broadly) position. Part of the trouble, though, is that the sexual revolution was not one movement. It was instead a set of movements, movements that were closely linked, even intertwined, but which often made uneasy bedfellows. Here I hope to do some untangling, laying out three of the most important strands of the sexual revolution and showing their historical origins, continuities, and disruptions.

The first strand, which transcended youth, might be cast as both evolutionary and revolutionary. Throughout the twentieth century, picking up speed in the 1920s, the 1940s, and the 1960s, we have seen a sexualization of America's culture. Sexual images have become more and more a part of public life, and sex—or more accurately, the representation of sex—is used to great effect in a marketplace that offers Americans fulfillment through consumption. Although the blatancy of today's sexual images would be shocking to someone transported from an earlier era, such representations developed gradually and generally did not challenge more "traditional" understandings of sex and of men's and women's respective roles in sex or in society.

The second strand was the most modest in aspect but perhaps the most revolutionary in implication. In the 1960s and early 1970s an increasing number of young people began to live together "without benefit of matrimony," as the phrase went at the time. While sex was usually a part of the relationship (and probably a more important part than most people acknowledged), few called on concepts of "free love" or "pleasure" but instead used words like "honesty," "commitment," and "family." Many of the young people who lived together could have passed for young marrieds and in that sense were pursuing fairly traditional arrangements. At the same time, self-consciously or not, they challenged the tattered remnants of a Victorian epistemological and ideological system that still, in the early 1960s, fundamentally structured the public sexual mores of the American middle class.

The third strand was more self-consciously revolutionary, as sex was *actively claimed* by young people and used not only for pleasure but also for power in a new form of cultural politics that shook the nation. As those who threw themselves into the "youth revolution" (a label that did not stick) knew so well, the struggle for America's future would take place not in the structure of electoral politics, but on the battlefield of cultural meaning. Sex was an incendiary tool of a revolution that was more than political. But not even the cultural revolutionaries agreed on goals, or on the role and meaning of sex in the revolution.

These last two strands had to do primarily with young people, and that is significant. The changes that took place in America's sexual mores and behaviors in the sixties were *experienced* and *defined* as revolutionary in large part because they were so closely tied to youth. The nation's young, according to common wisdom and the mass media, were in revolt. Of course, the sexual revolution was not limited to youth, and sex was only one part of the revolutionary claims of youth. Still, it was the intersection of sex and youth that signaled danger. And the fact that these were often middle-class youths, the ones reared in a culture of respectability (told that a single sexual misstep could jeopardize their bright futures), made their frontal challenges to sexual mores all the more inexplicable and alarming. . . .

## BEFORE THE REVOLUTION: YOUTH AND SEX

Like many of the protest movements that challenged American tranquility in the sixties, the sexual revolution developed within the protected space and intensified atmosphere of the college campus. . . .

The media had a field day when the president of Vassar College, Sarah Blanding, said unequivocally that if a student wished to engage in premarital sex, she must withdraw from the college. The oftquoted student reply to her dictum chilled the hearts of middle-class parents throughout the country: "If Vassar is to become the Poughkeepsie Victorian Seminary for young Virgins, then the change of policy had better be made explicit in admissions catalogs."

Such challenges to authority and to conventional morality were reported to eager audiences around the nation. None of this, of course, was new. National audiences had been scandalized by the panty raid epidemic of the early 1950s; the antics and petting parties of college youth had provided sensational fodder for hungry journalists in the 1920s. The parents—and grandparents—of these young people had chipped away at the system of sexual controls themselves. But they had not directly and publicly denied the very foundations of sexual morality. With few exceptions, they had evaded the controls and circumvented the rules, climbing into dorm rooms through open windows, signing out to the library and going to motels, carefully maintaining virginity in the technical sense while engaging in every caress known to married couples. The evasions often succeeded, but that does not mean that the controls had no effect. On the contrary, they had a great impact on the ways people experienced sex.

There were, in fact, two major systems of sexual control, one structural and one ideological. These systems worked to reinforce one another, but they affected the lives of those they touched differently.

The structural system was the more practical of the two but probably the less successful. It worked by limiting opportunities for the unmarried to have intercourse. Parents of teenagers set curfews and promoted double dating, hoping that by preventing privacy they would limit sexual exploration. Colleges, acting in loco parentis, used several tactics: visitation hours, parietals, security patrols, and restrictions on students' use of cars. . . .

The myriad of rules, as anyone who lived through this period well knows, did not prevent sexual relations between students so much as they structured the times and places and ways that students could have sexual contact. Students said extended good-nights on the porches of houses, they petted in dormitory lounges while struggling to keep three feet on the floor and clothing in some semblance of order, and they had intercourse in cars, keeping an eye out for police patrols. What could be done after eleven could be done before eleven, and sex need not occur behind a closed door and in a bed—but this set of rules had a profound impact on the *ways* college students and many young people living in their parents' homes *experienced* sex. . . . The ideological system of controls was more pervasive than the structured system and probably more effective. This system centered on ideas of difference: men and women were fundamentally different creatures, with different roles and interests in sex. . . . Women did in fact have a different and more imperative interest in controlling sex than men, for women could become pregnant. Few doctors would fit an unmarried woman with a diaphragm, though one might get by in the anonymity of a city with a cheap "gold" ring from a drugstore or by pretending to be preparing for an impending honeymoon. . . . Women who were too "free" with sexual favors could lose value and even threaten their marriageability. . . . While a girl was expected to "pet to be popular," girls and women who went "too far" risked their futures. Advice books and columns from the 1940s and 1950s linked girls' and womens' "value" to their "virtue," arguing in explicitly economic terms that "free" kisses destroyed a woman's value in the dating system: "The boys find her easy to afford. She doesn't put a high value on herself." The exchange was even clearer in the marriage market. In chilling language, a teen adviser asked: "Who wants second hand goods?" . . .

For most middle-class youth in the postwar era, sex involved a series of skirmishes that centered around lines and boundaries: kissing, necking, petting above the waist, petting below the waist, petting through clothes, petting under clothes, mild petting, heavy petting. The progression of sexual intimacy had emerged as a highly ordered system. Each act constituted a stage, ordered in a strict hierarchy (first base, second base, and so forth), with vaginal penetration as the ultimate step. But in their attempts to preserve technical virginity, many young people engaged in sexual behaviors that, in the sexual hierarchy of the larger culture, should have been more forbidden than vaginal intercourse. One woman remembers: "We went pretty far, very far; everything but intercourse. But it was very frustrating. . . . Sex was out of the question. I had it in my mind that I was going to be a virgin. So I came up with oral sex. . . . I thought I invented it."

Many young men and women acted in defiance of the rules, but that does not make the rules irrelevant. The same physical act can have very different meanings depending on its emotional and social/cultural contexts. For America's large middle class and for all those who aspired to "respectability" in the prerevolutionary twentieth century, sex was overwhelmingly secret or furtive. Sex was a set of acts with high stakes and possibly serious consequences, acts that emphasized and reinforced the different roles of men and women in American society. We do not know how each person felt about his or her private acts, but we do know that few were willing or able to publicly reject the system of sexual controls.

The members of the generation that would be labeled "the sixties" were revolutionary in that they called fundamental principles of sexual morality and control into question. The system of controls they had inherited and lived within was based on a set of presumptions rooted in the previous century. In an evolving set of arguments and actions (which never became thoroughly coherent or unified), they rejected a system of sexual controls organized around concepts of difference and hierarchy. . . .

## REVOLUTIONARIES

All those who rejected the sexual mores of the postwar era did not reject the fundamental premises that gave them shape. *Playboy* magazine played an enormously important (if symbolic) role in the sexual revolution, or at least in preparing the ground for the sexual revolution, . . . Begun by Hugh Hefner in 1953 with an initial print run of 70,000, *Playboy* passed the one million circulation mark in three years. By the mid-1960s Hefner had amassed a fortune of $100 million, including a lasciviously appointed forty-eight-room mansion staffed by thirty Playboy "bunnies" ("fuck like bunnies" is a phrase we have largely left behind, but most people at the time caught the allusion). Playboy clubs, also staffed by large-breasted and long-legged women in bunny ears and cottontails, flourished throughout the country. Though *Playboy* offered quality writing and advice for those aspiring to sophistication, the greatest selling point of the magazine was undoubtedly its illustrations.

*Playboy,* however, offered more than masturbatory opportunities. Between the pages of coyly arranged female bodies—more, inscribed in the coyly arranged female bodies—flourished a strong and relatively coherent ideology. Hefner called it a philosophy and wrote quite a few articles expounding it (a philosophy professor in

North Carolina took it seriously enough to describe his course as "philosophy from Socrates to Hefner").

Hefner saw his naked women as "a symbol of disobedience, a triumph of sexuality, an end of Puritanism." He saw his magazine as an attack on "our ferocious anti-sexuality, our dark antieroticism." But his thrust toward pleasure and light was not to be undertaken in partnership. The Playboy philosophy, according to Hefner, had less to do with sex and more to do with sex roles. American society increasingly "blurred distinctions between the sexes . . . not only in business, but in such diverse realms as household chores, leisure activities, smoking and drinking habits, clothing styles, upswinging homosexuality and the sex-obliterating aspects of togetherness," concluded the "Playboy Panel" in June 1962. In Part 19 of his extended essay on the Playboy philosophy, Hefner wrote: "PLAYBOY stresses a strongly heterosexual concept of society—in which the separate roles of men and women are clearly defined and compatible."

Read without context, Hefner's call does not necessarily preclude sex as a common interest between men and women. He is certainly advocating heterosexual sex. But the models of sex offered are not partnerships. Ever innovative in marketing and design, *Playboy* offered in one issue a special "coloring book" section. A page featuring three excessively voluptuous women was captioned: "Make one of the girls a blonde. Make one of the girls a brunette. Make one of the girls a redhead. It does not matter which is which. The girls' haircolors are interchangeable. So are the girls."

Sex, in the Playboy mode, was a contest—not of wills, in the model of the male seducer and the virtuous female, but of exploitative intent, as in the playboy and the would-be wife. In *Playboy*'s world, women were out to ensnare men, to entangle them in a web of responsibility and obligation (not the least of which was financial). Barbara Ehrenreich has convincingly argued that *Playboy* was an integral part of a male-initiated revolution in sex roles, for it advocated that men reject burdensome responsibility (mainly in the shape of wives) for lives of pleasure through consumption. Sex, of course, was part of this pleasurable universe. In *Playboy*, sex was located in the realm of consumption, and women were interchangeable objects, mute, making no demands, each airbrushed beauty supplanted by the next month's model.

It was not only to men that sexual freedom was sold through exploitative visions. When Helen Gurley Brown revitalized the traditional women's magazine that was *Cosmopolitan* in 1965, she compared her magazine to *Playboy*—and *Cosmo* did celebrate the pleasure of single womanhood and "sexual and material consumerism." But before Brown ran *Cosmo*, she had made her contribution to the sexual revolution with *Sex and the Single Girl*, published in May 1962. By April 1963, 150,000 hard-cover copies had been sold, garnering Brown much media attention and a syndicated newspaper column, "Woman Alone."

The claim of *Sex and the Single Girl* was, quite simply, "nice, single girls *do*." Brown's radical message to a society in which twenty-three-year-olds were called old maids was that singleness is good. Marriage, she insisted, should not be an immediate goal. The Single Girl sounds like the Playboy's dream, but she was more likely a nightmare revisited. Marriage, Brown advised, is "insurance for the worst years of your life. During the best years you don't need a husband." But she quickly amended that statement: "You do need a man every step of the way, and they are often cheaper emotionally and more fun by the dozen."

That fun explicitly included sex, and on the woman's terms. But Brown's celebration of the joys of single life still posed men and women as adversaries. "She need never be bored with one man per lifetime," she enthused. "Her choice of partners is endless and they seek *her*. . . . Her married friends refer to her pursuers as wolves, but actually many of them turn out to be lambs—to be shorn and worn by her."

Brown's celebration of the single "girl" actually began with a success story—her own. "I married for the first time at thirty-seven. I got the man I wanted," begins *Sex and the Single Girl*. Brown's description of that union is instructive: "David is a motion picture producer, forty-four, brainy, charming and sexy. He was sought after by many a Hollywood starlet as well as some less flamboyant but more deadly types. And *I* got him! We have two Mercedes-Benzes, one hundred acres of virgin forest near San Francisco, a Mediterranean house overlooking the Pacific, a full-time maid and a good life."

While Brown believes "her body wants to" is a sufficient reason for a woman to have an "affair," she is not positing identical interests of men and women in sex. Instead, she asserts the validity of women's interests—interests that include Mercedes-Benzes, full-time maids, lunch ("Anyone can take you to lunch. How bored can you be for an hour?"), vacations, and vicuna coats. But by offering a female version of the Playboy ethic, she greatly strengthened its message.

Unlike the youths who called for honesty, who sought to blur the boundaries between male and female, *Playboy* and *Cosmo* offered a vision of sexual freedom based on difference and deceit, but within a shared universe of an intensely competitive market economy. They were revolutionary in their claiming of sex as a legitimate pleasure and in the directness they brought to portraying sex as an arena for struggle and exploitation that could be enjoined by men and women alike (though in different ways and to different ends). Without this strand, the sexual revolution would have looked very different. In many ways *Playboy* was a necessary condition for "revolution," for it linked sex to the emerging culture of consumption and the rites of the marketplace. As it fed into the sexual reconfigurations of the sixties, *Playboy* helped make sex more—or less—than a rite of youth.

In the revolutionary spring of 1968, *Life* magazine looked from the student protests at Columbia across the street to Barnard College: "A sexual anthropologist of some future century, analyzing the pill, the drive-in, the works of Harold Robbins, the Tween-Bra and all the other artifacts of the American Sexual Revolution, may consider the case of Linda LeClair and her boyfriend, Peter Behr, as a moment in which the morality of an era changed."

The LeClair affair, as it was heralded in newspaper headlines and syndicated columns around the country, was indeed such a moment. Linda LeClair and Peter Behr were accidental revolutionaries, but as *Life* not so kindly noted, "history will often have its little joke. And so it was this spring when it found as its symbol of this revolution a champion as staunch, as bold and as unalluring as Linda LeClair." The significance of the moment is not to be found in the actions of LeClair and Behr, who certainly lacked revolutionary glamour despite all the headlines about "Free Love," but in the contest over the meaning of those actions.

The facts of the case were simple. On 4 March 1968 the *New York Times* ran an article called "An Arrangement: Living Together for Convenience, Security, Sex." (The piece ran full-page width; below it appeared articles on "How to Duck the Hemline Issue" and "A Cook's Guide to the Shallot.") An "arrangement," the author informs us, was one of the current euphemisms for what was otherwise known as "shacking up" or, more innocuously, "living together." The article, which offers a fairly sympathetic portrait of several unmarried student couples who lived together in New York City, features an interview with a Barnard sophomore, "Susan," who lived with her boyfriend

"Peter" in an off-campus apartment. Though Barnard had strict housing regulations and parietals (the curfew was midnight on weekends
and ten o'clock on weeknights, and students were meant to live either
at home or in Barnard housing), Susan had received permission to
live off campus by accepting a job listed through Barnard's employment office as a "live-in maid." The job had, in fact, been listed by a
young married woman who was a good friend of "Susan's."

Not surprisingly, the feature article caught the attention of Barnard administrators, who had little trouble identifying "Susan" as
Linda LeClair. LeClair was brought before the Judiciary Council—
not for her sexual conduct, but for lying to Barnard about her housing arrangements. Her choice of roommate was certainly an issue;
if she had been found to be living alone or, as one Barnard student
confessed to the *Times,* with a female cat, she would not have been
headline-worthy. . . .

Two hundred and fifty students and faculty members attended
LeClair's hearing, which was closed to all but members of the college
community. Her defense was a civil rights argument: colleges had no
right to regulate nonacademic behavior of adult students, and housing
rules discriminated on the basis of sex (Columbia men had no such
regulations). After deliberating for five hours, the faculty-student judiciary committee found LeClair guilty of defying college regulations; but
it also called for reform of the existing housing policy. The punishment
they recommended for LeClair was a sort of black humor to anyone
who had been to college: they barred her from the Barnard cafeteria.

Linda LeClair had not done anything especially unusual, as several
letters from alumnae to Barnard's president, Martha Peterson, testified. But her case was a symbol of change, and it tells us much about
how people understood the incident. The president's office received
over two hundred telephone calls (most demanding LeClair's expulsion) and over one hundred letters; editorials ran in newspapers,
large and small, throughout the country. Some of the letters were
vehement in their condemnation of LeClair and of the college. Francis Beamen of Needham, Massachusetts, suggested that Barnard
should be renamed "BARNYARD"; Charles Orsinger wrote (on good
quality letterhead), "If you let Linda stay in college, I can finally prove
to my wife with a front page news story about that bunch of glorified
whores going to eastern colleges." An unsigned letter began: "SUB-
JECT: Barnard College—and the kow-tow to female 'students' who
practice prostitution, PUBLICLY!"

Though the term "alley cat" cropped up more than once, a majority of the letters were thoughtful attempts to come to terms with the changing morality of America's youth. Many were from parents who understood the symbolic import of the case. Overwhelmingly, those who did not simply rant about "whoredom" structured their comments around concepts of public and private. The word *flaunt* appeared over and over in the letters to President Peterson. Linda was "flaunting her sneering attitude"; Linda and Peter were "openly flaunting their disregard of moral codes"; they were "openly flaunting rules of civilized society." Mrs. Bruce Bromley, Jr., wrote her first such letter on a public issue to recommend, "Do not let Miss LeClair attend Barnard as long as she flaunts immortality in your face." David Abrahamson, M.D., identifying himself as a former Columbia faculty member, offered "any help in this difficult case." He advised President Peterson, "Undoubtedly the girl's behavior must be regarded as exhibitionism, as her tendency is to be in the limelight which clearly indicates some emotional disturbance or upset."

The public-private question *was* the issue in this case—the letter writers were correct. Most were willing to acknowledge that "mistakes" can happen; many were willing to allow for some "discreet" sex among the unmarried young. But Linda LeClair *claimed* the right to determine her own "private" life; she rejected the private-public dichotomy *as it was framed around sex,* casting her case as an issue of individual rights versus institutional authority.

But public response to the case is interesting in another way. When a woman wrote President Peterson that "it is time for these young people to put sex back in its proper place, instead of something to be flaunted" and William F. Buckley condemned the "delinquency of this pathetic little girl, so gluttonous for sex and publicity," they were not listening. Sex was not what Linda and Peter talked about. Sex was not mentioned. Security was, and "family." "Peter is my family," said Linda. "It's a very united married type of relationship—it's the most important one in each of our lives. And our lives are very much intertwined."

Of course they had sex. They were young and in love, and their peer culture accepted sex within such relationships. But what they claimed was partnership—a partnership that obviated the larger culture's insistence on the difference between men and women. The letters suggesting that young women would "welcome a strong rule against living with men to protect them against doing that" made no sense in LeClair's universe. When she claimed that Barnard's rules were discriminatory because Columbia men had no such rules, . . . and asked, "If women are able, intelligent people, why must we be supervised and curfewed?" she was denying that men and women had different interests and needs. Just as the private-public dichotomy was a cornerstone of sexual control in the postwar era, the much-touted differences between men and women were a crucial part of the system.

Many people in the 1960s and 1970s struggled with questions of equality and difference in sophisticated and hard-thought ways. Neither Peter Behr nor Linda LeClair was especially gifted in that respect. What they argued was commonplace to them—a natural language and set of assumptions that nonetheless had revolutionary implications. It is when a set of assumptions becomes natural and unself-conscious, when a language appears in the private comments of a wide variety of people that it is worth taking seriously. The unity of interests that Behr and LeClair called upon as they obviated the male-female dichotomy was not restricted to students in the progressive institutions on either coast.

In 1969 the administration at the University of Kansas (KU), a state institution dependent on a conservative, though populist, legislature for its funding, attempted to establish a coed dormitory for some of its scholarship students. KU had tried coed living as an experiment in the 1964 summer session and found students well satisfied, though some complained that it was awkward to go downstairs to the candy machines with one's hair in curlers. Curlers were out of fashion by 1969, and the administration moved forward with caution.

A survey on attitudes toward coed housing was given to those who lived in the scholarship halls, and the answers of the men survive.

The results of the survey go against conventional wisdom about the provinces. Only one man (of the 124 responses recorded) said his parents objected to the arrangement ("Pending further discussion," he noted). But what is most striking is the language in which the men supported and opposed the plan. "As a stereotypical answer," one man wrote, "I already am able to do all the roleplaying socially I need, and see communication now as an ultimate goal." A sophomore who listed his classification as both "soph." and "4-F I Hope" responded: "I believe that the segregation of the sexes is unnatural. I would like to associate with women on a basis other than dating roles. This tradition of segregation is discriminatory and promotes inequality of mankind." One man thought coed living would make the hall "more homey." Another said it would be "more humane." Many used the word "natural." The most eloquent of the sophomores wrote: "[It would] allow them to meet and interact with one another in a situation relatively free of sexual overtones; that is, the participating individuals would be free to encounter one another as human beings, rather than having to play the traditional stereotyped male and female roles. I feel that coed living is the only feasible way to allow people to escape this stereotypical role behavior."

The student-generated proposal that went forward in December 1970 stressed these (as they defined them) "philosophical" justifications. The system "would NOT be an arrangement for increased boy-meets-girl contact or for convenience in finding dates," the committee insisted. Instead, coed living would "contribute to the development of each resident as a full human being." Through "interpersonal relationships based on friendship and cooperative efforts rather than on the male/female roles we usually play in dating situations" students would try to develop "a human concern that transcends membership in one or the other sex."

While the students disavowed "'boy-meets-girl' contact" as motivation, no one seriously believed that sex was going to disappear. The most cogently stated argument against the plan came from a young man who insisted: "[You] can't ignore the sexual overtones involved in coed living; after all, sex is the basic motivation for your plan. (I didn't say lust, I said sex)." Yet the language in which they framed their proposal was significant: they called for relationships (including sexual) based on a common humanity.

Like Peter Behr and Linda LeClair, these students at the University of Kansas were attempting to redefine both sex and sex roles. Sex should not be negotiated through the dichotomous pairings of male and female, public and private. Instead, they attempted to formulate and articulate a new standard that looked to a model of "togetherness" undreamed of and likely undesired by their parents. The *Life* magazine issue with which this section began characterized the "sexual revolution" as "dull." "Love still makes the world go square," the author concluded, for the revolutionaries he interviewed subscribed to a philosophy "less indebted to Playboy than Peanuts, in which sex is not so much a pleasure as a warm puppy." To his amusement, one "California girl" told him: "Besides being my lover, Bob is my best friend in all the world," and a young man insisted, "We are not sleeping together, we are living together."

For those to whom *Playboy* promised revolution, this attitude was undoubtedly tame. And in the context of the cultural revolution taking place among America's youth, and documented in titillating detail by magazines such as *Life*, these were modest revolutionaries indeed, seeming almost already out of step with their generation. But the issue, to these "dull" revolutionaries, as to their more flamboyant brothers and sisters, was larger than sex. They understood that the line between public and private had utility; that the personal was political.

It was a "holy pilgrimage," according to the Council for a Summer of Love. In the streets of Haight-Ashbury, thousands and thousands of "pilgrims" acted out a street theater of costumed fantasy, drugs and music and sex that was unimaginable in the neat suburban streets of their earlier youth. Visionaries and revolutionaries had preceded the deluge; few of them drowned. Others did. But the tide flowed in with vague countercultural yearnings, drawn by the pop hit "San Francisco (Be Sure to Wear Flowers in Your Hair)" and its promise of a "love-in," by the pictures in *Life* magazine or in *Look* magazine or in *Time* magazine, by the proclamations of the underground press that San Francisco would be "the love-guerilla training school for dropouts from mainstream America . . . where the new world, a human world of the 21st century is being constructed." Here sexual freedom would be explored; not cohabitation, not "arrangements," not "living together" in ways that looked a lot like marriage except for the lack of a piece of paper that symbolized the sanction of the state. Sex in the Haight was revolutionary.

In neat suburban houses on neat suburban streets, people came to imagine this new world, helped by television and by the color pictures in glossy-paper magazines (a joke in the Haight told of "bead-wearing *Look* reporters interviewing bead-wearing *Life* reporters"). Everyone knew that these pilgrims represented a tiny fraction of America's young, but the images reverberated. America felt itself in revolution. . . .

Youth culture and counterculture were not synonymous, and for many the culture itself was more a matter of life-style than revolutionary intent. But the strands flowed together in the chaos of the age, and the few and the marginal provided archetypes that were read into the youth culture by an American public that did not see the lines of division. "Hippies, yippies, flippies," said Mayor Richard Daley of Chicago. "Free Love," screamed the headlines about Barnard's Linda LeClair.

But even the truly revolutionary youths were not unified, no more on the subject of sex than on anything else. Members of the New Left, revolutionary but rarely countercultural, had sex but did not talk about it all the time. They consigned sex to a relatively "private" sphere. Denizens of Haight-Ashbury lived a Dionysian sexuality, most looking nowhere but to immediate pleasure. Some political-cultural revolutionaries, however, claimed sex and used it for the revolution. They capitalized on the sexual chaos and fears of the nation, attempting to use sex to politicize youth and to challenge "Amerika." . . . Other counter-cultural seekers believed that they had to remake love and reclaim sex to create community. These few struggled, with varying degrees of honesty and sincerity, over the significance of sex in the beloved community.

For others, sex was less a philosophy than a weapon. In the spring of 1968, the revolutionary potential of sex also suffused the claims of the Yippies as they struggled to stage a "Festival of Life" to counter the "Death Convention" in Chicago. "How can you separate politics and sex?" Jerry Rubin asked with indignation after the fact. Yippies lived by that creed. Sex was a double-edged sword, to be played two ways. Sex was a lure to youth; it was part of their attempt to tap the youth market, to "sell a revolutionary consciousness." It was also a challenge, "flaunted in the face" (as it were) of America.

The first Yippie manifesto, released in January 1968, summoned the tribes to Chicago. It played well in the underground press, with its promise of "50,000 of us dancing in the streets, throbbing with amplifiers and harmony . . . making love in the parks." Sex was a politics of pleasure, a politics of abundance that made sense to young middle-class whites who had been raised in the world without limits that was postwar America.

Sex was also incendiary, and the Yippies knew that well. It guaranteed attention. Thus the "top secret" plans for the convention that Abbie Hoffman mimeographed and distributed to the press promised a barbecue and lovemaking by the lake, followed by "Pin the Tail on the Donkey," "Pin the Rubber on the Pope," and "other normal and healthy games." Grandstanding before a crowd of Chicago reporters, the Yippies presented a city official with an official document wrapped in a *Playboy* centerfold inscribed, "To Dick with love, the Yippies." The *Playboy* centerfold in the Yippies' hands was an awkward nexus between the old and the new sexuality. As a symbolic act, it did not proffer freedom so much as challenge authority. It was a sign of disrespect—to Mayor Richard Daley and to straight America.

While America was full of young people sporting long hair and beads, the committed revolutionaries (of cultural stripe) were few in number and marginal at best. It is telling that the LeClair affair could still be a scandal in a nation that had weathered the Summer of Love. But the lines were blurred in sixties America. One might ask with Todd Gitlin, "What was marginal anymore, where was the mainstream anyway?" when the Beatles were singing, "Why Don't We Do It in the Road?"

## CONCLUSION

The battles of the sexual revolution were hard fought, its victories ambiguous, its outcome still unclear. What we call the sexual revolution was an amalgam of movements that flowed together in an unsettled era. They were often at odds with one another, rarely well thought out, and usually without a clear agenda.

The sexual revolution was built on equal measures of hypocrisy and honesty, equality and exploitation. Indeed, the individual strands contain mixed motivations and ideological charges. Even the most heartfelt or best intentions did not always work out for the good when put into practice by mere humans with physical and psychological frailties. As we struggle over the meaning of the "revolution" and ask ourselves who, in fact, *won*, it helps to untangle the threads and reject the conflation of radically different impulses into a singular revolution.

# Part 5

# THE VIETNAM WAR

The war in Vietnam was America's longest and most agonizing war. More than anything else, it was the wedge that divided the nation in two during the turbulent years of the sixties. In many ways, the growing U.S. involvement in Vietnam illustrates the logic of the Cold War doctrine of containment. In the years following World War II, despite U.S. wartime promises to end colonialism in Southeast Asia, President Truman chose to support French colonial power in Indochina rather than the nationalist independence movement there led by Vietnamese insurgents and, significantly, *communist*, Ho Chi Minh. Truman believed it was crucial to secure European support for the United States in its growing conflict with the Soviet Union, and this was an attempt to mollify France. But the implications of this action would be enormous. When Ho Chi Minh and his followers defeated the French colonial power in 1954, the United States stepped into the breach, creating a divided Vietnam and setting up a puppet government friendly to the United States in South Vietnam.

As the Cold War escalated, President John F. Kennedy promised the world in his inaugural address that Americans were prepared to "pay any price" and "bear any burden" to contain the threat of communism. In the logic of this Cold War world view, Vietnam (like Korea and even the Bay of Pigs invasion of Cuba) was a hot battle in the Cold War. Relying on the belief that the struggles in Vietnam might prove the "domino" that began the fall of Southeast Asia to communism, John Kennedy sent increasing numbers of military "advisors" to Vietnam, launched programs of counterinsurgency, and greatly increased programs of financial and military aid to South Vietnam.

America's growing involvement in Vietnam may also be seen as a by-product of the "politics of affluence" discussed in Part 2. In creating a divided Vietnam, the United States launched an experiment in nation building. Could the United States, through its great resources,

technological expertise, and example of democracy, construct a democratic, free-market state that would serve as a bulwark against the
spread of communism in the region? The war had begun as a war for Vietnamese independence from
the French. It continued as a civil war between the Vietnamese peo-
ple, but also as a proxy war in the larger Cold War struggle between
the United States and the Soviet Union. Under John Kennedy, American troop presence grew from 900 to 15,000; under Lyndon Johnson,
from 15,000 to 555,000. The war had a devastating effect on the people of Vietnam. Perhaps one-third of the South Vietnamese population became refugees,
uprooted from their ancestral homes, surviving as beggars, criminals, and prostitutes in an alien urban culture. The use of napalm
and defoliants, and the dropping of more than seven million tons
of bombs on Indochina—three times the total tonnage of explosives
dumped on all the enemy nations during World War II—demolished Vietnam's agricultural base and crippled its economy. As one
American major declared after a particularly brutal battle, "We had
to destroy the village in order to save it."

The war also created profound conflict within the United States. A
significant portion of the American people came to distrust their government. More and more Americans—and not just the young—came
to believe that the war had no purpose, that it was without morality,
justification, even self-interest. As more and more young men came
home in body bags and "the light at the end of the tunnel" seemed
no closer, large numbers of Americans concluded, with CBS news
anchor Walter Cronkite, that the war was "mired in stalemate."

Not everyone, of course, came to oppose the war. Bumper stickers
proclaimed, "America, love it or leave it." The American public's division over the war in Vietnam coalesced with all the other divisions in
American society: over civil rights and Black Power, over feminism,
over what seemed the cultural revolution of youth. With tanks in the
streets of Chicago at the 1968 Democratic National Convention, it
seemed that the nation would be torn apart. And even within the antiwar movement, there was no unity. The small minority of the antiwar
movement that proclaimed solidarity with the Vietnamese National
Liberation Front (NLF) had little in common with most of the 61
percent of Americans who, by 1971, saw U.S. involvement in Vietnam
as a "mistake."

In the following readings, we try to capture some of the range of Americans' understandings of the Vietnam War, both then and now. In an excerpt from *We Were Soldiers Once . . . and Young,* readers are taken back to 1965, a moment when patriotic innocence seemed possible, and when Americans faced—for the first time—the realities of an escalating war. An SDS antiwar leaflet from the same year shows the early antiwar protestors' strength of commitment, as well as the larger concerns that led them to protest the war. Historian William Chafe's article on Allard Lowenstein and the Dump Johnson movement highlights the efforts of some Americans to bring about change through peaceful electoral means in an increasingly polarized nation. John Kerry's 1971 testimony before Congress on behalf of the Vietnam Veterans against the War takes us back to the experience of American servicemen in Vietnam and offers a window into the horror of the war for the Vietnamese people. And William Jefferson Clinton's letter to the director of the ROTC in 1969 shows how at least one young student chose to find a way out of fighting in Vietnam.

The American public has not come fully to terms with the legacy of the Vietnam War. Neither have its historians. The section ends with two very controversial pieces on the Vietnam War. Robert McNamara, secretary of defense under Kennedy and Johnson and a key architect of the nation's Vietnam policy, argues that the war was wrong and explains why. Journalist Michael Lind, in contrast, argues that although the war was a failure, it was both right and necessary.

The questions that arise from this section are not easy ones. What should be America's role in the world? How should the United States define its own self-interest? What are the proper limits of U.S. intervention? Does U.S. policy in Vietnam show a fatal flaw in the idea that America has the moral right to impose its own values and beliefs on other nations? If that is the lesson of Vietnam, how would the logic of that lesson shape our foreign policy?

Other critical questions remain. Why did the United States lose the Vietnam War? Was there ever a way that U.S. involvement could have led to a democratic government in Vietnam? How can we understand the atrocities committed against the Vietnamese and reported by John Kerry in his congressional testimony? Was American involvement in Vietnam a mistake, or was it a failure?

# We Were Soldiers Once . . . and Young

## Lt. Gen. Harold G. Moore and Joseph L. Galloway

*The Vietnam Memorial, a wall of polished black granite bearing the name of each and every American who fell in Vietnam, graphically illustrates the toll of the war in loss and heartbreak. The names are listed in the order that the men died, and the wall begins low, with just a handful of names from the years before 1960. It rises to tower above the people who stand reading the names before tapering down again with the names of those who died toward the end of the war.*

*It was on November 14, 1965, in Vietnam's Ia Drang Valley, that American servicemen began dying in large numbers. In the following excerpt from* We Were Soldiers Once . . . and Young, *the commander of the 1st Battalion, 7th Cavalry and the only journalist with the battalion tell the story of the first major battle of America's Vietnam War. Writing from hindsight, they attempt to show us a moment in time, a "watershed year when one era was ending in America and another was beginning."*

## PROLOGUE

*In thy faint slumbers I by thee have watch'd*
*And heard thee murmur tales of iron wars . . .*
—Shakespeare, Henry IV, Part One, Act II, Scene 3

This story is about time and memories. The time was 1965, a different kind of year, a watershed year when one era was ending in America

From *We Were Soldiers Once . . . and Young* by Lt. General H.G. Moore and Joseph L. Galloway, copyright © 1992 by Lt. General H.G. Moore and Joseph L. Galloway. Used by permission of Random House, Inc.

and another was beginning. We felt it then, in the many ways our lives changed so suddenly, so dramatically, and looking back on it from a quarter-century gone we are left in no doubt. It was the year America decided to directly intervene in the Byzantine affairs of obscure and distant Vietnam. It was the year we went to war. In the broad, traditional sense, that "we" who went to war was all of us, all Americans, though in truth at that time the larger majority had little knowledge of, less interest in, and no great concern with what was beginning so far away.

So this story is about the smaller, more tightly focused "we" of that sentence: the first American combat troops, who boarded World War II–era troopships, sailed to that little-known place, and fought the first major battle of a conflict that would drag on for ten long years and come as near to destroying America as it did to destroying Vietnam.

The Ia Drang campaign was to the Vietnam War what the terrible Spanish Civil War of the 1930s was to World War II: a dress rehearsal; the place where new tactics, techniques, and weapons were tested, perfected, and validated. In the Ia Drang, both sides claimed victory and both sides drew lessons, some of them dangerously deceptive, which echoed and resonated throughout the decade of bloody fighting and bitter sacrifice that was to come.

This is about what we did, what we saw, what we suffered in a thirty-four-day campaign in the Ia Drang Valley of the Central Highlands of South Vietnam in November 1965, when we were young and confident and patriotic and our countrymen knew little and cared less about our sacrifices.

Another war story, you say? Not exactly, for on the more important levels this is a love story, told in our own words and by our own actions. We were the children of the 1950s and we went where we were sent because we loved our country. We were draftees, most of us, but we were proud of the opportunity to serve that country just as our fathers had served in World War II and our older brothers in Korea. We were members of an elite, experimental combat division trained in the new art of airmobile warfare at the behest of President John F. Kennedy.

Just before we slipped out to Vietnam the Army handed us the colors of the historic 1st Cavalry Division and we all proudly sewed on the big yellow-and-black shoulder patches with the horsehead silhouette. We went to war because our country asked us to go, because our new President, Lyndon B. Johnson, ordered us to go, but more importantly because we saw it as our duty to go. That is one kind of love.

Another and far more transcendent love came to us unbidden on the battlefields, as it does on every battlefield in every war man has ever fought. We discovered in that depressing, hellish place, where death was our constant companion, that we loved each other. We killed for each other, we died for each other, and we wept for each other. And in time we came to love each other as brothers. In battle our world shrank to the man on our left and the man on our right and the enemy all around. We held each other's lives in our hands and we learned to share our fears, our hopes, our dreams as readily as we shared what little else good came our way.

We were the children of the 1950s and John F. Kennedy's young stalwarts of the early 1960s. He told the world that Americans would "pay any price, bear any burden, meet any hardship" in the defense of freedom. We were the down payment on that costly contract, but the man who signed it was not there when we fulfilled his promise. John F. Kennedy waited for us on a hill in Arlington National Cemetery, and in time we came by the thousands to fill those slopes with our white marble markers and to ask on the murmur of the wind if that was truly the future he had envisioned for us.

Among us were old veterans, grizzled sergeants who had fought in Europe and the Pacific in World War II and had survived the frozen hell of Korea, and now were about to add another star to their Combat Infantryman's Badge. There were regular-army enlistees, young men from American's small towns whose fathers told them they would learn discipline and become real men in the Army. There were other young men who chose the Army over an equal term in prison. Alternative sentencing, the judges call it now. But the majority were draftees, nineteen- and twenty-year-old boys summoned from all across America by their local Selective Service Boards to do their two years in green. The PFCs soldiered for $99.37 a month; the sergeants first class for $343.50 a month.

Leading us were the sons of West Point and the young ROTC lieutenants from Rutgers and The Citadel and, yes, even Yale University, who had heard Kennedy's call and answered it. There were also the young enlisted men and NCOs who passed through Officer Candidate School and emerged newly minted officers and gentlemen. All laughed nervously when confronted with the cold statistics that measured a second lieutenant's combat life expectancy in minutes and seconds, not hours. Our second lieutenants were paid $241.20 per month.

The class of 1965 came out of the old America, a nation that disappeared forever in the smoke that billowed off the jungle battlegrounds where we fought and bled. The country that sent us off to war was not there to welcome us home. It no longer existed. We answered the call of one President who was now dead; we followed the orders of another who would be hounded from office, and haunted, by the war he mismanaged so badly.

Many of our countrymen came to hate the war we fought. Those who hated it the most—the professionally sensitive—were not, in the end, sensitive enough to differentiate between the war and the soldiers who had been ordered to fight it. They hated us as well, and we went to ground in the cross fire, as we had learned in the jungles.

In time our battles were forgotten, our sacrifices were discounted, and both our sanity and our suitability for life in polite American society were publicly questioned. Our young-old faces, chiseled and gaunt from the fever and the heat and the sleepless nights, now stare back at us, lost and damned strangers, frozen in yellowing snapshots packed away in cardboard boxes with our medals and ribbons.

We rebuilt our lives, found jobs or professions, married, raised families, and waited patiently for America to come to its senses. As the years passed we searched each other out and found that the half-remembered pride of service was shared by those who had shared everything else with us. With them, and only with them, could we talk about what had really happened over there—what we had seen, what we had done, what we had survived.

We knew what Vietnam had been like, and how we looked and acted and talked and smelled. No one in America did. Hollywood got it wrong every damned time, whetting twisted political knives on the bones of our dead brothers.

So once, just this once: This is how it all began, what it was really like, what it meant to us, and what we meant to each other. It was no movie. When it was over the dead did not get up and dust themselves off and walk away. The wounded did not wash away the red and go on with life, unhurt. Those who were, miraculously, unscratched were by no means untouched. Not one of us left Vietnam the same young man he was when he arrived.

This story, then, is our testament, and our tribute to 234 young Americans who died beside us during four days in Landing Zone X-Ray and Landing Zone Albany in the Valley of Death, 1965. That is more Americans than were killed in any regiment, North or South, at the Battle of Gettysburg, and far more than were killed in combat in the entire Persian Gulf War. Seventy more of our comrades died in the Ia Drang in desperate skirmishes before and after the big battles at X-Ray and Albany. All the names, 305 of them including one Air Force pilot, are engraved on the third panel to the right of the apex, Panel 3-East, of the Vietnam Veterans Memorial in Washington, D.C., and on our hearts. This is also the story of the suffering of families whose lives were forever shattered by the death of a father, a son, a husband, a brother in that Valley.

While those who have never known war may fail to see the logic, this story also stands as tribute to the hundreds of young men of the 320th, 33rd, and 66th Regiments of the People's Army of Vietnam who died by our hand in that place. They, too, fought and died bravely. They were a worthy enemy. We who killed them pray that their bones were recovered from that wild, desolate place where we left them, and taken home for decent and honorable burial.

This is our story and theirs. For we were soldiers once, and young.

## HEAT OF BATTLE

*You cannot choose your battlefield,*
*God does that for you;*
*But you can plant a standard*
*Where a standard never flew.*
—Stephen Crane, "The Colors"

The small bloody hole in the ground that was Captain Bob Edwards's Charlie Company command post was crowded with men. Sergeant Herman R. Hostuttler, twenty-five, from Terra Alta, West Virginia, lay crumpled in the red dirt, dead from an AK-47 round through his throat. Specialist 4 Ernest E. Paolone of Chicago, the radio operator, crouched low, bleeding from a shrapnel wound in his left forearm. Sergeant James P. Castleberry, the artillery forward observer, and his radio operator, PFC Ervin L. Brown, Jr., hunkered down beside Paolone. Captain Edwards had a bullet hole in his left shoulder and armpit, and was slumped in a contorted sitting position, unable to move and losing blood. He was holding his radio handset to his ear with his one good arm. A North Vietnamese machine gunner atop a huge termite hill no more than thirty feet away had them all in his sights.

"We lay there watching bullets kick dirt off the small parapet around the edge of the hole," Edwards recalls. "I didn't know how badly I had been hurt, only that I couldn't stand up, couldn't do very much. The two platoon leaders I had radio contact with, Lieutenant William W. Franklin on my right and Lieutenant James L. Lane on Franklin's right, continued to report receiving fire, but had not been penetrated. I knew that my other two platoons were in bad shape and the enemy had penetrated to within hand-grenade range of my command post."

The furious assault by more than five hundred North Vietnamese regulars had slammed directly into two of Captain Edwards's platoons, a thin line of fifty Cavalry troopers who were all that stood between the enemy and my battalion command post, situated in a clump of trees in Landing Zone X-Ray, Ia Drang Valley, in the Central Highlands of South Vietnam, early on November 15, 1965.

America had drifted slowly but inexorably into war in this far-off place. Until now the dying, on our side at least, had been by ones and twos during the "adviser era" just ended, then by fours and fives as the U.S. Marines took the field earlier this year. Now the dying had begun in earnest, in wholesale lots, here in this eerie forested valley beneath the 2,401-foot-high crest of the Chu Pong massif, which wandered ten miles back into Cambodia. The newly arrived 1st Cavalry Division (Airmobile) had already interfered with and changed North Vietnamese brigadier general Chu Huy Man's audacious plans to seize the Central Highlands. Now his goal was to draw the Americans into battle—to learn how they fought and teach his men how to kill them.

One understrength battalion had the temerity to land by helicopter right in the heart of General Man's base camp, a historic sanctuary so far from any road that neither the French nor the South Vietnamese army had ever risked penetrating it in the preceding twenty years. My battalion, the 450-man 1st Battalion, 7th Cavalry of the U.S. Army, had come looking for trouble in the Ia Drang; we had found all we wanted and more. Two regiments of regulars of the People's Army of Vietnam (PAVN)—more than two thousand men—were resting and regrouping in their sanctuary near here and preparing to resume combat operations, when we dropped in on them the day before. General Man's commanders reacted with speed and fury, and now we were fighting for our lives.

One of Captain Edwards's men, Specialist 4 Arthur Viera, remembers every second of Charlie Company's agony that morning. "The gunfire was very loud. We were getting overrun on the right side. The lieutenant [Neil A. Kroger, twenty-four, a native of Oak Park, Illinois] came up in the open in all this. I thought that was pretty good. He yelled at me. I got up to hear him. He hollered at me to help cover the left sector."

Viera adds, "I ran over to him and by the time I got there he was dead. He had lasted a half-hour. I knelt beside him, took off his dog tags, and put them in my shirt pocket. I went back to firing my M-79 grenade launcher and got shot in my right elbow. The M-79 went flying and I was knocked down and fell back over the lieutenant. I had my .45 and fired it with my left hand. Then I got hit in the neck and the bullet went right through. Now I couldn't talk or make a sound.

"I got up and tried to take charge, and was shot a third time. That one blew up my right leg and put me down. It went in my leg above the ankle, traveled up, came back out, then went into my groin and ended up in my back, close to my spine. Just then two stick grenades blew up right over me and tore up both my legs. I reached down with my left hand and touched grenade fragments on my left leg and it felt like I had touched a red-hot poker. My hand just sizzled."

When Bob Edwards was hit he radioed for his executive officer, Lieutenant John Arrington, a twenty-three-year-old South Carolinian who was over at the battalion command post rounding up supplies, to come forward and take command of Charlie Company. Edwards says, "Arrington made it to my command post and, after a few moments of talking to me while lying down at the edge of the foxhole, was also hit and wounded. He was worried that he had been hurt pretty bad and told me to be sure and tell his wife that he loved her. I thought: 'Doesn't he know I'm badly wounded, too?' He was hit in the arm and the bullet passed into his chest and grazed a lung. He was in pain, suffering silently. He also caught some shrapnel from an M-79 that the North Vietnamese had apparently captured and were firing into the trees above us."

Now the North Vietnamese were closing in on Lieutenant John Lance (Jack) Geoghegan's 2nd Platoon. They were already intermingled with the few survivors of Lieutenant Kroger's 1st Platoon and were maneuvering toward Bob Edwards's foxhole. Clinton S. Poley, twenty-three, six feet three inches tall, and the son of an Ackley, Iowa, dirt farmer, was assistant gunner on one of Lieutenant Geoghegan's M-60 machine guns. The gunner was Specialist 4 James C. Comer, a native of Seagrove, North Carolina.

Poley says, "When I got up something hit me real hard on the back of my neck, knocked my head forward and my helmet fell off in the foxhole. I thought a guy had snuck up behind me and hit me with the butt of a weapon, it was such a blow. Wasn't anybody there; it was a bullet from the side or rear. I put my bandage on it and the helmet helped hold it on. I got up and looked again and there were four of them with carbines, off to our right front. I told Comer to aim more to the right. After that I heard a scream and I thought it was Lieutenant Geoghegan."

It wasn't. By now, Lieutenant Geoghegan was already dead. His platoon sergeant, Robert Jemison, Jr., saw him go down trying to help a wounded man. "Willie Godboldt was twenty yards to my right. He was wounded, started hollering: 'Somebody help me!' I yelled: 'I'll go get him!' Lieutenant Geoghegan yelled back: 'No, I will.' He moved out of his position in the foxhole to help Godboldt and was shot." Just five days past his twenty-fourth birthday, John Lance Geoghegan of Pelham, New York, the only child of proud and doting parents, husband of Barbara and father of six-month-old Camille, lay dead, shot through the head and back, in the tall grass and red dirt of the Ia Drang Valley. PFC Willie F. Godboldt of Jacksonville, Florida, also twenty-four years old, died before help ever reached him.

Sergeant Jemison, who helped fight off five Chinese divisions at Chipyong-ni in the Korean War, now took a single bullet through his stomach but kept on fighting. Twenty minutes later the order came down for every platoon to throw a colored smoke grenade to mark friendly positions for the artillery and air strikes. Jemison got up to throw one and was hit again, this time knocked down by a bullet that struck him in the left shoulder. He got up, more slowly now, and went back to firing his M-16. Jemison fought on until he was hit a third time: "It was an automatic weapon. It hit me in my right arm and tore my weapon all to pieces. All that was left was the plastic stock. Another bullet cut off the metal clamp on my chin strap and knocked off my helmet. It hit so hard I thought my neck was broke. I was thrown to the ground. I got up and there was nothing left. No weapon, no grenades, no nothing."

James Comer and Clinton Poley, thirty feet to Jemison's left, had been firing their M-60 machine gun for almost an hour, an eternity. "A stick-handled potato-masher grenade landed in front of the hole. Comer hollered, 'Get down!' and kicked it away a little bit with his foot. It went off. By then we were close to being out of ammo and the gun had jammed. In that cloud of smoke and dust we started to our left, trying to find other 2nd Platoon positions. That's when I got hit in the chest and I hit the ground pretty hard."

Poley adds, "I got up and then got shot in my hip, and went down again. Comer and I lost contact with each other in the long grass. We'd already lost our ammo bearer [PFC Charles H. Collier from Mount Pleasant, Texas], who had been killed the day before. He was only eighteen and had been in Vietnam just a few days. I managed to run about twenty yards at a time for three times and finally came to part of the mortar platoon. A sergeant had two guys help me across a clearing to the battalion command post by the large anthill. The battalion doctor, a captain, gave me first aid."

Meantime, Specialist Viera was witness to scenes of horror: "The enemy was all over, at least a couple of hundred of them walking around for three or four minutes; it seemed like three or four hours. They were shooting and machine-gunning our wounded and laughing and giggling. I knew they'd kill me if they saw I was alive. When they got near, I played dead. I kept my eyes open and stared at a small tree. I knew that dead men had their eyes open."

Viera continues, "Then one of the North Vietnamese came up, looked at me, then kicked me, and I flopped over. I guess he thought I was dead. There was blood running out of my mouth, my arm, my legs. He took my watch and my .45 pistol and walked on. I watched them strip off all our weapons; then they left, back where they came from. I remember the artillery, the bombs, the napalm everywhere, real close around me. It shook the ground underneath me. But it was coming in on the North Vietnamese soldiers, too."

All this, and much more, took place between 6:50 A.M. and 7:40 A.M. on November 15, 1965. The agonies of Charlie Company occurred over 140 yards of the line. But men were fighting and dying on three sides of our thinly held American perimeter. In the center, I held the lives of all these men in my hands. The badly wounded Captain Bob Edwards was now on the radio, asking for reinforcements. The only reserve I had was the reconnaissance platoon, twenty-two men. Was the attack on Charlie Company the main enemy threat? Delta

Company and the combined mortar position were also under attack now. Reluctantly, I told Captain Edwards that his company would have to fight on alone for the time being. The din of battle was unbelievable. Rifles and machine guns and mortars and grenades rattled, banged, and boomed. Two batteries of 105mm howitzers, twelve big guns located on another landing zone five miles distant, were firing nonstop, their shells exploding no more than fifty yards outside the ring of shallow foxholes.

Beside me in the battalion command post, the Air Force forward air controller, Lieutenant Charlie W. Hastings, twenty-six, from La Mesa, New Mexico, radioed a special code word, "Broken Arrow," meaning "American unit in danger of being overrun," and within a short period of time every available fighter-bomber in South Vietnam was stacked overhead at thousand-foot intervals from seven thousand feet to thirty-five thousand feet, waiting its turn to deliver bombs and napalm to the battlefield.

Among my sergeants there were three-war men—men who parachuted into Normandy on D day and had survived the war in Korea—and those old veterans were shocked by the savagery and hellish noise of this battle. Choking clouds of smoke and dust obscured the killing ground. We were dry-mouthed and our bowels churned with fear, and still the enemy came on in waves.

# March on Washington: The War Must Be Stopped (1965)

## Students for a Democratic Society

*On April 17, 1965, thousands of people came together in Washington, D.C., for the first national protest against the war in Vietnam. Few Americans questioned their government's actions in Vietnam at this point; for most, the war was a peripheral issue. There were very few American military personnel in Vietnam before 1965. But questions about the war had begun to surface, especially on the nation's college and university campuses. This first national protest was organized by Students for a Democratic Society, still a small and virtually unknown group. SDS members had come to believe that the war was immoral, a threat to the cause of democracy both at home and abroad, and they meant to shake the nation from what they saw as a dangerous complacency. In a stirring speech, Paul Potter, president of SDS, linked the war in Vietnam to failures of democracy within American society. American intervention in Vietnam, he argued that day, did not represent the will of the American people but instead the interests of an interlocking set of elites—military, financial, technocratic. "We must name the system," he declared.*

*The following document is an SDS leaflet from November 1965, calling for a second protest, a March on Washington. Some historians have argued that the sort of logic set forth in this leaflet represents a critical flaw in this strand of the American antiwar movement: some leaders drew a false equivalency— largely based on ignorance of Vietnam and its history—between social problems in the United States and the civil war in Vietnam, between civil rights protesters in America and the Vietnamese National Liberation Front. How might such an understanding of America's involvement in Vietnam shape the course of antiwar protest? Why might the authors of this leaflet have seen the relationship between domestic social problems and foreign policy this way?*

In the name of freedom, America is mutilating Vietnam. In the name of peace, America turns that fertile country into a wasteland. And in

Students for a Democratic Society, leaflet.

the name of democracy, America is burying its own dreams and suffocating its own potential.

Americans who can understand why the Negroes of Watts can rebel should understand too why Vietnamese can rebel. And those who know the American South and the grinding poverty of our northern cities should understand that our real problems lie not in Vietnam but at home—that the fight we seek is not with Communism but with the social desperation that makes good men violent, both here and abroad.


## THE WAR MUST BE STOPPED

Our aim in Vietnam is the same as our aim in the United States: that oligarchic rule and privileged power be replaced by popular democracy where the people make the decisions which affect their lives and share in the abundance and opportunity that modern technology makes possible. This is the only solution for Vietnam in which Americans can find honor and take pride. Perhaps the war has already so embittered and devastated the Vietnamese that that ideal will require years of rebuilding. But the war cannot achieve it, nor can American military presence, nor our support of repressive unrepresentative governments.

The war must be stopped. There must be an immediate cease fire and demobilization in South Vietnam. There must be a withdrawal of American troops. Political amnesty must be guaranteed. All agreements must be ratified by the partisans of the "other side"—the National Liberation Front and North Vietnam.

We must not deceive ourselves: a negotiated agreement cannot guarantee democracy. Only the Vietnamese have the right of nationhood to make their government democratic or not, free or not, neutral or not. It is not America's role to deny them the chance to be what they will make of themselves. That chance grows more remote with every American bomb that explodes in a Vietnamese village.

But our hopes extend not only to Vietnam. Our chance is the first in a generation to organize the powerless and the voiceless at home to confront America with its racial injustice, its apathy, and its poverty, and with that same vision we dream for Vietnam: a vision of a society in which all can control their own destinies.

We are convinced that the only way to stop this and future wars is to organize a domestic social movement which challenges the very legitimacy of our foreign policy; this movement must also fight to end racism, to end the paternalism of our welfare system, to guarantee decent incomes for all, and to supplant the authoritarian control of our universities with a community of scholars.

This movement showed its potential when 25,000 people—students, the poverty-stricken, ministers, faculty, unionists, and others—marched on Washington last April. This movement must now show its force. SDS urges everyone who believes that our warmaking must be ended and our democracy-building must begin, to join in a March on Washington on November 27, at 11 A.M. in front of the White House.

# "Dump Johnson"

## William H. Chafe

*For those young antiwar protesters who wished to retain "political viability within the system," Allard Lowenstein provided a powerful role model. A bundle of political energy and charismatic charm, Lowenstein through the late 1940s, 1950s, and 1960s had seemed like a youthful knight in shining armor, leading various student crusades for reforming the political process, and redeeming America's promise to the ideals of equal opportunity, peace, and justice.*

*Lowenstein's politics represented a perfect amalgam of anticommunism and social reform. As one of the first presidents of the National Student Association (NSA) in 1950–51, the young, New York City–raised graduate of the University of North Carolina had pioneered both a tough anticommunist position for NSA on foreign policy and a commitment to racial equality and social progress at home. His exposé of the evils of apartheid in South Africa in 1962 helped highlight the genius and moral passion of Nelson Mandela's fight for black majority rule in that country. Then, Lowenstein became the primary white leader stirring northern white students to go South to Mississippi and join the civil rights struggle. Now, in 1967, Lowenstein assumed the most daunting mantle of all—leading an insurgency from the left within the Democratic Party to end the war in Vietnam, all the while working within the system. The following selection describes Lowenstein's tactical and strategic brilliance in creating the move to "dump" Lyndon Johnson as the Democratic Party's standard bearer in 1968. But in the process, the article also raises the larger question of whether it is possible to walk the thin line between rebellion against a policy of a political regime, and operating within the ground rules of that same regime.*

Stunning in its tactics and bold in its assumptions about the vulnerability of those in power, the campaign to "Dump Lyndon Johnson" as the

Excerpted from William H. Chafe, *Never Stop Running: Allard K. Lowenstein and the Struggle to Save American Liberalism,* copyrighted in 1993 by Harper Collins. Reprinted by permission.

presidential nominee of the Democratic Party in 1968 was the effort of a few reformers, propelled by conscience, to marshal enough political power to achieve, in essence, a peaceful coup d'état. Led by the young reformer Allard Lowenstein, this insurgent movement pledged to accomplish radical ends through reformist means. Rarely, if ever, had political activists reposed more faith in the capacity of a democratic process to turn its leaders and policies upside down. Between 1966 and 1968, in effect, Lowenstein and his allies sought to transform American politics. The degree to which that effort was a success testified dramatically to the genius and political passion of Allard Lowenstein, and represented the apex of his political influence. The effort also ultimately defined the borderline between seeking change within the political system, and deciding that the system itself had to change.

In the aftermath of the student "teach-ins" and the onset of the draft resistance campaign, Lowenstein sought a viable plan to sustain and nourish a political alternative to radical confrontation with the government. Earlier meetings between Lowenstein and administration officials had left little hope that change could come from within the administration. In response, Lowenstein and his allies from various liberal organizations set upon a course of action based on their conclusion that Lyndon Johnson himself was the Achilles' heel of the Democratic Party and that with enough support, they might mobilize opposition to the president's renomination.

By May 1967, Lowenstein started broaching the nucleus of his emerging strategy to friends. "It is now clear what must be done," Lowenstein told two student associates at a meeting in Cambridge. "Dump Johnson. We can do it. No one wants him out there and all that we have to do is have someone say it. Like, 'The emperor has no clothes.' There's a movement within the party that is dying for leadership." Later in the summer—after returning from a trip to Africa—Lowenstein talked about this idea with other student allies.

In both cases, the first response was astonishment. "I've never had any questions about [Al's] political judgment in the past," student leader Barney Frank—later congressman—told one friend, "[but] I think he's crazy. The idea of upsetting a sitting president with the power of Lyndon Johnson . . . crazy." Others asked what kind of mushrooms Al had been eating in Africa. But Lowenstein persisted. The idea might sound brazen and bizarre when first set forth, he agreed; but his friends should think about the logical sequence. The public was changing its opinion on the war and had no enthusiasm for LBJ; all people needed was an outlet for their grievances. Momentum would develop, Johnson would plummet further in popularity, suddenly a candidate would emerge who "will get on the bandwagon that we've built," and voila! Johnson would fall. The idea suddenly sounded plausible, especially to those who were captured by the conviction and energy of the person presenting it.

Not surprisingly, Lowenstein used as his departure point the place from which he had first launched his political alternative to radical protest—the NSA. Why not mobilize these students as the vanguard for carrying the "dump Johnson" movement forward into the Democratic Party and the primary states. Thus when the NSA met for its annual Congress in August 1967, two headlines emerged: the student delegates had decided to sever their ties with CIA-supported international organizations; and they determined to organize an "alternative candidates task force" that would pave the way for unseating Lyndon Johnson. "This congress," Lowenstein told the delegates at College Park, Maryland, "can be a launching pad for a decision to make 1968 the year when students help change a society almost everyone agrees is headed for destruction."

Ironically, the attractiveness of Lowenstein's "dump Johnson" strategy was heightened by the dissension and disarray among radicals who met later that summer at the National Conference for New Politics (NCNP) convention. More than 3,000 delegates gathered in Chicago, representing a variety of antiwar, Black Power, and community action groups. Most appeared committed to a total overhaul of American society, rejecting the feasibility of working for change through existing institutions. Almost immediately, however, their deliberations were taken over by fractious infighting. A black caucus demanded unconditional acceptance of a thirteen-point ultimatum requiring 50 percent black representation on all committees (later expanded to require 50 percent voting power throughout the convention), support for all wars of national liberation, condemnation of Zionist imperialism, and creation of "white civilizing committees" to extirpate "the savage and beastlike character that runs rampant through America." In what seemed to many a paroxysm of guilt, the overwhelmingly white delegates accepted the black caucus's demands. But then the convention devoted most of its energies to discussing how to create a revolution and barely mentioned the 1968 election or presidential politics. Thus the "new politics," especially as conveyed by the mass media, seemed to boil down to two essentials: a willingness to embrace inflammatory rhetoric as long as the source of the rhetoric was black; and an insistence that "politics," at least as conventionally defined, was beneath radical contempt—a tool of the establishment that should be abandoned as irrelevant.

From the point of view of Lowenstein and his allies, the NCNP's activities simply confirmed the legitimacy of their own effort, while removing one source of possible competition for the loyalties of those who still wanted to make a political fight against the president. "The third party had died with the New Politics," one student leader noted. "The chance of denying the army the manpower to fight [through draft resistance] . . . was equally impossible." The counterculture's assertion that revolution would come "when you could fuck in the streets" was a disaster. "So Allard's stuff—even as implausible as it sounded—still made more sense than [anything else around]." Suddenly, Lowenstein's contention that mainstream college students could provide the organizational infrastructure for unseating the president became not only credible but, for many antiwar activists, the only ball game in town.

At just this critical juncture, other political voices began to provide reinforcement. Writing in the *New Yorker* under the pseudonym Bailey Laird, Richard Goodwin, a speech writer for Robert Kennedy and a former aide to John Kennedy, cleverly dissected the conventional wisdom that an incumbent president could not be unseated. "The rules [of politics]," Goodwin wrote, "are only a summary of what's happened before. The trick is in trying to see what's going to happen next." According to the "rules," John Kennedy could never have been elected because "he was too young and a Catholic." But Kennedy chose to ignore the rules and create his own new reality. So, too, with the 1968 election, Goodwin reasoned. "People just don't like [Johnson]," he pointed out. "You can go around the country and you just don't meet anyone who's enthusiastic about [him] . . . . People tend to vote against someone rather than for someone, and I think they could really turn on the President." Thus, Goodwin concluded, "this nomination is really up for grabs . . . . People are looking for a fresh face . . . a man who really stands for something. . . . I think someone like that would find help . . . in the most unexpected places."

Allard Lowenstein could hardly have asked for a more ringing endorsement of both his own political assessment and his plan of action. He had maneuvered much of the student leadership of the country into a position of supporting his mainstream political approach to the war. Now he had escalated that campaign to an explicit assault on the president himself. The challenge he faced was to use his student base as a foundation from which to build buttresses of support to other segments of the party. Goodwin had written that "once in a while you have to take a big chance. Knowing when that time has come is what separates the great ones from the others. [But] I tell you, the big prize is hanging right up there ready to be grabbed." Lowenstein had decided that *this* was the time to turn fantasy into reality and reach for the prize.

He coordinated a remarkable team effort. Forces in the field were deployed far beyond what anyone could imagine, based on the number of people involved, and the results were literally stunning. One group, working from their postage-stamp office at Union Theological Seminary, made contact with campuses where Al might speak, and lined up potential canvassers for primary campaigns. Harold Ickes (later in the Clinton administration) dropped out of law school to spend up to twenty hours a day as "dispatch central," his New York studio apartment serving as the headquarters for scheduling "dump Johnson" activities. "I would literally work as the sun moved," he recalled, "from the East Coast to the West Coast. Al would call in and give me names of people I should follow up with, whom I should call, introduce myself to, etc. There was just this bewildering array of people that I kept in touch with." Pivotal to the whole operation, of course, were Lowenstein himself and his coworker Curtis Gans, who resigned from his ADA job to devote all his time to the "dump Johnson" project he had helped to create. Gans in Washington and Lowenstein in New York would target key constituencies to visit, orchestrate their travel schedules, pool their political contacts and resources, then hit the road in a political assault pattern that might well have made old-time politicians feel outclassed.

The scenario became routine. Collecting lists of names and phone numbers of all the "friendlies" they could identify from sources like ADA, Women Strike for Peace, and antiwar advertisements, Gans and Lowenstein would schedule a series of meetings in a local area. Lowenstein was teaching constitutional law at City College every Tuesday and Thursday, so he made East Coast trips after class on Tuesday and on Wednesday, then headed west from Thursday night through Monday. "I never missed a class," he boasted. Gans's role was to "advance" the joint mission, meeting with local politicos, scouting the territory for potential allies as well as minefields, and setting up speaking locations and private meetings for Lowenstein. A few days later, Lowenstein would parachute in for his part of the tandem operation, while Gans moved on to prepare the next landing site. Lowenstein would meet privately with important political figures, give a public address about the "dump Johnson" campaign in a community setting, then sometimes speak to a university group. Always the message was the same: this campaign was a mainstream effort of concerned Democrats; its purpose was to save the country and the party, not destroy them; the nation was full of people convinced that Johnson's Vietnam policy was disastrous, and working together, these people could make a difference and turn the country in a new direction. As reassuring as it was bold, the Lowenstein message hammered home the theme that concerted political action—within the party—was the highest form of Democratic loyalty, and the only way to save the country.

Almost magically, the pieces started to fall into place. Right after the NSA meeting in August 1967, Lowenstein flew to California, where he enlisted the support of Gerald Hill of the California Democratic Council, along with a $1,000 donation from the council to help defray his travel expenses. Shortly thereafter, $5,000 was collected from an East Coast antiwar source. The actor Robert Vaughn helped establish a group called Dissenting Democrats for antiwar activists who were outside the Democratic Party structure. By early September, the "dump Johnson" forces took the first giant step toward credibility *within* the party structure when Donald Peterson, the Democratic Party chairman of the tenth congressional district in Wisconsin, signed on, soon to be joined by Alpha Smaby, a widely respected legislator from Hubert Humphrey's home state of Minnesota. Newspaper stories proliferated as the campaign took on a life of its own. "Al seemed to be at every airport, every college campus, every state," Harold Ickes said. "It was just amazing where you would get calls from."

By the end of October, the "dump Johnson" movement had achieved a momentum that even hardened politicians could no longer ignore. The state party chairman in Michigan—a critical Democratic stronghold—embraced the campaign, as did the "young Democrat" organizations in Iowa, Michigan, and Wisconsin. Affiliate organizations multiplied, from the Coalition for a Democratic Alternative (CDA) to the Conference of Concerned Democrats ("concerned demagogues," Ickes called them) and Concerned Democrats of America. In a devastating blow to traditional Democrats, the liberal *New Republic* endorsed the campaign in a front-page editorial—"We don't know whether Lyndon Johnson can be denied. . . . We do know the attempt must be made"—and public opinion polls showed a growing groundswell of support for an alternative to Johnson, accompanied by a near free-fall decline in Johnson's public standing. It was as if everything Lowenstein had predicted in August were a carefully drawn blueprint for what was happening in October and November.

All that was missing was a candidate. From the beginning, Lowenstein had argued—undoubtedly with greater self-assurance than he felt—that once his coalition of forces had proved the depth and breadth of political alienation in the land, a candidate would "jump on the bandwagon." Furthermore, he insisted that such a demonstration had to come from "responsible, broadly based" groups within the party who could not be dismissed as marginal—thus providing another persuasive argument for excluding the "crazies." "These [potential candidates] cannot be expected to undertake so gruelling a contest [as an assault on the president]," he wrote, "unless they can be shown that it will not be an act of political hari-kari." But now that demonstration had been made and it was time to deliver on the final promise, without which the entire "dump Johnson" edifice might crumble.

Throughout the campaign, it had been clear that Lowenstein's ideal candidate was Robert Kennedy. The two had initially been wary of each other when Kennedy ran for the U.S. Senate from New York in 1964, but rapidly they became closer, especially after Kennedy enlisted Lowenstein's aid in drafting his antiapartheid speech at the University of Capetown in South Africa in February 1966. "He and Bobby [developed] a tremendous affection for each other," columnist Jack Newfield commented. When Lowenstein found himself on the same plane Kennedy was taking to California in the spring of 1967, therefore, he took the opportunity to brief Kennedy on his plans. Student-manned organizations would drive Johnson from the presidential race during the primaries, he told the senator, and the nomination would then be wide open. Although he did not ask Kennedy to become a candidate at that point, he nevertheless hoped to plant a seed that would grow. Kennedy responded with interest but contented himself primarily with speculating about other potential candidates, especially General James Gavin, a prominent military hero who had turned against the war. Lowenstein viewed Kennedy's response overall as "very friendly."

In their next meeting, the issue was broached more directly. At Hickory Hill, Kennedy's house in McLean, Virginia, after the ADA's board meeting in September 1967, Lowenstein and Jack Newfield engaged in a three-hour debate with Arthur Schlesinger, Jr., and James Loeb on the merits of Kennedy entering the race. "Argue it out," Kennedy told them, and while Schlesinger and Loeb defended the tactic of supporting a peace plank, Lowenstein and Newfield— with Lowenstein doing most of the talking—insisted that Johnson was going to fall and that Kennedy had a moral and political responsibility to step in. "Al was eloquent," Newfield said; he pulled out all the stops. At different points, Kennedy made remarks suggesting his fundamental agreement with Lowenstein. "When was the last time millions of people rallied behind a plank?" Kennedy asked Schlesinger. He also agreed that Johnson was vulnerable, "I think Al may be right," he said. "I think Johnson might quit the night before the convention opens. I think he is a coward." But Kennedy also told Lowenstein and Newfield that he saw no politically convincing argument for jumping in. Mayor Richard Daley of Chicago and other politicos were giving him no encouragement. Furthermore, any action Kennedy took would be seen as "splitting the party" out of personal spite toward LBJ. As Newfield later wrote, Kennedy's gut instincts were all for going in. But he could not bring himself to make the leap. "You understand, of course, that there are those of us who think the honor and direction of the country are at stake," Lowenstein told Kennedy as he left. "We're going to do it without you, and that's too bad, because you could have become president of the United States." It was a poignant moment, two politicians in quest of redemptive meaning in their public lives exchanging bittersweet comments on the larger struggle of conscience that engulfed them both.

In the meantime, Lowenstein took Kennedy's advice and approached a series of other potential candidates. General Gavin was interested but, in Lowenstein's view, completely naive, and more important he indicated that he would run as a Republican if he ran at all. George McGovern also responded positively to the idea and was seen by some as the best overall candidate because he understood the need for far-reaching reform in the political system. But McGovern was deeply concerned about the impact a presidential candidacy would have on his chances for reelection to the Senate from conservative South Dakota. When Lowenstein went to Sioux Falls, he discovered a mood substantially different from that of the rest of the country. "The picture of [South Dakota] unravelling" under the impact of the war just was not present, Lowenstein concluded. For McGovern to run for both president and the Senate, therefore, would create a problem of "two vocabularies, two emotional tones"—a prospect that seemed to confirm McGovern's doubts.

That left the one name that was on everyone's list, Eugene McCarthy. The senior senator from Minnesota, McCarthy had once been a close ally of Lyndon Johnson. His eloquent nomination speech for Adlai Stevenson at the 1960 Democratic convention was widely viewed as a last-ditch effort to block the Kennedy juggernaut and buy time for Johnson. In 1964, moreover, LBJ had publicly toyed with the idea of McCarthy as his vice-presidential choice (going to Humphrey only at the last minute). On the other hand, McCarthy had become a powerful voice against the war. His daughter Mary served as a persuasive intermediary for the "dump Johnson" forces, having been deeply impressed by Lowenstein's NSA speech in August. From talking to Mary, it seemed clear to Lowenstein that McCarthy was more ready to make a positive decision than anyone else.

Pressed especially by Gans, Lowenstein finally agreed to initiate a formal approach to the Minnesota senator. A man of deep Catholic morality but appropriately moderate demeanor, McCarthy in many ways was the ideal torchbearer. He would scare no one with his gray hair, his gray suit, and his dignified appeal for people to "speak out if you agree . . . there is no justification for continuing this war." But he could also inspire audiences with the simplicity of his moral commitment. "There comes a time," he said repeatedly, "when an honorable man simply has to raise the flag." Now, when Lowenstein and Gans went to him, McCarthy appeared ready to raise his—and to carry the banner for the "dump Johnson" movement.

On a three-day trip through the Northeast to test the political winds, the response was overwhelmingly positive. At a hastily massed rally in Cambridge, hand-lettered signs proclaimed, "The war is obscene, we want Eugene." In response, McCarthy told the crowds, "Vietnam is part of a much larger question, which is, is America going to police the planet?" the crowd went wild. Political supporters of the "dump Johnson" effort began to believe in it. "A month back," observed Gerald Hill, "I would have said our effort was an attempt to modify Johnson's policies by giving him a scare. Now it is becoming a real attempt to beat him." Having already scheduled a national Conference of Concerned Democrats in Chicago for December on the presumption a candidate would have emerged by then, Lowenstein and Gans were now confident that they had their man. "There are some things that are just so wrong that you have to take a stand," McCarthy said as he left Boston, "no matter what." Eleven months after the student body presidents' letter to LBJ, six months after first articulating the idea of "dumping Johnson" to student allies, and four months after the NSA convention at College Park, the final piece of Lowenstein's "impossible" plan had fallen into place. A candidate had emerged "to jump on the bandwagon."

No matter what political observers or historians think about Allard Lowenstein's style and effectiveness, his success in putting together a mainstream Democratic effort to defeat a sitting president was one of the most remarkable political achievements of contemporary American history. With unerring singleness of purpose, Lowenstein identified his objective, created a brilliant strategy, and mobilized an elite battalion of supporters to achieve his goal.

At the root of Lowenstein's success was his passionate preoccupation with showing that protest could triumph within the system. Countless thousands of other opponents of the war believed that the political process was so contaminated by militaristic values and materialism that only a struggle to change the soul of America and destroy capitalism could bring about the kind of change that was necessary. But whatever sympathy Lowenstein occasionally showed for the genuine alienation and idealism of these antiwar critics, he refused to play in their ball game and, in the way he defined their tactics, made sure they would not be accepted in his. Lowenstein denounced the "hate philosophy" he identified with the New Left and dismissed the inflammatory rhetoric that first decried the "system" and then tried to trash it. "Al [not only] didn't have much use for [the hard left]," Greg Craig noted, "[he had] some contempt for [them]."

To isolate and defeat the left, however, Lowenstein had to show that the politics of the center could work in addressing grievances identified by the left and shared by liberals. Thus, he had to reach out to the mainstream and simultaneously move it leftward, cultivating a heightened consciousness among "moderates" about the dimension of the problems that existed. It was like an upward spiral: you appealed to people's traditional values as the basis for mobilizing them, then kept them activated and working inside the system, initially as a way to prevent the left from triumphing, but ultimately as the only means of defeating the warhawks on the right. In everything Lowenstein did, one student ally noted, "there was an ongoing assumption that he defined the limits of the [permissible] left, wherever he was. Beyond that [there'd] be dragons." Thus, Lowenstein made his program the definition of acceptable dissent, galvanizing support precisely because the effort was to make democracy work, not destroy it. As one student supporter said, "Al [gave] me a way to do what I believed, and honor where I came from at the same time. . . . There was no way I was going to go against the system altogether, because I knew what it had done for my family. And here was an opportunity to take the tools of the system and make it work for what I believed in. I always believed that was what he wanted to do."

At every stage, Lowenstein devised ways of proceeding that reinforced such instincts. Al emphasized what united people behind a common cause and how their collective commitment could be turned to practical effect. "Al's greatest contribution," the journalist David Halberstam said, "was in making people feel they were not alone. He once told me, 'You know, the students think they're the only ones who are angry, and the middle-class women in the suburbs think they're the only ones who don't like the war' . . . and what Al did was [make] those people feel they were not alone. He was the ultimate moralist-activist . . . and he could touch in you and evoke in you those things that you believed in when you were very young."

There were some who believed Lowenstein took too much credit for the "dump Johnson" movement. "If the author supplies the idea and the architect the blueprint," Curtis Gans said, "he was neither the author nor the architect" of the campaign. Clearly, countless individuals were involved, some—like Gans—more important than others. Still, Lowenstein was the source, the inspiration, and the genius that made it all happen. "Al had the ability of taking very complex issues," Harold Ickes said, "and redefining them so that people who were not that sophisticated . . . really understood them in a very profound way." He could translate the most byzantine political strategy into terms that others could immediately identify with. Others provided the mechanical skill, an associate pointed out, but Lowenstein had the creativity to make the impossible seem doable.

"He was articulate as hell . . . he knew a bunch of reporters, [and] he was eminently quotable," the associate observed, thus becoming the critical pivot around which the movement turned.

Because of his talents, Lowenstein may have been the only person who could have achieved the triumph of 1967. Acknowledged as a member of mainstream, anticommunist America, he could articulate his position without automatically incurring dismissal as a "crazy." Yet, as a perennial student leader and reformer, he could reach out to the angry young and get their attention. Combined with an extraordinary political intelligence, these qualifications placed him in the unique position of being able to chart, direct, and then put into place a plan to show that the American democratic system would work, and that people who cared could make a difference.

What had begun as "a classic Don Quixote maneuver that no one believed in except himself" was now on the verge of victory. The fall of 1967, *Newsweek* observed, had been "one of the most histrionic autumns America has ever known . . . a season of blustery rhetoric and even stormier deeds." Into that autumn, Allard Lowenstein had brought a vision of change. "He said that . . . we're going to organize the students of this country and go in and do the work that the political hacks normally do," the Amherst student body president said, "[and he said] the students of this country are going to bring it back to sanity . . . and the most marvelous thing . . . is that he really predicted [what was going to happen]. And then he said . . . 'It will be the biggest news story of 1968.'"

With astonishing insight, Allard Lowenstein had prophesied—then helped bring to reality—a program of political protest that promised to redeem the faith of Americans in peaceful change through democratic processes. In the parlance of the day, he had delivered a "heavy" message and done so with style, brilliance, and panache. What was not yet clear was whether 1968 would bring the fulfillment of the promise he had made.

# Vietnam Veterans against the War (1971)

*John Kerry*

*By the early 1970s the American people's initial support of the government policy in Vietnam had become a yearning for an end to what seemed an interminable and unwinnable war. Americans from all walks of life now openly questioned and protested against the war. The antiwar movement had come to include groups such as Business Executives Move for a Vietnam Peace, the Federation of American Scientists, and Another Mother for Peace.*

*Vietnam Veterans against the War was one of the most influential and controversial antiwar organizations. Created by six Vietnam Veterans in 1967, it had thousands of members by the end of the decade. In April 1971, more than one thousand VVAW members—many in wheelchairs or on crutches—joined a 200,000 strong antiwar protest in Washington, D.C. "Bring our brothers home," they chanted. On April 23, thousands of veterans gathered at the U.S. Capitol, took the medals they'd been given by their nation—including Purple Hearts and Silver Stars—and threw them away.*

*Inside the Capitol building that day, one of their own, John Kerry, testified before the Senate Foreign Relations Committee. Kerry, a graduate of Yale University, had joined the navy and served as an officer on a gunboat in the Mekong Delta. He had received a Silver Star, Bronze Star, and three Purple Hearts. What he told the Senate committee was devastating. "How do you ask a man to be the last man to die for a mistake?" he demanded.*

*John Kerry was elected to the U.S. Senate (D., MA) in 1984 and has served since that date. As Democratic nominee for president, Kerry was narrowly defeated in the 2004 election by the incumbent, George W. Bush. During that election, as the war in Iraq continued, dividing the American people, the meaning of Kerry's military service in Vietnam and his protest against that war became key issues in the national debate over who should lead the nation.*

From "Vietnam Veterans against the War" statement by John Kerry to the Senate Committee on Foreign Relations, April 23, 1971.

I would like to talk on behalf of all those veterans and say that several months ago in Detroit we had an investigation at which over 150 honorably discharged, and many very highly decorated, veterans testified to war crimes committed in Southeast Asia. These were not isolated incidents but crimes committed on a day-to-day basis with the full awareness of officers at all levels of command.

It is impossible to describe to you exactly what did happen in Detroit—the emotions in the room and the feelings of the men who were reliving their experiences in Vietnam. They relived the absolute horror of what this country, in a sense, made them do.

They told stories that at times they had personally raped, cut off ears, cut off heads, taped wires from portable telephones to human genitals and turned up the power, cut off limbs, blown up bodies, randomly shot at civilians, razed villages in fashion reminiscent of Genghis Khan, shot cattle and dogs for fun, poisoned food stocks, and generally ravaged the countryside of South Vietnam in addition to the normal ravage of war and the normal and very particular ravaging which is done by the applied bombing power of this country.

We call this investigation the Winter Soldier Investigation. The term Winter Soldier is a play on words of Thomas Paine's in 1776 when he spoke of the Sunshine Patriots and summertime soldiers who deserted at Valley Forge because the going was rough.

We who have come here to Washington have come here because we feel we have to be winter soldiers now. We could come back to this country, we could be quiet, we could hold our silence, we could not tell what went on in Vietnam, but we feel because of what threatens this country, not the reds, but the crimes which we are committing that threaten it, that we have to speak out. . . .

In our opinion and from our experience, there is nothing in South Vietnam which could happen that realistically threatens the United States of America. And to attempt to justify the loss of one American life in Vietnam, Cambodia, or Laos by linking such loss to the preservation of freedom, which those misfits supposedly abuse, is to us the height of criminal hypocrisy, and it is that kind of hypocrisy which we feel has torn this country apart.

We found that not only was it a civil war, an effort by a people who had for years been seeking their liberation from any colonial influence whatsoever, but also we found that the Vietnamese whom we had enthusiastically molded after our own image were hard put to take up the fight against the threat we were supposedly saving them from.

We found most people didn't even know the difference between communism and democracy. They only wanted to work in rice paddies without helicopters strafing them and bombs with napalm burning their villages and tearing their country apart. They wanted everything to do with the war, particularly with this foreign presence of the United States of America, to leave them alone in peace, and they practiced the art of survival by siding with whichever military force was present at a particular time, be it Viet Cong, North Vietnamese or American.

We found also that all too often American men were dying in those rice paddies for want of support from their allies. We saw firsthand how monies from American taxes were used for a corrupt dictatorial regime. We saw that many people in this country had a one-sided idea of who was kept free by our flag, and blacks provided the highest percentage of casualties. We saw Vietnam ravaged equally by American bombs and search-and-destroy missions, as well as by Viet Cong terrorism, and yet we listened while this country tried to blame all of the havoc on the Viet Cong.

We rationalized destroying villages in order to save them. We saw America lose her sense of morality as she accepted very coolly a My Lai and refused to give up the image of American soldiers who hand out chocolate bars and chewing gum.

We learned the meaning of free-fire zones, shooting anything that moves, and we watched while America placed a cheapness on the lives of Orientals.

We watched the United States falsification of body counts, in fact the glorification of body counts. We listened while month after month we were told the back of the enemy was about to break. We fought using weapons against "oriental human beings." We fought using weapons against those people which I do not believe this country would dream of using were we fighting in the European theater. We watched while men charged up hills because a general said that hill has to be taken, and after losing one platoon or two platoons they marched away to leave the hill for reoccupation by the North Vietnamese. We watched pride allow the most unimportant battles to be blown into extravaganzas, because we couldn't lose, and we couldn't retreat, and because it didn't matter how many American bodies were lost to prove that point, and so there were Hamburger Hills and Khe Sanhs and Hill 81s and Fire Base 6s, and so many others.

Now we are told that the men who fought there must watch quietly while American lives are lost so that we can exercise the incredible arrogance of Vietnamizing the Vietnamese.

Each day to facilitate the process by which the United States washes her hands of Vietnam someone has to give up his life so that the United States doesn't have to admit something that the entire world already knows, so that we can't say that we have made a mistake. Someone has to die so that President Nixon won't be, and these are his words, "the first President to lose a war."

We are asking Americans to think about that because how do you ask a man to be the last man to die in Vietnam? How do you ask a man to be the last man to die for a mistake? . . . We are here in Washington also to say that the problem of this war is not just a question of war and diplomacy. It is part and parcel of everything that we are trying as human beings to communicate to people in this country— the question of racism which is rampant in the military, and so many other questions such as the use of weapons; the hypocrisy in our taking umbrage at the Geneva Conventions and using that as justification for a continuation of this war when we are more guilty than any other body of violations of those Geneva Conventions: in the use of free-fire zones, harassment interdiction fire, search and destroy missions, the bombings, the torture of prisoners, the killing of prisoners, all accepted policy by many units in South Vietnam. That is what we are trying to say. It is part and parcel of everything.

An American Indian friend of mine who lives in the Indian Nation of Alcatraz put it to me very succinctly. He told me how as a boy on an Indian reservation he had watched television and he used to cheer the cowboys when they came in and shot the Indians, and then suddenly one day he stopped in Vietnam and he said "my God, I am doing to these people the very same thing that was done to my people," and he stopped. And that is what we are trying to say, that we think this thing has to end.

We are here to ask, and we are here to ask vehemently, where are the leaders of our country. Where is the leadership? We're here to ask where are McNamara, Rostow, Bundy, Gilpatrick, and so many others. Where are they now that we, the men they sent off to war, have returned. These are commanders who have deserted their troops. And there is no more serious crime in the laws of war. The Army says they never leave their wounded. The marines say they never leave even their dead. These men have left all the casualties and retreated behind a pious shield of public rectitude. They've left the real stuff of their reputations bleaching behind them in the sun in this country. . . .

We wish that a merciful God could wipe away our own memories of that service as easily as this administration has wiped away their memories of us. But all that they have done and all that they can do by this denial is to make more clear than ever our own determination to undertake one last mission—to search out and destroy the last vestige of this barbaric war, to pacify our own hearts, to conquer the hate and the fear that have driven this country these last ten years and more. And more. And so when thirty years from now our brothers go down the street without a leg, without an arm, or a face, and small boys ask why, we will be able to say "Vietnam" and not mean a desert, not a filthy obscene memory, but mean instead the place where America finally turned and where soldiers like us helped it in the turning.

# Letter to the Draftboard (1969)

## William Jefferson Clinton

*In many respects, the 1992 presidential campaign represented a referendum on how Americans felt about the 1960s, and even more important, on which perception of the 1960s would prevail—the one that saw it as an era of reform and optimism, or one which perceived it as a time of polarization and bitterness. Nothing better highlighted the relevance of the 1960s to the 1992 presidential race than the disclosure that Bill Clinton had consciously sought to evade the draft, and the possibility of serving in Vietnam.*

*On February 12, 1992—in the midst of the New Hampshire primary campaign—Clinton released a letter he had sent in December 1969 to the head of the Reserve Officers Training Corps (ROTC) at the University of Arkansas. In that letter (reprinted here in its entirety) Clinton described the anguish, ambivalence, and outrage he felt about the possibility of serving in Vietnam. Already a Rhodes Scholar at Oxford University in England, he had returned to the United States in the summer of 1969; while at home, he struck a bargain, agreeing to join the ROTC unit at the University of Arkansas after his return from England. This action won him a deferment from the draft and reduced the likelihood that he might have to go to Vietnam. Once back in England, however, Clinton decided upon reflection that this course of action was not consistent with his moral revulsion against the war; hence, he chose to renege on the commitment—although only after his deferment had gone through.*

*The Clinton letter can be read in either of two ways—as the clever footwork of a schemer willing to do anything in order to escape fighting; or as the principled and tortured confession of someone so deeply troubled by the issue of how to serve his conscience and country that he fell into a state of moral and intellectual paralysis. There is also a third option: that Clinton's letter reflects both motivations simultaneously.*

*Whatever the case, the key to Clinton's behavior seems contained in his overriding objective, stated in the letter, "to maintain my political viability within the system." While others either served in the military or engaged in outright*

Excerpted from *The New York Times*. February 13, 1992.

*resistance, Clinton chose a middle course. Readers of the letter today, who have witnessed an extended war fought by an all-volunteer force, might well ponder just what it tells us about the realities facing young men in the late 1960s.*

*As context, is it useful to know that of the 26.8 million American men who came of draft age during the Vietnam War, 16 million—legally—did not serve in the military. Another 2 percent evaded the draft illegally. Of the 26.8 million men of draft age, 2.7 million (or roughly 10 percent) served in Vietnam, approximately half of them in combat or close support for combat troups. Graduates of elite colleges—such as George W. Bush—were unlikely to see military service in Vietnam; Harvard's twelve-hundred-member graduating class of 1970 sent two men to Vietnam. One exception was Clinton's vice president, Al Gore, who graduated from Harvard in 1969 and enlisted in the army. He spent approximately six months of his twenty-two-month military service in Vietnam as a military journalist.*

I am sorry to be so long in writing. I know I promised to let you hear from me at least once a month, and from now on you will, but I have had to have some time to think about this first letter. Almost daily since my return to England I have thought about writing, about what I want to and ought to say.

First, I want to thank you, not just for saving me from the draft, but for being so kind and decent to me last summer, when I was as low as I have ever been. One thing which made the bond we struck in good faith somewhat palatable to me was my high regard for you personally. In retrospect, it seems that the admiration might not have been mutual had you known a little more about me, about my political beliefs and activities. At least you might have thought me more fit for the draft than for R.O.T.C.

Let me try to explain. As you know, I worked for two years in a very minor position on the Senate Foreign Relations Committee. I did it for the experience and the salary but also for the opportunity, however small, of working every day against a war I opposed and despised with a depth of feeling I had reserved solely for racism in America before Vietnam. I did not take the matter lightly but studied it carefully, and there was a time when not many people had more information about Vietnam at hand than I did.

I have written and spoken and marched against the war. One of the national organizers of the Vietnam Moratorium is a close friend of mine. After I left Arkansas last summer, I went to Washington to work in the national headquarters of the Moratorium, then to

England to organize the Americans here for demonstrations Oct. 15 and Nov. 16.

Interlocked with the war is the draft issue, which I did not begin to consider separately until early 1968. For a law seminar at Georgetown I wrote a paper on the legal arguments for and against allowing, within the Selective Service System, the classification of selective conscientious objection, for those opposed to participation in a particular war, not simply to "participation in war in any form."

From my work I came to believe that the draft system itself is illegitimate. No government really rooted in limited, parliamentary democracy should have the power to make its citizens fight and kill and die in a war they may oppose, a war which even possibly may be wrong, a war which, in any case, does not involve immediately the peace and freedom of the nation.

The draft was justified in World War II because the life of the people collectively was at stake. Individuals had to fight, if the nation was to survive, for the lives of their countrymen and their way of life. Vietnam is no such case. Nor was Korea an example, where, in my opinion, certain military action was justified but the draft was not, for the reasons stated above.

Because of my opposition to the draft and the war, I am in great sympathy with those who are not willing to fight, kill, and maybe die for their country (i.e., the particular policy of a particular government) right or wrong. Two of my friends at Oxford are conscientious objectors. I wrote a letter of recommendation for one of them to his Mississippi draft board, a letter which I am more proud of than anything else I wrote at Oxford last year. One of my roommates is a draft resister who is possibly under indictment and may never be able to go home again. He is one of the bravest, best men I know. His country needs men like him more than they know. That he is considered a criminal is an obscenity.

The decision not to be a resister and the related subsequent decisions were the most difficult of my life. I decided to accept the draft in spite of my beliefs for one reason: to maintain my political viability within the system. For years I have worked to prepare myself for a political life characterized by both practical political ability and concern for rapid social progress. It is a life I still feel compelled to try to lead. I do not think our system of government is by definition corrupt, however dangerous and inadequate it has been in recent years.

(The society may be corrupt, but that is not the same thing, and if that is true we are all finished anyway.)

When the draft came, despite political convictions, I was having a hard time facing the prospect of fighting a war I had been fighting against, and that is why I contacted you. R.O.T.C. was the one way left in which I could possibly, but not positively, avoid both Vietnam and resistance. Going on with my education, even coming back to England, played no part in my decision to join R.O.T.C. I am back here, and would have been at Arkansas Law School because there is nothing else I can do. In fact, I would like to have been able to take a year out perhaps to teach in a small college or work on some community action project and in the process to decide whether to attend law school or graduate school and how to begin putting what I have learned to use.

But the particulars of my personal life are not nearly as important to me as the principles involved. After I signed the R.O.T.C. letter of intent I began to wonder whether the compromise I had made with myself was not more objectionable than the draft would have been, because I had no interest in the R.O.T.C. program in itself and all I seemed to have done was to protect myself from physical harm. Also, I began to think I had deceived you, not by lies—there were none—but by failing to tell you all the things I'm writing now. I doubt that I had the mental coherence to articulate them then.

At that time, after we had made our agreement and you had sent my 1-D deferment to my draft board, the anguish and loss of my self-regard and self-confidence really set in. I hardly slept for weeks and kept going by eating compulsively and reading until exhaustion brought sleep. Finally, on Sept. 12 I stayed up all night writing a letter to the chairman of my draft board, saying basically what is in the preceding paragraph, thanking him for trying to help in a case where he really couldn't, and stating that I couldn't do the R.O.T.C. after all and would he please draft me as soon as possible.

I never mailed the letter, but I did carry it on me every day until I got on the plane to return to England. I didn't mail the letter because I didn't see, in the end, how my going in the army and maybe going to Vietnam would achieve anything except a feeling that I had punished myself and gotten what I deserved. So I came back to England to try to make something of this second year of my Rhodes scholarship.

And that is where I am now, writing to you because you have been good to me and have a right to know what I think and feel. I am writing too in the hope that my telling this one story will help you to understand more clearly how so many fine people have come to find themselves still loving their country but loathing the military, to which you and other good men have devoted years, lifetimes, of the best service you could give. To many of us, it is no longer clear what is service and what is disservice, or if it is clear, the conclusion is likely to be illegal.

Forgive the length of this letter. There was much to say. There is still a lot to be said, but it can wait. Please say hello to Col. Jones for me.

Merry Christmas.
Sincerely,
Bill Clinton

# In Retrospect

## Robert McNamara

*Robert McNamara, secretary of defense from 1961 through 1968, was one of the key architects of America's war in Vietnam. Though he at first supported escalation of America's involvement in Vietnam, growing doubts about the war led him to resign in 1968. In 1995, twenty years after the end of the Vietnam War, McNamara published* In Retrospect: The Tragedy and Lessons of Vietnam. *"We of the Kennedy and Johnson administrations who participated in the decisions on Vietnam acted according to what we thought were the principles and traditions of this nation. We made our decisions in light of those values," he wrote. "Yet we were wrong, terribly wrong." McNamara's book was controversial: some pointed to his role in the war and called his self-criticism "too little, too late"; others saw his analysis as a betrayal of those who fought and died in a far-off land. Such controversy shows how raw the wounds of Vietnam may still be. But questions of responsibility aside, McNamara's larger interpretation is very much in line with the interpretations of many historians of the war. In the following excerpt from his book, he lays out what he sees as the major causes for America's "disaster" in Vietnam. Compare McNamara's analysis here with the radically different one that follows, drawn from Michael Lind's* Vietnam: The Necessary War.

By the time the United States finally left South Vietnam in 1973, we had lost over 58,000 men and women; our economy had been damaged by years of heavy and improperly financed war spending; and the political unity of our society had been shattered, not to be restored for decades.

Were such high costs justified?

Dean Rusk, Walt Rostow, Lee Kwan Yew, and many other geopoliticians across the globe to this day answer yes. They conclude that without U.S. intervention in Vietnam, Communist hegemony—both Soviet and Chinese—would have spread farther through South and East Asia to include control of Indonesia, Thailand, and possibly India. Some would go further and say that the USSR would have been led to take greater risks to extend its influence elsewhere in the world, particularly in the Middle East, where it might well have sought control of the oil-producing nations. They might be correct, but I seriously question such judgments.

When the archives of the former Soviet Union, China, and Vietnam are opened to scholars, we will know more about those countries' intentions, but even without such knowledge we know that the danger of Communist aggression during the four decades of the Cold War was real and substantial. Although during the 1950s, 1960s, 1970s, and 1980s the West often misperceived, and therefore exaggerated, the power of the East and its ability to project that power, to have failed to defend ourselves against the threat would have been foolhardy and irresponsible.

That said, today I question whether either Soviet or Chinese behavior and influence in the 1970s and 1980s would have been materially different had the United States not entered the war in Indochina or had we withdrawn from Vietnam in the early or mid-1960s. By then it should have become apparent that the two conditions underlying President Kennedy's decision to send military advisers to South Vietnam were not being met and, indeed, could not be met: political stability did not exist and was unlikely ever to be achieved; and the South Vietnamese, even with our training assistance and logistical support, were incapable of defending themselves.

Given these facts—and they are facts—I believe we could and should have withdrawn from South Vietnam either in late 1963 amid the turmoil following Diem's assassination or in late 1964 or early 1965 in the face of increasing political and military weakness in South Vietnam. And, as the table opposite suggests, there were at least three other occasions when withdrawal could have been justified.

I do not believe that U.S. withdrawal at any of these junctures, if properly explained to the American people and to the world, would have led West Europeans to question our support for NATO and, through it, our guarantee of their security. Nor do I believe that Japan would have viewed our security treaties as any less credible. On the contrary, it is possible we would have improved our credibility by

| Date of Withdrawal | U.S. Force Levels in South Vietnam | U.S. Killed in Action | Basis for Withdrawal |
|---|---|---|---|
| November 1963 | 16,300 advisers[a] | 78 | Collapse of Diem regime and lack of political stability |
| Late 1964 or early 1965 | 23,300 advisers | 225 | Clear indication of South Vietnam's inability to defend itself, even with U.S. training and logistical support |
| July 1965 | 81,400 troops | 509 | Further evidence of the above |
| December 1965 | 184,300 troops | 1,594 | Evidence that U.S. military tactics and training were inappropriate for the guerrilla war being waged |
| December 1967 | 485,600 troops | 15,979 | CIA reports indicating bombing in the North would not force North Vietnam to desist in the face of our inability to turn back enemy forces in South Vietnam |
| January 1973 | 543,00 troops (April 1969) | 58, 191[b] | Signing of Paris Accords, marking an end of U.S. military involvement |

[a] *This and all subsequent figures in the table have been supplied by the U.S. Army Center of Military History, Washington, D.C.*

[b] *As of December 31, 1968, the number of U.S. killed in action in Vietnam totaled 30,568.*

withdrawing from Vietnam and saving our strength for more defensible stands elsewhere.

It is sometimes said that the post–Cold War world will be so different from the world of the past that the lessons of Vietnam will be inapplicable or of no relevance to the twenty-first century. I disagree. That said, if we are to learn from our experience in Vietnam, we must first pinpoint our failures. There were eleven major causes for our disaster in Vietnam:

1. We misjudged then—as we have since—the geopolitical intentions of our adversaries (in this case, North Vietnam and the Vietcong, supported by China and the Soviet Union),

and we exaggerated the dangers to the United States of their actions.

2. We viewed the people and leaders of South Vietnam in terms of our own experience. We saw in them a thirst for—and a determination to fight for—freedom and democracy. We totally misjudged the political forces within the country.

3. We underestimated the power of nationalism to motivate a people (in this case, the North Vietnamese and Vietcong) to fight and die for their beliefs and values—and we continue to do so today in many parts of the world.

4. Our misjudgments of friend and foe alike reflected our profound ignorance of the history, culture, and politics of the people in the area, and the personalities and habits of their leaders. We might have made similar misjudgments regarding the Soviets during our frequent confrontations—over Berlin, Cuba, the Middle East, for example—had we not had the advice of Tommy Thompson, Chip Bohlen, and George Kennan. These senior diplomats had spent decades studying the Soviet Union, its people and its leaders, why they behaved as they did, and how they would react to our actions. Their advice proved invaluable in shaping our judgments and decision. No Southeast Asian counterparts existed for senior officials to consult when making decisions on Vietnam.

5. We failed then—as we have since—to recognize the limitations of modern, high-technology military equipment, forces, and doctrine in confronting unconventional, highly motivated people's movements. We failed as well to adapt our military tactics to the task of winning the hearts and minds of people from a totally different culture.

6. We failed to draw Congress and the American people into a full and frank discussion and debate of the pros and cons of a large-scale U.S. military involvement in Southeast Asia before we initiated the action.

7. After the action got under way and unanticipated events forced us off our planned course, we failed to retain popular support in part because we did not explain fully what was happening and why we were doing what we did. We had

not prepared the public to understand the complex events we faced and how to react constructively to the need for changes in course as the nation confronted uncharted seas and an alien environment. A nation's deepest strength lies not in its military prowess but, rather, in the unity of its people. We failed to maintain it.

8. We did not recognize that neither our people nor our leaders are omniscient. Where our own security is not directly at stake, our judgment of what is in another people's or country's best interest should be put to the test of open discussion in international forums. We do not have the God-given right to shape every nation in our own image or as we choose.

9. We did not hold to the principle that U.S. military action—other than in response to direct threats to our own security—should be carried out only in conjunction with multinational forces supported fully (and not merely cosmetically) by the international community.

10. We failed to recognize that in international affairs, as in other aspects of life, there may be problems for which there are no immediate solutions. For one whose life has been dedicated to the belief and practice of problem solving, this is particularly hard to admit. But, at times, we may have to live with an imperfect, untidy world.

11. Underlying many of these errors lay our failure to organize the top echelons of the executive branch to deal effectively with the extraordinarily complex range of political and military issues, involving the great risks and costs—including, above all else, loss of life—associated with the application of military force under substantial constraints over a long period of time. Such organizational weakness would have been costly had this been the only task confronting the president and his advisers. It, of course, was not. It coexisted with the wide array of other domestic and international problems confronting us. We thus failed to analyze and debate our actions in Southeast Asia—our objectives, the risks and costs of alternative ways of dealing with them, and the necessity of changing course when failure was clear—with the intensity and thoroughness that

characterized the debates of the Executive Committee during the Cuban Missile Crisis.

These were our major failures, in their essence. Though set forth separately, they are all in some way linked: failure in one area contributed to or compounded failure in another. Each became a turn in a terrible knot.

# The Genuine Lessons of the Vietnam War

## Michael Lind

*In his "reinterpretation" of the Vietnam War, Michael Lind rejects what he sees as the dominant interpretations of the war—left, liberal, and conservative—and returns to the Cold War vision of the men who committed America to the course that proved so disastrous. In the context of the Cold War, he argues, the Vietnam War was not a "tragic error" or an "inexplicable mistake." It was failure, but it was a just and necessary war.*

*Lind, who has written both for the left-progressive* Nation *and for the right-conservative* National Review, *is difficult to pigeonhole ideologically, but his book has been highly controversial among historians of the Vietnam War. It is useful to contrast the "lessons" Lind draws from America's experience in Vietnam with those outlined by McNamara in the previous selection. What are the implications of Lind's "lessons" for American foreign policy in the post–Cold War world?*

In the mid-1960s, the sound and ultimately successful Cold War grand strategy of global military containment of the communist bloc required Presidents Kennedy and Johnson to escalate the U.S. involvement in Vietnam rather than withdraw without a major effort. Any president in office at the time probably would have done so. On February 17, 1965, former president Dwight Eisenhower told President Johnson that "the U.S. has put its prestige onto the proposition of keeping SE Asia free. . . . We cannot let the Indo-Chinese peninsula go. [Eisenhower] hoped it would not be necessary to use the six to eight divisions mentioned, but if it should be necessary then so be it." Similarly, any president in the 1960s probably would have led the United States to war if North Korea had invaded South Korea a second time, or if China had invaded Taiwan. In the circumstances of the Cold War, a president who abandoned any of the three fronts in Asia to the communist bloc without a major struggle would have been guilty of dereliction of his duties as commander-in-chief and leader of the worldwide American alliance system. To argue otherwise is ahistorical. If the United States today, a decade after the demise of the Soviet Union, is prepared to go to war on behalf of South Korea and possibly Taiwan as well, then it makes no sense to argue that it was irrational for the United States to defend its Indochinese protectorate at the height of the Third World War.

Once the Vietnam War is viewed in the context of the Cold War, it looks less like a tragic error than like a battle that could hardly be avoided. The Cold War was fought as a siege in Europe and as a series of duels elsewhere in the world—chiefly, in Korea and Indochina. Both the siege and the duels were necessary. Power in world politics is perceived power, and perceived power is a vector that results from perceived military capability and perceived political will. The U.S. forces stationed in West Germany and Japan demonstrated the capability of the United States to defend its most important allies. U.S. efforts on behalf of minor allies in peripheral regions such as South Korea and South Vietnam and Laos proved that the United States possessed the will to be a reliable ally. Had the United States repeatedly refused to take part in proxy-war duels with the Soviet Union, and with China during its anti-American phase, it seems likely that there would have been a dramatic pro-Soviet realignment in world politics, no matter how many missiles rusted in their silos in the American West and no matter how many U.S. troops remained stationed in West Germany.

Most of the major duels between the American bloc and the communist bloc took place in countries that were peripheral (so that proxy wars between the superpowers would be unlikely to escalate into all-out global war) and symbolic (because they were divided between communist and noncommunist states). Along with China, which was divided between the communist mainland and Nationalist Taiwan, and partitioned Korea, Vietnam was one of a handful of front-line countries. The argument that the United States should have "chosen its battles" more carefully and avoided peripheral regions in which its allies were at a disadvantage posits a false alternative.

It would have been foolish for Moscow or Beijing to risk general war by attacking major U.S. allies, or to sponsor military challenges to the U.S. alliance system in places where the United States and its allies had a clear military and political advantage. The United States, then, was fated to forfeit the Cold War, or to fight in difficult conditions in battlefields that its enemies chose.

While the need to preserve a surplus of American credibility required the United States to escalate its involvement in Indochina by going to war, the need to preserve a surplus of American public support for the Cold War in its entirety required the U.S. government to avoid escalating the war in Indochina too much. Presidents Johnson and Nixon defended America's Cold War credibility, at the cost of eroding America's Cold War consensus. The high costs of the Vietnam War between 1965 and 1968 destroyed U.S. public support for an open-ended commitment to the defense of the noncommunist states of Indochina, while the additional costs of the prolonged withdrawal between 1968 and 1973 endangered public support for the Cold War on any front.

In the United States, the domestic result of the Vietnam War was a neoisolationist consensus in the 1970s. Disaffected moderate supporters of the Cold War teamed up with the permanent antiinterventionist made up of mostly northern progressive isolationists and Marx-influenced leftists. The neoisolationism of the U.S. Congress and the Carter administration in its first years permitted and encouraged the Soviet Union, with the assistance of its Vietnamese and Cuban auxiliaries, to engage in empire-building in the Third World without fear of American reprisal. The perception of rising Soviet power and American retreat inspired European appeasement of Moscow in the mid-seventies and also inspired bandwagoning with Moscow on the part of Third World states in the UN General Assembly. Only the Second Cold War of 1979–89, orchestrated in the face of significant leftist and neutralist opposition by Ronald Reagan, Margaret Thatcher, Helmut Kohl, François Mitterrand, and other western democratic leaders, reversed the pro-Soviet trend in world politics and drove the Soviet Union into bankruptcy by raising the costs of its bid for world military primacy. Far from having no affect in world politics, the U.S. defeat in Indochina inaugurated a period in which the relative power, influence, and ambition of the Soviet empire peaked. . . .

## THE VERDICT ON VIETNAM

In the House of Commons on April 4, 1940, Winston Churchill described the British retreat from Dunkirk: "We must be careful not to assign to this deliverance the attributes of a victory." Indochina was the Dunkirk of the American effort in the Cold War. The Vietnam War will never be understood as anything other than a horrible debacle. At the same time, it cannot be understood except as a failed campaign in a successful world war against imperial tyrannies that slaughtered and starved more of their own subjects than any regimes in history.

For the past generation, the Vietnam War has been considered not only a disastrous defeat (which it was), but an easily avoidable mistake (which it was not, any more than was the Korean War) and a uniquely horrible conflict (more Americans were killed in three months in the trenches in World War I than in a decade in Vietnam). The anti–Vietnam War orthodoxy is so exaggerated, and so implausible, that it is certain to change as younger historians uninfluenced by the partisan battles of the Vietnam era write a more accurate and dispassionate history.

In the long run, the greatest danger is that the Vietnam War will be treated by mainstream historians as an inexplicable mistake. It is only a slight exaggeration to say that academic historians are paid to explain why what happened had to happen more or less as it did happen. Historians tend to applaud success and to condemn failure without considering that a successful policy may have been a mistake and that a failed policy might have been worth attempting. . . .

How will the Vietnam War be considered a generation or two from now? It seems likely that historians free from the biases of Marxist leftism, liberal isolationism, and minimal realism will consider the Korean and Vietnam Wars to have been comparable Cold War proxy battles between the United States and the Soviet Union and China. It will be taken for granted that the United States was able to bring about a stalemate in the Korean War in large part because the enemy was vulnerable to American conventional forces backed by nuclear threats. The United States won a Pyrrhic victory in Indochina and withdrew because the U.S. military's misguided conventional-war approach to combating what, in the early years, was predominantly an insurgency piled up American casualties too quickly and destroyed American public support, first for the U.S. commitment to Indochina and then, temporarily, for the Cold War in general. Disinterested historians of the twenty-first century will also take it for granted that similar coalitions of progressive isolationists, Marxist radicals, and pacifists opposed U.S. intervention in World War I, World War II, and the major and minor conflicts of the Cold War, the Gulf War, and no doubt wars yet to come. The continuities in the ethnic and regional influences on isolationists and interventionists in the American population will be understood just as well.

Here, then, is a provisional verdict. The Vietnam War was a just, constitutional and necessary proxy war in the Third World War that was waged by methods that were often counterproductive and sometimes arguably immoral. The war had to be fought in order to preserve the military and diplomatic credibility of the United States in the Cold War, but when its costs grew excessive the war had to be forfeited in order to preserve the political consensus within the United States in favor of the Cold War.

The Vietnam War was neither a mistake nor a betrayal nor a crime. It was a military defeat.

# Part 6

# CONFRONTATIONS AND NEW LIMITS

To many Americans, the 1970s seemed the end of an era. Throughout the thirty years following World War II, American politics functioned on the premise that nothing was impossible if America wished to achieve it. Americans would be the guardians of freedom, send a man to the moon, conquer social injustice, eliminate poverty, and develop new technology that would change the shape of everyday life. That sense of confidence and power had been embraced not only by Great Society planners and politicians, but also by the young radicals who believed they could change the world.

In the 1970s, however, a new sense of limits struck home. The United States suffered its first loss in war. Richard Nixon became the first president forced to resign in disgrace, in large part because he himself had no sense of limits to his own presidential power. The Arab oil-producing countries quickly made Americans conscious of their dependence on the rest of the world during the 1973–74 oil boycott (staged in reaction to U.S. support of Israel during the October 1973 Yom Kippur War) and the enormous price hikes thereafter. When Iranian revolutionaries held American diplomats hostage for 444 days, the sense of being subject to powers beyond one's control was reinforced by every newscast. The American tendency toward hubris—the arrogant confidence that one can do anything—had come face to face with the realities of global competition, interdependency, and domestic failures.

By the time President Nixon resigned in disgrace, Americans' basic faith in their political system had been shaken and American society was more profoundly divided than at any time since the Civil War. As the peaceful petitions of the nonviolent Civil Rights movement were joined (or replaced) by Black Power slogans in the mid-1960s, white support plummeted and racial tensions grew. The emergence of feminism created profound divisions over traditional family roles and definitions of proper masculinity and femininity. The student movement began as a request for moderate changes, but with the growing crisis over Vietnam it challenged the very structure of the university. As the protests over Vietnam grew, many cities and university campuses became domestic battlefields. And as more and more evidence of political wrongdoing surfaced—Nixon's secret bombing of Cambodia; Watergate—many Americans felt betrayed.

Jimmy Carter spoke directly to that sense of betrayal when in 1976 he told the American people that they deserved a government as good as they were, one based upon faith, honesty, integrity, dignity, and respect for traditional American values. Gerald Ford, Nixon's vice president (who had replaced Spiro Agnew, who had resigned in scandal), had done an honorable job of healing the immediate wounds left by Watergate, but Carter offered an almost religious salve designed to reverse the damage. Running on the platform of an outsider who would bring a fresh perspective to Washington, Carter—a southerner and our first "born again" president—seemed to represent the simplicity and decency that would restore the faith of Americans in their political process.

The problem was that Carter knew very little about getting along in Washington. Often insensitive toward Congress, he helped to create a deadlock between the executive and legislative branches. Although he made some significant strides in American foreign relations, particularly with the Camp David accords on the Middle East, he was never able to fulfill his pledge to transform American government. While he diagnosed and articulated the crisis of confidence that existed in the American political process in the post-Nixon years, he was unable to mobilize support for constructive solutions to that crisis. He was stymied by economic "stagflation," in which a stagnant economy with rising unemployment joined with rapid inflation to create a rapidly rising "misery index" for the American people. And the intractable problems of energy and Iran seemed to paralyze his administration.

This section builds on previous sections—those on postwar affluence, civil rights and racial justice, the women's movement and sexual liberation, and the Vietnam war—to trace the increasing polarization of American society. By the end of the 1960s, the moderate reformism of Students for a Democratic Society had given way to the militant and violent rhetoric of the Weathermen. And as struggles over race and gender polarized Americans, so too did what people at the time called the "generation gap." The gulf between youth and their elders involved not only political disagreements, but also fundamental conflicts over "lifestyle." The counterculture spread rapidly, and Americans were as likely to find "hippie" communities in Atlanta, Georgia, and Lawrence, Kansas, as in San Francisco or New York. Culture and politics were increasingly intermixed; long hair, marijuana use, more casual attitudes toward sex, and rejection of middle-class values became associated with the antiwar and student movements. In the meantime, reaction against youthful protest and the counterculture grew. A new phrase—"Middle America"—came into use, describing those who defended "middle-class values" and rejected the claims of the counterculture and the political left. Spiro Agnew, Nixon's original vice president, made a cottage industry out of denouncing antiwar protesters as "ideological eunuchs" who were encouraged in their rabble-rousing "by an effete corps of impudent snobs who characterize themselves as intellectuals."

This section begins with a manifesto originally written by the San Francisco counterculture group, the Diggers, in 1966 and republished in *The Digger Papers* in August 1968. Next is the "Weatherman" manifesto, which marks a newly radical and violent turn chosen by some members of Students for a Democratic Society. It is useful to compare this statement to the original (1962) SDS manifesto; the shift illustrates how a faction of the SDS moved from a vision of social transformation through participatory democracy to an ideology that justified violent revolution. Another piece from that same year, Peter Schrag's 1969 article for *Harper's Magazine,* describes the American counterrevolt against counterculture and radical left in his portrait of "the forgotten America."

Next, historian Kim McQuaid analyzes the culminating event of this era of division: Watergate. Following Watergate, the polarized and shaken nation confronted new challenges: a major economic crisis, the oil embargo, the taking of American hostages in Iran. Historian David Farber describes the Iran hostage crisis, putting it into the larger context of an America confronting new limits. Finally, President Jimmy Carter's "Crisis of Confidence" speech captures the spirit of the nation and helps to explain why America might be drawn to the simple verities and optimism offered by presidential candidate Ronald Reagan.

In reading these analyses and historical documents, think about the following questions. How did America become so polarized? Was such polarization unavoidable? Did the intransigence of those in power make the shift toward more radical positions necessary? Was the counterculture really a challenge to the values and ways of life of mainstream America, or was it simply a lifestyle, built around its own forms of consumption? Is the "forgotten American" Peter Schrag describes still a force in American politics today? What role has public disillusionment played in our political system? Did Americans' confrontation of new limits in the 1970s have any lasting impact on American society and politics?

# Trip without a Ticket (1968)

## The Diggers

*In "the Sixties," many young men and women devoted themselves to creating a counterculture. They meant to overthrow the dominant Cold War culture, just as the New Left meant to challenge the political establishment.*

*The American counterculture was never consistent or coherent, but to the extent it was a movement, the Diggers came closest to being what historian David Farber called its "visionary core." Taking their name from a group of seventeenth-century English utopians, the few dozen men and women who formed the Diggers attempted to forge a "Free City" in the Haight-Ashbury district of San Francisco. They meant to create a community free of money and the profit motive, in which the boundaries between performer and audience, spectacle and viewer, were erased. They created "free" stores, provided free food, and sought to create lives as "edge-walkers" who combined communitarian commitments with a "do-your-own-thing" spirit of adventure.*

*Thousands of young people flooded into San Francisco during the "Summer of Love" in 1967. Unlike the Diggers and others who had helped create the Haight-Ashbury community over the previous three years, many of them were not equipped to handle the world they found. As groups like the Diggers tried to hold things together, predators found easy prey. Bad drug experiences, rape, disease, and violence escalated. At the end of the summer, the Diggers proclaimed the "death of Hippie," but the counterculture, in various forms, continued to spread through American society.*

*Many in the counterculture believed that mind-blowing experiences with drugs or sex or music were more likely to alter the world view of America's youth than all the earnest speeches and careful exhortations of the avowedly political strand of the movement. After reading the following document, do you think they were right? Was culture a more powerful transforming force than politics?*

Originally published by the Diggers, Winter, 1966–67; republished in *The Digger Papers*, August 1968.

*And as the counterculture espoused by the Diggers spread into the general youth culture, did it become less a "counter" culture and more a "lifestyle"?*

Our authorized sanities are so many Nembutals. "Normal" citizens with store-dummy smiles stand apart from each other like cotton-packed capsules in a bottle. Perpetual mental out-patients. Maddeningly sterile jobs for strait-jackets, love scrubbed into an insipid "functional personal relationship" and Art as a fantasy pacifier. Everyone is kept inside while the outside is shown through windows: advertising and manicured news. And we all know this.

How many TV specials would it take to establish one Guatemalan revolution? How many weeks would an ad agency require to face-lift the image of the Viet Cong? Slowly, very slowly we are led nowhere. Consumer circuses are held in the ward daily. Critics are tolerated like exploding novelties. We will be told which burning Asians to take seriously. Slowly. Later.

But there is a real danger in suddenly waking a somnambulistic patient. And we all know this.


**WHAT IF HE IS STARTLED RIGHT OUT THE WINDOW?**

No one can control the single circuit-breaking moment that charges games with critical reality. If the glass is cut, if the cushioned distance of media is removed, the patients may never respond as normals again. They will become life-actors.

*Theater is territory.* A space for existing outside padded walls. Setting down a stage declares a universal pardon for imagination. But what happens next must mean more than sanctuary or preserve. How would real wardens react to life-actors on liberated ground? How can the intrinsic freedom of theater illuminate walls and show the weakspots where a breakout could occur?

*Guerrilla theater intends to bring audiences to liberated territory to create life-actors.* It remains light and exploitative of forms for the same reasons that it intends to remain free. It seeks audiences that are created by issues. It creates a cast of freed beings. It will become an issue itself.

This is theater of an underground that wants out. Its aim is to liberate ground held by consumer wardens and establish territory without walls. Its plays are glass cutters for empire windows.

## FREE STORE/PROPERTY OF THE POSSESSED

The Diggers are hip to property. Everything is free, do your own thing. Human beings are the means of exchange. Food, machines, clothing, materials, shelter and props are simply there. Stuff. A perfect dispenser would be an open Automat on the street. Locks are time-consuming. Combinations are locks.

So a store of goods or clinic or restaurant that is free becomes a social art form. Ticketless theater. Out of money and control.

"First you gotta pin down what's wrong with the West. Distrust of human nature, which means distrust of Nature. Distrust of wildness in oneself literally means distrust of Wilderness."—Gary Snyder

Diggers assume free stores to liberate human nature. First free the space, goods and services. Let theories of economics follow social facts. Once a free store is assumed, human wanting and giving, needing and taking, become wide open to improvisation.

A sign: *If Someone Asks to See the Manager Tell Him He's the Manager.*

Someone asked how much a book cost. How much did he think it was worth? 75 cents. The money was taken and held out for anyone. "Who wants 75 cents?" A girl who had just walked in came over and took it.

A basket labeled *Free Money.*

No owner, no Manager, no employees and no cash-register. A salesman in a free store is a life-actor. Anyone who will assume an answer to a question or accept a problem as a turn-on.

Question *(whispered):* "Who pays the rent?"

Answer *(loudly):* "May I help you?"

Who's ready for the implications of a free store? Welfare mothers pile bags full of clothes for a few days and come back to hang up dresses. Kids case the joint wondering how to boost.

Fire helmets, riding pants, shower curtains, surgical gowns and World War I Army boots are parts for costumes. Nightsticks, sample cases, water pipes, toy guns and weather balloons are taken for props. When materials are free, imagination becomes currency for spirit.

Where does the stuff come from? People, persons, beings. Isn't it obvious that objects are only transitory subjects of human value? An object released from one person's value may be destroyed, abandoned or made available to other people. The choice is anyone's.

The question of a free store is simply: What would you have?

## STREET EVENT—BIRTH OF HAIGHT/FUNERAL FOR $ NOW

Pop Art mirrored the social skin. Happenings X-rayed the bones. Street events are social acid heightening consciousness of what is real on the street. To expand eyeball implications until facts are established through action.

The Mexican Day of the Dead is celebrated in cemeteries. Yellow flowers falling petal by petal on graves. In moonlight. Favorite songs of the deceased and everybody gets loaded. Children suck deathshead candy engraved with their names in icing.

A Digger event. Flowers, mirrors, penny-whistles, girls in costumes of themselves, Hell's Angels, street people, Mime Troupe.

Angels ride up Haight with girls holding *Now!* signs. Flowers and penny-whistles passed out to everyone.

A chorus on both sides of the street chanting *Uhh! —Ahh! —Shh be cool!* Mirrors held up to reflect faces of passersby. . . .

The burial procession. Three black-shrouded messengers holding staffs topped with reflective dollar signs. A runner swinging a red lantern. Four pall bearers wearing animal heads carry a black casket filled with blowups of silver dollars. A chorus singing *Get Out Of My Life Why Don't You Babe* to Chopin's *Death March*. Members of the procession give out silver dollars and candles.

Now more reality. Someone jumps on a car with the news that two Angels were busted. Crowd, funeral cortege and friends of the Angels fill the street to march on Park Police Station. Cops confront 400 free beings: a growling poet with a lute, animal spirits in black, candle-lit girls singing *Silent Night*. A collection for bail fills an Angel's helmet. March back to Haight and street dancing.

Street events are rituals of release. Reclaiming of territory (sundown, traffic, public joy) through spirit. Possession. Public NewSense.

Not street-theater, the street *is* theater. Parades, bank robberies, fires and sonic explosions focus street attention. A crowd is an audience for an event. Release of crowd spirit can accomplish social facts. Riots are a reaction to police theater. Thrown bottles and over-turned cars are responses to a dull, heavy-fisted, mechanical and deathly show. People fill the street to express special public feelings and hold human communion. To ask "What's Happening?"

The alternative to death is a joyous funeral in company with the living.

## WHO PAID FOR YOUR TRIP?

Industrialization was a battle with 19th-century ecology to win break-fast at the cost of smog and insanity. Wars against ecology are suicidal. The U.S. standard of living is a bourgeois baby blanket for executives who scream in their sleep. No Pleistocene swamp could match the pestilential horror of modern urban sewage. No children of White Western Progress will escape the dues of peoples forced to haul their raw materials.

But the tools (that's all factories are) remain innocent and the ethics of greed aren't necessary. Computers render the principles of wage-labor obsolete by incorporating them. We are being freed from mechanistic consciousness. We could evacuate the factories, turn them over to androids, clean up our pollution. North Americans could give up self-righteousness to expand their being.

Our conflict is with job-wardens and consumer-keepers of a per-missive looney-bin. Property, credit, interest, insurance, installments, profit are stupid concepts. Millions of have-nots and drop-outs in the U.S. are living on an overflow of technologically produced fat. They aren't fighting ecology, they're responding to it. Middle-class living rooms are funeral parlors and only undertakers will stay in them. Our fight is with those who would kill us through dumb work, insane wars, dull money morality.

*Give up jobs, so computers can do them!* Any important human occupa-tion can be done free. Can it be given away?

Revolutions in Asia, Africa, South America are for humanistic industrialization. The technological resources of North America can be used throughout the world. Gratis. Not a patronizing gift, shared.

Our conflict begins with salaries and prices. The trip has been paid for at an incredible price in death, slavery, psychosis.

An event for the main business district of any U.S. city. Infiltrate the largest corporation office building with life-actors as nymphoma-niacal secretaries, clumsy repairmen, berserk executives, sloppy secu-rity guards, clerks with animals in their clothes. Low key until the first coffee-break and then pour it on.

Secretaries unbutton their blouses and press shy clerks against the wall. Repairmen drop typewriters and knock over water coolers. Executives charge into private offices claiming their seniority. Guards produce booze bottles and playfully jam elevator doors. Clerks pull out goldfish, rabbits, pigeons, cats on leashes, loose dogs.

At noon 1000 freed beings singing and dancing appear outside to persuade employees to take off for the day. Banners roll down from office windows announcing liberation. Shills in business suits run out of the building, strip and dive in the fountain. Elevators are loaded with incense and a pie fight breaks out in the cafeteria. *Theater is fact/ action*

Give up jobs. Be with people. Defend against property.

# You Don't Need a Weatherman to Know Which Way the Wind Blows (1969)

*Submitted by Karin Ashley, Bill Ayers, Bernardine Dohrn, John Jacobs, Jeff Jones, Gerry Long, Howie Machtinger, Jim Mellen, Terry Robbins, Mark Rudd, and Steve Tappis*

*Just seven years after the Port Huron Statement, SDS met again in national convention. In the intervening years the war in Vietnam had expanded dramatically, the integrationist petitions of the early Civil Rights movement had turned into demands for Black Power, and a movement for student autonomy had generated massive protests on university campuses. For at least some, the primary lesson of the sixties had been the impossibility of securing change peacefully. Teach-ins at universities had not changed the government's Vietnam policy; campaigns on behalf of antiwar candidates seemed an exercise in futility; for those who were most bitter and radicalized, revolution seemed the only answer. With young people as an advance party, these activists demanded that SDS support a worldwide revolution against capitalism and imperialism. The following selection from the Weatherman Manifesto—"You don't need a weatherman to know which way the wind blows"—appears, in retrospect, a hopelessly doctrinaire plea. Just one year later, three of those who endorsed it blew themselves to pieces making bombs in Greenwich Village. Yet the statement also reflects just how corrosive the 1960s had been in destroying the idealism of seven years earlier.*

Excerpted from Karin Ashley et al. "You Don't Need a Weatherman to Know Which Way the Wind Blows," mimeographed statement, 1969.

## INTERNATIONAL REVOLUTION

> *The contradiction between the revolutionary peoples of Asia Africa and Latin America and the imperialists headed by the United States is the principal contradiction in the contemporary world. The development of this contradiction is promoting the struggle of the people of the whole world against US imperialism and its lackeys.*
>
> Lin Piao
> *Long Live the Victory of People's War!*

People ask, what is the nature of the revolution that we talk about? Who will it be made by, and for, and what are its goals and strategy?

The overriding consideration in answering these questions is that the main struggle going on in the world today is between US imperialism and the national liberation struggles against it. . . .

So the very first question people in this country must ask in considering the question of revolution is where they stand in relation to the United States as an oppressor nation, and where they stand in relation to the masses of people throughout the world whom US imperialism is oppressing. . . .

It is in this context that we must examine the revolutionary struggles in the United States. We are within the heartland of a world-wide monster, a country so rich from its world-wide plunder that even the crumbs doled out to the enslaved masses within its borders provide for material existence very much above the conditions of the masses of people of the world. The US empire, as world-wide system, channels wealth, based upon the labor and resources of the rest of the world, into the United States. The relative affluence existing in the United States is directly dependent upon the labor and natural resources of the Vietnamese, the Angolans, the Bolivians and the rest of the peoples of the Third World. All of the United Airlines Astrojets, all of the Holiday Inns, all of Hertz's automobiles, your television set, car and wardrobe already belong, to a large degree, to the people of the rest of the world. . . .

The goal is the destruction of US imperialism and the achievement of a classless world: world communism. Winning state power in the US will occur as a result of the military forces of the US overextending themselves around the world and being defeated piecemeal; struggle within the US will be a vital part of this process, but when the revolution triumphs in the US it will have been made by the people of the whole world. For socialism to be defined in national terms within so extreme and historical an oppressor nation as this is only imperialist national chauvinism on the part of the "movement."

In this context, why an emphasis on youth? Why should young people be willing to fight on the side of Third World peoples?. . .

As imperialism struggles to hold together this decaying, social fabric, it inevitably resorts to brute force and authoritarian ideology. People, especially young people, more and more find themselves in the iron grip of authoritarian institutions. Reaction against the pigs or teachers in the schools, welfare pigs or the army is generalizable and extends beyond the particular repressive institution to the society and the State as a whole. The legitimacy of the State is called into question for the first time in at least 20 years, and the anti-authoritarianism which characterizes the youth rebellion turns into rejection of the State, a refusal to be socialized into American society. Kids used to try to beat the system from inside the army or from inside the schools; now they desert from the army and burn down the schools.

The crisis in imperialism has brought about a breakdown in bourgeois social forms, culture and ideology. The family falls apart, kids leave home, women begin to break out of traditional "female" and "mother" roles. There develops a "generation gap" and a "youth problem." Our heroes are no longer struggling businessmen, and we also begin to reject the ideal career of the professional and look to Mao, Che, the Panthers, the Third World, for our models, for motion. We reject the elitist, technocratic bullshit that tells us only experts can rule, and look instead to leadership from the people's war of the Vietnamese. Chuck Berry, Elvis, the Temptations brought us closer to the "people's culture" of Black America. The racist response to the civil rights movement revealed the depth of racism in America, as well as the impossibility of real change through American institutions. And the war against Vietnam is not "the heroic war against the Nazis"; it's the big lie, with napalm, burning through everything we had heard this country stood for. Kids begin to ask questions: Where is the Free World? And who do the pigs protect at home?

## THE RYM AND THE PIGS

A major focus in our neighborhood and citywide work is the pigs, because they tie together the various struggles around the state as the enemy, and thus point to the need for a movement oriented toward power to defeat it.

The pigs are the capitalist state, and as such define the limits of all political struggles; to the extent that a revolutionary struggle shows signs of success, they come in and mark the point it can't go beyond. . . . Our job is not to avoid the issue of the pigs as "diverting" from anti-imperialist struggle, but to emphasize that they are our real enemy if we fight that struggle to win.

The most important task for us toward making the revolution, and the work our collectives should engage in, is the creation of a mass revolutionary movement, without which a clandestine revolutionary party will be impossible. A revolutionary mass movement is different from the traditional revisionist mass base of "sympathizers." Rather it is akin to the Red Guard in China, based on the full participation and involvement of masses of people in the practice of making revolution; a movement with a full willingness to participate in the violent and illegal struggle. It is a movement diametrically opposed to the elitist idea that only leaders are smart enough or interested enough to accept full revolutionary conclusions. It is a movement built on the basis of faith in the masses of people.

The task of collectives is to create this kind of movement. (The party is not a substitute for it, and in fact is totally dependent on it.) This will be done at this stage principally among youth, through implementing the Revolutionary Youth Movement strategy discussed in this paper. It is practice at this, and not political "teachings" in the abstract, which will determine the relevance of the political collectives which are formed.

The strategy of the RYM for developing an active mass base, tying the city-wide fights to community and city-wide anti-pig movement, and for building a party eventually out of this motion, fits with the world strategy for winning the revolution, builds a movement oriented toward the power, and will become one division of the International Liberation Army, while its battlefields are added to the many Vietnams which will dismember and dispose of US imperialism. Long Live the Victory of People's War!

# The Forgotten American (1969)

## Peter Schrag

*Inevitably, the social protests of the 1960s provoked a counterresponse. By the end of the decade a group, dubbed "middle Americans" by the media, had rallied to the defense of the flag, traditional authority, and good manners. One definition of "middle Americans" was primarily economic. Earning between $5,000 and $15,000 a year, they made up 55 percent of the population. The majority were blue-collar workers, lower-echelon bureaucrats, schoolteachers, and white-collar employees. As they saw the federal government pour money into impoverished areas, they developed a sense of neglect and resentment, believing that they were being ignored while vocal protesters received all the attention. Just as important, however, was a sense of crisis in cultural values, a belief that the rules were being changed in midstream. As* Newsweek's *Karl Fleming observed, middle Americans felt "threatened by a terrifying array of enemies: hippies, Black Panthers, drugs, the sexually liberated, those who questioned the sanctity of marriage and the morality of work." Antiwar protests galvanized these middle Americans into action. From their perspective, it was blasphemy to wear the American flag on the seat of one's pants, burn one's draft card, or shout obscenities at authorities. In the following article, published in 1969, Peter Schrag describes the resentments and values of this group, illuminating just how profound the polarization of the 1960s was, and perceptively explaining why so many would turn from the party of the New Deal to increasingly conservative candidates.*

There is hardly a language to describe him, or even a set of social statistics. Just names: racist-bigot-redneck-ethnic-Irish-Italian-Pole Hunkie-Yahoo. The lower middle class. A blank. The man under whose hat lies the great American desert. Who watches the tube, plays the horses, and keeps the niggers out of his union and his neighborhood. Who might vote for Wallace (but didn't). Who cheers when the cops beat up on demonstrators. Who is free, white, and twenty-one, has a job, a home, a family, and is up to his eyeballs in credit. In the guise of the working class—or the American yeoman or John Smith—he was once the hero of the civics books, the man that Andrew Jackson called "the bone and sinew of the country." Now he is "the forgotten man," perhaps the most alienated person in America.

Nothing quite fits, except perhaps omission and semi-invisibility. America is supposed to be divided between affluence and poverty, between slums and suburbs. John Kenneth Galbraith begins the foreword to *The Affluent Society* with the phrase, "Since I sailed for Switzerland in the early summer of 1955 to begin work on this book. . . ." But *between* slums and suburbs, between Scarsdale and Harlem, between Wellesley and Roxbury, between Shaker Heights and Hough, there are some eighty million people (depending on how you count them) who didn't sail for Switzerland in the summer of 1955, or at any other time, and who never expect to go. Between slums and suburbs: South Boston and South San Francisco, Bell and Parma, Astoria and Bay Ridge, Newark, Cicero, Downey, Daly City, Charlestown, Flatbush. Union halls, American Legion posts, neighborhood bars, and bowling leagues, the Ukrainian Club and the Holy Name. Main Street. To try to describe all this is like trying to describe America itself. If you look for it, you find it everywhere: the rows of frame houses overlooking the belching steel mills in Bethlehem, Pennsylvania; two-family brick houses in Canarsie (where the most common slogan, even in the middle of a political campaign, is "curb your dog"); the Fords and Chevies with a decal American flag on the rear window (usually a cut-out from the *Reader's Digest,* and displayed in counter-protest against peaceniks and "those bastards who carry Vietcong flags in demonstrations"); the bunting on the porch rail with the inscription, "Welcome Home, Pete." The gold star in the window. . . .

He does all the right things, obeys the law, goes to church and insists—usually—that his kids get a better education than he had. But the right things don't seem to be paying off. While he is making more than he ever made—perhaps more than he'd ever dreamed—he's still struggling while a lot of others—"them" (on welfare, in demonstrations, in the ghettos) are getting most of the attention. "I'm working my ass off," a guy tells you on a stoop in South Boston. "My kids don't have a place to swim, my parks are full of glass, and I'm supposed to bleed for a bunch of people on relief." In New York a man who drives a Post Office trailer truck at night (4:00 P.M. to midnight) and a cab during the day (7:00 A.M. to 2:00 P.M.), and who hustles radios for his Post Office buddies on the side, is ready, as he says, to "knock somebody's ass." "The colored guys work when they feel like it. Sometimes they show up and sometimes they don't. One guy tore up all the time cards. I'd like to see a white guy do that and get away with it."

## WHAT COUNTS

Nobody knows how many people in America moonlight (half of the eighteen million families in the $5000 to $10,000 bracket have two or more wage earners) or how many have to hustle on the side. "I don't think anybody has a single job anymore," said Nicholas Kisburg, the research director for a Teamsters Union Council in New York. "All the cops are moonlighting, and the teachers; and there's a million guys who are hustling, guys with phony social security numbers who are hiding part of what they make so they don't get kicked out of a housing project, or guys who work as guards at sports events and get free meals that they don't want to pay taxes on. Every one of them is cheating. They are underground people—*Untermenschen*. . . . We really have no systematic data on any of this. We have no ideas of the attitudes of the white worker. (We've been too busy studying the black worker.) And yet he's the source of most of the reaction in this country."

The reaction is directed at almost every visible target: at integration and welfare, taxes and sex education, at the rich and the poor, the foundations and students, at the "smart people in the suburbs." In New York State the legislature cuts the welfare budget; in Los Angeles, the voters reelect Yorty after a whispered racial campaign against the Negro favorite. In Minneapolis a police detective named Charles Stenvig, promising "to take the handcuffs off the police," wins by a margin stunning even to his supporters: in Massachusetts the voters mail tea bags to their representatives in protest against new taxes, and in state after state legislatures are passing bills to punish student demonstrators. ("We keep talking about permissiveness in training kids," said a Los Angeles labor official, "but we forget that these are our kids.")

And yet all these things are side manifestations of a malaise that lacks a language. Whatever law and order means, for example, to a

man who feels his wife is unsafe on the street after dark or in the park
at any time, or whose kids get shaken down in the school yard, it also
means something like normality—the demand that everybody play it
by the book, that cultural and social standards be somehow restored
to their civics-book simplicity, that things shouldn't be as they are
but as they were supposed to be. If there is a revolution in this country—a revolt in manners, standards of dress and obscenity, and, more
importantly, in our official sense of what America is—there is also a
counter-revolt. Sometimes it is inarticulate, and sometimes (perhaps
most of the time) people are either too confused or apathetic—or
simply too polite and too decent—to declare themselves. In Astoria,
Queens, a white working-class district of New York, people who make
$7000 or $8000 a year (sometimes in two jobs) call themselves affluent, even though the Bureau of Labor Statistics regards an income of
less than $9500 in New York inadequate to a moderate standard of
living. And in a similar neighborhood in Brooklyn a truck driver who
earns $151 a week tells you he's doing well, living in a two-story frame
house separated by a narrow driveway from similar houses, thousands
of them in block after block. This year, for the first time, he will go
on a cruise—he and his wife and two other couples—two weeks in the
Caribbean. He went to work after World War II ($57 a week) and he
has lived in the same house for twenty years, accumulating two television sets, wall-to-wall carpeting in a small living room, and a basement
that he recently remodeled into a recreation room with the help of
two moonlighting firemen. "We get fairly good salaries, and this is
a good neighborhood, one of the few good ones left. We have no
smoked Irishmen around."

Stability is what counts, stability in job and home and neighborhood, stability in the church and in friends. At night you watch television and sometimes on a weekend you go to a nice place—maybe a
downtown hotel—for dinner with another couple. (Or maybe your
sister, or maybe bowling, or maybe, if you're defeated, a night at the
track.) The wife has the necessary appliances, often still being paid
off and the money you save goes for your daughter's orthodontist,
and later for her wedding. The smoked Irishmen—the colored (no
one says black; few even say Negro)—represent change and instability, kids who cause trouble in school, who get treatment that your
kids never got, that you never got. ("Those fucking kids," they tell
you in South Boston, "raising hell, and not one of 'em paying his own
way. Their fucking mothers are all on welfare.") The black kids mean

a change in the rules, a double standard in grades and discipline, and—vaguely—a challenge to all you believed right. Law and order is the stability and predictability of established ways. Law and order is equal treatment—in school, in jobs, in the courts—even if you're cheating a little yourself. The Forgotten Man is Jackson's man. He is the vestigial American democrat of 1840: "They all know that their success depends upon their own industry and economy and that they must not expect to become suddenly rich by the fruits of their toil." He is also Franklin Roosevelt's man—the man whose vote (or whose father's vote) sustained the New Deal. . . .

## AT THE BOTTOM OF THE WELL

American culture? Wealth is visible, and so, now, is poverty. Both have become intimidating clichés. But the rest? A vast, complex, and disregarded world that was once—in belief, and in fact—the American middle: Greyhound and Trailways bus terminals in little cities at midnight, each of them with its neon lights and its cardboard hamburgers; acres of tar-paper beach bungalows in places like Revere and Rockaway; the hair curlers in the supermarket on Saturday, and the little girls in the communion dresses the next morning; pinball machines and the *Daily News,* the *Reader's Digest* and Ed Sullivan; houses with tiny front lawns (or even large ones) adorned with statues of the Virgin or of Sambo welcomin' de folks home; Clint Eastwood or Julie Andrews at the Palace; the trotting tracks and the dog tracks—Aurora Downs, Connaught Park, Roosevelt, Yonkers, Rockingham, and forty others—where gray men come not for sport and beauty, but to read numbers, to study and dope. (If you win you have figured something, have in a small way controlled your world, have surmounted your impotence. If you lose, bad luck, shit. "I'll break his goddamned head.") Baseball is not the national pastime; racing is. For every man who goes to a major-league baseball game there are four who go to the track and probably four more who go to the candy store or the barbershop to make their bets. (Total track attendance in 1965: 62 million plus another 10 million who went to the dogs.)

There are places, and styles, and attitudes. If there are neighborhoods of aspiration, suburban enclaves for the mobile young executive and the aspiring worker, there are also places of limited expectation and dead-end districts where mobility is finished. But even there you can often find, however vestigial, a sense of place, the roots of old ethnic loyalties, and a passionate, if often futile, battle against intrusion and change. "Everybody around here," you are told, "pays his own way." In this world the problems are not the ABM or air pollution (have they heard of Biafra?) or the international population crisis; the problem is to get your street cleaned, your garbage collected, to get your husband home from Vietnam alive; to negotiate installment payments and to keep the schools orderly. Ask anyone in Scarsdale or Winnetka about the schools and they'll tell you about new programs, or about how many are getting into Harvard, or about the teachers; ask in Oakland or the North Side of Chicago, and they'll tell you that they have (or haven't) had trouble. Somewhere in his gut the man in those communities knows that mobility and choice in this society are limited. He cannot imagine any major change for the better; but he can imagine change for the worse. And yet for a decade he is the one who has been asked to carry the burden of social reform, to integrate his schools and his neighborhood, has been asked by comfortable people to pay the social debts due to the poor and the black. In Boston, in San Francisco, in Chicago (not to mention Newark or Oakland) he has been telling the reformers to go to hell. The Jewish schoolteachers of New York and the Irish parents of Dorchester have asked the same question: "What the hell did Lindsay (or the Beacon Hill Establishment) ever do for us?"

The ambiguities and changes in American life that occupy discussions in university seminars and policy debates in Washington, and that form the backbone of contemporary popular sociology, become increasingly the conditions of trauma and frustration in the middle. Although the New Frontier and Great Society contained some programs for those not already on the rolls of social pathology—federal aid for higher education, for example—the public priorities and the rhetoric contained little. The emphasis, properly, was on the poor, on the inner cities (e.g., Negroes) and the unemployed. But in Chicago a widow with three children who earns $7000 a year can't get them college loans because she makes too much; the money is reserved for people on relief. New schools are built in the ghetto but not in the white working-class neighborhoods where they are just as dilapidated. In Newark the head of a white vigilante group (now a city councilman) runs, among other things, on a platform opposing pro-Negro discrimination. "When pools are being built in the Central Ward—don't they think white kids have got frustration? The white can't get a job; we have to hire Negroes first." The middle class, said Congressman Roman Pucinski of Illinois, who represents a lot of it, "is in revolt. Everyone has been generous in supporting anti-poverty. Now the middle-class American is disqualified from most of the programs."

## "SOMEBODY HAS TO SAY NO . . . "

The frustrated middle. The liberal wisdom about welfare, ghettos, student revolt, and Vietnam has only a marginal place, if any, for the values and life of the workingman. It flies in the face of most of what he was taught to cherish and respect: hard work, order, authority, self-reliance. He fought, either alone or through labor organizations, to establish the precincts he now considers his own. Union seniority, the civil-service bureaucracy, and the petty professionalism established by the merit system in the public schools become sinecures of particular ethnic groups or of those who have learned to negotiate and master the system. A man who worked all his life to accumulate the points and grades and paraphernalia to become an assistant school princi-pal (no matter how silly the requirements) is not likely to relinquish his position with equanimity. Nor is a dock worker whose only estate is his longshoreman's card. The job, the points, the credits become property:

> Some men leave their sons money [wrote a union member to the *New York Times*], some large investments, some business connections, and some a profession. I have only one worthwhile thing to give: my trade. I hope to follow a centuries-old tradition and sponsor my sons for an ap-prenticeship. For this simple father's wish it is said that I discriminate against Negroes. Don't all of us discriminate? Which of us . . . will not choose a son over all others?

Suddenly the rules are changing—all the rules. If you protect your job for your own you may be called a bigot. At the same time it's per-fectly acceptable to shout black power and to endorse it. What does it take to be a good American? *Give the black man a position because he is black, not because he necessarily works harder or does the job better.* What does it take to be a good American? Dress nicely, hold a job, be clean-cut, don't judge a man by the color of his skin or the country of his origin. What about the demands of Negroes, the long hair of the students, the dirty movies, the people who burn drafts cards and American flags? Do you have to go out in the street with picket signs, do you have to burn the place down to get what you want? What does it take to be a good American? *This is a sick society, a racist society, we are fighting an immoral war.* ("I'm against the Vietnam war, too," says the truck driver in Brooklyn. "I see a good kid come home with half an arm and a leg in a brace up to here, and what's it all for? I was glad to see *my kid* flunk the Army physical. Still, somebody has to say no to these demonstrators and enforce the law.") What does it take to be a good American?

The conditions of trauma and frustration in the middle. What does it take to be a good American? Suddenly there are demands for Italian power and Polish power and Ukrainian power. In Cleveland the Poles demand a seat on the school board, and get it, and in Pittsburgh, John Pankuch, the seventy-three-year-old president of the National Slovak Society, demands "action, plenty of it to make up for lost time." Black power is supposed to be nothing but emulation of the ways in which other ethnic groups made it. But have they made it? In Reardon's Bar on East Eighth Street in South Boston, where the workmen come for their fish-chowder lunch and for their rye and ginger, they still identify themselves as Galway men and Kilkenny men; in the newsstand in Astoria you can buy *Il Progresso, El Tiempo,* the *Staats-Zeitung,* the *Irish World,* plus papers in Greek, Hungarian, and Polish. At the parish of Our Lady of Mount Carmel the priests hear confession in English, Italian, and Spanish and, nearby, the biggest attraction is not the stickball game, but the *bocce* court. Some of the poorest people in America are white, native, and have lived all of their lives in the same place as their fathers and grandfathers. The problems that were presumably solved in some distant past, in that prehistoric era before the textbooks were written—problems of assimilation, of upward mobility—now turn out to be very much unsolved. The melting pot and all: millions made it, millions moved to the affluent suburbs; several million—no one knows how many—did not. The median income in Irish South Boston is $5100 a year but the community-action workers have a hard time convincing the local citizens that any white man who is not stupid or irresponsible can be poor. Pride still keeps them from applying for income supplements or Medicaid, but it does not keep them from resenting those who do. In Pittsburgh, where the members of Polish-American organizations earn an estimated $5000 to $6000 (and some fall below the poverty line), the Poverty Programs are nonetheless directed primarily to Negroes, and almost everywhere the thing called urban backlash associates itself in some fashion with ethnic groups whose members have themselves only a precarious hold on the security of affluence. Almost everywhere in the old cities, tribal neighborhoods and their styles are under assault by masscult. The Italian grocery gives way to the supermarket, the ma-and-pa store and the walk-up are attacked by urban renewal. And almost everywhere, that assault tends to depersonalize and to alienate. It has always been this way, but with time the brave new world that replaces the old patterns becomes increasingly bureaucratized, distant, and hard to control.

Yet beyond the problems of ethnic identity, beyond the problems of Poles and Irishmen left behind, there are others more pervasive and more dangerous. For every Greek or Hungarian there are a dozen American-Americans who are past ethnic consciousness and who are as alienated, as confused, and as angry as the rest. The obvious manifestations are the same everywhere—race, taxes, welfare, students—but the threat seems invariably more cultural and psychological than economic or social. What upset the police at the Chicago convention most was not so much the politics of the demonstrators as their manners and their hair. (The barbershops in their neighborhoods don't advertise Beatle Cuts but the Flat Top and the Chicago Box.) The affront comes from middle-class people—and their children—who had been cast in the role of social exemplars (and from those cast as unfortunates worthy of public charity) who offend all the things on which working class identity is built: "hippies [said a San Francisco longshoreman] who fart around the streets and don't work"; welfare recipients who strike and march for better treatment; "all those [said a California labor official] who challenge the precepts that these people live on." If ethnic groups are beginning to organize to get theirs, so are others: police and firemen ("The cop is the new nigger"); schoolteachers; lower-middle-class housewives fighting sex education and busing; small property owners who have no ethnic communion but a passionate interest in lower taxes, more policemen, and stiffer penalties for criminals. In San Francisco the Teamsters, who had never been known for such interests before, recently demonstrated in support of the police and law enforcement and, on another occasion, joined a group called Mothers Support Neighborhood Schools at a school-board meeting to oppose—with their presence and later, apparently, with their fists—a proposal to integrate the schools through busing. . . .

**WHEN HOPE BECOMES A THREAT**

The imponderables are youth and tradition and change. The civics
book and the institution it celebrates—however passé—still hold the
world together. The revolt is in their name, not against them. And
there is simple decency, the language and practice of the folksy cliché,
the small town, the Boy Scout virtues, the neighborhood charity, the
obligation to support the church, the rhetoric of open opportunity:
"They can keep Wallace and they can keep Alabama. We didn't fight
a dictator for four years so we could elect one over here." What happens when all that becomes Mickey Mouse? Is there an urban ethic to
replace the values of the small town? Is there a coherent public philosophy, a consistent set of beliefs to replace family, home, and hard
work? What happens when the hang-ups of upper-middle-class kids
are in fashion and those of blue-collar kids are not? What happens
when Doing Your Own Thing becomes not the slogan of the solitary
deviant but the norm? Is it possible that as the institutions and beliefs
of tradition are fashionably denigrated a blue-collar generation gap
will open to the Right as well as to the Left? (There is statistical evidence, for example, that Wallace's greatest support within the unions
came from people who are between twenty-one and twenty-nine,
those, that is, who have the most tenuous association with the liberalism of labor.) Most are politically silent; although SDS has been trying to organize blue-collar high-school students, there are no Mario
Savios or Mark Rudds—either of the Right or the Left—among them.
At the same time the union leaders, some of them old hands from
the Thirties, aren't sure that the kids are following them either. Who
speaks for the son of the longshoreman or the Detroit auto worker?
What happens if he doesn't get to college? What, indeed, happens
when he does?

Vaguely but unmistakably the hopes that a youth-worshiping
nation historically invested in its young become threats. We have
never been unequivocal about the symbolic patricide of Americanization and upward mobility, but if at one time mobility meant rejection
of older (or European) styles it was, at least, done in the name of
America. Now the labels are blurred and the objectives indistinct. Just
at the moment when a tradition-bound Italian father is persuaded
that he should send his sons to college—that education is the only
future—the college blows up. At the moment when a parsimonious
taxpayer begins to shell out for what he considers an extravagant

state university system the students go on strike. Marijuana, sexual liberation, dress styles, draft resistance, even the rhetoric of change become monsters and demons in a world that appears to turn old virtues upside down. The paranoia that fastened on Communism twenty years ago (and sometimes still does) is increasingly directed to vague conspiracies undermining the schools, the family, order and discipline. "They're feeding the kids this generation-gap business," says a Chicago housewife who grinds out a campaign against sex education on a duplicating machine in her living room. "The kids are told to make their own decisions. They're all mixed up by situation ethics and open-ended questions. They're alienating children from their own parents." They? The churches, the schools, even the YMCA and the Girl Scouts, are implicated. But a major share of the villainy is now also attributed to "the social science centers," to the apostles of sensitivity training, and to what one California lady, with some embarrassment, called "nude therapy." "People with sane minds are being altered by psychological methods." The current major campaign of the John Birch Society is not directed against Communists in government or the Supreme Court, but against sex education. . . .

## CAN THE COMMON MAN COME BACK?

Beneath it all there is a more fundamental ambivalence, not only about the young, but about institutions—the schools, the churches, the Establishment—and about the future itself. In the major cities of the East (though perhaps not in the West) there is a sense that time is against you, that one is living "in one of the few decent neighborhoods left," that "if I can get $125 a week upstate (or downstate) I'll move." The institutions that were supposed to mediate social change and which, more than ever, are becoming priesthoods of information and conglomerates of social engineers, are increasingly suspect. To attack the Ford Foundation (as Wright Patman has done) is not only to fan the embers of historic populism against concentrations of wealth and power, but also to arouse those who feel that they are trapped by an alliance of upper-class Wasps and lower-class Negroes.

If the foundations have done anything for the blue-collar worker he doesn't seem to be aware of it. At the same time the distrust of professional educators that characterizes the black militants is becoming increasingly prevalent among the minority of lower-middle-class

whites who are beginning to discover that the schools aren't working for them either. ("Are all those new programs just a cover-up for
failure?") And if the Catholic Church is under attack from its liberal
members (on birth control, for example) it is also alienating the
traditionalists who liked their minor saints (even if they didn't actually exist) and were perfectly content with the Latin Mass. For the
alienated Catholic liberal there are other places to go; for the lower-
middle-class parishioner in Chicago or Boston there are none.
Perhaps, in some measure, it has always been this way. Perhaps
none of this is new. And perhaps it is also true that the American
lower middle has never had it so good. And yet surely there is a difference, and that is that the common man has lost his visibility and,
somehow, his claim on public attention. There are old liberals and
socialists—men like Michael Harrington—who believe that a new alliance can be forged for progressive social action:

> From Marx to Mills, the Left has regarded the middle class as a stra-
> tum of hypocritical vacillating rear-guarders. There was often sound
> reason for this contempt. But is it not possible that a new class is com-
> ing into being? It is not the old middle class of small property owners
> and entrepreneurs, nor the new middle class of managers. It is com-
> posed of scientists, technicians, teachers, and professionals in the
> public sector of the society. By education and work experience it is
> predisposed toward planning. It could be an ally of the poor and the
> organized workers—or their sophisticated enemy. In other words, an
> unprecedented social and political variable seems to be taking shape
> in America.
>
> The American worker, even when he waits on a table or holds open
> a door, is not servile; he does not carry himself like an inferior. The
> openness, frankness, and democratic manner which Tocqueville de-
> scribed in the last century persists to this very day. They have been a
> source of rudeness, contemptuous ignorance, violence—and of a cre-
> ative self-confidence among great masses of people. It was in this latter
> spirit that the CIO was organized and the black freedom movement
> marched.

There are recent indications that the white lower middle class is
coming back on the roster of public priorities. Pucinski tells you that
liberals in Congress are privately discussing the pressure from the
middle class. There are proposals now to increase personal income
tax exemptions from $600 to $1000 (or $1200) for each dependent,
to protect all Americans with a national insurance system covering catastrophic medical expenses, and to put a floor under all incomes. Yet

these things by themselves are insufficient. Nothing is sufficient without a national sense of restoration. What Pucinski means by the middle class has, in some measure, always been represented. A physician earning $75,000 a year is also a working man but he is hardly a victim of the welfare system. Nor, by and large, are the stockholders of the Standard Oil Company or U.S. Steel. The fact that American ideals have often been corrupted in the cause of self-aggrandizement does not make them any less important for the cause of social reform and justice. "As a movement with the conviction that there is more to people than greed and fear," Harrington said, "the Left must . . . also speak in the name of the historic idealism of the United States."

The issue, finally, is not *the program* but the vision, the angle of view. A huge constituency may be coming up for grabs, and there is considerable evidence that its political mobility is more sensitive than anyone can imagine, that all the sociological determinants are not as significant as the simple facts of concern and leadership. When Robert Kennedy was killed last year, thousands of working-class people who had expected to vote for him—if not hundreds of thousands—shifted their loyalties to Wallace. A man who can change from a progressive democrat into a bigot overnight deserves attention.

# Watergate

## Kim McQuaid

*The sixties, the era we remember for heroic struggles for civil rights and the polarization of the nation over the war in Vietnam, came to a kind of symbolic end in 1974, with the resignation of President Richard Nixon over his betrayal of the trust of the American people. Through a bizarre series of events, the Nixon administration found itself in a situation where, in order to cover up high-level White House involvement in a burglary, it created a set of circumstances that brought down the entire administration. The ironies of the situation were endless. Nixon had such a commanding lead over his opponents in the 1972 presidential election that no one could really challenge him, yet in order to gain a still greater edge, Nixon's political associates authorized a break-in at Democratic national headquarters in the Watergate Hotel. Even with the evidence turned up by journalists and congressional hearings, Nixon would probably have remained in office, yet the taping system he himself had installed in order to document his role in the nation's history tripped him up. Perhaps appropriately, the man who sought office in order to "bring us together again" accomplished his purpose by uniting most of the country in revulsion against his unconstitutional actions.*

*In the following excerpts from his much longer discussion in* The Anxious Years, *historian Kim McQuaid, a professor at Lake Erie College, speculates on the significance of Watergate. Focusing on the tapes, the Senate Judiciary Committee hearings, and finally Nixon's resignation (to avoid impeachment), McQuaid raises questions about what Americans expect of their president. Was Watergate, as he argues, a "watershed in American innocence"?*

## HISTORY AS KALEIDOSCOPE

It is easy to enunciate brittle profundities about Watergate. Americans who lived through over two years worth of break-ins, cover-ups,

Reprinted by permission of the author.

hearings, resignations, and on- and off-camera debates know that
this political trial of a president and his closest associates mattered.
We know it proved something about Richard Nixon, presidential
power, government in general, and the laws upon which the nation
is dependent. When it comes to being precise, however, eloquence
often evaporates into knee-jerk phrases: "Nixon is a crook"; "No one
is above the law"; "Nixon got railroaded"; "All politicians are only out
for themselves"; and so forth.

This imprecision is hardly surprising. Watergate was a many-sided
skirmish that roiled into a full-scale war. As combat proliferated,
utterly ambitious people found their careers in danger and fought
to protect them. Loyalties were strained or broken by fear; alliances
were formed and reformed; associates were destroyed and replaced;
and layers of rhetoric, lies, evasions, ad hominem abuse, guesstima-
tion, press leaks, and instantaneous analysis obscured the landscape.

It was, to millions of concerned Americans, just one damned thing
after another—surprises galore, a wildly burgeoning cast of characters, crisis rhetoric, and a review of basic principles about as easy to
keep straight as a catalog of volcanoes on Mars or gaseous layers of
Neptune. Watergate certainly wasn't the intellectualized government
of political-science textbooks. It was a soap opera come to life, with a
plot that was like the layers of an onion.

Watergate produced a result which Vietnam never had. The war
made the United States look ineffective and divided, but Watergate
made America look ridiculous in the eyes of its own people. The leaders often appeared to be buffoons, and the led hedged their political loyalties accordingly. The view that "government is the problem"
grew. Washington looked as illegitimate and pathetic as it did misguided or criminal. The process—full of fits, starts, alarms, and diver-
sions—took place in five major stages, which are summarized here
and will be discussed in detail later.

An initial judicial and journalistic stage of the Watergate investigation lasted for eleven months, from June 1972 to May 1973. Then,
during May, June, and July, the first stage of the political trial com-
menced before the Senate Watergate Committee. Once John Dean
and Alexander Butterfield did so much to legitimize the Watergate
investigation and to put the criminal spotlight on Richard Nixon himself, a second judicial and journalistic struggle took place from July to
October 1973. At issue was whether the courts could gain custody of
the Watergate tapes. After the first special prosecutor was fired for

his legal troubles in October, and continuing on until April 1974, political, judicial, and journalistic opposition gradually, and sometimes hesitantly, converged on the White House. Finally, from April to August 1974, this process of convergence had gone far enough so that the second and last stage of the political trial of Watergate drove Nixon from the presidency.

By the end, almost nobody felt triumphant and almost everybody was emotionally drained. Watergate, in this important sense, marked a watershed in American innocence. It symbolized the end of three decades when Americans could assume, in bland arrogance, that they were a special, powerful, and uniquely favored nation existing outside of history. If there was one thing that everybody, from Richard Milhous Nixon himself to the most thorough Nixon-hater, agreed with after two-and-one-third years of repeatedly failed cover-up, it was this maxim from La Rochefoucauld: "Almost all our failings are more pardonable than the means we use to hide them." The adage captured the mood of unflattering self-awareness that characterized the period.

Watergate was a twenty-seven-month struggle during which . . . America's constitutional system of checks and balances was faced with its most divisive and overt challenges since the Depression decade of the 1930s. In the process of attempting to resolve the conflict about the proper scope of presidential, congressional, and judicial power in the United States, the judges, legislators, and executive branch officials—with assists from investigative journalists—were faced with the fact that presidential power had vastly increased during the Cold War which had characterized United States foreign policy since the end of the Second World War. Watergate had flowed from Vietnam and from the polarized domestic politics the failed American war in Indochina had induced.

It was now up to the Congress and the courts to determine how far to scale back executive privileges and the assumptions about national security that rationalized so many of those privileges. The process was daunting and threatening. Courts and Congress alike proceeded carefully and often hesitantly. Had Richard Nixon not made the incredible error of tape-recording his own conversations, and then of needlessly alienating many of his own congressional allies—as, for example, by claiming a right to impound funds—it is more than likely that he would have survived Watergate and that only a relatively small number of deniable intermediaries would have been punished for activities in which he was fully implicated. . . .

On April 29th, [1974,] Nixon went on prime-time TV to announce he was freely making available information about his knowledge and actions relating to the Watergate break-in and cover-up which would demonstrate that both were "just as I have described them to you from the very beginning." Framing the president as he spoke were several score bound volumes of transcript, or so it appeared. The volumes were stage props. Four-fifths of their pages were empty. The 1,200 pages remaining were heavily edited. Even with the White House's editing, however, the transcripts demonstrated no such "from the very beginning" honesty as Nixon claimed before an audience of over half the nation's adult population.

Honesty, however, was the last thing on the president's mind. Nixon was using his office as an "electronic pulpit" to make it appear that he was doing what he was not, in fact, doing—that is, providing evidence long desired by the courts and two special prosecutors and which had been demanded of him only two weeks earlier by a Congressional Judiciary Committee subpoena. All presidents engage in this sort of prevarication, but Nixon's lies were more brazen than most. For not quite ten months, the tapes had been a slowly tightening noose around his neck. So Nixon finally tried to slip the noose by "letting the people know" what was on the growing numbers of tapes the special prosecutor and Congress wanted to see, in hopes that his judicial and political opponents would then be forced to stop pressing for genuine evidence.

The strategy almost worked. Nixon gave one of his better Watergate performances, one good enough to elicit kudos from the *Washington Post* and the *New York Times*. He did this because he was initially able to make it appear as though he was finally obeying the law, and the appearance briefly cast Nixon's opponents as partisan villains. Here was the president giving everyone all anybody could ask for, so who was Congress to refuse it? Who was the special prosecutor to keep insisting on more? Congress now had all it needed to determine whether an impeachment trial was necessary.

Nixon's was a bold and unexpected stroke which only just failed. Had the House Judiciary Committee accepted the edited transcripts that Nixon advertised as genuine, Nixon could have eviscerated the political trial, continued to stymie criminal justice as it applied to himself, and kept his presidency alive. But the committee's staff, of course, knew that appearances were not realities. They knew that Nixon had released only sanitized versions of the tapes—including those which Sirica, grand jury members, the special prosecutor's lawyers, and the committee had seen entire—to avoid a clear refusal to obey a special congressional subpoena for many Watergate tapes which the Judiciary Committee had finally made on April 11th. Nixon submitted his *sanitized* transcripts the day before the deadline which the House Judiciary Committee had set for their receipt of the *unsanitized* evidence. . . .

They knew all of that. Still, they almost played Nixon's game. . . . On the evening of May 1st, the House Judiciary Committee's members were called upon to decide. Would they accept the transcripts Nixon had made public several days before as sufficient, or would they not? They wouldn't, but only just. By a vote of 20 to 18, the committee refused to allow Nixon to set the terms of his own investigation any longer. . . . They guessed what the public's reaction to Nixon's edited tapes might be, and they guessed right. Within two weeks after Nixon released his version of Watergate, his presidency was on the road toward dissolution.

Nixon's staff had deleted a lot from the transcripts—pithy instructions, for example, which the president gave John Mitchell on March 22, 1973, one day after his "cancer on the presidency" meeting with John Dean: "I want you all to stonewall it, let them plead the Fifth Amendment, cover up or anything else" to "save the plan." But the transcripts were peppered with "(expletives deleted)" and the expletives mattered. Off-color expressions, present and absent, shocked the majority of Americans who did not then believe that their presidents swore.

The idea seems quaint now, yet it existed then. The United States of 1974 was steeped in an era of American Greatness, weaned during decades when presidents loomed ever larger in the nation's political imagination. America had become the greatest country in the world, a land with missions to match its greatness. Majesty was accordingly expected of the men who led that nation and who symbolized it to hundreds of millions at home and abroad—and majesty meant moral grandeur and spotless behavior. "Give 'em Hell" Harry Truman had used salty language, but Richard Nixon and many another rising politician had pilloried such verbal pyrotechnics as unacceptable. Truman was common, and the day of the common president who used common language was over. Nixon and others cast their words and actions in heroic styles pioneered by successful presidents like Franklin Delano Roosevelt and John F. Kennedy. Heroic strategies paid off for presidents. It gave them a divinity which doth hedge kings and leaders of nations with thermonuclear arsenals. It allowed their power and repute to survive shocks which other leaders, like "fixer" Lyndon Johnson, did not survive.

But it also exacted a price. Richard Nixon paid that price after April 30th, 1974. Politicians who knew what presidential image making was all about guessed what was coming, as House Judiciary Committee member James Mann of South Carolina did when he talked with journalist Elizabeth Drew on the eve of the committee's crucial vote of May 1st. Mann referred, Drew wrote:

> as people have been doing all day, to the "(expletive deleted)"s. They all seem curious to know what those parentheses are hiding. "The more that people know about him, it seems, the more trouble he's in," he says. "It's not that they think he's guilty of an impeachable offense, necessarily, but that he's not the man they thought he was."

No, Nixon wasn't the man they thought he was, any more than Jack Kennedy had been, but Kennedy hadn't been exposed while still in office. And it cost Nixon heavily with those who had come to expect their president to be a democratic monarch. Nixon's image problem then was a major reason that the Judiciary Committee risked moving ahead—though only just—on May 1st. Enough members believed that Nixon's edited words would explode in his face. Congress fought to replace Nixon's evidentiary agenda with its own and, during the next several weeks, the truth of perceptions like Representative Mann's was borne out. Mann's constituents didn't like what they read or heard about the tapes, and they heard and read lots more than the White House reckoned they would.

The reading began when the *New York Times,* in a repeat of its Pentagon Papers revelations, serialized the White House's transcripts verbatim. On May 1st, CBS News broadcast a prime-time special in which reporters read segments of the tape transcripts. Three days later, NBC News used professional actors to do the same thing. Meanwhile, both the *Washington Post* and the *New York Times* rushed the transcripts into paperback, with commentaries to help readers make sense of seven hundred pages of text. Both books, available on newsstands by May 14th, quickly became best-sellers.

The more exposure Nixon's edited transcripts got, the less willing congressional Republicans and conservative Democrats were to defend their content. Republican House Minority Leader John

Rhodes of Arizona and his Senate counterpart, Hugh Scott of Pennsylvania, somersaulted from complimenting the president for supplying bowdlerized evidence to damning what Nixon had made public. Rhodes branded the transcripts a "deplorable, shabby, disgusting, and immoral performance by all," and later added that he'd be willing to accept Nixon's resignation if Nixon chose to offer it. Such strategic withdrawals by Congress's Republican leadership sent strong messages to fence sitters on the House Judiciary Committee. . . . The more Republicans who were willing to go after Nixon, the better for the Democrats. The Judiciary Committee would become a Chinese army, and Nixon simply couldn't shoot them *all*. . . .

For six months, the House Judiciary Committee moved glacially. . . . Through all of this, Washington's power brokers watched public-opinion polls like hawks, especially after Nixon's tape transcripts gambit failed. . . . Never before had the grass roots wanted Nixon out so badly. "Expletive deleted"s and a lot else besides had undermined Nixon to a point that a political indictment and a political trial were now acceptable. . . .

Thirty-eight percent believed Nixon should be impeached at the beginning of May, while 49 percent did not and 13 percent had no opinion. By mid-May, 48 percent wanted Nixon tossed out, 37 percent didn't, and 15 percent weren't sure. At the end of May, 44 percent wanted Nixon removed, 41 percent didn't, and the remainder stayed bemused. Six percent more of the adult population wanted Nixon tried at the end of May than at its start. Six percent more also believed that Nixon was guilty of crimes unbecoming a president, 9 percent ceased their opposition to trying Nixon, and 8 percent ceased opposing his impeachment. The release of the tapes had backfired. Millions of Americans had believed the president when he'd stated repeatedly that he hadn't been involved in Watergate at *all*. Nixon might be a dupe, but they didn't think of him as a liar or crook. Even with excisions, however, the White House tapes showed that Nixon *had* been involved. Sloughing everything off on bad advisers like John Dean no longer worked: the question was no longer whether Nixon was involved, but how involved he was. . . .

[Finally, on July 24th, 1974,] it was the Supreme Court's turn to make political determinations. This it did by deciding by a vote of 8 to 0 (one justice excusing himself) that Nixon must obey the subpoenas obtained by the special prosecutor for more Watergate tapes. Both the judicial trial and the political trial of the Watergate case, the judges had decided, required the best evidence available. The justices made a political decision that removed most of the final executive privilege and national security barriers to the impeachment trial. The power circle ringing Richard Milhous Nixon had finally closed—a year after the existence of the White House tapes had first become known.

No one recognized this better than the men and women of the House Judiciary Committee. Once the Court ruled unanimously against a president who had appointed four of its members, including Chief Justice Warren Burger, Nixon had few political friends left. Within hours, southern Democrats and moderate Republicans on the committee met to determine strategies for the impeachment debates that began the same evening.

## THE JUDICIARY COMMITTEE DECIDES

What followed focused the country's attention as nothing about Watergate had before. Not even the Senate Watergate Committee hearings of the summer of 1973 became an instantaneous folk event the way the week-long House Judiciary Committee debates and votes on five separate impeachment articles did. Via live television and radio, interested citizens were symbolically and actually admitted into the elite regions of their political order. In the process, it was easy— even natural—for tens of millions of people to think of themselves, too, as members of the political grand jury debating and deciding the issues before them.

Realities were otherwise, and very much went on behind the scenes, but Watergate was visible as it had never been before. The fundamental question the House Judiciary Committee had to decide was whether Richard Nixon still deserved to lead. The audience knew that, whether they had ever read the Constitution or not, or whether they knew much about the nuances of the many different aspects of the case. Everyone—audience and participants—was a part of history now. This vote mattered.

Rarely before had members of Congress played to such a large, diverse, and involved national audience. The experience was heady and intimidating. Fundamental issues of political power and privilege were very clearly at issue. The thirty-eight committee members at the center of the national stage worried, therefore. They would not have been human—or politically successful—if they had not. Sandwiched between an opening speech by Democrat Committee Chair Peter Rodino of New Jersey and a closing speech by ranking committee Republican Edward Hutchinson of Michigan, all the members—Democrat and Republican alternating—were given fifteen minutes to make an opening statement of their views on the overall case for or against Richard M. Nixon.

Nine and one-half hours of speechifying by thirty-eight people could have induced yawns or worse, but it didn't. For, in giving each member a quarter-hour before the cameras, the Judiciary Committee made itself known to a national audience for the first time. The committee became less of an abstract whole and much more a collection of individuals arguing different views in differing ways. Moreover, the opening statements were, in effect, a poll of a political grand jury, and the tens of millions in the television and radio audiences, listening to the general arguments for and against, could more easily understand and identify with the process of judgement.

The audience was also a jury, of course, one which would soon deliver electoral judgements on all of the assembled members of Congress. So all the committee's members did their best to couch their opening statements in fashions which would best make their case and best reflect upon their motives in arguing as they did. They sought to involve their electorates on their behalf. The president's opponents provided long sequences of details about his involvement in the cover-up. The president's defenders countered that the committee's Democratic majority was mostly engaged in a partisan vendetta using a "grab bag of allegations.". . .

The process was full of last-minute fits and starts. After the nine-and-one-half hours of nationally televised opening statements were completed on the evening of July 25th, Nixon's defenders on the House Judiciary Committee knew they didn't have the votes to stop the committee from voting out some impeachment charges. Representative Charles Sandman of New Jersey said as much near the start of the proceedings, but by their conclusion, the numbers were clear. The twenty-one Democratic members all intended to charge Nixon with something and six of the seventeen Republicans were off the reservation. Three were leaning strongly toward indictment, and another three (Cohen of Maine, Hogan of Maryland, and Railsback of Illinois) were definitely going to vote to indict.

At long last, the Democrats had the bipartisan alliance they had been trying to create for more than six months. The eleven Republicans who intended to vote against any and all charges hadn't convinced a single Democrat that Nixon had done nothing wrong, but the president's defenders did not lack for political energy. They intensified their efforts to make whatever charges were brought as innocuous and narrowly drawn as possible. As so often before, Nixon's defenders were arguing that the president should enjoy every conceivable benefit of a criminal justice system he had repeatedly flouted. With the last act in the Watergate drama about to be played, Nixon's congressional supporters kept on defending him.

They were not fools, these people. They mixed ideals with self-interest, just as their opponents did. Regarding interests, most feared that the Republican Party would be branded as the "party of Watergate" for as long as the Democrats could get away with it and that this political equation would cost the G.O.P. and themselves dearly.

Their ideals enabled them to rationalize and explain their concerns about their political interests and also to express some legitimate indignation. Hypocrisy and double standards were the charges the president's defenders hurled at his attackers, privately and publicly. Nixon was no saint and nobody was arguing that he was. But he hadn't done anything that every recent president before him hadn't also done, and most of these presidents had been Democrats. "Post-Watergate morality" was all very well, but all the Democrats were doing was obscuring their own domestic dirty tricks by blaming Nixon (and, through him, the Republicans) for everything, just as they had earlier done about sins committed in Vietnam.

These charges had substance, enough to make it clearer why Watergate took so long, and why a Democratic Congress was so very often hesitant to proceed quickly or expeditiously to resolve the case. Watergate had evolved out of the Vietnam War and the divisions and fears spawned by it. The politics of fear and discord that Nixon exploited was no peculiar creation of his. He was more its creation than its creator. So it appeared unfair to make Nixon what Democrat John Conyers of Michigan had called him at the start of the House Judiciary Committee's debates: "in a very real sense a casualty of the Vietnam war."

Nixon's defenders also opposed making Nixon a casualty because of his various domestic sins. Lyndon Johnson had been a thief and worse, but the Democratic congressional leaders who had known that hadn't mounted any sort of coup against him. Instead, they had stonewalled Republican efforts to trace millions of dollars in kickbacks and favoritism and misuse of government property and corruption of favored subordinates like Bobby Baker in the White House inner sanctum. Now these same people, joined by journalists and bureaucrats and uppity lawyers and judges, were out to get Nixon. They were mounting a coup because they were "marinated in hatred" for Nixon and all he stood for. So, thinking in this way, it was comparatively easy for some Republican members of Congress to keep fighting for Nixon. Watergate was, in this view, merely a skirmish in a much wider Cold War. If Nixon were denied office because he had mismanaged a skirmish, the nation might lose its war against foreign and domestic radicalism, and America could swiftly return to the bad old days of 1968.

Had Watergate not happened when and how it had, this hypocrisy and double-standard argument of the president's defenders might have had far more force. But popular fears about Vietnam, Black Power, and the New Left were passé in July 1974. Moreover, the White House had blundered far too many times in its efforts to squelch the case. The combination of these two factors removed just enough of the inhibitions within the House Judiciary Committee against charging Nixon with broadly defined political crimes. . . .

The resignation came first. On the morning of August 8th, people learned that Nixon had finally given up. In a televised address to the country at 9 P.M. that evening, Nixon gave his explanation of what had happened. "In all the decisions I have made in my political life," he began, "I have always tried to do what was best for the Nation." Regarding Watergate, Nixon had had a "duty to persevere" to "complete the term of office to which you elected me." But perseverance was no longer possible. Congressional support had eroded to such a point that there was no more point in fighting against what might be a "dangerously destabilizing precedent [impeachment] for the future," much as he "would have preferred to carry through to the finish." "I have never been a quitter. . . But, as President, I must put the interests of America first. America needs a full-time President and a full-time Congress" to deal with pressing national and international problems. Vice President Ford would be president as of noon on August 9th. Ford should be supported because a "process of healing" was "desperately needed in America." Nixon had made wrong judgements and some of these had hurt people, but all he had done had been done for America, not for himself. . . .

Nixon's more revealing statements came later. At 9:30 A.M. on August 9th, Nixon gathered his Cabinet and staff around him for the last time as president. Here, before what remained of his administration, Nixon came as close as he ever did to explaining himself as a human being during the entire twenty-six months of the Watergate struggle. It wasn't a neat performance; such public intimacies rarely are. Nixon mixed gallant gestures, self-justification, hope, and anger in about equal proportions. . . .

Nixon was leaving the presidency, but not disappearing from political life. A defeat was not an end. "It is only a beginning always." Only those who have "been in the deepest valley can . . . even know how magnificent it is to be on the highest mountain." Every one in government should remember this. They also needed to realize something else, Nixon added as he closed: "Always give your best, never get discouraged, never get petty; always remember, others may hate you; but those who hate you don't win unless you hate them, and then you destroy yourself."

There, finally, amidst tears and the more hard-eyed emotions, was the distilled personalized wisdom of the Watergate case. Nixon had hated well and excessively. That hate, in turn, had destroyed him. Minutes later, Richard Nixon and his family left the White House for a plane trip home to San Clemente, California, on a presidential aircraft named the Spirit of '76. In flight, shortly after noon on August 9th, 1974, Nixon's presidency ended.

# Taken Hostage

## David Farber

*The only major historical account of the seventies to appear before the year 2000 was titled* It Seemed Like Nothing Happened. *But our perception of history changes as events unfold, and after the terrorist attacks on the United States on September 11, 2001, the events of the 1970s came into a different focus. We look back to the OPEC oil embargo of 1973–74 as a critical moment. Access to oil would henceforth play a critical role in America's foreign policy. Skyrocketing oil prices helped shift economic wealth and power—as well as population and resulting political might—from the Rust Belt of the Midwest and Northeast to the rapidly growing Sun Belt in the South and West. The seventies saw the end of virtually guaranteed upward mobility; average weekly earnings (adjusted for inflation) peaked in 1973. In the decades that followed, the divide between the richer and the poorer grew. And finally, the Iranian hostage crisis no longer seems simply a difficult but isolated episode in the nation's history. Instead, it must be woven into a longer and more complex story about oil, U.S. relations with Muslim nations in the Middle East, and the significance of political Islam.*

*In the following excerpt from* Taken Hostage, *historian David Farber explains how hard times in the seventies made it difficult for either President Jimmy Carter or the American people to meet the challenge of an Islamic revolution in Iran.*

In the 1970s, Americans too often felt that they faced nothing but bad choices. It was not one of those *Tale of Two Cities* eras, like the 1960s, with its "best of times," "worst of times." Especially in the last years of the decade, it was mainly just hard times. Events lent themselves to a litany of despair: inflation up, employment down; oil prices out of control, American-made automobiles breaking down; factories closed, marriages over, homicide rates soaring; President Gerald Ford. A band of snarling British musicians made a trans-Atlantic name for themselves singing in 1977, "No future for you, no future for me." By the late 1970s, industrial workers, home buyers, grocery shoppers, factory owners, store-keepers, and young people looking for their first real jobs were treading water, trying to find their way to a distant shoreline. While they struggled for direction, an unlikely leader named Jimmy Carter had an uneasy hold on the ship of state.

In 1976, after a parade of disasters—Watergate, the fall of Saigon, President Ford's pathetically ineffective Whip Inflation Now campaign—the former one-term Georgia governor, Jimmy Carter, had surprised everyone but himself by becoming president of the United States. In Democratic primaries and then in the general election he'd won voters to his side by telling them again and again: "I'll never lie to you." Just a couple of years after Richard Nixon ("I am not a crook") had been forced to resign from the presidency, personal honesty seemed the stuff of presidential heroism. Carter combined his campaign promises with an unbroken record of never having served the United States in any position of national leadership. In an era that had seen traditional leaders and established authorities lose much of their credibility, Carter's "outsider" candidacy won the day.

Though relatively untested, President Carter, not surprisingly, was a man of many gifts. He would never have risen so far and so fast without them. His modesty veiled a rapier sharp intelligence. His decency was as deep as his Baptist faith. Though fiercely ambitious, he was also incorruptible and incontestably dedicated to serving the people of the United States. If a measure of integrity, tenacity, discipline, and IQ points added up to presidential greatness, then Jimmy Carter would have been one of America's most extraordinary leaders.

Alas, in the game of presidential leadership, brainpower and character usually count for less than political skill. And in the latter category, Carter was no genius. . . . [And] " President Carter, during his one term in office, would face events through "time and chance" that allowed for no easy answer and, too often, for no solution at all.

The fall of the Shah of Iran and the subsequent taking of American hostages at the U.S. embassy in Tehran by followers of the Islamic fundamentalist Ayatollah Ruhollah Khomeini, on top of and in the midst of many other national difficulties, was President Carter's most agonizing problem. In his memoirs, Carter blamed the 444-day-long hostage crisis for destroying his chances of winning a second term in office. For tens of millions of Americans, the 1979–1981 hostage crisis marked the spectacular failure of the Carter administration. Worse, it hammered home how far the American nation had fallen in the 1970s. Neither the president nor the American people knew that the fierce conflict between Iranian revolutionaries and the American government was just the first, relatively distant skirmish in America's ongoing struggle to resolve its differences with the Islamic world.

For Americans, the Iran hostage crisis came suddenly, claiming attention in the midst of all the other worries of a difficult decade. The first media reports were sketchy. On the morning of November 4, 1979, a mob rallied outside the American embassy in Tehran. There were thousands of people; they appeared to be students, mostly men but women, too. The women were in black, shrouded in chador. A small group cut the thick chain that secured the main gates and filed into the twenty-seven-acre embassy compound. Hundreds, then thousands, followed them, swarming over the eight-foot fence that guarded the embassy grounds. Iranian police, supposedly there to protect the American property, offered no resistance, called for no assistance, and received no support from other Iranian security forces. Compared to its heyday just a year earlier, the embassy was nearly deserted. And the few dozen U.S. embassy personnel who were still there were no match for the angry mob. They were grabbed and blindfolded. Their captors tied their hands behind their back. The 444 days of captivity had begun.

Americans watched the first news reports with indignation, as day after day the nightly news showed pictures of angry mobs at the U.S. embassy, waving crude anti-American placards and shouting anti-American slogans. The hostage-taking was an open wound on the American body politic and the press, politicians, and the American people could not leave it alone.

Walter Cronkite, anchor of the *CBS Evening News* and the most trusted man in American broadcasting, brought almost ritual quality to the passing days. . . . Night after night, until the 444th night when the hostages were at last freed, Walter Cronkite counted the days of America's humiliation, feeding Americans' angry preoccupation with the Iranian hostage-takers and their captives.

While November 4, 1979, marked the beginning of the crisis for America, Iranians (at least those who cheered on the takeover) saw it differently; they would choose other days to mark the beginning of all that followed. The student militants who took the embassy insisted that the crisis began on October 23, 1979. That was the day the American president allowed the deposed Shah of Iran, a man these militants saw as corrupt and evil, to seek sanctuary in the United States. "By allowing the shah to enter the U.S. the Americans have started a new conspiracy against the revolution," said one of these young militants in the days leading up to the embassy takeover. "If we don't act rapidly, if we show weakness, then a superpower like the U.S. will be able to meddle in the internal affairs of any nation." The takeover, said the militants, was the second act of the drama, a defensive act to protect the Iranian revolution from American interference.

Following this model of causality, Iranians also pointed much further back. The crisis really began, the student militants explained to the world's media, on August 19, 1953. On that day the Iranian government of Muhammad Mossadegh, the Soviet-friendly, nationalist prime minister, was overthrown. Muhammad Reza Pahlavi, the Shah of Shahs, regained control of Iran. Operation Ajax, as it was known, had been approved by President Eisenhower and smartly directed by Kermit Roosevelt of the relatively new American Central Intelligence Agency (and grandson of President Theodore Roosevelt). Old hands at the British Secret Intelligence Service assisted where they could. According to the militants' logic, the U.S. embassy, from 1953 through November 1979, was not the home of American officials correctly pursuing proper missions of diplomacy. It was, as they said again and again, "a nest of spies" whose intelligence agents must be stopped before they plotted another coup against Iranian self-determination. . . .

Each of these beginnings—and others, as well—suggests a particular historical trajectory, a different set of "what-if" questions, a specific political or ideological focus. Each reveals its own truths or half-truths. Nonetheless, the meaning and impact of the hostage crisis in the United States cannot be reduced to the events of any one day, . . . or even the bilateral history of Iran and America.

Americans perceived the outrageous treatment of their countrymen at the hands of Iranian Islamic fundamentalists as a national crisis because they believed that the United States, at the end of the 1970s, was already a nation in crisis. The American captives in Iran became a living symbol and a pointed daily reminder of what had gone wrong in the United States. . . . Without a feel for the causes and character of what some then called America's national "malaise,"

Americans' angry preoccupation with the hostage crisis cannot be understood.

Given the bad name the 1970s have in most pop histories of the recent American past, it is worth at least noting that life in post-Watergate America was not all bad clothes, bad hair, and bad times. Compared to almost any other nation in the world, much was still very right about the United States in the fall of 1979. Plenty of people around the world looked with envy at Americans' standard of living, the nation's cultural vitality, and the recent progress American society had made in rectifying some of its more obvious flaws. It does no interpretative good to paint too overly bleak a picture of the 1970s in order to set off the angry hues of the hostage crisis. That said, Americans had plenty in the 1970s about which to complain.

In the 1970s, almost every certainty Americans brought to their everyday lives was up for grabs. Economic expectations were upended. America's global role was under fire. Culture wars were breaking out at school board meetings and around dining room tables. The president committed felonies, children smoked marijuana, men wore gaudy jewelry around their necks, and communist Chinese pandas were the star attraction at the National Zoo.

In the 1970s Americans began to work out the practical legacy of the radical mass movements and the liberal federal legislation of the 1960s. It was not easy. In most regards, the fireworks were over: nobody was going to sic German Shepherds on little black children seeking a modicum of social justice; white politicians were not going to stand in schoolhouse doors screaming racial epithets; and women had the legal right to equal treatment in the workplace. But no consensus had emerged in the United States about how to implement all the new laws or how far to carry the vaguely accepted new ideals of tolerance and inclusivity. What should equality before the law mean? Affirmative action? School busing? Was Black Power just a discredited slogan or a new political agenda? From whom and what should women be liberated? All women? Who else got a place at the table where decisions were made and resources allocated? Above all, these changes in the 1970s were personal; they affected people's families, their workplaces, their churches, their schools, and their intimate lives. Depending on your point of view, the cultural and political changes were exhilarating, unsettling, or frightening.

In the 1970s, building on the grassroots activism, liberal federal legislation, and the countercultural movements of the prior twenty years, Americans had made stunning progress in bringing to life ideals of civic inclusivity, economic opportunity, and cultural diversity. It was good news for some; it was disquieting or even infuriating to others. At a minimum, in the 1970s no one could declare (as so many had done in the 1950s) that the nation enjoyed a calm, confident cultural consensus.

Similarly, the cold war ideological unity that had ruled American foreign policy from the Truman administration onward had broken apart. America's failed war in Vietnam had, obviously, done much to break the ideological spell of anti-communism. John Kennedy's thrilling certainties—"we shall bear any burden, pay any price" to defeat global communism—had died with America's failed commitment to Vietnam. In 1975, Americans watched in horror and embarrassment shocking images of Americans fleeing Saigon on overloaded helicopters, beating off terrified South Vietnamese allies, just moments before the city fell to communist forces. The "victory culture" that had emerged out of World War II and the first two decades of America's cold war battle against the Soviet Union and international communism was largely discredited. Pundits described a "Vietnam syndrome": defeat haunted America and made Americans across the political spectrum loathe to make strong international commitments to anyone.

In the early 1970s, President Richard Nixon and his key advisor, Henry Kissinger, had tried, with cunning and brilliance, to replace simple anti-communism with a more pragmatic realpolitik. Disregarding all pretenses of operating American foreign policy on the basis of morality, Nixon had embraced anyone in the world who gave the United States even short-term advantages. Thus, Nixon sidled up to racist regimes in Rhodesia and South Africa (though support was later tempered when events changed). Nixon further demonstrated his flexibility by seeking a measure of cooperation with the Soviet Union and opening up relations with the long despised and unrecognized communist government of mainland China. Nixon built American foreign policy on issues of expediency and narrowly cast national self-interest. . . .

In 1974, at the tail end of the scandal-ridden Nixon presidency, investigative journalist Seymour Hersh revealed that the CIA, at Nixon's bidding, had helped overthrow the legally elected Chilean government and had, as well, engaged in numerous illegalities in the United States. Idaho Senator Frank Church followed up Hersh's reporting with a Senate investigation that revealed decades of CIA involvement in coups and covert operations against numerous foreign governments, including those of Guatemala, Ecuador, Cuba, Indonesia, and, of course, Iran. While radicals in the United States and around the world had long decried such CIA involvements, few Americans had ever heard their charges and most of those that had felt confident in dismissing them as communist propaganda. The charges were all true. Liberals, as well as many conservatives, were shocked. What was America's role in the world? Was it the defender of democracy and freedom, fighting against the tyranny of communism? Or was it just another underhanded nation that sought advantage wherever it could, however it might? The combined force of the "Vietnam syndrome," Nixon's nasty, if usually effective, *realpolitik*, and the revelations about CIA covert operations around the world left many Americans with a bad taste in their mouths. The uncertain role of the United States in the world did not have the same immediacy for most Americans as did the more pressing concerns of the culture wars and domestic politics, but it was one more haunting problem with no obvious solution.

While America's uncertain role in the world was disquieting and the often harsh and divisive struggles over equality, inclusivity, and cultural standards were a part of the atmospherics, affecting how Americans responded to the Iranian hostage crisis, Americans in every income bracket in the late 1970s were far more anxious about economic issues. Here is where the larger crisis in American society lay. In America, people had come to expect that each generation would do better than the one that preceded it. The economic pie was supposed to increase every year so that everyone's piece of the American dream got at least a little bigger. But in the 1970s the dream looked like a fool's fantasy. The economy wasn't working. Prices were increasing, income was stagnating, personal debt was exploding, foreign goods were flooding the American marketplace, and third-world nations had organized cartels to put the squeeze on the United States. Americans looked outward at their newly fierce economic competitors like Japan and Germany and at the evermore powerful petroleum exporting countries such as Saudi Arabia, Kuwait, Iraq, and Iran with escalating fears and simmering hostility. More than anything, Americans felt betrayed by the nation's economic reversals.

Even here, however, it's imperative to see the totality of the picture. In 1979 the United States was a very wealthy nation. Nobody outside the nation's borders looked at America with pity. Throughout the 1970s, even during the periods of economic downturn, America's extraordinary wage scale drew in immigrants from around the world, especially those from nations just south of the United States. At the end of the decade, U.S. households ranked in the bottom 20 percent had an average annual income of $15,374, more money than the richest 20 percent earned in all but a few countries in the world. From 1969 to 1979 the percentage of people in poverty declined in the United States, the number of Americans who went to college increased, the percentage who owned automobiles rose, and life expectancy lengthened. By world scales and historic comparisons, America was—as a nation—doing extraordinarily well. And with the great benefit of hindsight, we know today that in the two decades that followed the Iran hostage crisis American wealth would, with a hitch or two, explode upward, blowing ahead of even the most optimistic projections of 1970s era economists, pundits, and campaigning politicians.

Of course, such long-term trends about aggregate national wealth and a few cherry-picked statistics tell little about how it felt to be an American in 1979 and 1980. After the long economic boom of the postwar years, roughly 1945 to 1971, the 1970s (and, in fact, even more so the early 1980s) were a period of slow or negative growth. Wages were stuck throughout most of the late 1970s and sharply declined in the election year of 1980. Working-class Americans were particularly hard hit. Under intense pressure from international competition, factories closed in the Northeast and Midwest, "dislocating," as the jargon of the times put it, hundreds of thousands of industrial, unionized workers and producing a downward economic spiral that affected millions of Americans and crushed numerous communities. In Youngstown, Ohio, so many people were out of work that the town had been forced to close the decaying bridges over the Mahoning River because there was no money to fix them. In Aurora, Minnesota, a town dependent on mining the iron ore no longer needed to feed America's dying steel industry, people desperately tried to sell their houses so they could start over somewhere else—but there were no takers. The American dream of owning one's own home had become, in Aurora, a millstone around the necks of desperate people. Those companies that fled high-wage, regulatory-oriented states like Michigan, Pennsylvania, Ohio, and New Jersey and reopened their plants in the South and the West almost always paid lower wages with fewer benefits to a non-unionized workforce. The movement and growth of businesses into what came to be called the "Sunbelt" contributed to a sharp reduction of Southern poverty (the South was the poorest region in the nation), but the Northeast, in turn, saw its poverty rates creep upward and unemployment boom.

Even in those parts of the nation that did well in the late 1970s, such as oil-producing Texas, uncertainty and even a certain pessimism about the economic future shadowed most American homes. In the 1970s, America was becoming a different kind of economic nation. People talked about the rise of a "service economy." So called "Rust-Belt" industries like steel making, appliance manufacturing, and textiles, which had long been at the heart of the American economy, were hemorrhaging jobs. While new hi-tech companies that would eventually lead to economic renaissance were starting up in the late 1970s, few Americans saw their potential and they employed a relative handful of people. Almost nobody knew what was next. Even people with good jobs were scared. By the end of the decade only 12 percent of Americans told pollsters that they were satisfied with the "state of the country"; 84 percent grimly stated that they were dissatisfied.

Two seemingly intractable problems fueled people's economic distress. The first was an unrelenting inflationary spiral that had begun at the tail end of the 1960s. Prices in the 1970s skyrocketed. The cost of the humble hamburger more than doubled; the price of coffee more than tripled. In a country used to cheap food it was like a slap in the face. With prices sometimes jumping more than 15 percent a year, the cost of credit raced to stay ahead of the declining buying power of the dollar. By the end of the decade interest rates for home mortgages and car loans hit 17 percent. That meant that the monthly payment on a thirty-year $100,000 home mortgage was $1,425 and the total amount in interest the holder of that mortgage would pay the bank by the time he or she owned that house free and clear was $413,243. A generation earlier people had paid as little as $421 a month on the same $100,000 mortgage, with a total of only $51,177 in interest over the course of the loan. Millions of people couldn't afford home mortgages in the 1970s.

Young people's dreams of becoming home owners were crushed; elderly people on fixed incomes watched their standard of living decline month in and month out; and people who needed to borrow money to invest in new businesses that could provide work for the growing number of unemployed were stopped in their tracks by sky-high loan rates.

The causes of inflation were complicated. Economists argued with each other about its primary causes, but most agreed that inflation had been unleashed when President Lyndon Johnson had pushed the federal budget into deficit by insisting on "guns and butter"—an expensive war in Vietnam and expansive social programs—without a balancing tax hike. And there was no doubt that Nixon had made the problem worse by refusing to make unpopular budget cuts and by not pushing for a tight monetary policy that would have slowed down the economy and, thereby, reduce price and wage increases.

Other factors played in: Americans were buying huge quantities of foreign-made goods, which meant that they were sending more and more dollars overseas, creating in 1971 (and then for most of the rest of the decade), for the first time since the late nineteenth century, a trade deficit. And because corporate America refused to invest sufficiently in new technology and facilities, productivity (the measure of output per worker) was on the decline, even as wages (slowly) increased. . . . Most economists were perplexed: price inflation was not supposed to occur when economic growth was slow or negative. A new term, "stagflation," was coined to describe the arresting phenomenon. . . . When Iranian militants grabbed American hostages in Tehran, inflation in the United States was racing along at a 17 percent annual rate.

Inflation and its evil cousin, stagflation, were bad enough. Just as destructive to the national spirit was the energy crisis that both contributed to the inflationary spiral and exacerbated Americans' sense that they had lost control of their national economic destiny to foreigners who competed unfairly and conspired against them. And while language about conspiracies sounds suspiciously like a kind of paranoia, in the 1970s conspiracy-spouting Americans were not exhibiting signs of stress-induced mental instability. They were right.

Spiking oil prices and gasoline shortages plagued the United States in the 1970s. This crisis had a villain Americans could identify: the Organization of the Petroleum Exporting Countries, better known as OPEC. Iran was in the thick of what many Americans considered this den of thieves.

Americans' exuberant use of cheap petroleum had helped fuel the fantastic economic growth of the post–World War II years. The great land yachts of the late 1950s and early 1960s, gaudily tail finned, chromed, and 1,000 pounds heavier than they had been just a decade earlier, symbolized American prosperity. They also exacerbated

Americans' great and growing dependence on refined oil. The average family auto in the early 1960s got about 12 miles per gallon of gas; by 1973 Americans had put a man on the moon but passenger cars averaged only 13.4 miles to the gallon. Gasoline consumption in the United States more than doubled between 1950 and 1970. By 1979 Americans, constituting less than 6 percent of the world's population, sucked up almost 30% of the world's oil production. As American oil demand increased, more and more of the petroleum Americans needed was imported. In 1969, the United States was still a net exporter of oil. By 1970 the scale had tipped, and between January 1973 and January 1977 alone, oil imports had shot up from 35 percent to 50 percent of domestic consumption. In large part, until the 1970s Americans could afford to ignore their growing oil habit because oil was so cheap that profligate use caused no pain. In January 1971 a barrel of oil imported from Saudi Arabia cost all of $1.80.

The first oil crisis came in October 1973 at the tail end of the Israeli-Arab Yom Kippur War. Arab nations launched an oil embargo to punish the United States for providing Israel, hard-pressed by Egyptian and Syrian forces, with military equipment in the middle of the conflict. By year's end the price of a barrel of oil had risen to $12. President Nixon had called for voluntary rationing and limited sales at gas stations. Instead, nervous car owners lined up at the pumps to "top off" their gas tanks in case supplies dried up. The "oil panic" temporarily tripled the price of gasoline, sending prices from around thirty-four cents a gallon to over a dollar, compounding inflationary pressures. Government attempts to address the exploding costs and shortages seemed only to make things worse. By February 1974, motorists in some states routinely waited in line two or three hours to fill their tanks. Fights broke out in gas station lines. Truck drivers, angry over poorly handled emergency gas rationing, struck.

Americans did make some half-hearted responses to the soaring price of oil. For a while at least, Americans began buying more fuel-efficient Japanese-made cars: little, boxy Toyotas and Datsuns. (This helped with energy consumption and saved money for individual drivers. However, rising purchases of foreign-made cars worsened the trade deficit and hurt the American auto industry, which was vital to the American economy.) Responding to the crisis, Congress mandated that car manufacturers make more energy-efficient autos and passed the 1974 Emergency Highway Energy Conservation Act, which set a maximum national highway speed limit of fifty-five miles per hour. In general, Americans felt like they had lost what many considered their birthright: cheap gas, high speeds, and plush rides. The Arab nations that led OPEC—Saudi Arabia, Kuwait, and Iraq—took great satisfaction in their successful action. OPEC had been founded in the early 1960s but had, up until 1973, failed in lining up member nations to act as a price-setting cartel. Their anger at the United States for aiding Israel, however, had unified them. And the embargo proved how vulnerable the industrialized nations of the world were to the oil producers. OPEC was, suddenly, a force in the world. The oil-consuming nations would have to meet the cartel's price. The Shah of Iran, though not directly involved in the decision to embargo oil, did take pleasure in admonishing the United States and other energy guzzling nations: "The industrial world will have to realize that the era of their terrific progress and even more terrific income and wealth based on cheap fuel is finished. They will have to find new sources of energy and tighten their belts." The OPEC nations had learned how to run a cartel and Americans could only watch, seething with resentment.

Between the spring of 1974 and the last days of 1977, OPEC successfully stabilized oil prices at record levels. Americans, rather than radically overhaul their energy patterns, essentially accepted the new terms. Americans spent three times as much as they once had on gasoline, heating oil, and other petroleum products—sending billions of dollars to the oil-producing nations. (Of course, many billions of dollars simply moved within the United States from non-oil-producing regions to those states, such as Texas and Oklahoma, blessed with the "black gold.") . . . The high cost of energy and the gleeful avarice of oil producers, both foreign and domestic, were, in the middle 1970s, just two more indignities most Americans felt forced to accept. People were angry but they also felt impotent.

Given Americans' grumpy resignation about the situation, Jimmy Carter had not headlined energy issues when he ran for the presidency in 1976. However, after being elected but even before taking office, Carter was confronted by another kind of energy shortage— this time natural gas—and he decided to put America's dependence on imported oil and its wasteful energy habits at the top of his White House agenda.

Carter, in his inaugural address, had hinted at a new spirit of sacrifice. In the best remembered passages of the somewhat lack-luster speech he suggested: "We have learned that 'more' is not necessarily 'better,' that even our great Nation has its recognized limits, and that we can neither answer all questions nor solve all problems. We cannot afford to do everything, nor can we afford to lack boldness as we meet the future. So, together, in a spirit of individual sacrifice for the common good, we must simply do our best." These honest but not particularly inspiring words set the tone for the Carter presidency. They were a far cry from John Kennedy's limitless New Frontier or Lyndon Johnson's passionate Great Society. America had entered a new era and it took an unusual kind of American to feel good about it.

# The "Crisis of Confidence" Speech: President Carter's Address to the Nation (1979)

*Jimmy Carter*

*At the end of a difficult decade, President Jimmy Carter did something American presidents rarely do. He spoke what he saw as hard truths to the American people, and he called for shared sacrifice. In particular, Carter pointed out that Americans' profligate use of oil made America dependent on foreign suppliers and so endangered American economic stability. America's dependence on oil from OPEC producers thus played a too powerful role in shaping the nation's international policies and practices.*

Good evening. This is a special night for me. Exactly three years ago, on July 15, 1976, I accepted the nomination of my party to run for president of the United States.

I promised you a president who is not isolated from the people, who feels your pain, and who shares your dreams and who draws his strength and his wisdom from you.

During the past three years I've spoken to you on many occasions about national concerns, the energy crisis, reorganizing the government, our nation's economy, and issues of war and especially peace. But over those years the subjects of the speeches, the talks, and the press conferences have become increasingly narrow, focused more and more on what the isolated world of Washington thinks is important. Gradually, you've heard more and more about what the government thinks or what the government should be doing and less and less about our nation's hopes, our dreams, and our vision of the future.

Ten days ago I had planned to speak to you again about a very important subject—energy. For the fifth time I would have described the urgency of the problem and laid out a series of legislative recommendations to the Congress. But as I was preparing to speak, I began to ask myself the same question that I now know has been troubling many of you. Why have we not been able to get together as a nation to resolve our serious energy problem?

It's clear that the true problems of our Nation are much deeper— deeper than gasoline lines or energy shortages, deeper even than inflation or recession. And I realize more than ever that as president I need your help. So I decided to reach out and listen to the voices of America.

I invited to Camp David people from almost every segment of our society—business and labor, teachers and preachers, governors, mayors, and private citizens. And then I left Camp David to listen to other Americans, men and women like you.

It has been an extraordinary ten days, and I want to share with you what I've heard. First of all, I got a lot of personal advice. Let me quote a few of the typical comments that I wrote down.

This from a southern governor: "Mr. President, you are not leading this nation—you're just managing the government."

"You don't see the people enough any more."

"Some of your Cabinet members don't seem loyal. There is not enough discipline among your disciples."

"Don't talk to us about politics or the mechanics of government, but about an understanding of our common good."

"Mr. President, we're in trouble. Talk to us about blood and sweat and tears."

"If you lead, Mr. President, we will follow."

Many people talked about themselves and about the condition of our nation.

This from a young woman in Pennsylvania: "I feel so far from government. I feel like ordinary people are excluded from political power."

And this from a young Chicano: "Some of us have suffered from recession all our lives."

"Some people have wasted energy, but others haven't had anything to waste."

And this from a religious leader: "No material shortage can touch the important things like God's love for us or our love for one another."

And I like this one particularly from a black woman who happens to be the mayor of a small Mississippi town: "The big-shots are not the only ones who are important. Remember, you can't sell anything on Wall Street unless someone digs it up somewhere else first."

This kind of summarized a lot of other statements: "Mr. President, we are confronted with a moral and a spiritual crisis."

Several of our discussions were on energy, and I have a notebook full of comments and advice. I'll read just a few.

"We can't go on consuming 40 percent more energy than we produce. When we import oil we are also importing inflation plus unemployment."

"We've got to use what we have. The Middle East has only five percent of the world's energy, but the United States has 24 percent."

And this is one of the most vivid statements: "Our neck is stretched over the fence and OPEC has a knife."

"There will be other cartels and other shortages. American wisdom and courage right now can set a path to follow in the future."

This was a good one: "Be bold, Mr. President. We may make mistakes, but we are ready to experiment."

And this one from a labor leader got to the heart of it: "The real issue is freedom. We must deal with the energy problem on a war footing."

And the last that I'll read: "When we enter the moral equivalent of war, Mr. President, don't issue us BB guns."

These ten days confirmed my belief in the decency and the strength and the wisdom of the American people, but it also bore out some of my long-standing concerns about our nation's underlying problems.

I know, of course, being president, that government actions and legislation can be very important. That's why I've worked hard to put my campaign promises into law—and I have to admit, with just mixed success. But after listening to the American people I have been reminded again that all the legislation in the world can't fix what's wrong with America. So, I want to speak to you first tonight about a subject even more serious than energy or inflation. I want to talk to you right now about a fundamental threat to American democracy.

I do not mean our political and civil liberties. They will endure. And I do not refer to the outward strength of America, a nation that is at peace tonight everywhere in the world, with unmatched economic power and military might.

The threat is nearly invisible in ordinary ways. It is a crisis of confidence. It is a crisis that strikes at the very heart and soul and spirit of our national will. We can see this crisis in the growing doubt about the meaning of our own lives and in the loss of a unity of purpose for our nation.

The erosion of our confidence in the future is threatening to destroy the social and the political fabric of America.

The confidence that we have always had as a people is not simply some romantic dream or a proverb in a dusty book that we read just on the Fourth of July.

It is the idea which founded our nation and has guided our development as a people. Confidence in the future has supported everything else—public institutions and private enterprise, our own families, and the very Constitution of the United States. Confidence has defined our course and has served as a link between generations. We've always believed in something called progress. We've always had a faith that the days of our children would be better than our own.

Our people are losing that faith, not only in government itself but in the ability as citizens to serve as the ultimate rulers and shapers of our democracy. As a people we know our past and we are proud of it. Our progress has been part of the living history of America, even the world. We always believed that we were part of a great movement of humanity itself called democracy, involved in the search for freedom, and that belief has always strengthened us in our purpose. But just as we are losing our confidence in the future, we are also beginning to close the door on our past.

In a nation that was proud of hard work, strong families, close-knit communities, and our faith in God, too many of us now tend to worship self-indulgence and consumption. Human identity is no longer defined by what one does, but by what one owns. But we've discovered that owning things and consuming things does not satisfy our longing for meaning. We've learned that piling up material goods cannot fill the emptiness of lives which have no confidence or purpose.

The symptoms of this crisis of the American spirit are all around us. For the first time in the history of our country a majority of our people believe that the next five years will be worse than the past five years. Two-thirds of our people do not even vote. The productivity of American workers is actually dropping, and the willingness of Americans to save for the future has fallen below that of all other people in the Western world.

As you know, there is a growing disrespect for government and for churches and for schools, the news media, and other institutions.

This is not a message of happiness or reassurance, but it is the truth and it is a warning.

These changes did not happen overnight. They've come upon us gradually over the last generation, years that were filled with shocks and tragedy.

We were sure that ours was a nation of the ballot, not the bullet, until the murders of John Kennedy and Robert Kennedy and Martin Luther King, Jr. We were taught that our armies were always invincible and our causes were always just, only to suffer the agony of Vietnam. We respected the presidency as a place of honor until the shock of Watergate.

We remember when the phrase "sound as a dollar" was an expression of absolute dependability, until ten years of inflation began to shrink our dollar and our savings. We believed that our nation's resources were limitless until 1973, when we had to face a growing dependence on foreign oil.

These wounds are still very deep. They have never been healed. Looking for a way out of this crisis, our people have turned to the Federal government and found it isolated from the mainstream of our nation's life. Washington, D.C., has become an island. The gap between our citizens and our government has never been so wide. The people are looking for honest answers, not easy answers; clear leadership, not false claims and evasiveness and politics as usual.

What you see too often in Washington and elsewhere around the country is a system of government that seems incapable of action. You see a Congress twisted and pulled in every direction by hundreds of well-financed and powerful special interests. You see every extreme position defended to the last vote, almost to the last breath by one unyielding group or another. You often see a balanced and a fair approach that demands sacrifice, a little sacrifice from everyone, abandoned like an orphan without support and without friends.

Often you see paralysis and stagnation and drift. You don't like it, and neither do I. What can we do?

First of all, we must face the truth, and then we can change our course. We simply must have faith in each other, faith in our ability to govern ourselves, and faith in the future of this nation. Restoring that faith and that confidence to America is now the most important task we face. It is a true challenge of this generation of Americans. . . .

We are at a turning point in our history. There are two paths to choose. One is a path I've warned about tonight, the path that leads to fragmentation and self-interest. Down that road lies a mistaken idea of freedom, the right to grasp for ourselves some advantage over others. That path would be one of constant conflict between narrow interests ending in chaos and immobility. It is a certain route to failure.

All the traditions of our past, all the lessons of our heritage, all the promises of our future point to another path, the path of common purpose and the restoration of American values. That path leads to true freedom for our nation and ourselves. We can take the first steps down that path as we begin to solve our energy problem.

Energy will be the immediate test of our ability to unite this nation, and it can also be the standard around which we rally. On the battlefield of energy we can win for our nation a new confidence, and we can seize control again of our common destiny.

In little more than two decades we've gone from a position of energy independence to one in which almost half the oil we use comes from foreign countries, at prices that are going through the roof. Our excessive dependence on OPEC has already taken a tremendous toll on our economy and our people. This is the direct cause of the long lines which have made millions of you spend aggravating hours waiting for gasoline. It's a cause of the increased inflation and unemployment that we now face. This intolerable dependence on foreign oil threatens our economic independence and the very security of our nation. The energy crisis is real. It is worldwide. It is a clear and present danger to our nation. These are facts and we simply must face them.

# Misery Index

*During the 1970s, Americans suffered through economic "stagflation": a "stagnant" economy caused high unemployment rates, while inflation spiraled out of control. This chart combines unemployment rates with inflation rates to create an economic "misery index"—one that helps to explain why Jimmy Carter lost his reelection bid in 1980.*

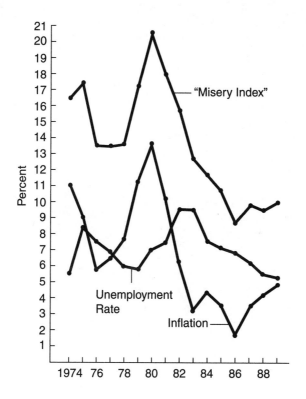

Adapted from Economic Report of the President, 1992 [Washington, D.C., 1992] pp. 340, 365.

# Part 7

## A NEW ERA OF CONSERVATISM

The 1970s and '80s represented the end of one era and the beginning of another. Indeed, the election of Ronald Reagan in 1980 represented the culmination of perhaps the most important development in the years after 1968—the triumph of a new conservatism. Reagan—originally a Hollywood actor—could communicate what he saw as simple vertities. America should be strong. Communism represented a false God and the Soviet Union an "evil empire." Free enterprise worked. And every individual should be responsible for him- or herself. With remarkable skill, the new president pushed through legislation to cut taxes—and social welfare benefits—while dramatically increasing military spending.

Ever since the Cold War began, American politics had been governed by what the British journalist Godfrey Hodgson called "the liberal consensus." It consisted of a series of axioms about America: a) the country and society were fundamentally sound; there was nothing organically or structurally wrong with the nation; b) capitalism was the best economic system in the world; c) democracy was the best political system; d) whatever problems did exist could be handled by incremental reform, e.g., civil rights legislation; e) economic growth was the best way of handling issues like poverty; and f) all of this was anchored and held together by a bipartisan commitment to anticommunism—the Soviet Union was the enemy; all Americans must unite in opposing Russia, and in defending freedom. As a result of the "liberal consensus," dissent against American foreign policy became virtually impossible, since it would mean one was being "soft on communism"; support for "leftist" domestic programs like national health insurance was also difficult because such programs could be associated with "socialism"; and progress on issues such as race or poverty had to be framed as consistent with traditional American values.

In the years after 1968, a new conservatism took over. It built on the economic views of the old right, led by Barry Goldwater—a belief in limited government, a strong military, deregulation of business, and minimal taxation. But starting with the campaign of Richard Nixon in 1968, the new conservatism more and more focused on cultural values. Nixon talked about "law and order," the "silent majority," people who believed in God and family. Adopting a southern strategy of appealing to whites who disapproved of busing and affirmative action, he built a new Republican Party.

In the 1970s, the conservatism that Nixon represented broadened still further, grounded less in free-market or libertarian philosophies and more in the convictions of evangelical, often fundamentalist Christianity. Whether galvanized by opposition to the Equal Rights Amendment, abortion, school busing, homosexuality, or the desire to preserve prayer in the schools, New Right groups added a new dimension to the American political scene. Working-class Americans were now as likely to vote based on their attitudes toward homosexuality or abortion as on their economic interests—hence the growing appeal of Republicans as the party of traditional values. Though America appeared less divided during the 1970s and '80s by protests and police barricades, a deeper division began to appear in the society—one that came to be described as the "culture wars." On the one side were the more cosmopolitan, sophisticated elites; on the other, the former bedrock of the Democratic Party, those who represented "middle America" and believed in family and religious values. As a result, the balance of national politics shifted.

The following articles and documents address this move toward conservatism. Dan Carter assesses how Governor George Wallace successfully moved his narrow, Alabama-based racist politics to a national stage, all the while leaving issues associated with race as a primary focus. Lisa McGirr discusses the broader trends in conservatism over this period, and especially the development of a broad coalition of forces from suburbia to evangelical fundamentalists. E. J. Dionne, Jr., analyzes the rise of the New Right and its connection to religious groups like Jerry Falwell's "Moral Majority." And William Berman assesses the economic context within which this all occurred. Ronald Reagan's 1985 State of the Union address illustrates the ideas and the optimism of the "Reagan Revolution," while Newt Gingrich's "Contract with America" shows how a resurgent political conservatism spiked in the early 1990s.

The questions that emerge from this section are ones that still remain with us. How can we function as a national community if we are divided by fundamental conflicts over social values? What role do race, religion, and issues of sexuality and gender play in our national politics? What role should they play? And how is it possible for either or both parties to embody values that most Americans will embrace, and at the same time advance political programs that offer different options to the American people?

# The Politics of Anger, 1963–1968

*Dan Carter*

*In the evolving strength of a grassroots conservative movement in America during the 1960s and '70s, race played a crucial role. With an instinctive sense of how to exploit a volatile issue, George Wallace, elected governor of Alabama in 1962, quickly seized on the quest of black Americans for freedom to create a politics of white resentment. Delivering on his earlier promise "never again to be outniggered" by a white politician, Wallace first solidified a base of those white southerners discomforted by black strides toward freedom, then carried his message of speaking on behalf of "common" white people to northern cities and states. "You know," he once told a political associate, "the whole country is southern."*

*By 1968, Wallace had become a viable third-party candidate, threatening to win numerous southern states and up to 20 percent of the national vote. Although his choice of General Curtis LeMay as his vice presidential candidate—LeMay wanted to "nuke" the Vietnamese and give field commanders authorization to use atomic weapons—eroded his base of support, Wallace succeeded in becoming a national voice for those who stood for traditional values, opposed black militancy, and rejected the liberalism of the "northeastern establishment" and the radicalism of hippies and the counterculture. Even after an assassination attempt in 1972 that left him confined to a wheelchair, Wallace continued to galvanize white support across the nation for new and more vibrant conservative movement.*

*In the following article, Dan Carter of the University of South Carolina traces the pivotal role played by Wallace in shaping the agenda of the new conservatism. Carter demonstrates the ways in which Wallace utilized the growing religious right for his own purposes, connected to those upset by liberal decisions of the Supreme Court, and came to speak for a coalition of nationalist and traditionalist groups. Some questions raised by his article include: how did Wallace succeed in translating his bare-bones Alabama racism into a national issue; what explains the links between religious groups, anti-ERA*

From *George Wallace to Newt Gingrich: Race in the Conservative Counterrevolution, 1963–1994* (Baton Rouge: Louisiana State University Press, 1996).

*forces, and those opposed to racial busing and affirmative action; and how did a politics of culture replace a politics of economic concerns?*

In 1963, George Wallace moved from the stage of regional politics into the national consciousness. Only a small number of Americans had heard him before his inauguration as governor of Alabama in January of 1963, when the ferocity of his defense of the white South captured their attention. Then and now, most Americans remember little about his inaugural address beyond the famous line, "Segregation now . . . segregation tomorrow . . . segregation forever." All three major networks used the "segregation forever" section of his speech in their evening broadcast. The Associated Press, United Press International, The New York Times and both major afternoon papers in Alabama opened with the segregation quote. That amnesia has allowed Wallace to insist that his defense of segregation was a symbolic issue; his struggle was to preserve states' rights against the overweening power of the federal government. As he said on several occasions in attempting to dismiss the significance of that speech, he should have said "states' rights now . . . states' rights tomorrow . . . states' rights forever." He was never against black people; his oratory had nothing to do with race.

Nothing could be further from the truth.

By the Deep South standards of the 1950s, the Alabamian had been a liberal on economic issues and a moderate on race, but his bitter loss to John Patterson in June of 1958 marked a turning point. After early returns made it clear that he would lose decisively, a depressed Wallace waited with several close friends in a car parked outside the Jefferson Davis Hotel, postponing the dreaded concession speech he would have to make to his followers. "Well boys," he said tightly as he snuffed out his cigar, "no other son-of-a-bitch will ever out-nigger me again."

The man who wrote George Wallace's inaugural address was Asa Carter, founder and co-editor of *The Southerner,* one of the most racist magazines published in the 1950s. While Carter publicly described himself as a White Citizens Council leader, he was in reality a professional anti-Semite and hard-line racial terrorist, the organizer of a secret para-military force with the romantic name of the "Original Ku Klux Klan of the Confederacy." His speech at Clinton, Tennessee, in March of 1957 kicked off a violent race riot, and—on one occasion—he shot and seriously wounded two Klan followers who challenged his leadership. Carter's Klan group helped organize the riots at the University of Alabama which led to Autherine Lucy's expulsion in February of 1956. The following month six of his men carried out an assault on black singer Nat King Cole as he performed before an all-white audience in Birmingham, and four hard-core members of the Klavern seized, at random, a Birmingham black handyman as he walked along a country road and castrated him as a warning to civil rights activists.

This was the man Wallace chose as his main speechwriter for the 1962 governor's race; this was the man he chose to write the defining speech of his life. Racial purity lay at the very core of Southern defiance. A "basically ungodly government," led by the United States Supreme Court, warned Wallace, sought to "play at being God . . . without faith in God . . . and without the wisdom of God." That governmental apparatus fed and encouraged "everything degenerate and base in our people" with its substitution of "what it calls 'human rights' for individual rights. . . ."

Communism was winning the world, Wallace told a cheering audience of 12,000. America was being betrayed by the liberals who followed the "false doctrine of communistic amalgamation." And "if we amalgamate into the one unit as advocated by these communist philosophers . . . then the enrichment of our lives . . . the freedom for our development . . . is gone forever. We become, therefore a mongrel unit of one under a single, all powerful government. . . ."

The reckless course embarked on by the nation's leaders was worse than that of the Nazis. The "national racism of Hitler's Germany persecuted a national minority to the whim of a national majority . . . ," noted Wallace, but the "international racism of the liberals seek to persecute the international white minority to the whim of the international colored majority. . . ."

To make certain that no-one had any doubts about what he meant, Wallace pointed to the recent black violence which had claimed the lives of whites living in the former Belgian Congo. "Those Belgian survivors of the Congo," Wallace reminded his listeners, could not present their case to a "war crimes commission." And neither, he added, could the citizens of Oxford, Mississippi. It is doubtful if Wallace realized the implication of his subtly invidious comparison between racial liberals and Nazis, but Carter—a devoted anti-Semite and secret defender of Hitler—certainly did.

During the next decade, political observers would concoct fanciful scenarios in which a minority of voters elected the Alabama governor as President; even Wallace, in his unguarded moments, would seriously entertain the belief that he might someday be the nation's chief executive.

It was fantasy. If most Americans, indeed most Alabamians, remembered few of the details of his oration, the racial implications of his segregation pledge were clear enough. Wallace's 1963 inaugural speech was his Faustian bargain. It guaranteed his national notoriety; it also doomed him to work along the boundaries of American politics. But what a periphery it was! In the months after his inauguration, Wallace demonstrated his political skills as he brilliantly repositioned himself away from the narrowly racial rhetoric of his 1962 gubernatorial campaign and adopted a kind of soft-porn racism in which fear and hatred could be mobilized without mentioning race itself (except to deny that he was a racist). The key turning point—his "Stand in the Schoolhouse Door"—lets us see something of the critical interaction between the issues of race and politics and the increasingly powerful role played by television.

In June of 1963, George Wallace fulfilled his pledge to block the entrance of two black students to the University of Alabama. Over 200 newspaper reporters converged on the Tuscaloosa campus for this highly-staged event. Our collective memory is shaped not by words, however, but by the grainy black-and-white images of that day's television news cameras. United States Assistant Attorney General Nicholas Katzenbach strides up the long walkway to the entrance of Carmichael Hall; Wallace stands in the blistering summer heat and sternly raises one hand like an irascible traffic cop; the governor attacks the "illegal usurpation of power by the Central Government" and insists that he will stand firm to "forbid this illegal and unwarranted action by the Central Government."

It was, of course, a theatrical performance, staged for the benefit of a national television audience. Within two hours, the federal government had nationalized the Alabama National Guard, Wallace had backed down, the students had been enrolled, and the governor had returned to Montgomery. Leaders of both parties, the media, and national opinion leaders all agreed the Stand in the Schoolhouse Door was simply one more shabby charade in a long line of presentations by Southern demagogues. Wallace, predicted one usually astute reporter, would soon be "placed beside that old broken musketeer, Ross Barnett, in Dixie's wax museum.

They were wrong. George Wallace instinctively understood the lesson that media specialists would slowly grasp: in the world of television, viewers' opinions were shaped by the powerful totality of visual and verbal "impressions," impressions which could be molded and directed in such a way as to overwhelm earlier notions and ideas, particularly those not firmly fixed in the viewer's mind.

First, the television coverage gave him stature. According to an old Arab proverb: "A man with powerful enemies is a powerful man." By claiming center stage with the representative of the President of the United States, who had to treat him with respect and even deference, Wallace transformed himself into a major player in American politics.

Secondly, by producing a relatively dignified media event, the Alabama governor showed that he understood the old adage: a picture (or, in this case, a series of pictures) is worth a thousand words. The print media might describe the complexities of Wallace's involvement in racist politics, but what 78 million viewers saw on the three major networks' evening news programs were clips which ranged in length from four minutes and 20 seconds to six minutes and 35 seconds. George Wallace appeared indignant, but poised; his language, a little stilted and pretentious, but nothing like the raving demagoguery most Americans expected to hear.

Attorney General Robert Kennedy had elected to position Vivian Malone and Jimmy Hood off stage in a government sedan at the curb to shield them from a direct confrontation with the governor. It was a long-range blunder for the Kennedy administration. If the two had stood beside Katzenbach, viewers, rather than seeing George Wallace make a declaration of "constitutional principles," would have seen him holding up his hand, physically blocking two qualified black applicants. In the short run, the presence of Malone and Hood would have helped Wallace. In the long run, their presence would have made it difficult to insist that race was irrelevant.

But the performance succeeded. Few non-Southerners wanted to embrace overt racism in 1963. Wallace's use of non-racial language allowed a substantial minority of Americans to maintain the illusion that the issue was indeed an abstract constitutional question. In the week following his television performance, over 100,000 congratulatory telegrams and letters flooded the office of the Alabama governor. Over half came from outside the South, and 95 percent supported George Wallace.

As NBC news correspondent Douglas Kiker said, it was a moment of epiphany for George Wallace. He had looked out upon those white Americans north of Alabama and suddenly been awakened by a blinding vision: "they all hate black people, all of them. They're all afraid, all of them. Great God! That's it! They're all Southern! The whole United States is Southern!"

Most Americans, of course, continued to regard him with disdain, but the response to his Tuscaloosa performance confirmed the governor's belief that a large floating constituency awaited a champion. Six months earlier, he had discussed the possibility of a presidential campaign to mobilize opposition to racial integration, but it is not clear that he intended his candidacy as more than a symbolic gesture. In the 24 hours preceding his inauguration in 1963, Wallace quietly met with a group of segregationist Southern political leaders to hear a proposal from a right-wing Virginia newspaperman, John Synon. Synon had been inspired by the 1960 Presidential election; an election so close that the electoral votes of Mississippi, Alabama, South Carolina, Louisiana, Arkansas and Georgia could have held the balance of power. Synon's original plan was to push a group of favorite sons from each deep South state such as Barnett in Mississippi, Wallace in Alabama, Strom Thurmond in South Carolina, Harry Byrd in Virginia. Wallace was interested, but uncertain that the Synon plan would promote his ambitions. In the aftermath to the Stand in the Schoolhouse Door, George Wallace began to gear up for a national campaign.

There is today a great debate about the space which should be allowed between a candidate's public and private positions. No one who knew Wallace well ever took seriously his earnest professions—uttered a thousand times after 1963—that he was not a racist, or, as he put it in a line which reporters ultimately lip-synced to amuse themselves: "I have never made a speech or statement in my life that reflected on any man because of his race, color, creed or national origin." It is difficult to know how Americans would have reacted had they been able to glimpse the private Wallace. He was—like many Southern white politicians of his class and generation—simply incapable of avoiding racial epithets. Tony Heffernan, a UPI reporter in the 1960s (and a native New Yorker), covered Wallace at close range throughout the 1960s. He "never said anything but Negro in public," recalled Heffernan, "but in personal conversation, they were 'niggers.'" The staple of humorous conversation was the "nigger joke." A decade later, *New York Times* reporter Jim Wooten—no virgin on the subject of racism—was as much stunned as appalled when Wallace casually referred to Edward W. Brooke as that "nigger senator from Massachusetts."

Very occasionally an interpretive piece in a major newspaper or magazine would repeat one of the Alabama governor's imprudent remarks. ("All these countries with niggers in 'em have stayed the same for a thousand years. . . .") Most racist slurs went unreported; the rules among newsmen in the 1960s for the most part were crudely simple, recalled one freelance writer. "You didn't report who was f—king whom, and you didn't print [those kind of] indiscreet comments of politicians." Occasionally, carefully avoiding the "n" word, local reporters managed to convey some sense of the ugly contours of Wallace's racial outlook. "I read where a Uganda [*sic*] leader said he didn't like the Birmingham racial situation," Ramona Martin of the *Montgomery Journal* quoted the Alabamian as telling a Mississippi audience in 1963. "I guess he [Kenya's President Jomo Kenyatta] was leaning on his spear when he said it." That anyone might find such an observation offensive bewildered him.

He seemed genuinely to believe that blacks were a separate race, inferior and threatening. In an unguarded moment early in his national political career, Wallace confided to a Canadian social studies teacher that the only hope for the nation was complete segregation. Not only were blacks criminally predisposed, he wrote, they were prone to commit the most "atrocious acts of [in]humanity, such as rape, assault and murder." Such antisocial behavior was a reflection of the fact that a "vast percentage of people who are infected with venereal diseases are people of the Negro race. . . ." In addition to their criminality and sexual promiscuity, blacks were lazy and shiftless. If black and white mingled in the schools, inevitably "this mixing will result in the races mixing socially which fact will bring about intermarriages of the races, and eventually our [white] race will be deteriorated [*sic*] to that of the mongrel complexity."

The depth of Wallace's racism—the degree to which it was part of his core beliefs—was always unclear. He sometimes manifested an air of apologetic cynicism; when forced to break away from informal gatherings because of a speaking engagement, he would often turn to his friends and ask to be excused with a sheepish grin and a half-embarrassed explanation: "I got to go give 'em a little nigger-talk." . . .

That such a Southern politician should gain a national hearing suggests the extent to which "white backlash" had begun to stretch beyond the Southern states. As school desegregation decisions, anti-discrimination housing ordinances, and race riots moved North in the mid-1960s, Americans soon discovered there was a bit of redneck in Grand Rapids as well as in Birmingham. When Lyndon Johnson took office in 1963, only 31 percent of the nation's adults felt that the federal government was pushing integration "too fast." By 1968, that figure had grown to more than 50 percent. The Kennedy/Johnson civil rights measures, however limited in their impact, had reached beyond the South and confronted the existence of racial discrimination in the North in housing and employment.

What is perhaps less understandable is how George Wallace tapped into those fears and escaped Dixie's history which had trapped in re-gional amber such fellow demagogues as Orval Faubus, Ross Barnett and Lester ("Axe Handle") Maddox. His enemies—and they were legion—attributed his success in transcending his regional roots to a combination of two factors: first, the existence of racism outside the South, and second, the support of ultra-right activists and financial contributors who equated Wallace's attacks on the federal govern-ment with their hostility to "liberal" economic legislation.

It is certainly true that a sizable number of right wing/nouveau riche politicos supported the Alabama governor out of a hard-nosed assess-ment of the financial benefits his candidacy offered. Many members of the ultra-right were equally attracted to Wallace's semi-hysterical anti-communism. As a former assistant remembered, any trip out to meet the Wallace faithful was a tour of the radical right bestiary: John Birchers (whose administrative skills rescued the Alabamian's 1968 Presidential campaign from absolute chaos), the Minutemen, Ku Klux Klansmen, the White Action Movement, and a dozen other fringe hate groups who emerged and then disappeared into the cauldron of the politics of the 1950s and 1960s.

For most liberals of the 1960s and 1970s it was an article of faith that Wallace was funded by such right-wing patrons as Texas millionaire H. L. Hunt and Louisiana segregationist/oil man Leander Perez, but they were mistaken. Hunt's eccentric son, Bunker, once handed over a briefcase filled with hundred dollar bills (variously said to be

$300,000 or $400,000). But no individual or group ever controlled Wallace. If he used and manipulated them, the course he charted was never dictated by anyone but George Wallace. . . .

Wallace, with his unadorned lust for public office, was his own secret weapon. In the 1950s, '60s and '70s, every courthouse philosopher in Alabama had stories to tell of this relentless pursuit of votes and public adulation. Blessed with that memory for names and faces essential to any Southern politician, he could walk into a crowded room and identify individuals—some of whom he had met only briefly eight or ten years earlier. If his first biographer, Marshall Frady, was sometimes imaginative in his poetic descriptions and a little creative in his dialogue, he accurately sketched the broad contours of his subject's skills and his politics—even when he did not always understand their roots. . . .

In the army he made friends with G.I.'s from all over the country. He had never been particularly conscious of his "Southernness," but the ribbing of Northern soldiers about his accent and provincialism often rankled and helped to shape the way in which he looked at the world.

His sensitivity to being "looked down upon" and his identity as a beleaguered white Southerner strengthened his appeal to ethnic minorities and working class Americans. Many of his followers were, in the parlance of the social scientists: "alienated." Like the Populists of the late nineteenth century, Wallace supporters—North and South— felt psychologically and culturally isolated from the dominant currents of American life in the 1960s. In contrast to the earlier Populists, neither Wallace nor his followers had any understanding of, or deep interest in, the workings of the American economic system. But like the Populists, they were deeply embittered over the way in which respectable folk sniggered at their lack of cultural sophistication. No Wallace speech was complete without the defensive claim that he and his supporters were "just as cultured and refined" as those "New York reporters."

The peculiar complexity of "provincial" Alabama politics both strengthened and limited Wallace's national role. We tend to forget that he began his career as a protege of one of the most liberal Southern politicians in modern history, James ("Big Jim"—"Kissing Jim") Folsom. As a delegate to the 1948 national Democratic Convention, Wallace stayed with the party loyalists and refused to join the racist Dixiecrat walkout for Strom Thurmond. In the state legislature, he consistently introduced legislation to aid disadvantaged Alabamians. Even on racial issues he was a moderate, conscientiously serving as a member of the Board of Trustees of all-black Tuskegee Institute (though he later tried to make light of his apostasy with crude jokes among fellow politicians about "spending weekends with those 'high-yaller' majorettes").

Alabama, whatever its racist crudities, was not Mississippi. For more than one hundred years, yeoman farmers from the northern counties had waged a political guerrilla war against the reactionary Black Belt gentry, and the state had by Southern standards a substantial organized labor movement and a vigorous tradition of working-class political activism. Few other Southern states had furnished liberal politicians to match Hugo Black, "Big Jim" Folsom, Lister Hill and John Sparkman. Wallace's early past support for New Deal liberalism (or "progressivism," as he preferred to call it) gave him an ear for the complex variant of Populist conservatism that characterized blue-collar workers and disenchanted Democrats all over the nation.

His appeal to ethnic voters in the urban Northeast and Midwest initially confounded political observers. In retrospect, it is not that surprising that he drew support from these groups. The often blue-collar ethnic neighborhoods of Boston, New York, Philadelphia, Cleveland, Gary and Chicago had borne the brunt of social transformation as the black community expanded outward into once stable neighborhoods. Many, though certainly not all such ethnic voters, saw in Wallace a kindred spirit: a man despised and dismissed by distant social planners all too ready to sacrifice working-class families on the altar of upper middle-class convictions.

All of these factors help to explain his appeal, but there is something more. The files of Governor Wallace's–chief of staff, General Taylor Hardin, describe the way in which as early as 1966 and 1967 several Wallace staffers drew upon the computer expertise of Oklahoma preacher Billy James Hargis's Christian Anti-Communist Crusade to develop their own direct-mail fund-raising program. The portly Tulsa evangelist has long since been overshadowed by Oral Roberts, the Bakkers, Jimmy Swaggart and Pat Robertson. In the mid-1960s he had 212 radio outlets and twelve television stations, however, and was well on his way to becoming the first of the big-time Christian broadcasters before a disgruntled associate disclosed his somewhat unfatherly interest in younger students. His fall from grace should not obscure the fact that Hargis was one of the first to grasp the way in which weekly doses of apocalyptic warnings, accompanied by computer-generated "personalized" mailings, could help charismatic demagogues tap the pocketbooks of frightened television viewers.

The red-baiting rhetoric that dominated every aspect of Wallace's anti-civil rights rhetoric during these years served him well. It allowed him to use the cold war fears of international communism to discredit the civil rights movement. And the cadences of anti-communism gave him a rhetorical bridge to a national audience. In the early 1960s, most non-Southerners were still ambiguous in their attitudes toward the rising civil rights movement; they were not ambigious in their hatred for the red menace.

Such anti-communist rhetoric also allowed Wallace to link his crusade against black Americans to a long historical tradition of paranoia in which Americans viewed politics not as a conflict between different visions of the common good, but as a moral tableau, a religious struggle of conspiracy and betrayal in which the forces of light must constantly struggle against those of the darkness.

And Wallace was, of course, the ultimate beneficiary of a series of wrenching events in the 1960s: the race riots of the long hot summers which spread pillars of fire across America's urban landscape; the explosion of the anti-war movement as the conflict in Vietnam accelerated after 1965; and the general sense of a collapse in traditional values in the nation's homes and streets. Liberal academics and journalists might speak even-handedly—even approvingly—of the emergence of a counterculture. But as George Wallace looked out upon the disordered political landscape of the 1960s, he sensed that millions of Americans felt betrayed and victimized by the sinister forces of change. He knew that a substantial percentage of the American electorate despised the civil rights agitators and anti-war demonstrators as symptoms of a fundamental decline in the traditional cultural compass of God, family and country, a decline reflected in rising crime rates, the legalization of abortion, the rise in out-of-wedlock pregnancies, the increase in divorce rates, and the proliferation of "obscene" literature and films. And moving always beneath the surface was the fear that blacks were moving beyond their safely encapsulated ghettos into "our" streets, "our" schools, "our" neighborhoods.

The Wallace campaign had begun long before 1968. His 1964 foray in the Democratic Primaries of Wisconsin, Indiana and Maryland had convinced the Alabamian that his basic strategy was sound; by the spring of 1965, he and several members of his staff were talking guardedly about a third-party run. The leadership of both parties was the same, Wallace complained in the summer of 1966 as he traveled throughout the country. "You could put them all in an Alabama cotton picker's sack, shake them up and dump them out; take the first one to slide out and put him right back into power and there would be no change." The ultraliberalism of the two major parties might make it necessary for him to sacrifice himself on the altar of national politics as a third-party candidate, he hinted in one speech late in 1966.

Wallace handily survived one political scare on his home grounds after a handful of legislative opponents filibustered legislation which would have allowed him to succeed himself. He boldly nominated his shy wife, Lurleen, to run as his stand-in. She obliterated a field of eight Democratic opponents and one hapless Republican. With Alabama safely under control and state contractors and suppliers pouring in seed money, the Wallace presidential campaign was underway by the fall of 1967.

There is no evidence that Wallace genuinely believed (despite his statements to the contrary) that he had a chance to win. His goals were to position himself for 1972 and, if the cards came up right, to throw the 1968 election into the House of Representatives. Even that possibility seemed far-fetched in the fall of 1967. Polls showed his support to be non-existent on the West Coast and in the Rocky Mountain states and less than 6 percent in the East and Midwest. Even on his home ground in the South, he would run a poor third to almost any Republican or Democratic candidate.

Against all the odds, however, Wallace cobbled together the American Independent Party and fought his way onto the ballot of all fifty states. Flying in an obsolete turbo-prop airplane and almost no professional advance staff, the candidate careened around the nation. Missed luggage, botched schedules, and non-existent speech texts frustrated journalists, already angry that the Wallace plane was dry. But across the nation, his support grew steadily through the spring and summer of 1968. Attacking Republicans and Democrats alike, he saved his choicest barbs for former Vice-president Richard Nixon, who ultimately won his party's nomination. Nixon and the Republicans had been fighting for the "colored vote" since 1953, when Eisenhower had appointed Earl Warren to write the *Brown v. Board of Education school* decision, Wallace told the *New York Times*. "Nixon is just like the national Democrats. He's for all this Federal invasion of the state's right to run their own affairs."

The war in Vietnam, a contributory factor to inflation and the economic slowdown of the 1960s and 1970s, fueled additional resentment, although its immediate political impact was cultural rather than economic. Despite the opportunity it offered for a crusade against Godless, atheistic Communism, the war itself was never very popular with Wallace supporters. Their quarrel was with the protest movement led by privileged elites (or, as Wallace called them, "silver-spooned brats") who rejected patriotism and a whole range of American cultural and religious values. Wallace and his followers had decidedly ambiguous views on the war. He often urged more aggressive prosecution of the war but, as a group, Wallace voters in 1968 were much more likely to agree with the proposition that the United States should never have become involved in the Vietnam conflict.

The candidate seldom raised explicitly issues of race, but more fastidious political observers shuddered at his attacks on the federal courts for their busing orders, and his threats against "lawless street punks and demonstrators" repeatedly kindled the rage of his audiences.

George Wallace was one of the last grand masters of the kind of foot-stomping public speaking that characterized American politics—particularly Southern American politics—in the age before television. Thousands of stump speeches, from county fair grounds to Kiwanis Clubs, had given him an unerring sense of what would "play." He was, in the vocabulary of the students of rhetoric, the perfect "mimetic orator," probing his audiences' fears and passions and articulating those emotions in a language and style they could understand. Despite the amateurish operation of his political campaigns, Wallace was no political luddite as Marshall Frady suggests in his biography of the Alabama Governor. Wallace paid close attention to political polling and adopted sophisticated computer mailings in order to build a political and financial base for his campaigns. . . .

Wallace skillfully pulled from the American political fabric the strands of xenophobia, racism, and a "plain folk" cultural outlook which equated the cosmopolitan currents of the 1960s with moral corruption and weakness. His genius was his ability to voice his listeners' sense of betrayal—of victimhood—and to refocus their anger. Instead of the New York bankers and moneyed interests feared by his nineteenth century counterparts, or the shadowy "commies" of the McCarthy era, Wallace warned of the danger to the American soul posed by civil rights agitators and anti-war demonstrators who flaunted their contempt for the law and mocked patriotic and "Christian" values, the federal officials who threatened the property rights of home-owning Americans and the union seniority system of blue collar workers, and federal judges who protected the criminal and penalized the victim with their obsession with civil liberties. Because of the Supreme Court's paramount role in challenging segregation in the 1950s and 1960s, it was an obvious target for Wallace the segregationist. What is striking, however, is the shift which takes place after 1964 in Wallace's rhetoric. His attacks on the federal courts continue to have a racial theme (bussing, early efforts at affirmative action, etc.), but much of his anger is focussed on the court's betrayal of "moral" and "traditional values." Wallace talked about the court's decision to outlaw school prayer as much as he did its role in integrating public schools.

He might begin with abstract attacks on the "power of the central government," but he turned to earthy sarcasm as he sneered at the "so-called intelligentsia," the "intellectual snobs who don't know the difference between smut and great literature," the "hypocrites who send your kids half way across town while they have their chauffeur drop their children off at private schools," the "briefcase-carrying bureaucrats" who "can't even park their bicycles straight."

On paper his speeches are stunningly disconnected, even incoherent, but on flickering television screens and in giant political rallies he offered frightened and insecure millions a chance to strike back—if only rhetorically—at the enemy. To Hunter Thompson, the counter-culture journalist who covered the 1968 and 1972 presidential campaigns, a Wallace performance was awe-inspiring, a political "Janis Joplin Concert." There was a sense, Thompson said, "that the bastard had somehow levitated himself and was hovering over us."

In the election of 1968, George Wallace became the voice of this political upheaval and for a while it seemed that he would succeed in accomplishing his most ambitious goal: throwing the election into the House of Representatives. Through the summer and fall of 1968, the Harris and Gallup pollsters had tracked Wallace's support as it grew from less than 10 percent in April, to 14 percent in mid-June, to 18 percent in mid-July, to 21 percent in late September. By October 1, a plurality—in some cases a majority—of Deep South voters supported the Alabama governor, who was closing in on Nixon in the border states of Virginia, Tennessee, Kentucky and Florida. Irrefutable polling evidence that Nixon was the second choice of seventy to eighty percent of the Wallace voters frustrated Republican campaign staffers. Their candidate still held the lead in the popular vote and in the electoral college, but the race was much closer. When Hubert Humphrey began a comeback in the traditional Democratic strongholds of the North in mid-October, Nixon's comfortable lead began to evaporate.

Then, at a critical moment in the campaign, the Wallace effort faltered. The Alabama governor's choice for vice-president, retired Air Force General Curtis LeMay, proved to be disastrous. (Like a stuck phonograph needle, LeMay kept returning to his favorite subject: American's "irrational" fear of nuclear weapons. Hubert Humphrey began referring gleefully to the Wallace-LeMay ticket as "the Bombsey Twins.") And many of Wallace's supporters, when faced with the prospect of dividing the conservative vote and electing Humphrey, voted for Richard Nixon.

Nor did Wallace's passionate level of support from his followers prove to be an unmixed blessing. As much religious exorcism as political exercise, the giant Wallace rallies unleashed both his power and the limitations of that power. Few can match his appearance in Madison Square Garden on October 24, 1968. On an unusually warm fall evening in New York City, four hundred policemen—nearly a hundred on horseback—lined up on Seventh Avenue between West 31st and 33rd Streets, as crowds began to pour into the city's largest indoor arena.

Across the street an astonishing array of fringe groups gathered: a caravan of Ku Klux Klansmen from Louisiana; a delegation of followers of the "Minutemen of America," with neatly printed signs and armloads of brochures; a dozen jackbooted members of the American Nazi Party who sported swastika armbands and "I like Eich" buttons, worn in memory of Nazi war criminal, Adolph Eichmann. New York police separated this motley crew from more than two hundred members of the Trotskyite Workers World Party and several hundred young people of the SDS who waved the black flag of anarchy. Altogether, more than two thousand black and white New Yorkers—most in their early twenties—brandished picket signs and shouted their conflicting chants. From the left: "Seig Heil! Seig Heil!" From the right: "Commie Faggots! Commie Faggots!"

By 8 P.M., 20,000 of the faithful, the largest political gathering in New York City since Franklin Roosevelt had spoken from the same stage in 1936, packed the Garden. Former Alabama Governor George Wallace, candidate for President on the American Independent Party ticket, claimed the stage at 8:20 P.M. The audience erupted. Although the campaign had another week to run, for Wallace, the rally was the emotional climax of his remarkable Presidential race. Earlier in the summer he had drawn 70,000 supporters to the Boston Commons, more than any rally ever put on by the Kennedys, as he constantly reminded reporters. In October—outside the South—he had spoken to crowds of 15,000 in Pittsburgh's Arena Auditorium, 16,000 at an outdoor rally in Baltimore, 12,000 in the San Francisco Cow Palace, 10,000 in the San Diego Sports Arena, 15,000 in Detroit's Cobo Hall, and 16,000 in Cincinnati's Convention Hall. And now—20,000 in the heartland of the enemy.

While a brass band played a medley of patriotic songs, Wallace threw kisses to a crowd which roared his name again and again in a chant which could be heard by demonstrators a half-block away. Curtis LeMay, his vice-presidential running mate, and LeMay's wife, Helen, joined him on the stage, but his supporters continued to whistle and shout. After more than fifteen minutes, Wallace finally brought the crowd to order by having a country singer perform "God Bless America."

He began awkwardly, seemingly overwhelmed by the fervor of his admirers. In the southwest balcony of the Garden, a squarely-built black man stood and held up a poster proclaiming "Law and Order— Wallace Style." Underneath the slogan was the outline of a Ku Klux Klansman holding a noose. At his side, another demonstrator turned on a portable bull horn and began shouting: "Wallace talks about law-and-order! Ask him what state has the highest murder rate! The most rapes! The most armed robberies."

A squadron of police hurried toward the balcony to eject the hecklers as the crowd exploded in a rage which seemed to ignite the Alabama governor. "Why do the leaders of the two national parties kowtow to these anarchists?" he demanded, gesturing toward the protesters. "One of 'em laid down in front of President Johnson's limousine last year," continued Wallace with a snarl. "I tell you when November comes, the first time they lie down in front of my limousine it'll be the last one they'll ever lay down in front of; their day is over!"

The crowd leaped to its feet in the first of more than a half-dozen standing ovations and 30 interruptions for applause as Wallace poured out his proven applause lines.

"We don't have a sick society, we have a sick Supreme Court," he said, as he scornfully described "perverted" decisions which disallowed prayer in the classrooms even as they defended the right to distribute "obscene pornography."

Fifteen minutes into his talk, he shed his jacket as he weaved and bobbed across the stage, his right fist clenched, his left jabbing out and down as if in the midst of a boxing match. "We don't have riots in Alabama," he shouted. "They start a riot down there, first one of 'em to pick up a brick gets a bullet in the brain, that's all. And then you walk over to the next one and say, 'All right, pick up a brick. We just want to see you pick up one of them bricks, now!'"

The crowd went berserk. Richard Strout, the genteel columnist of the *New Republic*, watched the spectacle that night with a mixture of fascination and horror. Never again, he told his readers, would he think about Germany in the 1930s without remembering this wild eruption of hatred.

It is hardly a revelation to note the connection between power, politics and sexuality. (In one of his stories of Washington politics and power, novelist Ward Just simply called it "the hots.") Wallace's appeal seemed to lurch uncertainly between eroticism and violence, closer to that of the outlaw country music singer Waylon Jennings than to the suave John Kennedy whom the Alabama governor envied for his effortless grace. The energy flowed back and forth between Wallace and his audience in a performance which was palpably sexual, bizarrely blending the sacred—God, Mother and Country and the profane— with calls for violence and retribution, the damning of "the other."

Gerald Wallace bluntly acknowledged his brother's "mean streak." He was a first-rate amateur boxer, twice winning the state's Golden Gloves bantam weight championship. When he walked into the ring, the smiling, pleasant "old George" disappeared. He was "like an animal," a friend remembered uneasily. "Everybody's always trying to psychoanalyze George," his second wife Cornelia recalled in 1989. But if you "really want to understand him, just look at this." She held out a photograph of Wallace in a boxing ring, his face grimacing with concentration while he pummelled a blood-covered opponent.

He loved talking on the telephone or speaking to a crowd, Cornelia shrewdly observed, because there was always a safe distance between himself and those who adored him. But her former husband could not tolerate genuine intimacy, she said. "He couldn't stand to get emotionally close to people." That was true with each of his three wives; it was equally true of his relationship with his children. Until the last few years when he became reconciled with George, Jr., Wallace had only the most superficial contacts with his son and his daughters. (It was years before George, Jr., forgave his father for pressuring the dying Lurlene to run for governor in 1966.) "Daddy and I don't have time to share many activities," one of his daughters said in an unguarded interview as she described a father distant and uninvolved even after her mother had died. George Wallace, Jr., is dutifully loyal to his father in his account, *The Wallaces of Alabama,* but the thread that runs throughout the book is one of a son isolated from a father far too concerned with collecting votes to be a father. (The book opens with an unconsciously revealing description of a near death experience by George, Jr. at age 21. As he fought a gulf coast undertow his only concern was how much he had loved his father and how he had failed to accomplish enough in his young life to earn reciprocated pride and love from his father.)

George Wallace never lost a political race in Alabama after 1958, but he came closest when he ran against Albert Brewer in 1970. Brewer, the faithful successor as governor to the late Mrs. Wallace, seemed just the ticket for a state temporarily sated with Wallace's political acrobatics. He almost eliminated Wallace from the campaign in the first primary in May and led by a wide margin going into the run-off. As the election drew near, however, one of Brewer's strongest supporters in eastern Alabama confided her fears of a Wallace victory to Anniston newspaper editor Brandy Ayers.

"Is it because of the race thing?" asked Ayers, in a reference to Wallace's attacks on Brewer as the tool of the black vote.

No, she replied, as she spread her thumb and pointer finger. "The problem is that the voters think that Albert has a tee-tee about this long."

Crude? Indeed, but her off-color observation accurately captured the musky chauvinism which characterized George Wallace's political identity.

Journalists of the time marveled at his ability to transcend his Southern roots by appealing to working-class voters outside the region. What they seldom observed, however, were the particular contours of that appeal. Wallace as the pugnacious Southern bad boy heavily drew his support from young white men between the ages of 18 and 35. As late as three weeks before the election of 1968 he outdrew Humphrey and Nixon in that segment of the voting population. The basic bond between Wallace and his audience was the ethos of the locker room, of a man's world free from the constraints of women and their weaknesses. In the 1960s, race was, after all, still a male prerogative.

Alienated Americans who mobbed Wallace at his rallies or cheered his television performances were thrilled at having found a champion. Still, what most American voters—even many of the Wallace voters—wanted was a return to a time of safety and stability, not a program of unending struggle. As the campaign of 1968 drew to a close, it was clear that George Wallace had been the first politician to sense and then to exploit the changes America came to know by many names: white backlash, the silent majority, the alienated voters. Like other political insurgents, his threatening demeanor and fiery personality limited him to the role of redneck poltergeist. As George Wallace neared the limits of his political popularity, however, he opened the door for his successors to manipulate and exploit the politics of rage.

# Piety and Property: Conservatism and Right-Wing Movements in the Twentieth Century

## Lisa McGirr

*As the new conservatism made its way across the country, it drew support from a variety of constituencies. In addition to those white Americans distressed by black demands for racial equality and a larger share of the national economic pie, conservatives appealed to the "silent" Americans Richard Nixon had galvanized—people who believed in law and order, "middle Americans" who earned less than $40,000 a year and were fed up with protesting students and young radicals denouncing capitalism, traditional marriage, and the ethos of hard work.*

*The new conservatism, as McGirr shows, grew out of antistatist origins associated with the Republican Party of the late 1940s and early '50s. Intellectuals argued for libertarian policies and opposed the growth of the federal government. The John Birch Society seized on the nation's fixation with the threat of communism to suggest that anyone favoring a large federal establishment was suspect. The first stage of a resurgent conservatism came to a culmination with the nomination of Senator Barry Goldwater in 1964 as the Republican candidate for president. Arguing for reconsideration of Social Security, the possible use of nuclear weapons in Vietnam, and a return to laissez-faire individualism in the economy, Goldwater represented the essence of the Old Right.*

*But soon the Old Right was broadened to embrace new converts. In addition to those galvanized by George Wallace's attacks on racial liberals were a number of other groups. Of particular importance in this new coalition were those (women and men) who were profoundly alienated by feminism, the movement for an Equal Rights Amendment, and legal abortion—the demand that women be given the choice whether to continue a pregnancy. They were*

Lisa McGirr. "Piety and Property: Conservatism and Right-Wing Movements in the Twentieth Century." In *Perspectives on Modern America: Making Sense of the Twentieth Century,* edited by Harvard Sitkoff, pp. 33–54 (New York: Oxford University Press 2001).

*joined by straight Americans who were offended by the growing movement that called for gay rights, homosexual marriages, and the celebration of a "queer" lifestyle.*

*Pivotal to this conservative coalition was the emergence in the 1970s of a new, politicized evangelical religious movement. Led by people like Jerry Falwell and his "Moral Majority," and TV evangelist Pat Robertson, the religious New Right helped provide an organizational infrastructure for those devoted to preserving traditional values.*

*In this article, Lisa McGirr helps place all these forces into perspective, providing a context and analysis that illuminate the emergence of one of the most profound political and cultural movements of recent history. How did this movement become a national force, joining California suburbanites to rural southern farmers? Which parts of the new conservatism played the most critical role? And how might liberals have better answered the conservative assault?*

World War II effectively ended the reformist spirit of the New Deal, but it also solidified the recast world of the New Deal Order by vastly expanding the role of the federal government bureaucracy in national life. The postwar world thus posed new challenges and new opportunities for conservatives. Conservative politicians within the Republican party had since the 1930s kept up their tirades against the New Deal, struggling on the side of "liberty against socialism." In 1946, building on public resentment toward rationing, high meat prices, and the Office of Price Administration, Republicans succeeded in recapturing Congress, bringing to Washington a group of influential conservatives. The "class of 1946" included Richard Nixon of California, William Jenner of Indiana, William F. Knowland of California, Joe McCarthy of Wisconsin, and John Bricker of Ohio. Resurgent Republicans allied with conservative Democrats in seeking to roll back wartime labor gains. They successfully contained the power of organized labor through the Taft-Hartley Act (1947), with devastating implications for the labor movement in the post–World War II era. Yet if Republicans believed that their victory in 1946 represented a mandate for laissez faire individualism and hostility to the New Deal, a mandate that would herald a GOP presidential victory in 1948, they were wrong. Truman's victory in 1948 and the Democrats return to dominance in Congress that same year demonstrated that there was little electoral support for ending state benevolence. The old slogan "liberty against socialism" failed to galvanize more than a core constituency of conservatives.

The Republican party increasingly split into two factions. Its eastern internationalist wing sought containment of the New Deal, while the Republican "Old Guard," largely centered in its midwestern wing, demanded nothing less than rollback. During these same years, right-wing intellectuals, convinced that Americans were falsely under the sway of liberal ideas, sought to alter the climate of debate. Working largely in isolation from one another, in fits and starts, these intellectuals sought to build a philosophical basis for American conservatism. They founded journals and wrote books navigating the new world that had come out of the 1930s and 1940s. No single person articulated right-wing concerns with this new order, especially the trend toward centralized state planning, as sharply as Friedrich Hayek. Hayek, an economist and émigré from Austria who fled after Hitler invaded his country, was hailed by many as the intellectual father of postwar libertarianism. Hayek's most important work, a small book named *The Road to Serfdom* (1944), argued that centralized state planning leads inevitably to totalitarianism. Lauding free competition and the market economy to maintain freedom, which in his eyes meant freedom from government constraint, Hayek argued that economic planning and social welfare in the hand of government would produce dictatorship. Journals ranging from *Human Events* (1944), *Plain Talk* (1946), and the *Freeman* (1950), while hardly influential voices, echoed Hayek's concerns and championed classical liberalism along with a virulent anticommunism.

At the same time that Hayek and libertarian conservatives developed their ideas, as historian George Nash has chronicled, Russell Kirk and a group of conservative "traditionalists" forged an ideology that was soon to become a distinctive segment in a burgeoning conservative intellectual movement. Kirk sought to debunk criticisms that conservatism in America was merely a defense of materialistic businessmen or the dogma of Manchesterian economics. In *The Conservative Mind* (1953) he argued, instead, for a philosophical conservatism grounded in religiosity, authority, traditionalism, and a rejection of liberal egalitarianism. Confined to the circles of academia, however, these intellectuals were scattered voices of protest against what seemed like a very real hegemony of vital center liberalism.

Despite the Right's sense of beleaguerment, conservatives received a boost for a moment by the rising tide of anticommunism that swept the United Stated during the 1950s. Concerns over Communist gains internationally since World War II, especially the Soviet's Union's dominance in Eastern Europe, the "loss" of China in 1949, and Russia's obtainment of the atom bomb that same year, contributed to the rise of Senator Joseph McCarthy to national prominence during the early 1950s. Right-wingers who had hawked conspiracy theories since the 1930s found new audiences for their allegation of Communist infiltration into government, the mass media, unions, schools, and other vital institutions. Their audiences, moreover, went well beyond the core base of the Republican party. Catholic ethnics still linked to the New Deal, for example, found in Joe McCarthy, with his vigorous anticommunism and attacks on effeminate liberal elites, a hero.

McCarthyism, however, represented a phenomenon that went far beyond the man for whom the red scare was named. McCarthyism was not a mass movement with membership organizations or meetings but rather a political tendency rooted in popular anxieties of the postwar years generated by the cold war and broader social and cultural change. It was, moreover, a political tendency that had grave consequences for American public life in these years. Its targets were as often liberals, progressives, and civil libertarians as Communists. California's mini-House Un-American Activities Committee, for example, cast its net so widely that at one point it declared the American Civil Liberties Union a "communist front or transmission belt organization." The same committee agitated against sex education in public schools, programs they accused of following "the Communist Party line for the destruction of the moral fiber of American youth." Yet, the all-consuming atmosphere of anticommunism in the late 1940s and particularly the early 1950s gained its strength in large part because it represented a consensus ideology shared by Democrats and Republicans alike. The marginal difference between soft and hard anticommunism was insufficient to stir the public at large to join conservative ranks and embrace its broader agenda.

Despite the stranglehold McCarthy put on the expansion of liberal goals in the 1950s, McCarthyism could not stem the historical tide that, for the moment, lay with the expansion of liberalism. The undercurrent of discontent that McCarthyism evinced with the world of the New Deal liberal state and the events of the cold war did not coalesce for political purposes. Conservatives once dominant in the halls of Washington and the nation were still playing a reactive role, seeking to stem calls for expansion of Social Security and public housing, and for civil rights and health insurance legislation. A broad segment of the American public still had a fundamental stake in New Deal social reforms.

Demonstrating the limits of conservatives' political influence even further was their loss of control over the Republican party. The political strength they had enjoyed during the early 1950s in the national Republican party through their champions Senator Robert Taft of Ohio and Senator Joe McCarthy of Wisconsin vanished by the mid-1950s. It was Dwight D. Eisenhower, not Robert Taft, who won the Republican party primary battle of 1952. Indeed, the death of Taft one year later and McCarthy's censure in 1954 left conservatives without powerful spokesmen in Washington. The triumph of liberalism was symbolically confirmed when Supreme Court Justice Earl Warren, appointed by Republican president Dwight D. Eisenhower, presided over *Brown* v. *Board of Education* in 1954. Supreme Court decisions in 1957, moreover, dismantled the remains of McCarthyism, limiting state activity against "subversion." As a result, by the late 1950s the New Deal Order with its commitment to an activist state and Keynesian economic policies seemed to be deeply embedded in the institutions of the American state and central to the nation's dominant political ideology. This seemed like a hopeless situation for the remaining critics of liberalism. Bereft of powerful spokespersons in Congress, the executive, and the media, the outlook for the Right's political success seemed bleak. It was indeed at this moment that liberal intellectuals like Daniel Bell, Seymour Martin Lipset, and Richard Hofstadter dissected those remaining conservative impulses and organizations and described them as fanatics without a future.

How is it that history turned out to be so different from what most reasonable observers expected in the late 1950s? How did these marginalized conservatives turn themselves into a viable political movement that only some thirty years later would bring Ronald Reagan to the White House? It was a combination of changing social and economic conditions fueled by the New Deal state itself and conservatives' own strategies that eventually brought them back into political power.

For one, the late 1950s and early 1960s saw a revitalization of a newly reformist liberalism. Democrats substantially increased their majorities in both houses of Congress in 1958, and John F. Kennedy's election to the presidency in 1960 symbolized the triumph of an assertive, internationalist liberalism that had a strong faith in the ability of the federal government to manage capitalism in order to solve social as well as economic problems. This newly assertive liberalism also championed a new set of individual and personal freedoms. While the student movement antiwar protests had yet to heat up, the civil rights movement made its first mark on the national scene already in the 1950s with the Montgomery bus boycott (1956) and Little Rock school crisis (1957). By the early 1960s, with sit-ins across the South and freedom riders' journeys into the heartland of segregation, change beckoned on the horizon. While the Right had already been dissatisfied with the moderate Republicanism of Eisenhower, the election of a liberal Democrat to the presidency and the deepening penetration of liberal ideas into the nation's schools, churches, and communities created a sense of urgency, encouraging conservatives to organize against what they perceived with increasing alarm as dangerous developments.

Businessmen and intellectuals were the first to act. Perceiving their weakness within the halls of power in Washington, as well as in the Republican party, they saw the need for new strategies to make their influence felt. Some sought to effect a revolution of ideas, and the burgeoning number of conservative books and journals testify to their efforts. William Buckley began publishing *National Review* in 1955 to help usher in a "new era of conservatism." Russell Kirk followed in 1957 with the more scholarly quarterly *Modern Age* to "forthrightly oppose . . . political collectivism, social decadence and effeminacy." While the journals began an effort to formulate a set of conservative ideas and policies, a spate of national organizations followed suit to translate ideas into politics. In 1958 conservative Republican party politicians and business leaders created Americans for Constitutional Action to help repeal "the socialistic laws now on our books." A group of conservatives meeting in Indiana in December of the same year founded the John Birch Society. And finally, in 1960 William F. Buckley together with a group of conservative students founded Young Americans for Freedom (YAF) in 1960 to provide a vehicle for conservative youth to work for "economic freedom," "state rights," and "the destruction of international communism." Older groups also grew by leaps and bounds. The Christian Anti-Communism Crusade, conceived in 1953, held its first week-long "Anti-Communism Schools" in 1958. On the upswing in the late 1950s and early 1960s, it doubled its receipts each year. In 1961, sparked by its successes in places in the Southwest, where sympathizers were able to back their support with money, the Crusade took in over one million dollars.

These organizations, along with the resources that backed them, invigorated a grass-roots movement that had begun to mobilize in local schools and communities to reverse the tide of liberalism. In the booming Sunbelt, most especially, in places like Southern California, Arizona, and Texas, middle-class men and women organized study groups, opened "Freedom Forum" bookstores, filled the rolls of the John Birch Society, entered school-board races, and worked within the Republican party, all in an urgent struggle to safeguard their particular vision of freedom and the "American heritage." The high-tech suburbs of Southern California, in particular, proved to be a hotbed for conservative activism in the 1960s. Here, the largely white-collar, educated, and often technologically skilled women and men embraced right-wing politics not least because they saw their own lives and the booming communities where they made their homes as tributes to the possibilities of individual entrepreneurial success. Regional business leaders, moreover, promulgated a staunch libertarian ethos that helped to lead citizens to an unabashed celebration of the free market. At the same time, the men and women who had come to the burgeoning Southland were often steeped in a strident nationalism, staunch moralism, and religious piety that was part of the woof and weave of the communities from which they haled. While this cultural conservatism had been tenored by an earlier linkage to New Deal reforms, it took on aggressive new meanings in the places they now made their home, sharpened by their new affluence and their discomfort with the prevalent liberalism in state and national politics in the 1960s.

The most vigorous organized expression of this conservative resurgence was the rise of the extremist John Birch Society. Its rapid growth evinced that not one but two variants of radicalism characterized the 1960s. Though derided by liberals and the national media, the organization gained strength, developing into one of only a few conservative political vehicles concerned with developing a mass base. Candy manufacturer Robert Welch, a man long active in Massachusetts Republican party politics and in the leadership of the National Association of Manufacturers, had founded the organization in December 1958. Disillusioned with the moderate leadership of the Republican party, Welch saw the need to build an organization to thwart the growth of "socialism" and "communism"—which, in his eyes, included all aspects of the welfare state whose progress, he claimed, was rooted in Communist conspiracy. He sought to develop a national mass membership organization of dedicated anti-Communist patriots who would work to shift the political direction of the nation. Choosing the name "John Birch Society" after a Baptist missionary killed by Chinese Communists, Welch linked the society to cold war events, a link that would inform its activities throughout the decade.

The Birch Society, originally an organ of an older midwestern conservatism, mushroomed in the South and West and, especially, in the rising Sunbelt. Eight years after its founding, the society drew approximately 80,000 to 100,000 members (exact membership has always been kept secret). Indeed, at its height it rivaled the peak membership strength of the Communist Party U.S.A. during the Popular Front period. Moreover, like the Communist party, the John Birch Society flourished in supportive ideological waters of "fellow travelers." In 1962 Welch stated that the society was growing fastest in the Southwest, contrasting this area with his home state of Massachusetts, where it encountered much less favorable terrain. Its members, solidly middle-class men and women, were often active in broader conservative circles. They played important roles as both rank-and-file volunteer activists and leaders of the Goldwater movement.

The John Birch Society linked an older and a newer Right. Inheriting the language, targets, and symbols of McCarthyism, the society's mission was increasingly fueled by concerns over the social and cultural changes of the 1960s. The organization profited from anxieties over social and cultural change by establishing a "Task-Force on Civil Disorder," programs to "Impeach Earl Warren," and campaigns to "Support Your Local Police." Indeed the growing number of adherents by mid-decade suggests that these appeals bore fruit. Not only were the society's set of concerns or the geographic areas that fueled its growth novel, but it also embraced a pluralist religious appeal, something the old Christian Right had refused to do. In contrast to the Right prior to World War II, the John Birch Society sought to curb the anti-Semitic tendencies its members sometimes evinced. More important, the society drew not only conservative Protestants to its ranks but a significant number of Catholics. Indeed Robert Welch, the leader of the society, claimed that 40 percent of its members were Catholics.

The John Birch Society embraced a fusionist variant of conservatism that linked libertarian economic ideas, a moral traditionalism, and virulent anticommunism. Although propelled in no small part by conservative concerns with the ever more assertive civil rights movement, it distinguished itself sharply from the "racist right" of the White Citizen's councils, States' Rights parties, and Ku Klux Klan. These organizations also flourished in the wake of civil rights gains. The first White Citizen Council, for example, was established in Indianola, Mississippi, in the wake of the *Brown* decision in 1954 and expanded rapidly thereafter. Integration, in the eyes of the Citizen's councils, represented regimentation, totalitarianism, communism, and destruction. The revived Far-Right Ku Klux Klan embraced violence and terrorism against African Americans and civil rights workers to achieve its goals. These organizations tapped into a long tradition of populist racism in the South. This politics of white supremacy flourished in the Deep South where race had been a determinant marker of populist politics through the twentieth century. While these organizations mirrored northern and western conservatives' hostility to federal control and liberal elites, their overt racism, for the most part, did not resonate beyond the Deep South. Acknowledging the narrow regional appeal of the movement's shrill racist messages, the broader conservative movement, even the conspiratorial John Birch Society, wrapped its hostility toward civil rights in a language of anti-communism, opposition to federal control, and fear of collectivism. It was this more muted and thus supposedly more respectable opposition to enabling African Americans to obtain their constitutional rights that carried the day in the conservative movement during the 1950s and 1960s.

If the formation of *National Review,* Young Americans for Freedom, and the John Birch Society were signs of a revival on the Right in the realm of civil society, conservatives were well aware that to exert significant political power they would have to gain influence over the institutions of the state. And this influence could best be exerted by gaining control of the Republican party. During the 1960s, an amalgam of conservatives contributed to the effort "to take back" the party. Utilizing the networks and experiences forged in the grassroots mobilizations earlier in the decade, a new generation of conservative Republicans with a strong southern and western regional bent challenged the eastern wing for control of the party. And they won. In 1964, backed by powerful new centers of regional capital in the rising Sunbelt and by the deeply segregationist sentiments of white Southerners, they succeeded in capturing the Republican party for their standard bearer, Barry Goldwater, in 1964. This "takeover" signified a historic power shift in the party. The party of Lincoln, now captured by southern and western interests, would in the decades to follow become the party of evangelical Christians and cowboy capitalists.

Yet ironically, Goldwater's nomination almost doomed conservatism as a national movement. After all, Goldwater went down to monumental defeat in November of 1964. The election was in many ways a debacle for conservatives: Goldwater lost by 15,951,220 votes. Johnson won the greatest number of votes, the greatest margin, and the greatest percentage any president has ever drawn from the American people, confirming that most citizens in 1964 optimistically embraced the possibilities of the liberal promise in a period of national affluence. Goldwater, in effect, had failed utterly to reach beyond his core constituencies in the Deep South and the Southwest. And even in the Deep South, the strength of Goldwater's vote was due to his strong states' rights stance rather than his broader conservative agenda. In all, his strident anticommunism, pronouncements on "conventional nuclear weapons," and "low-yield nuclear bombings" shocked a nation already anxiously living under the threat of nuclear warfare. His unmitigated hostility to the welfare state and to Social Security failed to resonate in an era of affluence. Goldwater's rhetoric, indeed, not only failed to appeal to a broader constituency, it scared many people outright. "When in all our history," prominent historian Richard Hofstadter asked only weeks before the election, "has anyone with ideas so bizarre, so archaic, so self-confounding, so remote from the basic American consensus, ever gotten so far?" In a similar vein, one prominent Republican branded "Goldwaterism" a "crazy-quilt collection of absurd and dangerous positions." The respectable political spectrum in the 1960s shared a consensus that the federal government was needed to resolve problems that free-market capitalism could not. In a decade of liberal achievements, right-wing pronouncements on turning back the welfare state and conservatives' belief that the government had no place in redressing social and economic inequities were considered among liberal Democrats, moderate Republicans, and the left alike as "extremist," so farfetched and radical did they seem.

Moderate Republicans, as well as Democratic liberals and the Left, frequently characterized the conservative movement in the 1960s with reference to its most extremist component: the conspiratorial John Birch Society. Yet, it is misleading to equate the movement as a whole with the society. Conservatives within the Republican party certainly had beliefs that meshed well with those of the John Birch Society—virulent anticommunism, laissez faire economics, and a staunch moralism. But many right-wing proponents were repelled by the conspiratorial aspects of the Birch philosophy, and felt that Welch's erratic leadership of the society had damaged the movement as a whole. Whereas some conservatives criticized the society's conspiratorial vision, on the other hand, conservatives from William Buckley to Barry Goldwater and Ronald Reagan were quick to distinguish between its leader and its members whom they considered to be "some of the solidest conservatives in the country."

Still, the "Birch" or "extremist" tag hounded the conservative movement through the mid-1960s, a constant reminder that the movement's ideas lay outside the bounds of respectable political discourse. And indeed, the rhetoric of the John Birch Society and the ideas expressed in their journal, *American Opinion*, were, despite some conservatives claims to the contrary, extreme. At their more radical edge, they evinced a mixture of blood-and-soil nationalism and traditionalism with an antidemocratic free-market ethos. The Birch Society's calls to "impeach Earl Warren" moreover, its "scoreboards of Communist conquest," exposes of "treasonous networks in the state department," calls for "getting the U.S. out of the U.N.," and tirades against what one *American Opinion* writer asserted was the liberal "goal" of "one world, one race," "one world, one government," smacked of a zaniness that was easily lampooned by liberals. Taken together, it contributed to marginalizing the conservative movement in these years.

How would the Right be able to leave their ghetto behind and expand their influence? Two factors contributed to conservative ascendancy in the second half of the 1960s. First, cultural, social, and political changes played a major role. And second, the Right itself, by muting its own rhetoric and rethinking its strategies, picked up on these new opportunities, transforming itself into a viable electoral contender by decade's end.

A sign of the conservative reorientation in the wake of Goldwater's defeat and the new opportunities provided by the social and cultural upheavals came when a b-rate movie actor named Ronald Reagan ran in 1966 for the governorship of California, the most populous state of the nation. Reagan scored a clear victory for conservatives. Importantly, in the wake of Goldwater's defeat Reagan and other conservatives had refashioned their discourse, moving away from tirades on socialism and communism and toward attacks on liberal "permissiveness," "welfare chiselers," and "runaway spending." Reagan, a man attuned to package himself for his public, was able to sustain a right-wing politics while at the same time attracting a broader group of constituents whose loyalties were up for grabs.

Reagan succeeded not only by embracing a repackaged conservatism, but also because large-scale cultural and social changes made it easier for him to attract voters critical of the New Deal Order. The boiling cauldron of concerns about morality, law and order, and race generated in the two years between Goldwater and Reagan's campaign played into their hands. In effect, just as the Right was moving into the respectable mainstream, the mainstream moved toward them.

Reagan's victory exhibited most of the elements that have come to characterize conservatism since the 1960s. It symbolized, for example, the growing importance of the Sunbelt and West to modern conservatism. Moreover, it showed that conservative support came most easily from the newly affluent suburbs of the region. In these places, highly skilled men and women, many of whom worked as engineers, doctors, and dentists, fueled the right-wing upheaval. Embracing modern lifestyles, these newly mobilized men and women were far removed from the status-anxious conservatives left behind by modernity that Bell and others had described. They forwarded a virulent brand of cultural conservatism linked to a staunch economic libertarianism sustained and deepened by regional business leaders.

Importantly, the increasing tilt of the Republican party Right toward the South and West amplified the unambivalent statist posture the Right had adopted in terms of defense. An older Taftite conservatism had tenored its anticommunism with concerns over state spending, including military spending. By the 1960s, however, such qualms disappeared, not least because conservatives drew their strength from a region where lives were closely linked to the cold war military-industrial complex.

The social and cultural upheavals that benefited Reagan presaged the rise of a majoritarian conservatism that would make itself felt on the national scene in the 1968 presidential election. National political contenders like Nixon and Wallace picked up on the discourse of "morality," "law and order," "welfare chiselers," and "liberal permissiveness," and rode a tide of popular middle- and lower-middle-class resentment toward the social changes of the decade. While neither Nixon nor

Wallace represented quintessential Republican conservatism—Wallace with his southern segregationist, harsh antielitist rhetoric, and Nixon with his conservative pragmatism and internationalist centrism—both put forward their own brand of conservative populist lingo that spoke to some, if not all, of right-wing concerns.

By the late 1960s, the Right had made important political gains. Ronald Reagan, an unabashed right-wing ideologue, had won a resounding victory in his run for governor. Richard Nixon, a centrist Republican who courted the Republican's right wing, had gained his party's presidential nomination with the strong backing of conservatives and had won the election through an embrace of a new middle-class conservatism. And George Wallace, a law-and-order populist, had garnered 13 percent of the national vote on a third-party ticket. In effect, by the late 1960s the Right refashioned itself and gained new political respectability. News of antiwar protests, hippie youth culture, and riots in the nation's inner cities filled the evening news, and the conservative critique of liberalism resonated with an increasing number of Americans.

Already in the 1960s, the conservative revival had been propelled in no small part by cultural and social issues. A series of Supreme Court decisions that took prayer out of schools and expanded personal rights and freedoms, a growing youth culture, and women's liberation generated anxieties among cultural conservatives about the preservation of family values. By the early 1970s these concerns became ever more prominent. In March 1972, the Senate overwhelmingly passed the Equal Rights Amendment, and in 1973 the Supreme Court legalized abortion in its famous *Roe v. Wade* decision.

The rise of a new social issues conservatism had an uneven impact on the Right. On the one side, older organizations that had been so critical to the mobilizations earlier in the decade experienced decline. On the other side, new conservative initiatives sprang up. These initiatives moved the center of activity away from the anticommunism that was so much a part of the mobilization in the early 1960s and instead embraced new single-issue campaigns as well as a newly politicized evangelical Christianity. As a result of this reorientation, the John Birch Society, an organization that had played such an important role in channeling grass-roots activity earlier in the decade, experienced the greatest decline. Despite the social upheavals of the decade, the society was running into trouble. In the wake of the conservative reorientation after their monumental defeat in 1964, the

John Birch Society, with its apocalyptic utterances and its belief in a Communist conspiracy, turned into more of a liability than an aid to the conservative movement and it was increasingly marginalized.

Yet it was many of the men and women who had been foot soldiers in the Goldwater mobilization who now turned their wrath against "secular humanism." Phyllis Schlafly, who had been a prominent Goldwater supporter in the 1960s and who wrote *A Choice Not an Echo* to generate support for his presidential run, now turned her attention to the increasingly assertive feminist movement. In 1973, Schlafly created a national network to oppose ratification of the ERA (Equal Rights Amendment). In 1975 she changed the name of her "Stop ERA" campaign to the "Eagle Forum." Her organization represented one of the opening battles of a Right increasingly focused on family and reproductive issues.

The concern over sexual permissiveness, women's liberation, homosexuality, and threats to the "traditional family" that propelled the Eagle Forum also fueled the politicization of conservative evangelical Christians and their reentry into politics. Religious conservatives saw the deep social changes of the 1960s and 1970s as an assault on their values and beliefs, propelling their reentry into politics. Yet while the new crusades of the Religious Right drew upon the ideological inheritances of their evangelical forbears in the 1920s, they were also distinct in important ways. The militant fundamentalists in the 1920s were strongest in the rural and small-town Midwest and South—but in the 1970s and beyond it was the affluent suburbs of the Sunbelt and West with their huge corporate-like megachurches that would drive fundamentalism into its newly assertive political posture.

The prominence of evangelicals in politics by the late 1970s drew strength from the growth of evangelical and fundamentalist Christianity nationally. Beginning in the mid-1960s, the number of adherents in mainline Protestant denominations declined, while theologically conservative churches flourished. Many of these churches became the organizational bastions for the Christian Right's political mobilizations. Eventually, these religious conservatives succeeded not least because they built powerful institutions that disseminated their message. The Moral Majority, the Christian Voice, and Concerned Women for America, all of which were established in the late 1970s, brought their vision of religious traditionalism and a staunch economic conservatism to the halls of Congress and the White House.

The Religious Right's new prominence in Republican party politics was also boosted by a group of politically experienced conservatives who saw the social conservatives as natural allies in building a broad-based electoral coalition. A small coterie of influential conservative political operators including Richard Viguerie, Howard Phillips, and Paul Weyrich sought to capitalize on the importance of new social issues. In doing so, they tried to distinguish themselves from traditional Republican conservatives who had emphasized economic issues and anticommunism. This group, which adopted the "New Right" label, exaggerated the newness of their politics for strategic purposes. Their mobilization represented a repackaged fusion of anticommunism, libertarianism, and traditionalism. Its core organizers, moreover, had first delved into politics in the conservative revival of the 1960s. Indeed, it is interesting to note that the term *New Right* had first been used by Lee Edwards in 1962 when he proposed a conservative platform for Young Americans for Freedom. Still, the New Right's use of the term did reflect the new prominence of the organized Religious Right within the conservative coalition. Indeed, Kevin Phillips popularized the term to refer to the new prominence of social conservatives on the Right in 1975.

But the success of the Right in the 1970s cannot only be explained by the preferences, aims, and aspirations of its rank-and-file constituency nor by a group of politically savvy conservative operators in Washington, D.C. At least as essential for the new prominence of the Right in American life in the 1970s was the reorientation of American business. A segment of conservative business leaders had long been central to conservative causes. Among them, wealthy millionaires like J. Howard Pew backed such policy organizations as the American Enterprise Institute, in the early 1960s, at a time when few businessmen offered such support. He also provided significant backing for the evangelical flagship journal *Christianity Today* and journals of opinion ranging from *Human Events* to *National Review*. But in the 1970s, driven by sweeping economic changes, a much broader segment of the business community mobilized to assert their recast political interests. New conservative think tanks such as the Heritage Foundation began their work, and older ones like the American Enterprise Institute and the Hoover Institution saw vast infusions of money. The AEI, for example, which had a budget of less than 300,000 dollars in 1960, expanded dramatically in the 1970s. By 1977 it boasted a budget of five million dollars, and four years later that number had doubled, backed by six hundred corporate donors.

This new expansion of conservative institutions earned the Right increasing visibility and helped to bring antistatist ideas into the mainstream of American intellectual life and policy discussions. Additionally, a broader middle-class economic preservationism, symbolized best by California's Proposition 13 tax revolt, encouraged an increasing number of Americans to move away from an embrace of the liberal project and to search for a new political home. Suddenly, laissez faire ideas seemed to make as much "common sense" to many Americans as the New Deal Order had during the 1950s and 1960s.

The reorientation of the conservative movement, then, along with the social, cultural, and economic changes that marked the 1960s and 1970s, transformed conservatism from a marginal movement preoccupied with communism into a viable electoral contender. As a result, by 1980 conservatives were able to bring their vision of national identity and their prescriptions for a free and just society to the White House. Twenty years later, a vision that once had been outside the bounds of respectable discourse and was so contrary to post-war liberal conceptions of the American past and its future, has become the dominant discourse in the halls of Congress and the nation.

Since their rise to national power in the early 1980s, conservatives have seen both successes and failures. Indeed, their new position of dominance in itself has opened rifts in places where conservatives had once been united against a common enemy. Free marketeers, the senior partners in the conservative coalition, have been at the cutting edge of recent historical change. Religious conservatives, while obtaining new access to the corridors of power, are still waiting to see their concerns over abortion, homosexuality, and obscenity reflected in public policy. Indeed, some politically oriented religious conservatives' disillusionment with their ability to "Christianize America" has led to a reconsideration of their political activism and a proposal to withdraw once more from politics. Even if a segment of the Religious Right does retreat, however, the history of the past one hundred years should assure us that such a retreat would be momentary and incomplete. If the past is any guide to the future, then the deep and tenacious roots of conservatism in this country over the past one hundred years suggests that we can expect the Right to have a continued and vital presence on the national stage as we enter the new millennium.

# The Religious Right and the New Republican Party

## E. J. Dionne, Jr.

*As the young conservatives who wrote the Sharon Statement (Part 2) discovered when they worked for Goldwater's election in 1964 and found many supporters motivated by anti-integration States' Rights doctrines rather than by belief in the free market, American conservatism is not a single, coherent movement. The tensions within conservatism—and, by extension, within the Republican Party—have played a major role in shaping American politics in the last half of the twentieth century and beyond. In this excerpt from his bestselling book,* Why Americans Hate Politics, *E. J. Dionne explores some of these tensions and their implications, focusing on the rise to power of the Religious Right in the 1970s and 1980s.*

*Dionne's analysis was published near the end of the era of Reagan and Bush, Sr. How did the New Right continue to influence American politics during the Clinton and Bush, Jr., administrations? Is the troubled relationship Dionne describes between "Old" and "New" Right resolved, or does it still play a role in the nation's political life?*

In 1965, a young Baptist minister explained why he felt it inappropriate for fundamentalists such as himself to become involved in politics. "We have few ties to this earth," the minister explained. "Believing in the Bible as I do, I would find it impossible to stop preaching the pure saving Gospel of Jesus Christ and begin doing anything else, including fighting communism or participating in civil rights reforms," he said. "Preachers are not called upon to be politicians but to be soul winners. Nowhere are we commissioned to reform the externals." The minister who spoke these words was the pastor of the Thomas Road Baptist Church in Lynchburg, Virginia, the Reverend Jerry Falwell.

Falwell's statement is remarkable only in light of his subsequent history. At the time he spoke, his words were well within the fundamentalist and evangelical mainstream. Until the 1970s, a polite disrespect for politics characterized much of the fundamentalist and evangelical movement. If Christ's Kingdom was not of "this world," then His followers had no political obligations beyond a relatively narrow definition of what they should "render unto Caeser." Baptists, whether fundamentalist such as Falwell or not, had long been the most ardent advocates of separating church and state, even on the touchiest issues such as prayer in public schools and abortion. The Baptists' dissenting, popular tradition and their mistrust of state religion had deep roots. In colonial America, the Established churches had been the churches of the upper classes. Baptists, with their deep belief in individual conscience and their disdain for hierarchy, knew instinctively that if a religion was established by the state, it would not be theirs.

But there were other reasons for the fundamentalists' mistrust of politics.

Fundamentalism was plunged into crisis by its two great public crusades of the teens and twenties, the wars against evolution and alcohol. Ironically, both wars initially appeared successful. Prohibition was enacted into law, passed with the support of the culturally "advanced" as well as the culturally "backward." . . . Prohibition, of course, proved to be a disaster and was forever after invoked by all who insisted that government efforts to regulate personal morality were doomed.

The Scopes "monkey trial" actually ended in the conviction of John T. Scopes for teaching evolution, another fundamentalist victory. But few victories better deserved to be called Pyrrhic. The fundamentalists' claims about evolution were held up for scorn throughout the nation. . . . And so the fundamentalists went underground, disdaining a presence in public life that had done their movement so much harm. . . .

Yet in 1980, the entire nation was discussing the fundamentalists and the evangelicals—vaguely aware that the two groups overlapped but were not quite the same. A religious movement that the broader society had dismissed as hopelessly unsophisticated proved exceptionally adept at using the tools of modern politics: television, precinct organization, direct mail. The religiously hip and liberal had drawn much notice in the 1960s. But by the 1970s, the declining churches were the liberal churches, which had rejected the "fundamentals" of Christianity, as the fundamentalists saw it. The churches on the rise were the most *conservative*—those preaching the most old-fashioned Gospel, those demanding adherence to the strictest moral codes. . . .

Still, the growth of conservative churches was one thing; the rise of a *politicized* Christian right was something else again. The apparent power of the Religious Right caused alarm around the nation. Books with titles such as *God's Bullies* and *Holy Terror* warned that tolerance and individual freedom were in jeopardy.

Some of the Religious Rights' leaders did indeed sound alarming. . . . "We have enough votes to run the country," said the Reverend Pat Robertson. "And when the people say, 'We've had enough,' we are going to take over."

If Americans outside the fundamentalist and evangelical communities were worried by what was going on, they were also baffled. After all, most of what had happened in the 1960s and 1970s moved the country in a *liberal* direction. In this "greening of America," sexual attitudes were freer, drugs were more widely used, abortion was legal, women were marching toward equality. If America was indeed as dangerously secularized as the leaders of the Religious Right proclaimed, how could their movement sneak up on the country and become so powerful? . . .

In light of the growth experienced by the evangelical and fundamentalist movements through the 1970s, a political reassertion by conservative Protestantism was inevitable. But the insurgency need never have been as loud, as widespread, or as right wing as it proved to be. The sparks that inflamed the Religious Right came from the judiciary—specifically, the Supreme Court's decisions on issues such as school prayer, abortion, pornography, and government aid to religious schools. *The paradox of the Religious Right is that it became an important factor in American politics primarily because of liberal victories.* . . .

Jerry Falwell himself wrote in his autobiography that he began changing his mind about the involvement of preachers in politics on January 23, 1973, the day the Supreme Court issued the *Roe v. Wade* decision that struck down the nation's abortion laws. If advocates of the Social Gospel had spoken of "social sin," Falwell began to speak of "national sin." A new Prohibitionist movement was about to be born. . . .

If Jerry Falwell began moving toward political action in 1973 because of the *Roe* decision on abortion, an influential group of conservatives were ready to encourage him. Falwell arrived on the scene at precisely the point when conservative political operatives were searching for new political constituencies and new ways to move them. . . .

Class resentment clearly played a key role in New Right politics and its founders. They were eager to identify with George Wallace and his followers among both the working class and the unvarnished new rich. Among the key figures was Richard Viguerie, a onetime direct-mail fund-raiser for Young Americans for Freedom who was hired by George Wallace to handle his mail solicitations. "Compared to a William Buckley . . . ," wrote Paul Gottfried and Thomas Fleming, two conservative historians, "Viguerie resembles a car salesman attending, uninvited, a formal dinner." Among Viguerie's direct-mail clients and allies was Paul Weyrich, a former congressional staffer who helped found two new conservative institutions in the early 1970s. The Committee for the Survival of a Free Congress was the forerunner to the dozens of conservative political action committees that would proliferate in the 1970s. . . . Weyrich's other creation was the Heritage Foundation, which he set up with Ed Feulner, another Capitol Hill veteran. Heritage was to be a militant think tank that would feed ideas directly to the conservative movement and to its allies in Congress. . . . Heritage wanted political victory *now!* Weyrich saw little point in the niceties of academic debate, since he took the warfare analogy to heart. "It may not be with bullets," he was once quoted by Viguerie as saying, "and it may not be with rockets and missiles, but it is a war nevertheless. It is a war of ideology, it's a war of ideas, and it's a war about our way of life. And it has to be fought with the same intensity, I think, and dedication as you would fight a shooting war."

Clearly, the stylistic differences between *National Review* and the New Right were profound, and they betrayed a fundamental difference in emphasis between the two schools of conservatism. For *National Review* conservatives, the centerpiece of postwar conservatism had been anticommunism. Despite *National Review*'s traditionalism, it was still more comfortable with libertarian antigovernment themes than with the New Right's "populism." Following their hero George Wallace, the New Rightists were much more prepared than the older conservatives to use government for their own ends. Kevin Phillips noted that the New Right, while sharing with the Old Right a sympathy for a strong military and a suspicion of government, believed that the primary political questions were "domestic social issues." What he really had in mind were domestic social *resentments*. He listed these as "public anger over busing, welfare spending, environmental extremism, soft criminology, media bias and power, warped education, twisted textbooks, racial quotas, various guidelines and an ever-expanding bureaucracy." It is no accident that Phillips's list seemed to define the difference between Barry Goldwater and George Wallace.

. . . "The New Right is looking for issues that people care about," Weyrich said. "Social issues, at least for the present, fit the bill." The Moral Majority was born out of a series of meetings among Falwell, Viguerie, Howard Phillips, another early New Right leader, and others. Falwell credits Weyrich with coming up with the name, though Howard Phillips appears to have used it first. "Jerry, there is in America a moral majority that agrees about the basic issues," Weyrich told Falwell in 1979. "But they aren't organized. They don't have a platform. The media ignore them. Somebody's got to get that moral majority together."

For the New Right, religious issues offered an opportunity to expand the movement's social-issue repertoire. Abortion had emerged first during the Nixon campaign in 1972. After the 1973 Supreme Court decision, all the pressure on the issue moved right, since the *Roe v. Wade* decision gave liberals what they thought was the decisive victory; now it was the conservatives who had to organize against the status quo.

The Falwell movement also allowed the New Right to speak more effectively on a host of other issues. Where George Wallace's attacks on the educational establishment could not help but smack of racism, the Religious Right's approach emphasized not race but values—the right of parents to influence the content of their children's education, the right of schoolchildren to recite prayers. The Moral Majority was also a natural complement to the antifeminist movement. Support for Phyllis Schlafly's campaign against the Equal Rights Amendment was especially strong among women with conservative religious commitments. With Schlafly concentrating her efforts in states where the ERA was up for ratification, the Moral Majority helped give her sympathizers elsewhere an alternative organizational voice.

The Moral Majority gave bite to the political approach that F. Clifton White had proposed to Barry Goldwater when he made his "Choice" documentary on declining American values. White's film spoke to a generalized unease that many Americans felt about the country's moral direction. But in 1964, those Americans were unorganized, and the evangelicals and fundamentalists had still not achieved their political breakthrough. Falwell's activities gave Weyrich and his allies a chance to turn vague discontent into a real lever of political power. And with the growth of the evangelical and fundamentalist churches, such a movement had more political potential than ever.

It is a sign of the distance between the Old and New Right that in 1980, Ronald Reagan was not the first choice of many of the conservatives who gathered around Viguerie and Weyrich. For them, Reagan was a throwback to the Goldwater campaign, a champion of the Buckleyite past rather than the populist future. . . .

The populism of the Religious Right made the conservatives affiliated with *National Review* uncomfortable. Russell Kirk, for one, detested the very idea of a "populist conservatism," calling populism "the ignorant democratic conservatism of the masses." But the *National Review* conservatives could put their doubts aside because they understood the political potential of the Religious Right and its electoral sympathizers. Here, at last, was the mass constituency that traditionalist conservatism had lacked. In the 1950s, traditionalism seemed to be a hopelessly antiquated creed, an antidemocratic doctrine supported by a handful of marginal conservative intellectuals. It turned out that traditionalism had a genuine base among those who looked to the Bible rather than Edmund Burke for authority. . . .

For conservative evangelicals and fundamentalists, the elections of 1976 and 1980 created a sense of triumph. The first had allowed evangelicals to rejoin the political mainstream. The second confirmed their power. . . . Yet in retrospect, it is clear that the Religious Right was never as powerful as it claimed to be, or as its liberal critics feared. . . .

For example, the notion that the Moral Majority had "elected" Ronald Reagan is almost certainly wrong. The evidence suggests strongly that Reagan would have won with or without the Moral Majority. According to the *New York Times*/CBS News poll surveying over 12,000 voters after they had cast their ballots in 1980, "born-again white Protestants" accounted for 17 percent of the electorate. Reagan carried this group over Carter 61 percent to 34 percent. *Even if Carter had defeated Reagan by the same 61 to 34 percent among born-again white Protestants, Reagan would still have won.* And this analysis makes every effort to *exaggerate* rather than underestimate the Moral Majority's influence. For example, it assumes that *all* born-again white Protestants were influenced by the Moral Majority, which was certainly not the case, since polls showed that substantial numbers of born-again white Protestants actually disagreed with the Moral Majority on many issues. . . .

What happened in 1980, then, was not a Republican breakthrough but a ratification of earlier trends toward the Republicans that had been interrupted by Jimmy Carter in 1976. White evangelicals and fundamentalists had begun backing Republicans long before anyone outside of Lynchburg, Virginia, had heard of Jerry Falwell. These shifts did not occur because a group of preachers told their followers to abandon the party of Roosevelt. Nor did Republican politicians win the evangelical vote on the basis of conservative religious themes alone. Most of the evangelical conservatives were white Southerners who *began voting against the Democrats because of civil rights*. Many of them did so when not a campaign word was spoken about faith or morals. Even in his 1964 landslide victory, Lyndon Johnson could not manage a majority in the nation's most heavily Baptist counties. Johnson's share of the Baptist vote was 13 percentage points *lower* than his share in the nation as a whole. . . .

What is important about the Religious Right, then, is not that it created new political facts, but that it reinforced trends that had begun long ago because of the reaction of conservative Southern whites to civil rights. In the process, the Religious Right transformed both the Republican Party and the conservative movement. At least as late as 1976, it was possible for a candidate with moderate—which is to say nonconservative—views on social issues to win the Republican nomination. By 1980, that had become virtually impossible. . . .

Nonetheless, for all the much-touted strength of the Religious Right, the movement's successes during the 1980s were actually quite modest. Reagan proved himself to be very much a man of the Old Right, just as some of the New Right leaders had feared. Although Reagan could speak as movingly about traditional values as he spoke about everything else, his priorities were elsewhere: in cuts in domestic programs, in reductions in marginal tax rates, and in large increases in military spending to counter the Soviet threat. In the meantime, abortions continued, women kept flooding the workplace—and not a word of prayer was recited in the schools to petition the Almighty to turn these trends around.

Reagan himself, moreover, seemed to embody the broader society's ambivalence in the battle between modernity and traditionalism; he seemed very much the sort of person who could pray for Prohibition and vote for Gin. He was the nation's first divorced president. He rarely attended church. He had been formed by Hollywood and demonstrated enormous personal tolerance for "alternative" lifestyles. As one Republican put it, young voters who liked Reagan but were liberal on the social issues always sensed that Reagan was winking at them when he tossed a rhetorical bone to the Religious Right. How serious could a man of his experience and background really be about Jerry Falwell's agenda?

Indeed, the 1980s could hardly be seen as a time when the nation embraced the old Protestant virtues of thrift, self-denial, and self-discipline. The Republican Party abandoned dour, if "responsible," fiscal policies for deficit spending. The dominant ethos of the age seemed to be acquisitive, materialistic, self-indulgent. The clichés of the 1980s were Madonna's "Material Girl," insider trading, MTV, MBAs, BMWs, yuppies. The traditionalists who streamed to evangelical churches could no more identify with these symbols than they could with the Rolling Stones, LSD, or the yippies of the 1960s. . . .

For the more ardent religious conservatives, many of whom repaired to Pat Robertson's candidacy in 1988, the Reagan years had meant little progress at all. . . . They sought much firmer commitments from conservatives to social and religious traditionalism. To the extent that they passed their demands too forcefully, they threatened the Republican coalition and conservatism's delicate philosophical balance. For the rise of the Religious Right had strengthened the hand of the traditionalist wing of conservatism—the wing that had always seen values as more important than markets, religious faith as more important than economic growth, tradition more important than progress. As a result, the old conservative war between traditionalists and libertarians that Frank Meyer and *National Review* conservatives had tried to settle was raging with greater ferocity than ever. For the libertarians, who profoundly disagreed with the traditionalists on many issues, had also made real gains under Reagan. Many conservatives sensed danger ahead.

# America's Right Turn

*William C. Berman*

America's Right Turn, *by William C. Berman, broadly examines the economic, cultural, and racial causes for the end to Democratic hegemony and the dominance of Republican conservatism from the late 1960s to the 1990s. While acknowledging the key roles played by the white backlash to the civil rights revolution and by those drawn to the New Right's family and moral values, emphasized by the previous authors in this section, Berman focuses on the ways in which inflation and globalization, and an improving national economy, led to conservatism's notable successes during the presidency of Ronald Reagan.*

*Following President Reagan's election in 1980, Congress supported his proposal to slash federal income taxes on individuals and businesses. "Reaganomics" and "supply-side" economics rested on the assumption that people would invest their tax savings, thereby creating jobs, increasing consumer spending, and generating higher tax revenues. In the short term, however, as military spending increased, many government programs had to be abolished or reduced—particularly for the poor, for unskilled workers in the inner cities, and for African Americans and Hispanic Americans— to keep the deficit in the federal budget from ballooning enormously. Other key elements of the "Reagan Revolution" included reducing the powers and membership of organized labor, lowering the inflation rate, and deregulating major industries.*

*In the following excerpt, Berman, formerly a professor of recent U.S. history at the University of Toronto, describes Reagan's economic program and its political consequences—conservatism's triumph over liberalism.*

Reagan's triumph in 1980 ushered in a new era in American politics and life, giving confident conservatives a unique opportunity to offer their programmatic alternatives to the largely discredited liberalism of the seventies. While Reagan supplied the uplifting rhetoric and vision, others in his administration, coming from conservative think tanks, provided the necessary details and approach for dealing with the most pressing matter on the domestic agenda, the state of the American economy. They soon crafted a program that went far to incorporate the supply-side argument for corporate and personal tax cuts, which was also consistent with the objectives sought by such influential business lobbyists as Charls Walker and the powerful business coalition he represented. . . .

At one time a student radical at Michigan State and later a divinity student at Harvard, Stockman also served for a time in the House of Representatives, where he made friends with fellow Republican Jack Kemp, that chamber's leading supply-sider. Because he possessed both talent and good connections, Stockman was brought into the Reagan administration to serve as its budget director. After producing a plan calling for substantial tax cuts and a reduction or elimination of funding for many Great Society programs, he hoped that his efforts would lead in the direction of a balanced budget in the near term. Given the military spending priorities of the Reagan White House and Congress's refusal or inability to make even deeper cuts in domestic programs that had already been sliced, the goal of a balanced budget was soon out of reach. . . .

[The] tax cut was at the top of Reagan's domestic legislative agenda. Along with the military buildup, it was the common denominator that united the various elements of his coalition and a key to his program of producing economic growth and abundance at home. . . .

Reagan's call for tax cuts hit home for millions of citizens who had suffered a serious erosion in purchasing power resulting from persistent inflation, which, among other consequences, had placed them in higher tax brackets. So the argument that a readjustment in tax rates would benefit them made good sense to many Americans during a period of declining living standards. At the same time, corporate America felt that it, too, was entitled to tax relief and other benefits in order to compete more effectively in the now-globalized market place. Consequently, the supply side argument carried the day, with corporate spokesmen arguing that a tax cut would serve as an incentive to spur fresh investment in productive facilities, while blue-collar and middle-class Americans hoped that it would reduce the pressure on their pocketbooks.

Thus, with the ideological and political foundations for a tax cut now firmly in place, the Reagan administration maneuvered a willing Congress to act in accord with David Stockman's design, which included a tax cut of roughly 25 percent spread over three years, as well as a significant reduction in federal spending for many domestic social programs. The fulfillment of a supply-sider's dream, the Economic Recovery Tax Act of 1981 (ERTA) served as the centerpiece of the Reagan administration's effort to stimulate growth and to produce new investment. . . .

As the administration intended, the chief beneficiaries of this supply-side windfall were wealthy Americans as well as the American business community, the major constituents of Reaganomics. In general terms, the 1981 tax act mandated that rates would be reduced over a three-year period by 25 percent, with the top rate coming down from 70 to 50 percent. Or to put it in more class-oriented terms, estate taxes were substantially reduced, and rates on unearned income and capital gains were also targeted for relief. As a result of such action, the income of the top 0.2 percent of all income filers had increased by 21 to 26 percent by 1984, whereas the gain in disposable income for those at the median point was a nominal 3.5 percent. Meanwhile, families under $10,000 lost more than 15 percent of their income due to various tax and budget changes enacted in 1981. Such, in general terms, were the economic and social results of the $750 billion cut that ERTA had projected and authorized over a three-year period.

Business, too, benefited from the tax legislation of 1981. Corporate taxes were substantially reduced, and individual sectors such as energy received special consideration from Congress resulting from the competition between Democrats and Republicans seeking the favor of business. In addition, business was aided by legislation designed to accelerate the rapid depreciation allowance, and investment tax credits were also included in the package that was drafted after much consultation with business lobbyists. All in all, a unified corporate America received a handsome reward, amounting to a $150 billion tax cut over a five-year period, for services rendered to the Republican party by business PACs and other forms of corporate financing and endorsements during the 1980 presidential campaign.

From Reagan's perspective, that reduction in personal and corporate taxes was a positive act because it reduced the amount of money available to the government that otherwise might have been spent on unwanted social programs. With ERTA on the books, the federal government lost an estimated $600 billion in tax revenues by 1986. . . .

Reagan's desire to roll back or cut governmental services was just as intense as his support of a tax cut. In his mind, each was an integral part of the larger process of liberating the private sector and individual initiative from the nefarious grip of big government and its attendant bureaucracies. He had, after all, campaigned in 1980 on the theme of "getting government off our backs." This message was well received across the country, especially with those audiences least in need of governmental support and help for personal and social survival. . . .

Once OBRA cleared Congress, it was signed into law by President Reagan on August 13, 1981. This legislation marked a major turning point in the recent social history of the United States, going far to reduce or abolish governmental support for the most politically unpopular Great Society programs of the sixties, at a time when the United States already possessed the weakest and most stingily funded welfare state among any of the major industrial democracies of the West. Along with ERTA, it served notice that the United States government, under Ronald Reagan's symbolic leadership, was well disposed to aid and support the most powerful and wealthy elements in the country at the expense of those least able to fend for themselves. Such was the new economic and social gospel according to those supply-siders and the many neoconservative intellectuals located in the White House, the various conservative think tanks, and universities across the country. . . .

[T]he Reagan administration broke with the informal working arrangements that had largely characterized government-business-labor relations of the sixties and seventies: it now deliberately sought to undercut, if not destroy, the position and authority of organized labor in order to weaken its bargaining position vis-à-vis business.

A major step in that direction was taken in August 1981 when President Reagan broke the back of the air traffic controllers' union (PATCO) after it had launched an illegal strike against the government. By moving very quickly to decertify this union, which had supported his election bid in 1980, Reagan served notice to the country that a new day in government-labor-management relations had dawned. Organized labor would no longer have privileged entrée into the inner sanctum of government, as had formerly been the case beginning in the 1930s. Nor would its claims be given serious respect or consideration from an administration eager to convert the

National Labor Relations Board into an adjunct of business. Labor's failure or inability to contest Reagan's antiunion moves was a fresh indication of the depth of the current crisis of American liberalism, a crisis that preceded the Carter years and was magnified by the events of the Reagan era. . . .

Plans to deregulate the American economy were also high on the administration's agenda to help business. For years Reagan himself had been saying that government had "overspent, overestimated, and overregulated." . . .

[B]uilding on the legacy of Jimmy Carter, who had earlier pursued the deregulation of the airline and trucking industries, the White House sought to free the market from what it considered to be a variety of unnecessary restraints imposed on business by governmental regulatory agencies. It moved, accordingly, to weaken the regulatory reach and authority of a number of key agencies, including the Occupational Safety and Health Administration and the Environmental Protection Agency, by reducing their budgets and staff. In addition, it worked hard to simplify and reduce the number of rules and regulations, numbering in the thousands, with which business had to comply. At the same time, it staffed other key regulatory agencies, including the Federal Trade Commission and the Federal Communications Commission, with people sympathetic to its point of view and goals. Those appointments were clearly made with the intention of promoting the Reagan agenda from the inside out. . . .

[A] majority of Americans in 1981 thought that inflation was their number one problem; based on the high and persistent inflation rates of 1980–81, they had good reason to believe it. Thus aware of their concerns, President Reagan was eager to wrestle this monster to the ground—and he was prepared to pay the political and economic price to defeat it. Convinced that the country had to take strong medicine after what he called its thirty-year "binge," which he associated with wasteful governmental spending and Great Society programs, Reagan felt confident that a hard-line monetarist approach would go far to lick inflation, allowing him to reach his twin goals of economic stability and noninflationary growth in time for the 1984 election. . . .

A dynamic surge of entrepreneurship and eighties-style ostentation soon converged, thanks to the new mood of optimism unleashed by the Reagan boom. As John Kennedy's victory in 1960 had opened space on the left for a host of emerging liberal-radical ideologies and movements, so too did Reagan's rhetoric and politics provide an opportunity and the context for the emergence of new men of power, wealth, and connections, who would thrive in an economic climate that he did much to create. Indeed, the tax cut of 1981, the high interest rates of 1981–82, and the growing federal deficit went far to generate new sources of wealth for those who already had more money than virtually everyone else in America. It is no surprise, then, that since a redistribution of wealth in an upward direction had been a major goal of Reaganomics, the chief beneficiaries were those already at the top of the income pyramid. . . .

Reagan's domestic policies inspired similar loyalty and support from people who could be classified as Reagan Democrats. For instance, many working-class and lower-middle-class whites, whose political loyalties went back to Franklin Roosevelt, closely identified with his attack on big government and his demand for lower taxes, for these perspectives captured well their own changing attitudes toward the welfare state and race. Like many others, they were tired of seeing their tax dollars spent on poor blacks, who did not seem to benefit from the various welfare programs sponsored by the government: black street crime was still very much on the increase, while the inner cities continued to rot away.

# "The Second American Revolution": President Reagan's State of the Union Address (1985)

## Ronald W. Reagan

*Whether political observers are hostile or friendly to Ronald Reagan, nearly every political commentator agrees that Reagan possessed extraordinary skill in articulating his point of view and rallying support for it. Although Reagan retained a level of popular backing usually reserved for "consensus" politicians of a moderate persuasion, he presented, and argued effectively for, a singularly partisan definition of America's purpose and goals. Reagan had clear ideas, many of them in deep conflict with the direction of American government and policies since the New Deal. He wished to dismantle the "welfare state," cut taxes severely, restore a laissez-faire economy, and simultaneously construct a huge new military machine. In fact, Reagan did seek a new American revolution, one that would alter dramatically the shape and substance of American politics. Here in his State of the Union Address in 1985, the dimensions of that revolution are outlined, suggesting the degree to which Reagan sought publicly to build support for his strong ideas.*

Mr. Speaker, Mr. President, distinguished members of the Congress, honored guests and fellow citizens. I come before you to report on the state of our union. And I am pleased to report that, after four years of united effort, the American people have brought forth a nation renewed—stronger, freer and more secure than before.

Four years ago, we began to change—forever, I hope—our assumptions about government and its place in our lives. Out of that change has come great and robust growth—in our confidence, our economy and our role in the world. . . .

Four years ago, we said we would invigorate our economy by giving people greater freedom and incentives to take risks, and letting them keep more of what they earned.

We did what we promised, and a great industrial giant is reborn. Tonight we can take pride in 25 straight months of economic growth, the strongest in 34 years: a three-year inflation average of 3.9 percent

385

the lowest in 17 years; and 7.3 million new jobs in two years, with more of our citizens working than ever before. . . .

We have begun well. But it's only a beginning. We are not here to congratulate ourselves on what we have done, but to challenge ourselves to finish what has not yet been done.

We are here to speak for millions in our inner cities who long for real jobs, safe neighborhoods and schools that truly teach. We are here to speak for the American farmer, the entrepreneur and every worker in industries fighting to modernize and compete. And, yes, we are here to stand, and proudly so, for all who struggle to break free from totalitarianism; for all who know in their hearts that freedom is the one true path to peace and human happiness. . . .

We honor the giants of our history not by going back, but forward to the dreams their vision foresaw. My fellow citizens, this nation is poised for greatness. The time has come to proceed toward a great new challenge—a Second American Revolution of hope and opportunity; a revolution carrying us to new heights of progress by pushing back frontiers of knowledge and space; a revolution of spirit that taps the soul of America, enabling us to summon greater strength than we have ever known; and, a revolution that carries beyond our shores the golden promise of human freedom in a world at peace.

Let us begin by challenging conventional wisdom: There are no constraints on the human mind, no walls around the human spirit, no barriers to our progress except those we ourselves erect. Already, pushing down tax rates has freed our economy to vault forward to record growth.

In Europe, they call it "the American Miracle." Day by day, we are shattering accepted notions of what is possible. . . .

We stand on the threshold of a great ability to produce more, do more, be more. Our economy is not getting older and weaker, it's getting younger and stronger; it doesn't need rest and supervision, it needs new challenge, greater freedom. And that word—freedom—is the key to the Second American Revolution we mean to bring about.

Let us move together with an historic reform of tax simplification for fairness and growth. Last year, I asked then-Treasury Secretary Regan to develop a plan to simplify the tax code, so all taxpayers would be treated more fairly, and personal tax rates could come further down.

We have cut tax rates by almost 25 percent, yet the tax system remains unfair and limits our potential for growth. Exclusions and exemptions cause similar incomes to be taxed at different levels. Low-income families face steep tax barriers that make hard lives even harder. The Treasury Department has produced an excellent reform plan whose principles will guide the final proposal we will ask you to enact.

One thing that tax reform will not be is a tax increase in disguise. We will not jeopardize the mortgage interest deduction families need. We will reduce personal tax rates as low as possible by removing many tax preferences. We will propose a top rate of no more than 35 percent, and possibly lower. And we will propose reducing corporate rates while maintaining incentives for capital formation. . . .

Tax simplification will be a giant step toward unleashing the tremendous pent-up power of our economy. But a Second American Revolution must carry the promise of opportunity for all. It is time to liberate the spirit of enterprise in the most distressed areas of our country.

This government will meet its responsibility to help those in need. But policies that increase dependency, break up families and destroy self-respect are not progressive, they are reactionary. Despite our strides in civil rights, blacks, Hispanics and all minorities will not have full and equal power until they have full economic powers. . . .

Let us resolve that we will stop spreading dependency and start spreading opportunity; that we will stop spreading bondage and start spreading freedom.

There are some who say that growth initiatives must await final action on deficit reductions. The best way to reduce deficits is through economic growth. More business will be started, more investments made, more jobs created and more people will be on payrolls paying taxes. The best way to reduce government spending is to reduce the need for spending by increasing prosperity. . . .

To move steadily toward a balanced budget we must also lighten government's claim on our total economy. We will not do this by raising taxes. We must make sure that our economy grows faster than growth in spending by the federal government. In our fiscal year 1986 budget, overall government program spending will be frozen at the current level; it must not be one dime higher than fiscal year 1985. And three points are key:

First, the social safety net for the elderly, needy, disabled and unemployed will be left intact. Growth of our major health care programs, Medicare and Medicaid, will be slowed, but protections for the elderly and needy will be preserved.

Second, we must not relax our efforts to restore military strength just as we near our goal of a fully equipped, trained and ready professional corps. National security is government's first responsibility, so, in past years, defense spending took about half the federal budget. Today it takes less than a third.

We have already reduced our planned defense expenditures by nearly $100 billion over the past four years, and reduced projected spending again this year. You know, we only have a military industrial complex until a time of danger. Then it becomes the arsenal of democracy. Spending for defense is investing in things that are priceless: peace and freedom.

Third, we must reduce or eliminate costly government subsidies. For example, deregulation of the airline industry has led to cheaper airfares, but on Amtrak taxpayers pay about $35 per passenger every time an Amtrak train leaves the station. It's time we ended this huge federal subsidy.

Our farm program costs have quadrupled in recent years. Yet I know from visiting farmers, many in great financial distress, that we need an orderly transition to a market-oriented farm economy. We can help farmers best, not by expanding federal payments, but by making fundamental reforms, keeping interest rates heading down and knocking down foreign trade barriers to American farm exports. . . .

In the long run, we must protect the taxpayers from government. And I ask again that you pass, as 32 states have now called for, an amendment mandating the federal government spend no more than it takes in. And I ask for the authority used responsibly by 43 governors to veto individual items in appropriations bills. . . .

Nearly 50 years of government living beyond its means has brought us to a time of reckoning. Ours is but a moment in history. But one moment of courage, idealism and bipartisan unity can change American history forever. . . .

Every dollar the federal government does not take from us, every decision it does not make for us, will make our economy stronger, our lives more abundant, our future more free. . . .

There is another great heritage to speak of this evening. Of all the changes that have swept America the past four years, none brings greater promise than our rediscovery of the value of faith, freedom, family, work and neighborhood.

We see signs of renewal in increased attendance in places of worship; renewed optimism and faith in our future; love of country rediscovered by our young who are leading the way. We have rediscovered that work is good in and of itself; that it ennobles us to create and contribute no matter how seemingly humble our jobs. We have seen a powerful new current from an old and honorable tradition—American generosity. . . .

I thank the Congress for passing equal access legislation giving religious groups the same right to use classrooms after school that other groups enjoy. But no citizen need tremble, nor the world shudder, if a child stands in a classroom and breathes a prayer. We ask you again—give children back a right they had for a century-and-a-half or more in this country.

The question of abortion grips our nation. Abortion is either the taking of human life, or it isn't; and if it is—and medical technology is increasingly showing it is—it must be stopped. . . .

Of all the changes in the past 20 years, none has more threatened our sense of national well-being than the explosion of violent crime. One does not have to have been attacked to be a victim. The woman who must run to her car after shopping at night is a victim; the couple draping their door with locks and chains are victims; as is the tired, decent cleaning woman who can't ride a subway home without being afraid.

We do not seek to violate rights of defendants, but shouldn't we feel more compassion for victims of crime than for those who commit crime? For the first time in 20 years, the crime index has fallen two years in a row; we've convicted over 7,400 drug offenders, and put them, as well as leaders of organized crime, behind bars in record numbers.

But we must do more. I urge the House to follow the Senate and enact proposals permitting use of all reliable evidence that police officers acquire in good faith. These proposals would also reform the *habeas corpus* laws and allow, in keeping with the will of the overwhelming majority of Americans, the use of the death penalty where necessary.

There can be no economic revival in ghettos when the most violent among us are allowed to roam free. It is time we restored domestic tranquility. And we mean to do just that. . . .

Tonight I have spoken of great plans and great dreams. They are dreams we can make come true. Two hundred years of American history should have taught us that nothing is impossible. . . . Anything is possible in America if we have the faith, the will and the heart.

History is asking us, once again, to be a force for good in the world. Let us begin—in unity, with justice and love.

Thank you and God bless you.

# The Republican Contract with America (1994)

## Newt Gingrich

*Despite the presidential election of Bill Clinton, the conservative coalition that had arisen in the 1960s and 1970s, captured the White House in 1980, and flexed its muscles at the 1992 GOP convention scented victory as the 1994 midterm elections approached. The failure of the Clinton administration's health care plan, as well as allegations of financial and sexual wrongdoing by the president, highlighted the Democrats' vulnerability.*

*Georgia congressman Newt Gingrich, seizing the moment, drafted a conservative manifesto he called the Republicans' "Contract with America." It turned the midterm elections, usually dominated by local issues and personalities, into a national ideological referendum.*

*Running on the Contract, the Republicans won control of both houses of Congress in 1994, forcing Clinton to tack to the right and break with the Democratic Party's liberal tradition. Among other measures, he signed a crime-sentencing bill aimed at "getting tough on criminals" and a historic welfare reform bill that ended "welfare as we know it," slashed the capital gains tax, and embraced the Contract's goal of a balanced budget and fiscal restraint. "I hope you're all aware," the president told his aides, "we're all Eisenhower Republicans . . . fighting the Reagan Republicans."*

As Republican Members of the House of Representatives and as citizens seeking to join that body we propose not just to change its policies, but even more important, to restore the bonds of trust between the people and their elected representatives. That is why, in this era of official evasion and posturing, we offer instead a detailed agenda for national renewal, a written commitment with no fine print.

This year's election offers the chance, after four decades of one-party control, to bring to the House a new majority that will transform

From http://www.townhall.com/documents/contract.html.

the way Congress works. That historic change would be the end of government that is too big, too intrusive, and too easy with the public's money. It can be the beginning of a Congress that respects the values and shares the faith of the American family. . . .

On the first day of the 104th Congress, the new Republican majority will immediately pass the following major reforms, aimed at restoring the faith and trust of the American people in their government:

First, require all laws that apply to the rest of the country also apply equally to the Congress;

Second, select a major, independent auditing firm to conduct a comprehensive audit of Congress for waste, fraud, or abuse;

Third, cut the number of House committees, and cut committee staff by one-third;

Fourth, limit the terms of all committee chairs;

Fifth, ban the casting of proxy votes in committee;

Sixth, require committee meetings to be open to the public;

Seventh, require a three-fifths majority vote to pass a tax increase;

Eighth, guarantee an honest accounting of our Federal Budget by implementing zero base-line budgeting.

Thereafter, within the first 100 days of the 104th Congress, we shall bring to the House Floor the following bills, each to be given full and open debate, each to be given a clear and fair vote and each to be immediately available this day for public inspection and scrutiny.

1. *The Fiscal Responsibility Act.* A balanced budget/tax limitation amendment and a legislative line-item veto to restore fiscal responsibility to an out-of-control Congress, requiring them to live under the same budget constraints as families and businesses.

2. *The Taking Back Our Streets Act.* An anti-crime package including stronger truth-in-sentencing, "good faith" exclusionary rule exemptions, effective death penalty provisions, and cuts in social spending from this summer's "crime" bill to fund prison construction and additional law enforcement to keep people secure in their neighborhoods and kids safe in their schools.

3. *The Personal Responsibility Act.* Discourage illegitimacy and teen pregnancy by prohibiting welfare to minor mothers and denying increased AFDC for additional children while

on welfare, cut spending for welfare programs, and enact a tough two-years-and-out provision with work requirements to promote individual responsibility.

4. *The Family Reinforcement Act.* Child support enforcement, tax incentives for adoption, strengthening rights of parents in their children's education, stronger child pornography laws, and an elderly dependent care tax credit to reinforce the central role of families in American society. . . .

6. *The National Security Restoration Act.* No U.S. troops under U.N. command and restoration of the essential parts of our national security funding to strengthen our national defense and maintain our credibility around the world. . . .

9. *The Common Sense Legal Reform Act.* "Loser pays" laws, reasonable limits on punitive damages and reform of product liability laws to stem the endless tide of litigation.

10. *The Citizen Legislature Act.* A first-ever vote on term limits to replace career politicians with citizen legislators.

# Part 8

## THE UNITED STATES AND THE WORLD IN THE POST–COLD WAR ERA

In the aftermath of the September 11 terrorist attacks on the United States, commentators rushed to predict that everything about American life—from popular culture to foreign policy—had been changed forever. The attacks *were* unprecedented, and lives *were* forever changed, especially those of people who survived the attacks or who lost loved ones that day. But the longer term impact of what came to be called "9/11" is complicated. Fairly quickly, for the vast majority of Americans, daily life returned to normal.

But the attacks would have an enormous impact on American politics, policies, and foreign affairs. George Bush, whose presidency was widely perceived as ineffectual in early September 2001, became a "war president," pledged to defend and protect his country. Following U.S. attacks on Afghanistan, whose Taliban leaders had given refuge to Osama bin Laden and other members of Al Qaeda, the Bush administration shifted the focus of "the war on terror" to Iraq. Claiming that Saddam Hussein possessed weapons of mas destruction, the United States broke with precedent and began a "preemptive" war in Iraq in March 2003. While Saddam was quickly deposed, no weapons of mass destruction were found and U.S. troops (along with the small number of troops pledged by other nations) found themselves in an ongoing struggle with insurgents, caught in the middle of what many argued was a civil war.

The 2004 presidential election turned largely on issues of national security, and George Bush won reelection. In subsequent months, the Bush administration struggled with Congress and the courts over the limits of the war powers the president could claim. Could he bypass legal requirements for search warrants to eavesdrop on American citizens? Could individuals be held without appeal if the administration deemed them "enemy combatants"? The attacks on the World Trade Center and the Pentagon created possibilities for radical shifts in the nation's actions in the world, and began difficult debates over the balance between security and civil liberties, presidential versus congressional power, and the transparency (and honesty) of government officials who make major decisions about the nation's future. Dissatisfied with President Bush's answers to these questions, and with the course of the war in Iraq, the American people sent a powerful message to the Bush administration in the 2006 midterm elections and returned both houses of Congress to Democratic control.

In an even larger sense, the attacks of September 11, 2001, pointed to an irrefutable fact about the world at the beginning of the new millennium: its peoples and nations are increasingly connected. Political and national borders are compromised by global economies, by global communications, by global travel, by the global environmental impact of national decisions, and by the proliferation of weapons of mass destruction. Despite unprecedented power, the United States is increasingly subject to global forces, and to the consequences of decisions made and actions taken in far-off places. Possible consequences are not only economic: the appearance of bird flu in Asia threatened a global pandemic, and the spread of AIDS throughout the world had already demonstrated that political borders have little impact on the transmission of disease.

In the last decades of the twentieth century, the United States led the world in the development of a "new economy," one driven by global capital, heavily reliant on new technologies, dynamic, flexible, and highly competitive. By the dawn of the twenty-first century, the economies of the world had become increasingly interdependent, with the economic fortunes of the United States tied directly to a growing number of nations. Europeans created a common market, with most members of the European Union moving to a single currency in January 2002, and the United States opened trade borders with Mexico and Canada with the 1994 North American Free Trade Agreement (NAFTA).

Throughout the 1990s, the American economy showed unparalleled sustained growth. The stock market climbed steadily and rapidly, "dot.com" companies founded by twenty-something entrepreneurs made instant millionaires in a generation of computer-savvy youth.

Unfounded assumptions about never-ending economic growth and rising prosperity were tempered by the recession that began in 2000 and that was exacerbated by the events of 9/11/01. But there were downsides to the new economy well before the recession. During the 1990s, the benefits of economic growth were not distributed equally: the top 1 percent of American households claimed more wealth than the lower 95 percent. Between 1980 and 1996, the real income of the top 5 percent grew 58 percent, while the income of the bottom 60 percent rose by just 4 percent. By 2000, the poverty rate had reached a low of 11.3 percent, close to the 1973 all-time low of 11.1 percent. But that 11.3 percent represented 31.1 million people, and it hid further inequities. More than 20 percent of African Americans and Latinos fell below the poverty line. While that figure represented an all-time low for both groups, it scarcely suggested economic equality.

In addition, because of the flow of global capital and the interdependence of markets in the new economy, the United States' economy cannot be insulated. Developing countries in Latin America, Africa, and South Asia increasingly compete for the same jobs as do the older industrialized countries—jobs that at an ever-increasing rate are leaving America and other "first world" countries. Global systems of transportation and communication have made it possible for the United States to import goods made much more cheaply elsewhere; they also mean that even goods "made in the U.S." may be assembled from parts constructed in distant nations, and that companies may well "outsource" white-collar work to nations such as India. In 2005, China's economic growth rate was 9.8 percent (compared to the United States' 3.5); China's rapid growth suggests there will be major changes in the world economy in coming years.

As the global economy changes, so too has the structure of world geopolitics. The attacks in the United States in 2001, followed by those in Spain and Great Britain, are evidence of the instability of the post–Cold War world and of the threat of nonstate actors in a world at least presumably stabilized by an alliance of nations. When, nearly three-quarters of a century after having come into existence, the Soviet Union suddenly dissolved in 1991, the United States became the only remaining superpower, the "winner" of the Cold War with the Soviet Union. It seemed a moment of triumph and possibility, but that confidence quickly faded as it became apparent that the end of the Cold War did not promise peace and stability. New international problems proliferated, with ethnic nationalism, indigenous civil wars, and religiously driven conflict souring hopes for a post–Cold War peace. Some even voiced nostalgia for the certainties of Cold War ideology. How was it possible to determine what was morally correct or politically advantageous when the choices in international affairs were so murky and muddled?

The readings in this section focus on the United States and the world, both in terms of foreign affairs and geopolitics and in terms of economic relations. Historian of international relations George Herring analyzes the impact of 9/11 in the context of post–Cold War foreign policy, providing a context for the documents that follow. The experience of 9/11 is captured in the accounts of two New Yorkers who were at Ground Zero the day of the attack. A segment from President George Bush's State of the Union address describes his vision of a larger "war on terror" and lays the groundwork for the American invasion of Iraq. A letter to President Bush from Cindy Sheehan, mother of a Marine killed during his duty in Iraq, represents domestic protest against the war in Iraq.

Turning back to questions of domestic security, a "report card" created by former members of the 9/11 Commission points to the enormous gap between the key actions the commission recommended as necessary to prevent future terrorist attacks and improve American security, and the actions taken by the Bush administration and Congress as of December 2005. Looking outside the United States, a major poll conducted by the Pew Foundation reveals attitudes of other nations toward the United States and its people.

Two documents offer different perspectives on globalization. An interview with Thomas Friedman, author of *The World Is Flat,* explores Friedman's overall embrace of the force of globalization, while a document created by the group Global Exchange rejects the vision of globalism it sees manifested by the powerful World Trade Organization.

In reading the documents that follow, students should consider the changing place of the United States in the larger world. What is "globalization," and what impact do the processes of globalization have on the United States and on other nations of the world? What drives the increasing interdependence of nations? Technology? Economics? The traditional sorts of national interests that have structured foreign policy over the past century? Is globalization inevitable? How has the web of changes the term sums up affected American security and the ways in which war is waged in the contemporary world?

# From Gulf War I to Gulf War II: Confronting the Post–Cold War World Order

*George C. Herring*

*When the Cold War came to an end, millions of Americans believed—perhaps understandably—that foreign policy issues no longer would dominate American political discussion and decision making. For almost fifty years, a bipolar Cold War vision had shaped American foreign policy. Now the situation was dramatically different. But in many ways, the end of the Cold War simply made geopolitics and American international relations much more complex.*

*There was only a decade between the end of the Cold War and the terrorist attacks of September 11, 2001. That decade, as historian George Herring demonstrates in his analysis of post–Cold War foreign policy, was far from peaceful, and the foreign policy issues facing the United States were far from easy. In the following piece, Herring moves beyond the complexities of post–Cold War foreign policy to analyze the post-9/11 Bush doctrine (which he characterizes as "a radically new national security doctrine"). Having read his analysis, do you think that the world was more stable at the height of the Cold War or in the first decade of the twenty-first century?*

For a fleeting moment in the early 1990s, peace and world order seemed within reach. The end of the Cold War and the subsequent collapse of the Soviet Union removed the major cause of international tension for the past half century and eased, if they did not eliminate altogether, the dreadful threat of a nuclear holocaust. The emergence of democracies and market economies in the former Soviet satellites, Latin America, and even in South Africa offered the hope of a new age of freedom and prosperity. The victory in the 1991

Persian Gulf War of a powerful allied coalition, headed by the United States and working under the aegis of the United Nations, seemed to hail the triumph of Woodrow Wilson's dreams of collective security where peace would be maintained and aggression repelled by international collaboration. In the aftermath of the Gulf War, President George Bush proclaimed the birth of a new world order under American leadership. State Department official Frances Fukayama went farther, exulting in the "end of history," the absolute triumph of capitalism and democracy over fascism and communism and the promise of a just and peaceful world made up of stable and prosperous democracies in which geopolitics would be a thing of the past.

It did not take long for such prophecies to be exposed as at best wishful thinking, at worst, absolute folly. The Cold War had imposed a crude form of order on inherently unstable regions of the world, and its end unleashed powerful forces that had been held in check for years. Especially in Central Europe, the Middle East, and Central Asia, national loyalties gave way to explosive ethnic rivalries and secessionist movements. Most prominent were the brutal wars between Serbs, Croats, and Muslims in the former Yugoslavia and the conflict between Sunni and Shiite Muslims and Kurds in the Middle East, but the *New York Times* counted in early 1993 forty-eight such conflicts scattered across the globe. "Get ready for fifty new countries in the world in the next fifty years," a pessimistic New York Senator Daniel P. Moynihan admonished, most of them "born in bloodshed." Wilson's ideal of self-determination seemed to have returned with a vengeance, threatening to tear the world apart rather than bring it together.

Other commentators predicted even more gloomy scenarios. Some warned that the Cold War struggle between East and West would give way to a new conflict between North and South, between the haves and have-nots of the world, "the West and the rest." Runaway population growth in the developing countries portended a possibly disastrous drain on already scarce resources, enormous environmental crises that could afflict the entire globe, and the rampant spread of crime, disease, and war. Some commentators warned that international migration would be the greatest problem of the twenty-first century and foresaw an assault on the borders of developed countries through massive emigration. Others predicted that the anarchy already gripping Africa would spread across the globe, the chaos in less-developed countries eventually contaminating the developed ones. Although such predictions appeared unnecessarily pessimistic and even reflected a false nostalgia for the "order" of the Cold War, it seemed clear that the end of history was not in view. Conflict and disorder would characterize the post–Cold War era.

The position of the United States in the new world order was paradoxical. During the 1990s, America enjoyed a preponderance of power unprecedented in world history. Its economy was 40 percent larger than that of the second ranked nation, its defense spending six times that of the next six nations combined. Because of its wealth and security, it had unrivaled freedom of action. Ironically, however, it seemed less threatened by and had less to gain from the world and therefore was less disposed to act. The "central paradox of unipolarity," according to political scientist Stephen Walt, was that the United States "enjoys enormous influence but has little idea what to do with its power or even how much effort it should expend."[1] These peculiar conditions caused an always fickle American public to lose interest in the world. Both reflecting and shaping public opinion, the media drastically reduced its coverage of developments abroad, and Congress slashed the foreign affairs budget.

Not surprisingly, the United States responded uncertainly to the new world order. Its contours were fuzzy at best, and Americans lacked any sort of blueprint for dealing with it. The absence of an obvious threat to national security removed any compelling inducement to take the lead in solving world problems. Americans recognized that there could be no return to isolationism in a world shrunken by technology and bound by economic interdependence, but after forty years of international commitment and massive Cold War expenditures they yearned for normalcy and relief from the burdens of leadership. As in the aftermath of World Wars I and II, they preferred to focus on domestic problems, and support for foreign policy ventures waned. Bitter memories of the Vietnam debacle haunted the nation for a quarter century after the event, adding yet another restraint against global involvement.

The halting response of the Bush administration to the new order it had once hailed foreshadowed the difficulties of the post–Cold War era. If the administration looked to the future and reassessed America's global role, it did not reach any firm conclusions or confront in any

---

1. Stephen Walt, "Two Cheers for Clinton," *Foreign Affairs* (March/April 2000), 64–65.

fundamental way such urgent issues as world population growth and the environment. After its forceful leadership in the Persian Gulf War, it did little to address longer-range but still pressing problems in the Middle East. Its response to a mounting crisis in Bosnia in the Balkans suggested its hesitancy. Despite warnings from some quarters of a new holocaust and its own bold rhetoric, it did nothing to halt Serbia's "ethnic cleansing." "Where is it written that the United States is the military policeman of the world?" State Department spokesperson Margaret Tutwiler asked. "We don't have a dog in that fight," her boss, Secretary of State James Baker, curtly proclaimed. In his last days in office, President Bush authorized a humanitarian rescue mission in Somalia, sending troops to prevent rivalries among local warlords from causing mass starvation. But the administration appears never to have decided whether it was really committed to the new world order under American leadership that its rhetoric claimed, or, because of domestic constraints, it preferred retrenchment and retreat.

Even more than its predecessor, the administration of William Jefferson Clinton found adjustment to the new world order vexing and difficult. Clinton's aides had run their campaign on the slogan "It's the economy, stupid," and in many ways the new administration seemed more attuned to the new era, making clear its preeminent concern with domestic issues. Having spent his entire political career in state politics, the former governor of Arkansas was plainly less interested in, experienced with, and informed on foreign policy. At least at the outset, he appeared to hope that this team could hold the world at bay while he implemented an ambitious domestic agenda. His few campaign pronouncements on foreign policy seemed to promise more forthright U.S. leadership and a more active role in volatile areas such as Bosnia. Yet his foreign policy advisers came mainly out of the liberal Democratic mold—burned by Vietnam, nervous about unilateral interventions, and committed to working through the United Nations and persuading allies to share the burden of world leadership.

Clinton and his advisers quickly discovered the perils of the new world order. The administration was deeply committed to promoting domestic prosperity through the expansion of foreign trade. The president himself was an unabashed enthusiast for globalization, seeing trade as a primary means to promote free markets, democracy, and eventually peace and prosperity. "Since we don't have geopolitics any more," one Clinton adviser pronounced, "trade is the name of the game," and in embassies across the world diplomats turned their attention to economics. Clinton cashed in all his political chips to secure congressional passage in 1993 of the North American Free Trade Agreement (NAFTA). He also vigorously promoted the Asia-Pacific Economic Community as a modern economic NATO and the General Agreement on Tariffs and Trade (GATT). The Clinton administration eventually presided over the greatest expansion of foreign trade in U.S. history, helping to fuel the nation's most prolonged period of economic growth.

Promoting trade expansion raised all sorts of problems, however. Whatever its long-term benefits, it also brought huge short-term trade-offs and costly job displacement. NAFTA contributed significantly to the prosperity of the 1990s, but it also eliminated more jobs in the nation's already moribund manufacturing sector. In the new world economy, promotion of trade often involved unprecedented and unwelcome intrusion into the internal politics of other nations, and globalization, which to many peoples meant Americanization, provoked a growing backlash abroad.

Committed to promoting human rights as well as expanding trade, the administration quickly discovered that the two might not always be compatible. Exports were increasingly important to domestic prosperity. In the most prominent cases, the administration therefore bowed to expediency without totally abandoning its principles. Two hundred thousand Americans were employed in the sale of some $9 billion worth of exports to China, for example, yet that country's abuses of human rights offended the sensibilities of pressure groups and some Washington officials. After much agonizing, the administration normalized trade relations with China, accepting more or less at face value that nation's promises to improve its human rights record.

Clinton also quickly discovered the painful truth that in foreign policy American presidents do not have to seek out trouble, it finds them. The administration was even less surefooted on the increasingly difficult questions posed by world order: peacekeeping and what came to be called humanitarian intervention to prevent human suffering in areas torn by ethnic conflict. In the campaign and in its early days in office, it sounded at least mildly interventionist. Clinton himself scored Bush's inaction on Bosnia and affirmed that "no national security issue is more urgent than securing democracy's triumph around the world." National security adviser Anthony

Lake coined vague phrases such as "enlargement of democracy" and "pragmatic Wilsonianism" to describe an approach that hinted at greater activism. Before the end of its first year in office, however, the administration had beaten a hasty retreat. Unable to persuade its European allies to lift an arms embargo against Bosnia, it would go no further than sanction harmless NATO air strikes to defend embattled UN peacekeepers. It went along with expansion of the UN role in Somalia, but when eighteen American GIs were killed in bloody fighting in Mogadishu on October 3, 1993, it immediately scaled back the U.S. role and promised an alarmed Congress and public that Americans would be out of Somalia in six months. A week later, closer to home, and even more humiliating, a shipload of American soldiers and technicians dispatched to troubled Haiti as part of a larger effort to unseat a cruel military government turned back in the face of armed and jeering mobs on the docks at Port-au-Prince.

While rampant instability wracked the globe, the administration developed guidelines for intervention some critics denounced as "self-containment." The United States would only intervene in cases where international security was gravely threatened, a major disaster required urgent relief, or gross violation of human rights had occurred. Other nations would have to share the costs, but American troops would participate only under U.S. command. In response to proliferating UN commitments, the administration in May 1994 spelled out a total of seventeen even more restrictive guidelines for support of these peacekeeping operations. Making clear in the aftermath of Somalia its lack of enthusiasm for UN enterprises, it vowed that it would commit troops only in cases where vital U.S. interests were threatened. Congress would have to approve the mission, and funds would have to be available. Such missions must have a clearly stated objective, a reasonable assurance of success, and a strategy for completing the job. They must pose a major threat to international peace and security or gross violations of human rights. At the same time, Clinton urged the UN to scale back its own ambitions: "If the American people are to say yes to UN peacekeeping, the United Nations must know when to say no." Parodying John F. Kennedy's inaugural address, critics claimed that in a troubled world Clinton's United States was willing to "pay only some prices, fight only some foes, and bear only some burdens in the defense of freedom." It was all but admitting to potential adversaries that when the going got tough, the United States would go home.

Not surprisingly in view of these guidelines, the United States and the rest of the world looked the other way in 1994 when ethnic rivalries in Rwanda in central Africa produced "the fastest, most efficient killing spree of the twentieth century."[2] While the world did nothing, the revenge-bent Hutu tribe murdered an estimated 800,000 rival Tutsis, some of them with machetes. It was a case where even a relatively small intervention might have made a difference, but the world chose to do nothing. Paralyzed by memories of Somalia and Haiti, the Clinton administration did not even discuss the possibility of intervention. As if to insulate themselves from guilt and responsibility, U.S. officials refused even to use what was called "the g-word," resorting instead to the euphemistic "acts of genocide" to describe what was happening. Their main concern was to get Americans out of Rwanda as quickly as possible.

The Clinton administration began to shift gears in the fall of 1994. After months of soul-searching, imposition of sanctions that hurt victims more than oppressors, and warnings that were ignored, it used the threat of a full-scale invasion of Haiti to remove a brutal military dictatorship and restore to power the erratic—but elected—president Jean-Bertrand Aristide. Clinton justified the move as necessary to "restore democracy" and, more pragmatically, to prevent a massive flight of Haitians to U.S. shores. To the shock of some observers, this time U.S. troops met a warm reception from Haitians, and after tense negotiations the military government agreed to leave. The intervention did not bring democracy to Haiti or lead to a new policy toward humanitarian interventions, but it probably spared some suffering in that troubled land and helped burnish a badly damaged Clinton image.

After years of hesitation, the United States in the summer of 1995 finally made its weight felt in the former Yugoslavia. The Serb massacre of a Bosnian Muslim enclave in the village of Srebrenica, after three years of shelling with artillery, aroused anger throughout the world. In the United States a new coalition of liberal and neoconservative interventionists began to push the administration to do something. Humiliated by Somalia and Haiti, three years of inaction in the Balkans, and the blatant defiance of Serb leader Slobodan

---

2. Samantha Power, "Bystanders to Genocide: Why the United States Let Rwanda Tragedy Happen," *The Atlantic Monthly* (September 2001), 84.

Milosevic, the president himself was moved to exclaim: "The United States cannot be a punching bag in the world anymore." In August 1995, with full U.S. backing, NATO began intensive bombing of Serb positions using the most modern technology and eventually taking out Milosevic's communications center. This decisive action forced the warring parties to the conference table in Dayton, Ohio, where U.S. diplomat Richard Holbrooke brokered "an imperfect peace to a very imperfect part of the world after an unusually cruel war."[3] Clinton followed by sending U.S. troops to participate in a Bosnian peacekeeping mission, to cover his political flanks limiting the commitment to twelve months (subsequently extended).

Clinton was reelected by a substantial margin in 1996, but foreign policy played an insignificant role in the campaign, and the election victory did not bring a firmer hand to the foreign policy wheel. In the absence of any clear threat and with the nation more prosperous than at any time in the twentieth century, there was little incentive for engagement. The result on the part of the American public was a form of "apathetic internationalism." A band of highly nationalist Republicans in Congress flaunted their hostility toward the outside world, boasting of not having passports. Republican House of Representatives leader Richard Armey of Texas even claimed that he did not need to go to Europe because he had already been there once. Network news focused increasingly on entertainment and trivia and further slashed its foreign coverage. After January 1998, moreover, Clinton was increasingly crippled when he first denied and then, faced with incontrovertible evidence, admitted, an affair with a young White House intern, Monica Lewinsky, prompting his foes in Congress to initiate impeachment proceedings.

While the administration was preoccupied with its own survival, the Balkans continued to seethe with violence. This time it was in Kosovo, the most volatile part of a most explosive region, with its own long and bitter history of ethnic hatreds. Populated predominantly by Kosovar Albanians who were also Muslims, Kosovo was viewed as sacred turf by Serbs. Left out of the Dayton discussions, it exploded in crisis shortly after. In 1997, the Kosovars began to form a Kosovo Liberation Army (KLA) to win their independence and launched guerrilla warfare

---

3. David Halberstam, *War in a Time of Peace: Bush, Clinton, and the Generals* (New York, 2001), 358.

against local Serbs. The Serbs struck back with a vengeance, burning villages and murdering those Kosovars they could get their hands on. At first, they moved slowly—"a village a day keeps NATO away"—was their sardonic slogan. Their intent was nevertheless unmistakable, and the results devastating. An especially bloody massacre at the village of Racak in late 1998 again provoked cries for international action.

Once more in early 1999, a reluctant administration was moved to do something. The Senate finally acquitted Clinton of impeachment charges in February 1999, freeing his hands. Still smarting from Vietnam and uneager to get entangled in a Balkans quagmire, the military stubbornly resisted calls for intervention. Within and outside the government, however, pressures grew. Some advocates of intervention compared the Serbs' ethnic cleansing to the Holocaust. The new Secretary of State, Madeline Albright, who had grown up in pre–World War II Czechoslovakia and viewed the United States as the "indispensable nation," fervently warned of another Munich and ridiculed the military's caution. Why do you insist on having all those modern forces if you are unwilling to use them, she once asked General Colin Powell. So important was her role that when war came it was known as "Madeline's War."

In March 1999, the administration finally went to war over Kosovo. If memories of World War II helped push the United States to do something, more recent and haunting memories of Vietnam dictated the way it fought. Clinton also hoped to repeat the Bosnian experience where a modest effort had forced Milosevic to the conference table. To assuage fears in Congress and among the European allies, the administration relied exclusively on airpower. In what turned out to be a huge miscalculation, the president even publicly vowed: "I do not intend to put ground troops into Kosovo to fight a war."

As is so often the case, the war turned out to be much more complicated than had been anticipated. The bombing was implemented gradually and the Serbs stubbornly withstood it, evoking memories of the Vietnam quagmire. As the war dragged on, Clinton and the NATO allies drastically escalated the bombing. It was a new kind of high-tech war, virtual war it seemed, fought by professional forces, waged from 50,000 feet, with no sacrifice required of the American people and little intrusion upon their lives. Using precision-guided weapons, U.S. aircraft attacked Serb airfields and ground forces and eventually Belgrade itself, causing troops to mutiny and political opposition to form. To increase the pressure, Clinton finally reneged on his promise not to use ground forces, warning that "all options are on the table." Milosevic conceded in June.

The war was fought clumsily—a "textbook case of how not to fight a war," in the words of two experts—and the results were less than satisfactory.[4] The always clever Milosesvic used the onset of war to drive the Albanians out of Kosovo, inflicting a great deal more human suffering and creating a million new refugees. A war fought to minimize Western military losses resulted in the death of an estimated 10,000 people, many of them civilians. As the war ended, the KLA seized the opportunity to drive the remaining Serbs out of Kosovo, ensuring further conflict. The war at least resolved the immediate problem without providing a long-term solution, and ultimately contributed to the removal of Milosevic.

The Clinton legacy in foreign policy was at best mixed. The administration took some measures in association with Russia to reduce the huge nuclear inventories left over from the Cold War, and opened a dialogue with North Korea to check its nuclear threat. It used American influence with some short-term success to try to settle longstanding disputes in Northern Ireland and the Middle East. It normalized relations with Vietnam, ending more than twenty-five years after the fall of Saigon the crippling and vindictive postwar sanctions imposed by loser on winner. It enlarged NATO to include some former Soviet satellites, rewrote the longstanding treaty with Japan, and sent warships in 1996 to defuse a dangerous crisis in the Taiwan Straits.

In the 1990s, as in the 1920s, the business of America was business, and in foreign policy as in domestic policy the administration's major claim to success was in the realm of economics. A timely bailout loan of $25 billion helped avert economic disaster in Mexico in 1995, and by keeping American markets open even at the cost of a huge short-term balance of payments deficit the administration helped contain the impact of the Asian economic meltdown of 1997. During the Clinton years, the United States concluded more than 300 trade agreements. While the United States prospered, however, there was little sign that globalization was producing the democratizing and stabilizing results its enthusiasts claimed. On the contrary, by the end of the century it had provoked a strong backlash from labor unions and some liberals at home and from leaders of the developing nations

---

4. Ivo Daalder and Michael O'Hanlon, *Winning Ugly: NATO's War to Save Kosovo* (Washington, D.C., 2000).

who on the one hand resented the competitive edge it gave the rich nations and on the other feared reformers from outside who sought to impose labor and environmental standards. Warfare in the streets of Seattle during the WTO meeting in November 1999 symbolized a clash that was likely to grow in the years ahead.

In the realm of international politics, as Garry Wills observed, Clinton was a "foreign policy minimalist, doing as little as possible as late as possible in place after place."[5] The administration responded perfunctorily to terrorist attacks on American interests in Saudi Arabia, New York City, and Africa, and on a U.S. Navy destroyer in Yemen, a sign of things to come unheeded. Clinton later felt compelled to apologize for U.S. inaction in Rwanda. He eventually employed U.S. power along with NATO to impose an uneasy peace on the Balkans, but the long-term prospects were still highly uncertain and the human cost of the delay was enormous. The administration never developed a doctrine for humanitarian intervention or a broader rationale for the use of American power in the new world order.

Without firm presidential leadership, the nation drifted. The mood in the aftermath of the Cold War was one of triumphalism and smug, insular complacency. In a 1998 poll, Americans did not even list foreign policy among their major problems. On college campuses, the teaching of foreign languages decreased drastically, and area studies gave way to modeling and game theory. Support for military spending, foreign aid, and the United Nations plummeted, and there was little backing for the use of ground troops abroad. Foreign policy played no more than a peripheral part in the 2000 presidential campaign. Self-indulgent Americans reveled in their prosperity, a minority of the world's population recklessly consuming a huge proportion of the world's limited resources.

Much would soon change. After a period of stumbling and uncertainty, the new Republican administration of George W. Bush would use the opportunity created by devastating terrorist attacks on the United States on September 11, 2001, to effect the most revolutionary changes in U.S. foreign policy since the Truman administration.

Narrowly elevated to the presidency in a contested election settled by the Supreme Court, the younger Bush gave little hint in his

---

5. Garry Wills, "The Clinton Principle," *New York Times Magazine* (January 19, 1997), 44.

campaign what was to come. Compared to his internationalist father, his experience and mindset were parochial. A graduate of Yale University and the Harvard Business School, he had traveled little, worked mostly in business, and served only as governor of Texas. In the campaign, he distanced himself from the Wilsonian label he sought to pin on Clinton, expressing skepticism about humanitarian intervention and disdain for nation-building. Bush sought to make up for his own lack of experience by naming a veteran foreign policy team. Appointment of the immensely popular Colin Powell as secretary of state, the first African American to hold that position, cheered liberal internationalists more than it should have given his staunch opposition to using force for humanitarian purposes. But the real center of power in policy making rested with Secretary of Defense Donald Rumsfeld and Vice-President Dick Cheney. The two had worked closely since the Nixon years. They had been deeply disturbed by America's failure in Vietnam, the denouement of which they had witnessed first-hand from the Ford White House. They shared Reagan's conviction that American ideals and power were a force for good in the world. They believed that the United States must maintain military supremacy and use it to promote its own interests, not permitting the scruples of allies to stand in the way. Less noticed at the outset but equally important was the presence in key second-level positions of Paul Wolfowitz, Douglas Feith, John Bolton, and other neoconservatives, former liberals who fervently believed that America's power should be used to reshape the world in its image.

From the start, the administration took a decidedly unilateralist approach. It gave top priority to developing a missile defense system that was intended to make the United States invulnerable but also violated treaties with the former Soviet Union. Without any consultation, it withdrew from the 1997 Kyoto Protocol on global warming and suspended talks aimed at stopping North Korea's development of long-range missiles. State Department spokesperson Richard Haas labeled the new approach "a la carte multilateralism," but critics at home and abroad denounced the administration's rude manners and go-it-alone approach as a new isolationism.

Early in the morning on September 11, 2001, nineteen Arab terrorists operating under the orders of Saudi Osama bin Laden and his Al Qaeda organization hijacked four commercial airliners and used them as missiles to strike New York's World Trade Center and the Pentagon. A planned attack on the Capitol or White House was aborted when a revolt of courageous passengers forced a crash landing on Pennsylvania farmland. After two enormous explosions, Manhattan's landmark twin towers crumbled to the ground, leaving a massive pile of rubble at what became known as Ground Zero. The attack caused major damage at the Pentagon. Almost three thousand people were killed.

9/11, as it came to be called, worked dramatic changes in American life. For the first time since 1814, the continental United States had come under brutal, devastating attack, and in one fiery moment the intellectual and emotional baggage left from Vietnam and the complacency that had marked the 1990s seemed swept aside in a surge of fear and anger. An already sluggish economy descended into what economists finally admitted was a recession. Americans felt vulnerable. Congress granted the president sweeping authorization to use American military forces to combat terrorism, and through the so-called Patriot Act vastly expanded powers that would be used in ways that infringed on traditional civil liberties. 9/11 worked a sea change in the mindset shaped by Vietnam and Watergate.

An administration that had seemed floundering suddenly found purpose and with broad popular support launched an all-out war against international terrorism. Seemingly confounding those who had dismissed him as a lightweight, Bush gave a powerful address before a joint session of Congress, rallying the nation behind the war. September 11 evoked an outpouring of sympathy and support from abroad, and under Powell's leadership, an administration that had only recently shunned multilateralism now began cobbling together an unwieldy coalition composed of old allies such as Britain and France, former enemies such as Russia and China, and pariah states such as Pakistan to attack in different ways on a variety of fronts a new kind of foe and its sources of support, hinting, mistakenly as it turned out, that the summer's unilateralism was a thing of the past. The president's stark and tactless warning that those who were not with him were against him, more accurately reflected the direction the administration would take.

The first phase of the war shocked many experts. Moving with great deliberateness, the United States mobilized military forces to strike at the immediate source of the threat, bin Laden's Al Qaeda and the fundamentalist Islamic Taliban that sheltered them in Afghanistan. In the parlance of the old West, Bush vowed to bring back "the evil one" dead or alive. Applying on a much larger scale the new high-tech methods of warfare first used in the Balkans, the United States relied on airpower and Afghan proxies to eliminate in less than four months the despised and surprisingly weak Taliban and destroy bin Laden's training camps. In December 2001, the United States installed a new interim government. Administration supporters cheered the victory and sneered at skeptics who had warned that the United States might get bogged down in Afghanistan as the Soviet Union had in the 1980s.

In fact, the administration made crucial errors that turned tactical success into a possible strategic failure. Worried about fighting in Afghanistan and determined to convert the armed forces to a new form of warfare, Rumsfeld relied on airpower and local forces to do what might have required large numbers of U.S. troops on the ground. Bin Laden and Taliban leader Mullah Omar, along with numerous of their followers, paid off or eluded Afghan soldiers and slipped into the rugged mountains along the Pakistan-Afghanistan border to fight another day. In time, they mounted an insurgency that jeopardized security in parts of Afghanistan. Never enthusiastic about the job of reconstruction, the Bush administration undertook what critics called "nation-building lite," making inadequate preparations and providing insufficient funds for an enormously challenging task. Large parts of the country fell under the sway of local warlords. In war, the law of unintended consequences usually prevails, and opium recaptured its accustomed place as the nation's major cash crop, further undercutting the by-now-forgotten U.S. war against drugs. Afghanistan soon disappeared from the front pages; an administration that had vowed to kill or capture "the evil one" stopped using bin Laden's name in public statements.

While the war in Afghanistan lagged amid claims of victory, the White House in September 2002 unveiled a radically new national security doctrine. Written, at Bush's instruction, in words the "boys in Lubbock" could understand, the National Security Strategy paper used 9/11 and the war on terrorism to implement ideas conservatives and neo-conservatives had been tossing around for years. It reflected an evangelical Christian president's taste for moral absolutes. It manifested the influence of Wolfowitz and other neo-conservatives who wished to use America's power to promote democracy abroad. It combined ringing affirmations of Wilsonian ideals with hard-nosed statements about the uses of American power. Admitting to only one "sustainable model for national success: freedom, democracy, and free enterprise," it vowed to "use this moment of opportunity to extend the benefits of freedom across the globe." It insisted that the United States must do what was necessary to maintain its military preeminence. It paid lip service to multilateralism, but made clear that the United States would "act apart when our interests and unique responsibility require." The nation could not wait until it had "absolute proof" of danger from weapons of mass destruction. Threats must be stopped before they reached American shores. The principles of military preeminence, unilateralism, and preemptive or even preventive war departed sharply from the ideas of containment and deterrence that had guided Cold War strategies. Praised by conservatives, what came to be called the Bush Doctrine was denounced by critics as striking a tone of arrogance worthy of the Roman Empire and "Wilsonianism in boots."

Long before it set forth the Bush Doctrine, the administration began to contemplate war to force regime change in Iraq. Dictator Saddam Hussein had somehow survived a crushing defeat in 1991 and a decade of UN sanctions. Even before 9/11, Bush administration officials talked of getting rid of him. Immediately after the terrorist attack, they tried desperately to link him to something for which he had no responsibility. Once the Afghan war appeared won, Iraq immediately resurfaced. Persuading themselves that Saddam was near getting weapons of mass destruction and might give them to terrorists, they decided to go to war by summer 2002 without searching internal debate or close examination of alternatives.

"Why Iraq, why now?" was a question asked often in the days ahead, and it will likely continue to be asked far into the future. The answers appear as varied and complex as the individuals who pushed for war. The easy response was oil, of course, and from the outset critics screamed "No blood for oil." But Bush, Cheney, and Rumsfeld appear to have been less worried about Iraqi oil for its own sake than about the threat an Iraq armed with weapons of mass destruction might pose to an oil-rich region. Assertive nationalists, Cheney and Rumsfeld saw an opportunity to complete the unfinished business of 1991, eliminate a nuisance and potential threat, and by demonstrating the efficacy of modern, high-technology warfare, put America's military might on full display. For the neo-cons, as they came to be called, war satisfied deep philosophical convictions as well as immediate practical concerns. The most hawkish of Reagan's advisers, they formed a highly influential cabal in the Bush administration. They believed that the United States had a moral duty to oppose tyranny and spread democracy. They shared the Cheney-Rumsfeld position that the nation must use its military preeminence to impose a "benign hegemony" across the world. Many of them had close ties to Israel, and they believed that the overthrow of Saddam and democratization of Iraq would promote that ally's security. They fantasized that through a reverse domino theory democracy would extend from Iraq to other Middle Eastern countries. If any individual or group bears primary responsibility for the second war with Iraq, it was Wolfowitz and the neo-conservatives.

Advocates of war found a receptive audience in the White House. Toppling Saddam would permit the president to succeed where his father had failed and avenge the Iraqi dictator's 1993 attempt on his father's life. Bush combined the cowboy mentality of his native Texas with the missionary spirit of evangelical Christianity. He was neither a deep thinker nor particularly curious and he abjured complexity— "I don't do nuance," he once snapped. At the same time, he could be forthright and bold. He saw the world in terms of good and evil and fervently believed that he had been "called" to defend the United States and extend "God's gift of liberty" to "every human being in the world." In Bush's worldview, a war with Iraq would protect the security of the United States, eliminate a major force of evil, and expand freedom.

In a strange, almost surreal way, the administration moved the nation toward its first preventive war with remarkably little debate or dissent. Exploiting still fresh memories of the horrors of 9/11, it ran roughshod over any and all opposition. Employing evidence that in most cases proved to be exaggerated or just plain wrong, it repeated over and over ominous warnings that Saddam had or would soon have weapons of mass destruction and would share them with terrorists, thus justifying preventive war. In the oft-quoted words of national security adviser Condoleezza Rice, "We don't want the smoking gun to be a mushroom cloud." Divided among themselves, nervous about dissent in wartime, and with mid-term elections approaching, the Democrats did not muster effective opposition. Even as U.S. troops poured into the Persian Gulf, Congress in October 2002 overwhelmingly passed a resolution authorizing the president to "use the armed forces of the United States as he determines to be necessary and appropriate . . . against the continuing threat opposed by Iraq."

The administration did not enjoy similar success at the United Nations. Powell preferred to wage war multilaterally, as in 1991, and persuaded a reluctant White House to take the issue to the United Nations. Among leading nations, however, only Britain went along, and France and Germany actively opposed the U.S. drive toward war. After months of bullying and arm-twisting tactics and a ballyhooed 75-minute speech by Powell purporting to make the case for war failed to produce backing for a UN resolution endorsing military action, the administration plunged ahead on its own. Gathering a ramshackle "coalition of the willing" composed of Britain and twenty-five small nations, most of whom provided only token contingents, it launched in March 2003 Operation Iraqi Freedom.

Much like Afghanistan except at far greater cost, the war against Iraq was a smashing, short-term military success, an enormously costly longer term political failure. A massive "shock and awe" bombing campaign knocked out Iraqi communications and destroyed crucial military installations at the start of the war. In one of the most rapid advances in military history, U.S. forces with only slight delays drove from Kuwait to Baghdad in less than three weeks. Although Saddam remained at large, the toppling of his statue in Baghdad on April 11 symbolized the fall of his regime. The United States suffered only 109 casualties in this phase of the war. On May 10, a jubilant Bush landed in full flight regalia aboard the aircraft carrier U.S.S. Ronald Reagan in San Diego Bay. Standing below a huge banner proclaiming "Mission Accomplished," the commander-in-chief hailed the success of his troops.

Within a very short time, the joy of victory turned into haunting fears of another Vietnam-like "quagmire." Largely because of decisions made by Rumsfeld, the coalition had ample forces to win the war, but not enough to secure the peace. In an act of remarkable fecklessness, the Defense Department's careful planning for military operations was not matched by equally systematic preparation for the postwar period. The result was an eruption of lawlessness, violence and looting, including the theft or destruction of priceless treasures from the national museum. Rumsfeld's flippant remarks that "stuff happens" and freedom was "messy" seemed to underscore the administration's callousness. Top officials had foolishly predicted that Americans would be welcomed as liberators in a "cakewalk," but the looting and lawlessness left Iraqis seething with anger. The inability of the "liberators" to put a shattered infrastructure back together increased the rage. In the months that followed, anarchy evolved into violent and sustained guerrilla opposition to what most Iraqis came to view as a foreign occupation. A task that would have been difficult at best was made much worse by poor planning and wishful thinking among Pentagon civilians, "a reckless evasion of responsibility," journalist James Fallows has concluded.[6]

Over the next two years, the insurgency grew in strength and a war seemingly over in weeks dragged on. Sunni Muslim followers of Saddam were joined in opposition to the United States by some Shiites and also by Al Qaeda and other militants who poured into Iraq as the insurgency took root. Using car bombs and improvised explosive devices with lethal effectiveness, they took a growing toll on U.S. and coalition troops, as well as Iraqi security forces hastily pressed into service and helpless Iraqi civilians.

As the fighting continued and the cost escalated, Americans soured on the commitment. Search as they might, U.S. forces could find no evidence of weapons of mass destruction, cutting the legs from beneath the administration's case for war. In the meantime, critics picked apart other evidence used to justify the nation's first preventive war. Often-used documents purporting to show that Saddam had attempted to buy uranium from Niger to produce nuclear weapons proved to be forgeries. Administration spokespersons fell back on the argument that the deposition of Saddam had removed a bloody tyrant and made the world safer. But the abuse of captives at Abu Ghraib prison by U.S. guards and the detention of other prisoners without trial raised questions about American claims to a higher morality. Bush managed to use continuing popular concerns about the terrorist threat and an appeal to stay the course to help secure reelection in 2004, but in the first year of his second term public approval for the war and his handling of it plummeted. Some Congressional critics even began to demand withdrawal. The administration rejected such demands out of hand, and with Republican majorities in both Houses of Congress any rash action seemed unlikely. In late 2005, the administration mounted an intensive public relations campaign to boost public support. To appease an increasingly anxious public, however, it did begin to speak of possible troop withdrawals and promoted a policy of Iraqization by which Iraqi forces would gradually take over from the Americans the burden of the fighting.

---

6. James Fallows, "Blind into Baghdad," *The Atlantic Monthly* (Jan/Feb, 2004), 73.

After three years of U.S. engagement in Iraq, it remained impossible to predict the outcome of the war. Saddam Hussein's reign of terror had ended, a source of enormous relief for many Iraqis, and the dictator himself had been captured and brought to trial. Elections had been held, a constitution drafted, and a government was being formed. But the Kurdish minority still seemed intent on creating an autonomous state. It was unclear whether the Sunni Arabs, who had dominated Iraqi politics for years, would take part in the new government. Civil war among Iraq's disparate religious groups remained a distinct possibility. Basic services still had not been restored in all areas, and the economy was running at much less than full steam. The insurgency remained a menacing presence and a formidable barrier to progress in other areas. Insurgent attacks hit record numbers in 2005. Without security, it was difficult to put the country back together. It was not clear whether democracy would take firm root in a land without a tradition for it, and if so whether it might produce a Shiite-dominated government closely tied to Iran.

The cost of these limited achievements was enormous. More than two thousand Americans had been killed. Many more suffered severe psychological wounds and horrible maiming from improvised explosive devices. Estimates of Iraqi dead ran as high as 200,000. By the end of 2005, the cost of military operations alone had reached $251 billion. Economists estimated that the direct, long-term cost of the war might reach as high as $1.3 trillion. The war and Iraqi reconstruction contributed to soaring U.S. deficits with the potential to do great long-term damage to the nation's economic well-being. The wars in Iraq and Afghanistan put enormous strain on the U.S. armed forces. A sharp decline in enlistments threatened the integrity of the volunteer army concept, the mainstay of post-Vietnam national security policy. National Guard units were stretched to the breaking point. A study leaked to the press in early 2006 warned that the "thin green line" might not be adequate to meet the nation's future security needs. The U.S. invasion of Iraq provoked widespread anger in the Muslim world, undermining U.S. efforts in the broader war against terrorism. The administration's arrogant unilateralism in going to war damaged the nation's image across much of the world. During his second term, the president and Rice, now secretary of state, set out to refurbish America's tarnished image, but much remained to be done. Popular disillusionment with the war in Iraq threatened an interventionist foreign policy, leading some experts to warn of a resurgence of isolationism.

No matter how the war in Iraq turns out, the United States will face major challenges in the years to come. By some estimates, the world is less violent now than at any time in recent memory. Armed conflicts are down 40 percent from 1992; wars causing more than 1,000 combat deaths are down 80 percent. International stability is enhanced by the emergence among the developed states of North America, Western Europe, and Japan of a "security community" of nations "among whom war is literally unthinkable."[7] At the same time, international health issues and global poverty pose serious threats to international security and equilibrium. The surging economies of China and India offer major competitive challenges for the United States. A leftward tilt in Latin American politics and economics with distinctively anti–United States overtones seems likely to bring that long forgotten continent back into U.S. consciousness. The voracious worldwide consumption of oil products raises concerns about U.S. dependence on limited petroleum resources located mainly in a region that will likely remain volatile. Peace between Israel and its Arab neighbors appears as remote as ever. It remains unclear whether U.S. intervention in Iraq has increased or decreased the dangers from the global war on terrorism, a shadowy conflict with no front lines waged mainly by elusive non-state actors. Above everything else looms the threat of nuclear proliferation, especially with Iran and North Korea, nations who seem on the verge of acquiring such weapons and who have already shown that they will be much more difficult to deal with than Saddam's Iraq. A world in which nation-states still predominate is rendered even more complex by the emergence of powerful non-state actors ranging from global financial markets to multinational corporations to bin Laden's sinister network. The claims of its enthusiasts to the contrary notwithstanding, the onrushing process of globalization without the development of accompanying political and civic institutions to curb its abuses seemed as likely to produce conflict and disorder as peace and stability.

Because of its enormous power and the pervasiveness of its culture, the United States will necessarily remain central to this sometimes baffling new world order. How it will respond to the global challenges of the twenty-first century is much less clear. The neo-con ideology and the Bush Doctrine, with their emphasis on primacy, unilateral-

---

7. Robert Jervis, *American Foreign Policy in a New Era* (New York, 2005), 12.

ism, and preventive war seem ill suited to address the major issues of the day. They have been thoroughly discredited by the continuing war in Iraq, which made amply clear that even superpowers must recognize the limits to their ability to control world events. Multilateralism, obviously, is no panacea, and working closely with other nations requires patience and a tolerance of sometimes messy results that bother restless Americans, but there seems no other way to deal with issues that stretch across international boundaries. It seems also essential to scrap the ideology that drove the Bush administration in its first years and return to America's more traditional pragmatism. The one thing that is certain is that, like it or not, foreign policy will remain central to America's survival and prosperity. It is more urgent than ever to understand the more complex and still dangerous world we live in and take a responsible and constructive role in addressing its major problems.

# 9/11

## Peter Coates and Vincent Vok

*On the morning of September 11, 2001, terrorists hijacked two civilian airliners and crashed first one, then the other, into the twin towers of New York's World Trade Center. Another plane slammed into the Pentagon. A fourth exploded in a Pennsylvania field, brought down by brave passengers who refused to let it become another weapon.*

*Historian George Herring has placed the events of 9/11 in a larger historical context. Here, though, are the stories of two men who were there, in New York, on that tragic day. Peter Coates's and Vincent Vok's stories are archived, along with many thousands more, by the on-line September 11 Digital Archive. This project, organized by the American Social History Project/Center for Media and Learning at the City University of New York Graduate Center and the Center for History and New Media at George Mason University, has collected the accounts of that day from people throughout the United States and around the world.*

**Contributed by:** Peter Coates
**Contributor's location on 9/11:** Lower Manhattan, New York, NY
September 12th 2001
Narrative of Tuesday Morning, September 11, 2001

I came up from the subway onto Wall Street and into a blizzard of paper—millions of sheets falling from high in the sky. A few were signed, but most simply floated here and there on the currents and eddies among the building. For a moment I thought it was a ticker-tape parade, but they're held on Broadway, two blocks to the west.

Permission granted by Peter Coates and Vincent Vok.
Peter Coates, Story #836, *The September 11 Digital Archive,* 27 June 2002, http://911 digitalarchive.org/stories/details/836.
Vincent Vok, Story #11035, *The September 11 Digital Archive,* 13 September 2004, http://911 digitalarchive.org/stories/details/11035.

High above the paper was a broad plume of smoke across a blue sky. Someone said it was coming from the World Trade Center, and that it had been hit by an airliner. It seemed unlikely—perhaps a Cessna or a helicopter.

My temporary office is to the east, at Wall and Water streets, but instead I walked north and west to the WTC plaza. I crossed the park diagonally and emerged from behind the large office building (1 Liberty Plaza) on the northern edge that hid the towers from view. The upper floors of the northern tower were in flames, spectacular, improbable, cinematic flames. Six or eight floors blazed, apparently filled completely, or nearly completely, with an orange glow that billowed out in huge puffs—not at all the flames of a normal building fire. An ordinary building fire is mostly smoke, with tongues of orange fire lacing through it; huge balls of flame poured out of the tower—billows of flame that rolled out into the sky.

The flames were perhaps 800 or 900 feet above the ground, and the foot of the tower perhaps 500 feet away, yet they were gigantic, utterly dwarfing the human scale. Terrified people in the floors above looked out and hung out from windows just above, barely noticeable in the vastness of the scale. Windows were shattered in floors above the flames—the people seemed to be seeking breathable air, or trying to escape heat; it was impossible to tell. The flaming floors, and the relatively undamaged portion above, clearly still filled with people made up only perhaps a fifth of the building. Everything appeared to be intact.

Few people on the ground seemed upset—a couple of hundred of us stood across the street transfixed by the spectacle, but most of us were oddly calm, as if watching news report of some distant disaster. A pedestrian falling on sidewalk or a minor traffic accident produces as much apparent alarm. There was little talking, no screaming, no "Oh the humanity." Among some, a snow-day mood was evident. Perhaps we were unable to feel, unable to imagine what to feel, at seeing those clinging to the windows, leap, or pass out, or simply fall, and tumble slowly to the ground. It takes a long time to fall so far plenty of time to see who they are, wonder about what they might be thinking and wonder if they are frightened. At the scale of the WTC, a sense of unreality is a nearly seamless defense against horror.

I don't think any of us—there weren't very many at that spot, directly in front of the northern tower at the corner of John and Church—heard or saw the second plane approach from behind the unharmed second tower. Certainly I didn't. When the face of the second tower exploded it was flabbergasting—there wasn't the slightest hint until the glass and the metal facing ribs bloomed out riding the front of an immense fireball—a mass of flame that seemed to form a roof across the whole plaza, closer the ground than the flames of the first tower, and immensely larger—smaller than, but similar in scale to that of the buildings, which was almost geologic. We were at the corner of a side street two narrow blocks below the northern edge of the tower and no one had to be told to run, or which way—there was nothing to hide behind. We sprinted, young and old. Several people fell, and those behind simply leapt over them, but the ugly panic one reads about wasn't seen on that street. For everyone that leapt over or ran around, at least one other stopped. A tiny woman tried to pull a very fat black woman in a pink dress to her feet, hopelessly outmatched. I grabbed too and we hauled her up and drove her before us. Then an slender older woman sprawled face down a dozen feet ahead, not even struggling to get up. A man leapt over her and kept going. With the famous strength of panic, I simply grabbed her by the waist and literally set her on her feet screaming at her to "run her ass off" and shoving her rudely. I could feel the mass of glass and steel coming after us—the fireball seemed to stretch forever, but the debris never reached us. Everyone made it safely to the corner.

The second building was now in worse shape than the first. The destruction was slightly closer to the ground, about 2/3 of the way up, and the billowing flames enormous. The first building seemed only to smolder in comparison. Large quantities of material had been ejected from the building across the plaza. Firemen still streamed toward it—brave men, for the second tower was raining glass, steel, people, and the contents of half a dozen devastated floors down on the plaza. Few people seemed to be coming out—certainly not crowds. I was looking for the flood of people one sees when a baseball stadium empties; this was a trickle, no greater than the numbers of firemen converging on the doors.

I went south again to the park at 1 Liberty Plaza behind the row of buildings that face the towers and screened them from view. Back at the southern edge of plaza it was instantly evident that it was not a bomb but another plane that had struck the tower: on the southern face of tower two was a clean, almost round hole six to ten stories high and wide that gaped on level with the blown out north and west faces. On opposing sides of the hole, tilted sharply from horizontal, were long slices where the wings had struck.

There was nothing to be done to help—hoards of firemen and police were arriving. There were few obvious injured—bodies littered the plaza, but the officials outnumbered the fleeing.

I moved back past Broadway, still directly opposite the towers, but behind a couple of blocks of buildings, watching the disaster from a distance. I chatted with a distinguished looking and confident man who pooh-poohed the idea that the tops might collapse. I told him I remembered the old west-side piers that burned—the steel looked like a mass of cooked spaghetti, but he was quite sure the WTC was built to withstand a fire. He said that much jet fuel might burn for hours. That much was believable. If there was to be a collapse, I pictured the tops falling off, like ice cream off a cone. Many people were horrified, but few were alarmed for themselves. Some still seemed almost gay, as if this, at last, was something really different.

I decided to leave, and walked further back, across the island to Water Street, still directly opposite the plaza, but half a dozen blocks away. The pedestrian walkway on the Brooklyn Bridge, a few blocks to the north, is the surest way to get across the East River. From Water Street, one could see the top third of the towers—enough to see the northern tower burning. The burning portion of the southern tower was obscured by buildings. Incredibly, cars and delivery trucks still drove in the direction of the towers, going about their ordinary business as if nothing out of the ordinary were occurring. A UPS driver honked, looking irritated, and turned west directly toward the WTC.

For many more minutes I stood watching from there. A woman approached and we talked about the disaster and watched. She told me she worked at Goldman Sachs further downtown at 1 New York Plaza—directly across from my own home office, as it happens. Mostly we watched quietly. Then as we gazed at the most awful thing we'd ever seen, the southern tower simply sank from view; it didn't fall over, it just sank. An immense plume of dust and smoked erupted in its place, but it immediately followed the tower below the buildings, sucked down as fast as it had bloomed to fill the vacuum left by the sinking building. The sky was clear where the tower had been.

In seconds, far up John Street the mass of dust reappeared as a solid wall rushing forward, filling the street, overtaking and instantly obscuring the pedestrians fleeing toward us. The air ahead of the cloud was crystalline, then people simply winked out as the cloud over-took them. The dust was so dense that it was as opaque as wallboard. The cloud came down the street like a piston, swallowing the terrified people fleeing it, coming faster than a car would travel. Attempting to outrun it was absurd, but that was most everyone's instinct.

Drivers stopped at the traffic light tried to cross the intersection, despite the blocked traffic ahead. Several of us beat on their hoods and yelled to stop them from blocking the intersection. Successfully, surprisingly: the drivers fled, not even closing their doors. When the cloud swept over the intersection, it was opaque, but only for a few minutes. And just around the corner the air was almost transparent again. I pulled my shirttail over my mouth and nose and shouted for people to come, and many did. We ducked into a garage where the air was breathable.

In minutes it cleared sufficiently to see ten or twenty feet. I ran back out, and people were stumbling out of the obscurity choking and gagging. The radius of vision was only a few feet. I ran into the cloud, my face covered with my shirt. A pretty Asian girl wearing only her underwear ran into my view. She shrieked on meeting me in the gloom. She couldn't be led, or even told—she just shrieked and shrieked, recoiling from my approach and even my words. But in her fright she ran in the right direction, so I just let her go. Everyone was filthy, but her panic was exceptional. A few were stunned, but most were remarkably cool and understood instantly when told where to go. One woman, dusty white from head to foot, seemed genuinely puzzled and a little annoyed to be taken for someone who might be in need of directions. Very New York.

It cleared rapidly—mostly it was dust, not smoke, and it simply fell to the ground or blew away. A young man, maybe thirty years old, was also running around dragging people into lobbies and shops. We introduced ourselves—he was Angelo—and ran together up John Street into the cloud, toward whatever was left of the WTC.

We stopped for a few seconds and he tore off the sleeve of his T-shirt and gave it to me for a mask. The T-shirt was hard to tear straight, so he opened his Swiss Army knife and cut it with scissors. We stopped again to loot an abandoned hotdog stand of a crate of cold Poland Spring bottled water, and carried it Jack and Jill style towards the towers. We opened the cooler and filled a milk crate with bottles. For an awkward moment I fumbled with some money to leave and Angelo laughed out loud. Along the way we passed out bottles right and left to crying, choking people, or squirted their eyes clear and hustled them into doorways. Many were unable to see, their eyes caked with powder. People seemed not to think of the most obvious thing—that it wouldn't be so dusty inside and that the air would clear quickly.

We made it back to the park at the southwest corner. The water supply was gone twice over. Hotdog stands across the island suffered at our hands. At the park there were a dozen firemen and many pieces of equipment, windows smashed, doors hanging open. The firemen were just milling around dazed and leaderless. Some of their crew were missing; most were missing, gone into the tower, but some of those left behind with the equipment were said to be missing too. The park was piled with debris, dust and trash as high as the benches in some places, as high as the hoods of cars in others. The fire trucks and police cars were badly battered and windowless. The long stainless steel ribs that sheath the towers were scattered everywhere. They're big, about sixteen inches square, and a dozen feet long: stainless steel sheet bent into a sleek cover for the vertical ribs of the building. It takes two hands to pick one up. The wind-borne debris had pushed most of the trees over to about 45 degrees. The stainless steel sheathing was piled in heaps along with tons of paper, steel and concrete. The dust was ankle deep in some places, feet deep in others, and everywhere, huge amounts of paper. Tons upon tons of forms, manuals, letters. Everything was under mounds of gray dust. . . .

I lost sight of Angelo. Seconds or minutes later the sliding, roaring sound of the second collapse began—there was a deep trilling sound under it, like the rolling of a Spanish "r." It was the scraping sound that a dump truck of gravel makes when it unloads, but infinitely bigger. I dashed for the colonnade. There was no one else in sight, and no time to look around. Instantly darkness swept over from the plaza. It was inky black—shockingly black to a city person, as black as a moonless night in the country. The roar of the collapse died down in seconds, but the air was so thick it seemed to resist motion through it. It fell so thickly that the air had weight. My shirt pocket got heavy with it in seconds. I started to draw a breath through the mask/respirator, which had somehow lost its patched up T-shirt filter, and I got a thick mouthful of ash and sand. I felt for the glass wall, inexplicably not broken, and felt my way down it to the revolving door, which was fortunately not jammed. Inside the triangular opening, light was faintly visible within.

A few people were in the lobby, all of us panicky, but we determined that to stay was pretty safe, and to leave almost impossible until the dust settled. The last dust had become passable in minutes, but this was far thicker.

But within five or ten minutes it was clear enough that an improvised T-shirt mask enabled me to go outside with a bull horn and begin calling to people to come to the sound. But after several minutes no one had come. I literally stumbled over the dropped respirator and patched up the filter with more T-shirt. There was nobody to look for, and the north was impassible, so I headed south. It was still dark as night, although it was still mid-morning on a day of clear blue skies.

Below the WTC on West Street, a block below the covered pedestrian bridge across the highway, firefighters, police and emergency crews were gathering. The road ahead was blocked with scores of burning trucks and cars. Everything was deep in ash—several inches covered the tops of cars and walls. Sporadic explosions of gas tanks and car tires made everyone jump. A man was walking around poking at suspicious lumps under the ash and marking those that appeared to be parts of bodies with traffic cones and tape. An office telephone, handset and all, lay in the dust, its lines spun round and round the sleeve a man's sport jacket. A little later the man came and marked it with a cone, for the jacket turned out not to be entirely empty.

Nearby one of the airplane wheels lay, tire and all, along with some of the attached gear, torn off in mid-axle. The tire was burst, but whole. Up the road, less recognizable if you hadn't seen the whole one, lay another, bare of rubber and smashed. They must have come from the plane that hit the North Tower. Pieces of sheathing, an airplane door and thousands of unidentifiable bits and pieces lay everywhere, blanketed by dust. In the middle of the highway is an underpass to nowhere—it emerges again a hundred yards or so down town. Three policemen were shuffling down the road into it, kicking through the dust in line looking for a service pistol one of them had dropped when fleeing the flow of dust. A woman yelled down to them from the upper roadway to knock it off and go do something useful. They looked sheepish and left, despite the evident lack of anything to do until the burning wrecks were extinguished. It did look a little foolish.

I waited an hour or two for the flames and dust to die down enough to do something useful, but they sprang up again, and again, and the adjacent building seemed in danger of collapse, so everyone moved further back. I killed time dragging some of the bigger chunks of sheathing out of the streets so vehicles would be able to pass, but it was pointless work. Little fires burned unattended all around. Window were blown out of the surrounding buildings to a height of perhaps twenty stories. The numbers of official relief people had grown to the hundreds and no prospect of doing anything useful appeared likely for many hours. Too much fire and smoke, and too many chunks of adjacent buildings still falling into the cauldron of the plaza and surrounding blocks. I headed up the street away from the scene of the disaster.

A couple of blocks away an old man was picking his way through the trash and debris. I had a last bottle of water in my pocket and I offered it to him. He said no thanks, he was fine, but could I direct him to an address on Liberty Street. I laughed and said I didn't think he'd have to go to work today, that everyone had gone home. But he told me he was a security guard there, and that it was necessary to report, especially now. He'd been there many years, but in all the smoke and trash he couldn't find it. Neither could I. We had to ask a cop.

**Contributed by:** Vincent Vok
**Contributor's location on 9/11:** Staten Island, New York
WTC—9/12

I work for a local hospital, and spent the 11th and 12th answering phone calls from people desperately looking for their loved ones. I had the late shift on the 12th, and that was the heaviest and hardest. Only one out of 200 names could be confirmed as treated and released. The unique grief of the hospitals in the area was that we stood ready for massive casualties, and there were none. My co-worker, a young man named Chris, and I were alone in the office for six hours, taking calls from every part of the country, not able to help them. We finally got out of there at 11:15 p.m. His girlfriend, Carolyn, an x-ray technician, had appeared out of nowhere, wearing a thin white sweater and green scrubs, with a very grim look on her face. "I was just there." She pointed to a building across the street. "From where we are, now, to there, there is the rubble, where the buildings used to be. But it's massive. It's so crazy. Everything is everywhere. I'm going back. They need eyewash." She said other things I can't remember, but the main thing was, she was going back. I toyed for a moment with going home and drinking myself to sleep in front of CNN, then looked at Chris and the three of us were in her Pathfinder, on our way to the ER for bottles of eyewash. Chris and I put on green scrubs and made sure our hospital badges were displayed, and we took off. It was midnight, and we were virtually alone on the road. They were in the front, talking quietly. I was in the back with my head against the cold glass window, tired, and anxious to see the destruction.

From the Verrazano Bridge, we got our first look at the massive cloud of smoke and dust, glowing white from the searchlights, spreading out into a thick gray fog. The remaining buildings were sharp, black silhouettes. We were stopped at the entrance of the Brooklyn Queens Tunnel by a police officer, who waved us through after he saw the supplies, badges and scrubs. We followed an empty flatbed through the tunnel and came out on the other side.

The Pathfinder we were in crawled knee-high through fire trucks, cranes, military vehicles and flatbed trucks, making tracks in the deep dust that covered everything and everyone. The landscape was foreign—gray and muffled. With a backdrop of a black night, reality was redefined as something hard to touch, hard to see and hard to swallow. It was the silence of an awful snowfall obliterating familiar ground. Green traffic signs hung sideways pointing down. Ghosts in colorless uniforms doing urgent jobs already routine. There was no point of reference, no relevant direction, no sense that anyone still alive had ever been there before.

"This is where I parked before. Look. There's that infant car seat I told you about." We parked in an empty area near a gray building with gray windows. Alone in the gray was a gray car seat on the gray ground. I stepped out of the car and onto the soft surface of a gray new world. "Come on."

We pulled the supplies out of the back, and followed her around the corner. Up until that point, there were glimpses, flashes of smoky light, empty spaces where I remembered walls. We turned the corner and shrank into specks of dust. The sad remains of a disturbed landscape leaned inside itself, supporting the weight of the smoke and bright lights, exposed from the inside out. Ruins and victims of violence and gravity lay mangled and random, twisted, charred, broken, betrayed, murdered and terrified, framed out by a cold night at the very edge of the ending day. Proportion was distorted by slashes across the face of a 30-story building that was left standing, cracks from sidewalk to roof. The sky was black, the smoke was gray, the twisted metal, concrete, glass, rubble, was sharpened and defined by the shadows cast by the brilliant white work-lights; no colors flowed, down through the black channels of the cracks made by the lights, through mounds, over down around, to the ground, which was covered with paper. Sheets of paper, memos, invoices, triplicate forms, records, 8½ × 11, untorn, unclaimed, unimportant pushed-out leaves fallen from shaken trees. The sounds I heard from machines, from people, from my own throat swallowing, were secrets whispered against the night dulled with dust. To breathe meant to taste the air, the sharp, unknown smells and floating particles and atoms of people and things once whole. The pull on my senses was so complete I felt the vacuum, the lack of space that pulled my breath, my lungs, my heart and essence in and out in waves, and I was replaced to the core by the absolute immensity of the cold intention of chaos.

The triage area where the first aid was occurring was set up in the lobby of a nearby building. We were given facemasks, goggles and rubber gloves, and were told where to put the supplies. Aside from a dog that was receiving aid for a cut paw, the only other medical activity was the washing out of the eyes of the rescue workers. This was being improvised by bending the sharp end of a hypodermic needle into an "L" shape, holding up the eyelid, and washing out the affected area. There were about a dozen volunteers walking around wearing scrubs of various colors, all from different hospitals. Among the firefighters in all their rescue gear, I felt incredibly underdressed.

Chris and I stood at the base of an escalator, looking for ways to help. We heard they needed an area cleared so that cots could be set up, so we decided to organize the space. There were large boxes of clothing, sweaters, t-shirts, socks and underwear, which had been piled up, unneeded, in the middle of the floor. There were blankets, toothbrushes, mouthwash, Band-Aids, half-eaten lunches and half-dozen stacks of Poland Spring bottled water scattered, gray and untouched. There were three or four unrecognizable gray mounds on the floor, which I thought were blankets but turned out to be sleeping firefighters.

Carolyn said "Come on," again, and we followed her up the unmoving escalator. "They told me about this." She led us to jagged-edged opening in a gray wall, and we looked down. From that view we could see the entire rescue effort taking place. If God and Creation are painted on the ceiling of the Sistine Chapel, this is the scene of Destruction Michelangelo would paint on the floors of Hell. Clusters of teams of firefighters, dogs, jackhammers, welders, flashlights, paramedics, crawling over the rubble of smoking, twisted-metal mounds, looking for signs of life, finding only bloody pieces of it.

We had to keep moving. No one stands in one place too long, especially to stare. All grief was in another gray pile somewhere, under some wall or stairway, not yet needed.

At one point we became part of a river of firefighters heading towards a point in the rubble where someone had been found. To my knowledge no one had said anything, yet they all moved as a single unit. We stood at the very edge of destruction, trying to see what they were seeing. Behind us a ten-story crane was pulling a mangled steel I-beam out of the ground and placing it on a truck. In front of us, firefighters were watching and waiting. Then, quite suddenly, as if released from a single string, they dispersed, going back to their tasks once again. Two of them came out of the debris, each with the handle of an orange body bag in hand. It was sagging very unnaturally in the middle. That was all. That was it. A piece at a time.

At 3 A.M., September 13, they gave the word to move the triage, and I heard the word "recovery" replace the word "rescue"—a significant change. We decided to go home. Our green scrubs were gray. My skin was gray. My thoughts . . . We retraced our steps, stepped around the gray car seat, got into the Pathfinder, followed a flatbed into the tunnel, and got stuck behind a slow-moving sanitation truck, which was spraying water down, to wash away the dust, before it escaped into the night.

We drove back across the bridge, looking back, always looking back. I sat in the back with the window down. The black cold night air washed out our lungs. My eyelids were heavy from the dust. We were there for three hours. There were people there spending a season in that Hell. God help them.

# The "Axis of Evil" Speech: President Bush's State of the Union Address (2002)

## George W. Bush

*On January 29, 2002, President George W. Bush addressed the U.S. Congress and the nation's citizens in his second State of the Union address. It was only four and a half months after the attacks of 9/11, and Bush began his speech with a reminder of the "unprecedented dangers" that faced the world. He claimed success in "Operation Enduring Freedom," the invasion of Afghanistan. And he moved quickly to call for American action to preempt future terrorism, in a statement that presaged "Operation Iraqi Freedom," the U.S. invasion of Iraq that began more than a year later.*

*In this speech, Bush branded three nations—North Korea, Iran, and Iraq—as the "axis of evil." The phrase, coined by then–Bush speechwriter David Frum, combined language from World War II (the Axis powers) with Ronald Reagan's description of the Soviet Union (the empire of evil). It was powerful rhetoric, but critics worried that it heightened emotions and so made international diplomacy more difficult, that it suggested that Iran, Iraq, and North Korea were operating as a group, when that was not the case, and that the use of inflammatory language may have increased the power of radical groups in Iran. Warren Christopher, secretary of state under President Clinton, said of the axis of evil: "It was a speechwriter's dream and a policy-maker's nightmare."*

*As you read this excerpt from Bush's speech, look back to George Herring's discussion of the United States' role in the post–Cold War world (pp. 397–417). Is Bush signaling a change in American foreign policy? How important do you think his choice of language was in shaping America's options in the post-9/11 world?*

THE PRESIDENT: Thank you very much. Mr. Speaker, Vice President Cheney, members of Congress, distinguished guests, fellow

The White House, online, 10 February 2002 [http://www.whitehouse.gov].

citizens: As we gather tonight, our nation is at war, our economy is in recession, and the civilized world faces unprecedented dangers. Yet the state of our Union has never been stronger.

We last met in an hour of shock and suffering. In four short months, our nation has comforted the victims, begun to rebuild New York and the Pentagon, rallied a great coalition, captured, arrested, and rid the world of thousands of terrorists, destroyed Afghanistan's terrorist training camps, saved a people from starvation, and freed a country from brutal oppression.

The American flag flies again over our embassy in Kabul. Terrorists who once occupied Afghanistan now occupy cells at Guantanamo Bay. And terrorist leaders who urged followers to sacrifice their lives are running for their own. . . .

Our cause is just, and it continues. Our discoveries in Afghanistan confirmed our worst fears, and showed us the true scope of the task ahead. We have seen the depth of our enemies' hatred in videos, where they laugh about the loss of innocent life. And the depth of their hatred is equaled by the madness of the destruction they design. We have found diagrams of American nuclear power plants and public water facilities, detailed instructions for making chemical weapons, surveillance maps of American cities, and thorough descriptions of landmarks in America and throughout the world.

What we have found in Afghanistan confirms that, far from ending there, our war against terror is only beginning. Most of the 19 men who hijacked planes on September the 11th were trained in Afghanistan's camps, and so were tens of thousands of others. Thousands of dangerous killers, schooled in the methods of murder, often supported by outlaw regimes, are now spread throughout the world like ticking time bombs, set to go off without warning.

Thanks to the work of our law enforcement officials and coalition partners, hundreds of terrorists have been arrested. Yet, tens of thousands of trained terrorists are still at large. These enemies view the entire world as a battlefield, and we must pursue them wherever they are. So long as training camps operate, so long as nations harbor terrorists, freedom is at risk. And America and our allies must not, and will not, allow it.

Our nation will continue to be steadfast and patient and persistent in the pursuit of two great objectives. First, we will shut down terrorist camps, disrupt terrorist plans, and bring terrorists to justice. And, second, we must prevent the terrorists and regimes who seek chemical, biological or nuclear weapons from threatening the United States and the world. . . .

My hope is that all nations will heed our call, and eliminate the terrorist parasites who threaten their countries and our own. Many nations are acting forcefully. Pakistan is now cracking down on terror, and I admire the strong leadership of President Musharraf.

But some governments will be timid in the face of terror. And make no mistake about it: If they do not act, America will.

Our second goal is to prevent regimes that sponsor terror from threatening America or our friends and allies with weapons of mass destruction. Some of these regimes have been pretty quiet since September the 11th. But we know their true nature. North Korea is a regime arming with missiles and weapons of mass destruction, while starving its citizens.

Iran aggressively pursues these weapons and exports terror, while an unelected few repress the Iranian people's hope for freedom.

Iraq continues to flaunt its hostility toward America and to support terror. The Iraqi regime has plotted to develop anthrax, and nerve gas, and nuclear weapons for over a decade. This is a regime that has already used poison gas to murder thousands of its own citizens— leaving the bodies of mothers huddled over their dead children. This is a regime that agreed to international inspections—then kicked out the inspectors. This is a regime that has something to hide from the civilized world.

States like these, and their terrorist allies, constitute an axis of evil, arming to threaten the peace of the world. By seeking weapons of mass destruction, these regimes pose a grave and growing danger. They could provide these arms to terrorists, giving them the means to match their hatred. They could attack our allies or attempt to blackmail the United States. In any of these cases, the price of indifference would be catastrophic.

We will work closely with our coalition to deny terrorists and their state sponsors the materials, technology, and expertise to make and deliver weapons of mass destruction. We will develop and deploy effective missile defenses to protect America and our allies from sudden attack. And all nations should know: America will do what is necessary to ensure our nation's security.

We'll be deliberate, yet time is not on our side. I will not wait on events, while dangers gather. I will not stand by, as peril draws closer and closer. The United States of America will not permit the world's most dangerous regimes to threaten us with the world's most destructive weapons.

Our war on terror is well begun, but it is only begun. This campaign may not be finished on our watch—yet it must be and it will be waged on our watch.

We can't stop short. If we stop now—leaving terror camps intact and terror states unchecked—our sense of security would be false and temporary. History has called America and our allies to action, and it is both our responsibility and our privilege to fight freedom's fight.

# An Open Letter to George W. Bush (2004)

*Cindy Sheehan*

*As it became clear in early 2003 that the United States planned to invade Iraq in a "preemptive" war (see pp. 429–432), the American people did not come together in support. The administration's argument that Saddam Hussein had weapons of mass destruction convinced many, but others argued that the United Nations' weapons inspections were working, or that a shift to preemptive war was a very bad move for the United States. As the war wore on, and it became clear first that there were no weapons of mass destruction and then that there would be no easy victory, more Americans began to ask why America had gone to war in the first place, and to wonder why those who planned the invasion had so poorly planned for securing the peace. As insurgents continued to resist and the death tolls of both Iraqis and Americans continued to climb, a majority of Americans told pollsters they did not support the Bush administration's handling of the war in Iraq.*

*One of the most powerful protests against the war came together around Cindy Sheehan, mother of Army Specialist Casey Sheehan. Casey Sheehan died in Baghdad's Sadr City on April 4, 2004; he was one of eight soldiers killed by small arms fire or rocket-propelled grenades that day. In early August 2005, Ms. Sheehan pitched a tent as close as she could get to President Bush's ranch in Crawford, Texas, where he was spending five weeks, and demanded to meet with the president. (President Bush had met with her, along with members of other families who had lost sons in Iraq, in June 2004; she later said that he seemed "detached from humanity" and that "there was nothing in his eyes or anything else about him that showed me he really cared or had any real compassion at all.") More antiwar protesters joined her at "Camp Casey," and antiwar protests were energized by the media attention she drew as a grieving and angry mother of a fallen soldier.*

From http://www.mfso.org/article.php?id=309.

*The letter that follows was written by Sheehan to President Bush and circulated publicly as an act of protest against the war. As context for this letter, compare what you know about protests against the war in Iraq with what you learned about American protests against the Vietnam War. How does Sheehan make her case? What do you see as this letter's strengths and weaknesses in approaching President Bush? Others who oppose the war? People with family members in Iraq? The general public? Why might this letter be more or less effective than a careful argument against the goals and conduct of the war in Iraq?*

## November 4, 2004
## An Open Letter to George W. Bush

Dear George,

You don't mind if I call you George do you? When you sent me a letter offering your condolences on the death of my son, Spc. Casey Austin Sheehan, in the illegal and unjust war on Iraq, you called me Cindy, so I naturally assume we are on a first name basis.

George, it has been seven months today since your reckless and wanton foreign policies killed my son, my big boy, my hero, my best-friend: Casey. It has been seven months since your ignorant and arrogant lack of planning for the peace murdered my oldest child. It has been two days since your dishonest campaign stole another election . . . but you all were way more subtle this time than in 2000, weren't you? You hardly had to get the Supreme Court of the United States involved at all this week.

You feel so proud of yourself for betraying the country again, don't you? You think you are very clever because you pulled the wool over the eyes of some of the people again. You think that you have some mandate from God . . . that you can "spend your political capital" any way that you want. George you don't care or even realize that 56,000,000 plus citizens of this country voted against you and your agenda. Still, you are going to continue your ruthless work of being a divider and not a uniter. George, in 2000 when you stole that election and the Democrats gave up, I gave up too. I had the most ironic thought of my life then: "Oh well, how much damage can he do in four years?" Well, now I know how much you have damaged my family, this country, and this world. If you think I am going to allow you another four years to do even more damage, then you truly are mistaken. I will fight for a true vote count and if that fails, your impeachment. Also, the impeachment of your Vice President. The only thing is, I'm not politically savvy, and I don't have a Karl Rove to plan my strategy, but I do have a big mouth and a righteous cause, which still mean something in this country, I hope.

All of this lying, fooling, and betraying must be "hard work" George. You really think you know what hard work is?

George, let me tell you what "hard work" really is.

Hard work is seeing your oldest son, your brave and honorable man-child go off to a war that had, and still has, no basis in reality. Hard work is worrying yourself gray and not being able to sleep for 2 weeks because you don't know if your child is safe.

Hard work is seeing your son's murder on CNN one Sunday evening while you're enjoying the last supper you'll ever truly enjoy again.

Hard work is having three military officers come to your house a few hours later to confirm the aforementioned murder of your son . . . your first born . . . your kind and gentle sweet baby.

Hard work is burying your child 46 days before his 25th birthday. Hard work is holding your other three children as they lower the body of their big "baba" into the ground. Hard work is not jumping in the grave with him and having the earth cover you both.

But, Dear George, do you know what the hardest work of all is? Trying to digest the fact that the leader of the country that your family has fought for and died for, for generations, lied to you and betrayed your dear boy's sense of honor and exploited his courage and exploited his loyalty to his buddies. Hard work is having your country abandon you after they killed your son. Hard work is coming to the realization that your son had his future robbed from him and that you have had your son's future and future grand-children stolen from you. Hard work is knowing that there are so many people in this world that have prospered handsomely from your son's death.

George, I must confess that I and my family worked very HARD to re-defeat you this time, but you refuse to stay defeated. Well, we are watching you very carefully. We are going to do everything in our power to have you impeached for misleading the American people into a disastrous war and for mis-using and abusing your power as Commander-in-Chief. We are going to scream until our last breath to bring the rest of our babies home from this quagmire of a war that you have gotten our country in to: before too many more families learn the true meaning of Hard Work. We know it is going to be an uphill battle, knowing how Republican Congress is, but thanks to you, we know the meaning of Hard Work and we're not afraid of hard work at all.

The 56,000,000 plus citizens who voted against you and your agenda have given me a mandate to move forward with my agenda. Also, thanks to you and your careless domestic policies, I am unemployed, so this will be my full-time job. Being your political downfall will be the most noble accomplishment of my life and it will bring justice for my son and 1125 (so far) other brave Americans and tens of thousands of innocent Iraqis your lies have killed. By the way, George, how many more innocent Iraqis are your policies going to kill before you convince them that you are better than Saddam? How many more of their cities are you going to level before you consider that they are liberated? If you really had any moral values, or if you were an honorable man at all you would resign. My son was a man who had high moral values and true courage. Humanity lost a bright light on April 04, 2004. I will live the rest of my life missing Casey desperately. Thank you for that, George. Have a nice day.

God Bless America!! We surely need it!

Cindy Sheehan

# Final Report on 9/11 Commission Recommendations (2005)

## The 9/11 Commission

*In November 2002, the United States Congress created the National Commission on Terrorist Attacks Upon the United States, charging it to investigate the "facts and circumstances" of the terrorist attacks of September 11, 2001. The commission, composed of five Democrats and five Republicans, and chaired by Thomas H. Kean and Lee H. Hamilton, interviewed more than twelve hundred people in ten different nations and examined more than 2.5 million pages of documents. The report they issued offered a compelling narrative of the events of 9/11, and of the steps leading to them. It became a surprise best-seller nationwide. But the report also made concrete recommendations, listing specific reforms the commissioners believed could help prevent another terrorist attack and save American lives.*

*After the publication of the 9/11 Commission Report, the commission reconstituted itself as a private, nonprofit organization whose purpose was to push for—and monitor—adoption of the commission's recommendations. In early December 2005, the group issued a final report, including a "report card" with letter grades indicating how well the Bush administration and Congress had responded to each of their forty-one suggested reforms. There was only one A (actually, an A–), earned for "vigorous effort against terrorist financing." On almost half the recommended reforms, the government earned Ds, Fs, or incompletes. The report card touched off a series of political charges and countercharges in Washington, D.C.*

*But some commentators looked beyond the report card and pointed, instead, to Hurricane Katrina. Even with advance warning, as in the case of Katrina, the government's response was inadequate at best, leading to needless deaths and human misery all along the Gulf Coast, especially in New Orleans. As the 9/11 Commission's report card, along with the human devastation following Katrina seemed to demonstrate, the nation was not at all ready to manage the threat—or the reality—of another terrorist attack.*

From 9/11 Public Discourse Project, http://www.9-11pdp.org/.

# Final Report on 9/11 Commission Recommendations   December 5, 2005

| HOMELAND SECURITY AND EMERGENCY RESPONSE | | INTELLIGENCE AND CONGRESSIONAL REFORM | | FOREIGN POLICY AND NONPROLIFERATION | |
| --- | --- | --- | --- | --- | --- |
| Radio spectrum for first responders | F/C* | Director of National Intelligence | B | Maximum effort to prevent terrorists from acquiring WMD | D |
| Incident Command System | C | National Counterterrorism Center | B | Afghanistan | B |
| Risk-based homeland security funds | F/A* | FBI national security workforce | C | Pakistan | C+ |
| Critical infrastructure assessment | D | New missions for CIA Director | I | Saudi Arabia | D |
| Private sector preparedness | C | Incentives for information sharing | D | Terrorist sanctuaries | B |
| National Strategy for Transportation Security | C– | Government-wide information sharing | D | Coalition strategy against Islamist terrorism | C |
| Airline passenger pre-screening | F | Northern Command planning for homeland defense | B– | Coalition detention standards | F |
| Airline passenger explosive screening | C | Full debate on PATRIOT Act | B | Economic policies | B+ |
| Checked bag and cargo screening | D | Privacy and Civil Liberties Oversight Board | D | Terrorist financing | A– |
| Terrorist travel strategy | I | Guidelines for government sharing of personal information | D | Clear U.S. message abroad | C |
| Comprehensive screening system | C | Intelligence oversight reform | D | International broadcasting | B |
| Biometric entry-exit screening system | B | Homeland Security Committees | B | Scholarship, exchange, and library programs | D |
| International collaboration on borders and document security | D | Unclassified top-line intelligence budget | F | Secular education in Muslim countries | D |
| Standardize secure identifications | B– | Security clearance reform | B | | |

* If pending legislation passes

# Image of the United States (2005)

*Pew Global Attitudes Project*

*The Pew Global Attitudes Project is a series of international public opinion surveys. Conducted by members of the Pew Research Center (which describes itself as a nonpartisan "fact tank"), these surveys began in the 1990s as a way to understand regional attitudes toward globalization and, in post–Cold War Europe, attitudes about democracy and international change. Following the September 11, 2001, attacks on the U.S. World Trade Center and the Pentagon, the Pew Global Attitudes Project began to attempt to measure attitudes toward the United States in different nations and regions. In all, the project has surveyed more than ninety thousand people in fifty countries.*

*The material that follows is drawn from a survey of sixteen nations and was released in June 2005. It attempts to understand the image of the United States and its people across the globe, and in comparison to the images of other major nations. In reading this report, think about why such research is done. Do you think this social science research would be useful to those who plan American international policies? If so, how? Are the attitudes toward "American Character" expressed in these surveys as significant as those toward U.S. actions (such as the war in Iraq)? What does such information tell us about America's place in the contemporary world?*

## I: IMAGE OF THE UNITED STATES

Even though the image of the United States has improved slightly in some parts of the world over the past year, this country's global approval ratings trail well behind those of other leading nations.

When the publics of the 16 nations covered by the survey were asked to give favorability ratings of five major leading nations—the United States, Germany, China, Japan, and France—the U.S. fared the worst of

Used with permission of the Pew Global Attitudes Project.

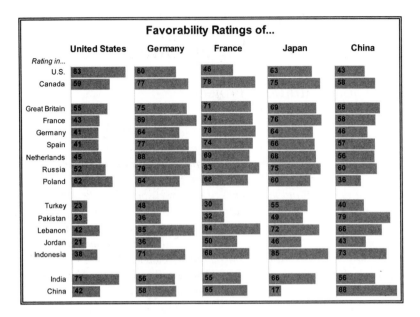

**Favorability Ratings of...**

| Rating in... | United States | Germany | France | Japan | China |
|---|---|---|---|---|---|
| U.S. | 83 | 60 | 46 | 63 | 43 |
| Canada | 59 | 77 | 78 | 75 | 58 |
| Great Britain | 55 | 75 | 71 | 69 | 65 |
| France | 43 | 89 | 74 | 76 | 58 |
| Germany | 41 | 64 | 78 | 64 | 46 |
| Spain | 41 | 77 | 74 | 66 | 57 |
| Netherlands | 45 | 88 | 69 | 68 | 56 |
| Russia | 52 | 79 | 83 | 75 | 60 |
| Poland | 62 | 64 | 66 | 60 | 36 |
| Turkey | 23 | 48 | 30 | 55 | 40 |
| Pakistan | 23 | 36 | 32 | 49 | 79 |
| Lebanon | 42 | 85 | 84 | 72 | 66 |
| Jordan | 21 | 36 | 50 | 46 | 43 |
| Indonesia | 38 | 71 | 68 | 85 | 73 |
| India | 71 | 56 | 55 | 66 | 56 |
| China | 42 | 58 | 65 | 17 | 88 |

the group. In just six of the 16 countries surveyed does the United States attract a favorability rating of 50% or above. By contrast, China receives that level of favorability rating from 11 countries, while Japan, Germany and France each receive that high of a mark from 13 countries.

The U.S. draws its most negative assessments from Muslim nations, with Jordan at just 21% favorable and Turkey and Pakistan at 23%. These ratings, while low, are better than they were at the start of the Iraq war. As in recent years, the U.S. draws only middling reviews from traditional allies in the West, with Canada at 59% favorable, Great Britain at 55%, the Netherlands at 45%, France at 43% and Germany and Spain each at 41%. It is considerably more popular in India (71%) and Poland (62%)....

### *Americans See U.S. as Unpopular*

Americans harbor no illusions about the popularity of their country around the world. Nearly seven-in-ten (69%) say the U.S. is "generally disliked" by people in other countries; this is the most downbeat assessment of global popularity given by any national public in the survey.

## How Others Feel About Your Country

| | We're disliked | We're liked |
|---|---|---|

| Country | We're disliked | We're liked |
|---|---|---|
| Canada | 4 | 94 |
| Jordan | 8 | 84 |
| Indonesia | 11 | 86 |
| India | 13 | 83 |
| Spain | 14 | 80 |
| Netherlands | 15 | 83 |
| China | 16 | 68 |
| France | 19 | 80 |
| Lebanon | 32 | 55 |
| Pakistan | 31 | 53 |
| Great Britain | 33 | 56 |
| Poland | 35 | 51 |
| Germany | 43 | 51 |
| Russia | 57 | 32 |
| Turkey | 66 | 30 |
| U.S. | 69 | 26 |

In just two other countries—Turkey and Russia—does a majority of the public believe that their country is generally disliked by people in other countries, with 66% of Turks and 57% of Russians holding this view.

At the other end of the scale, Canadians believe by an overwhelming margin (94%) that their country is popular. Other national publics that believe their countries are popular around the world include Indonesia (86% say their country is generally liked), Jordan (84%), India (83%), the Netherlands (83%), Spain (80%), France (80%) and China (68%).

As a group, the Muslim countries surveyed spread out across the spectrum of self-assessed popularity, with Indonesians and Jordanians

**Loathing or Loving the Homeland?**

| Rating given by . . . | Ratings for Own Country | | |
| | Favorable | Unfavorable | DK |
|---|---|---|---|
| | % | % | % |
| Chinese | 88 | 9 | 2 = 99 |
| Americans | 83 | 14 | 3 = 100 |
| French | 74 | 26 | 0 = 100 |
| Germans | 64 | 34 | 1 = 99 |

feeling extremely popular, while Pakistanis and Lebanese feel some-what popular. In Lebanon, notably, Muslims are less certain of their popularity with only 44% saying they are liked by others, while two-thirds of Christians say so. Turks, however, feel unpopular.

### Mirror, Mirror on the Wall

When it comes to people's attitudes toward their own countries, con-trary to common belief that the French have an inordinately high opinion of themselves and their culture, France does not lead the self-popularity parade. That honor belongs to China, where 88% of Chinese report holding a favorable attitude toward their country. Second in line comes the U.S., where 83% of Americans hold their country in favorable regard. By comparison, the French favor France by a 74%-26% margin. . . .


## II: IMAGE OF THE AMERICAN PEOPLE

In all Global Attitudes surveys dating back to 2002, the rest of the world has held the American people in higher esteem than it has held America. That is still the case now, but in several countries around the world, the gap has narrowed.

This shift in perceptions is most apparent in Indonesia, where since 2003 there has been a sharp increase in U.S. favorability rat-ings (to 38%, up from 15%) but a significant drop in the favor-ability ratings of Americans (to 46%, down from 56%). Whatever goodwill the U.S. gained in Indonesia from its tsunami relief efforts

### Declining View of the American People

| | % Favorable | | | |
|---|---|---|---|---|
| | **2002** | **2003** | **2004** | **2005** |
| Great Britain | 83 | 80 | 73 | 70 |
| Poland | 77 | – | – | 68 |
| Canada | 78 | 77 | – | 66 |
| Netherlands | – | – | – | 66 |
| Germany | 70 | 67 | 68 | 65 |
| France | 71 | 58 | 53 | 64 |
| Russia | 67 | 65 | 64 | 61 |
| Spain | – | 47 | – | 55 |
| Lebanon | 47 | 62 | – | 66 |
| Indonesia | 65 | 56 | – | 46 |
| Jordan | 53 | 18 | 21 | 34 |
| Turkey | 31 | 32 | 32 | 23 |
| Pakistan | 17 | 38 | 25 | 22 |
| India | 58 | – | – | 71 |
| China | – | – | – | 43 |

### Where America's Up, But Americans are Down

| | Favorability of the United States | | | Favorability of Americans | | |
|---|---|---|---|---|---|---|
| | 2003 | 2004 | 2005 | 2003 | 2004 | 2005 |
| | % | % | % | % | % | % |
| Russia | 36 | 47 | 52 | 65 | 64 | 61 |
| Turkey | 15 | 30 | 23 | 32 | 32 | 23 |
| Pakistan | 13 | 21 | 23 | 38 | 25 | 22 |
| Indonesia | 15 | – | 38 | 56 | – | 46 |

apparently did not improve the image that Indonesians have of the American people.

A similar pattern has played out in Russia, Turkey and Pakistan. In these three nations, the image of the United States has risen since 2003 while the image of Americans has declined.

The favorability ratings of Americans have declined since 2002 in 9 of the 12 countries for which trend data exists for that year. These include Great Britain, Poland, Canada, Germany, France, Russia, Indonesia, Jordan and Turkey. The three countries where the image of Americans has risen in that period are Pakistan, India and Lebanon.

*American Character Traits*

To find out what the world makes of the American character, respondents, including Americans themselves, were asked to rate Americans on seven character traits—three positives (hardworking, inventive and honest) and four negative (greedy, violent, rude and immoral).

The picture that emerges is both complex and nuanced. Some of the people around the world who have a generally unfavorable view of Americans are nonetheless inclined to acknowledge some strong Americans traits—for example, while just 46% of Indonesians have a favorable view of Americans, 84% say Americans are both hardworking and inventive. Likewise, many who admire Americans generally nonetheless discern weak points in their character. For example, two-thirds of the Dutch public has a favorable overall view of Americans, but an equal proportion say Americans are greedy and 60% say they are violent.

**Positive Characteristics Associated with Americans**

| Hardworking | | Inventive | | Honest | |
|---|---|---|---|---|---|
| France | 89 | India | 86 | U.S. | 63 |
| U.S. | 85 | Indonesia | 84 | India | 58 |
| Indonesia | 84 | U.S. | 81 | Great Britain | 57 |
| Netherlands | 84 | Canada | 76 | France | 57 |
| India | 81 | Germany | 76 | Germany | 52 |
| Jordan | 78 | France | 76 | Lebanon | 46 |
| Canada | 77 | Poland | 73 | Netherlands | 46 |
| Great Britain | 76 | China | 70 | Spain | 45 |
| Spain | 74 | Netherlands | 69 | Poland | 44 |
| Russia | 72 | Jordan | 68 | Canada | 42 |
| Lebanon | 69 | Great Britain | 64 | Jordan | 37 |
| Germany | 67 | Lebanon | 58 | China | 35 |
| Poland | 64 | Pakistan | 57 | Russia | 32 |
| Pakistan | 63 | Russia | 56 | Pakistan | 27 |
| Turkey | 61 | Turkey | 54 | Indonesia | 23 |
| China | 44 | Spain | 53 | Turkey | 16 |

**Negative Characteristics Associated with Americans**

| Greedy | | Violent | | Rude | | Immoral | |
|---|---|---|---|---|---|---|---|
| U.S. | 70 | Jordan | 73 | Jordan | 64 | Jordan | 69 |
| Turkey | 68 | Turkey | 70 | Indonesia | 56 | Lebanon | 64 |
| Netherlands | 67 | Indonesia | 67 | Turkey | 53 | Pakistan | 58 |
| Lebanon | 66 | Canada | 64 | Canada | 53 | Turkey | 57 |
| Great Britain | 64 | Lebanon | 63 | Pakistan | 51 | Indonesia | 48 |
| Jordan | 63 | Pakistan | 63 | Lebanon | 50 | China | 44 |
| Canada | 62 | France | 63 | Russia | 48 | Russia | 42 |
| Indonesia | 61 | China | 61 | China | 44 | U.S. | 39 |
| Russia | 60 | Spain | 60 | Spain | 39 | Netherlands | 38 |
| Pakistan | 58 | Netherlands | 60 | France | 36 | France | 37 |
| Spain | 58 | Russia | 54 | U.S. | 35 | India | 36 |
| China | 57 | Great Britain | 53 | Great Britain | 29 | Spain | 36 |
| Poland | 55 | U.S. | 49 | India | 27 | Canada | 34 |
| Germany | 49 | Germany | 49 | Netherlands | 26 | Poland | 33 |
| India | 43 | India | 39 | Poland | 21 | Germany | 31 |
| France | 31 | Poland | 33 | Germany | 12 | Great Britain | 26 |

*Hardworking* is the positive trait that people around the world most readily associate with Americans. A majority of every public save one agrees with that assessment, led by the French, who agree with it by a margin of nearly nine-to-one (89%). Just 44% of the Chinese see Americans as hardworking, however. A majority of every public also believes Americans are *inventive,* though by somewhat less lopsided margins. World views are more mixed about whether Americans are honest; only in the U.S., India, Britain, France and Germany is more than half of the public ready to use that word to describe Americans.

On the negative side of the ledger, people around the world are generally inclined to say Americans are greedy and violent. However, most people are not inclined to describe Americans as *rude* and *immoral.*

In all these character assessments, Americans generally fared worse in Muslim countries than they did among traditional allies.

Americans generally rate themselves better than does the rest of the world, but there are a couple of exceptions. Strikingly, Americans are more inclined than any other public in this survey to say their fellow Americans are *greedy.* Americans are about in the middle of the pack in rating their fellow Americans as *immoral.*

In weighing the relative importance of the rest of the world's assessments about each of these specific character traits, *rudeness* emerges in countries that are traditional U.S. allies as the trait most linked with a low regard for Americans. In Muslim countries as well, *rudeness* is an important link to low overall ratings for Americans, but so too is the perception that Americans are *violent* and *immoral.*

## III: OPINIONS OF U.S. POLICIES

A continuing source of resentment toward the U.S. is the view that America pays little if any attention to the interests of other countries in making international policy decisions. Americans, as might be expected, do not subscribe to this view. Two-thirds of the U.S. public says the United States pays either a great deal (28%) or a fair amount (39%) of attention to the interests of other nations.

Majorities in only three other countries now share that opinion; India, where 63% say the U.S. pays a great deal or a fair amount of attention to their country's interests, Indonesia (59%), and China (53%). In line with the general upsurge of positive feelings toward the

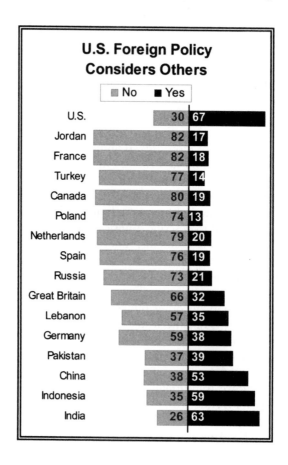

U.S. in both India and Indonesia, these percentages are up sharply from past Pew Global Attitudes surveys.

In addition, increasing numbers in Pakistan and Lebanon say the U.S. pays at least some attention to their countries' interests. About four-in-ten Pakistanis (39%) express that view, compared with 18% in 2004. There has been a comparable increase in Lebanon, though a majority of Lebanese still feel that the U.S. pays little or no attention to their interests. (However, among Lebanese Christians a solid majority (59%) feels that the U.S. is attentive to their country's concerns.) And, fewer than one-in-five in Jordan (17%) and Turkey (14%) think that the U.S. takes their interests into consideration in its international policymaking.

Perceptions of U.S. unilateralism remain widespread among the publics of America's traditional allies. In Germany, only 38% of respondents think the U.S. takes their country's interests into account, the highest percentage in Europe. In Canada, just 19% feel the U.S. takes Canadian interests into account to any substantial degree when making policy. While these views have remained fairly stable in France, Spain and Russia over the last few years, the numbers of those viewing the U.S. as self-centered in its foreign policymaking have risen substantially in Canada, Great Britain and Germany.

# "Why the World Is Flat": Interview with Thomas Friedman

## Daniel H. Pink

*The term* globalization *came into widespread use in the 1980s as a shorthand way to describe a rapidly escalating historical process. As people developed and adapted new technologies, they made possible the increasing integration of economies around the world. Trade and financial connections that transcend national boundaries are fundamental to globalization, but the term also describes the movement of people and knowledge across international borders, along with the cultural, political, and environmental implications of such movements and connections.*

*Globalization, at its most basic, allows markets to function more efficiently. Global competition fosters specialization and thus efficiency; global markets offer both cheaper imports and larger export markets, as well as greater access to investment capital and technological resources. The economic benefits of globalization, however, are not equally shared. The political, cultural, and environmental effects of globalization are significant and controversial.*

*Over the past decade or so, people worldwide have battled over globalization— in chambers where policy is made, and in the streets. Some embrace the benefits of globalization; others express concern about its inequities but see it as an inevitable historical process; others take strong stands against it, for reasons including concern about global poverty and international inequality, commitment to human rights and the protection of the environment, and worries that relatively unimpeded international competition—which allows manufacturing to follow cheap labor—destroys the possibility for well-paid factory or manufacturing jobs in wealthy nations such as the United States.*

*In the following interview from* Wired *magazine, New York Times columnist Thomas Friedman discusses the argument he made in his influential*

Daniel H. Pink (www.danpink.com) is the author of *A Whole New Mind*. This article originally appeared in *Wired* magazine (www.wired.com) and is reprinted with permission.

*book,* The World Is Flat. *Friedman offers the positive case for globalization—though with serious warnings about its implications for the United States. And in the piece immediately following this interview, Global Exchange offers their "Top Ten Reasons to Oppose the World Trade Organization." The argument about globalization is complex and widespread, with many variations, and these two pieces offer only a small piece of it. However, they are good starting points for discussion of a critically important issue in the contemporary world.*

Thirty-five years ago this summer, the golfer Chi Chi Rodriguez was competing in his seventh US Open, played that year at Hazeltine Country Club outside Minneapolis. Tied for second place after the opening round, Rodriguez eventually finished 27th, a few strokes ahead of such golf legends as Jack Nicklaus, Arnold Palmer, and Gary Player. His caddy for the tournament was a 17-year-old local named Tommy Friedman.

Rodriguez retired from golf several years later. But his caddy—now known as Thomas L. Friedman, foreign affairs columnist for *The New York Times* and author of the new book *The World Is Flat: A Brief History of the Twenty-First Century*—has spent his career deploying the skills he used on the golf course: describing the terrain, shouting warnings and encouragement, and whispering in the ears of big players. After 10 years of writing his twice-weekly foreign affairs column, Friedman has become the most influential American newspaper columnist since Walter Lippmann.

One reason for Friedman's influence is that, in the mid-'90s, he staked out the territory at the intersection of technology, financial markets, and world trade, which the foreign policy establishment, still focused on cruise missiles and throw weights, had largely ignored. "This thing called globalization," he says, "can explain more things in more ways than anything else."

Friedman's 1999 book, *The Lexus and the Olive Tree: Understanding Globalization,* provided much of the intellectual framework for the debate. "The first big book on globalization that anybody actually read," as Friedman describes it, helped make him a fixture on the Davos-Allen Conference-Renaissance Weekend circuit. But it also made him a lightning rod. He's been accused of "rhetorical hyperventilation" and dismissed as an "apologist" for global capital. The columnist Molly Ivins even dubbed top-tier society's lack of concern for the downsides of globalization "the Tom Friedman Problem."

After 9/11, Friedman says, he paid less attention to globalization. He spent the next three years traveling to the Arab and Muslim world trying to get at the roots of the attack on the US. His columns on the subject earned him his third Pulitzer Prize. But Friedman realized that while he was writing about terrorism, he missed an even bigger story: Globalization had gone into overdrive. So in a three-month burst last year, he wrote *The World Is Flat* to explain his updated thinking on the subject.

Friedman enlisted some impressive editorial assistance. Bill Gates spent a day with him to critique the theory. Friedman presented sections of the book to the strategic planning unit at IBM and to Michael Dell. But his most important tutors were two Indians: Nandan Nilekani, CEO of Infosys, and Vivek Paul, a top executive at Wipro. "They were the guys who really cracked the code for me."

*Wired* sat down with Friedman in his office at the *Times'* Washington bureau to discuss the flattening of the world.

**WIRED: What do you mean the world is flat?**
FRIEDMAN: I was in India interviewing Nandan Nilekani at Infosys. And he said to me, "Tom, the playing field is being leveled." Indians and Chinese were going to compete for work like never before, and Americans weren't ready. I kept chewing over that phrase—the playing field is being leveled—and then it hit me: Holy mackerel, the world is becoming flat. Several technological and political forces have converged, and that has produced a global, Web-enabled playing field that allows for multiple forms of collaboration without regard to geography or distance—or soon, even language.

**So, we're talking about globalization enhanced by things like the rise of open source?**
This is Globalization 3.0. In Globalization 1.0, which began around 1492, the world went from size large to size medium. In Globalization 2.0, the era that introduced us to multinational companies, it went from size medium to size small. And then around 2000 came Globalization 3.0, in which the world went from being small to tiny. There's a difference between being able to make long distance phone calls cheaper on the Internet and walking around Riyadh with a PDA where you can have all of Google in your pocket. It's a difference in degree that's so enormous it becomes a difference in kind.

**Is that why the Netscape IPO is one of your "10 flatteners"? Explain.**

Three reasons. Netscape brought the Internet alive with the browser. They made the Internet so that Grandma could use it and her grandchildren could use it. The second thing that Netscape did was commercialize a set of open transmission protocols so that no company could own the Net. And the third is that Netscape triggered the dotcom boom, which triggered the dotcom bubble, which triggered the overinvestment of a trillion dollars in fiberoptic cables.

**Are you saying telecommunications trumps terrorism? What about September 11? Isn't that as important?**

There's no question flattening is more important. I don't think you can understand 9/11 without understanding flattening.

**This is probably the first book by a major foreign affairs thinker that talks about the world-changing effects of ... supply chains.**

[*Laughs.*]

**Why are supply chains so important?**

They're incredible flatteners. For UPS to work, they've got to create systems with customs offices around the world. They've got to design supply chain algorithms so when you take that box to the UPS Store, it gets from that store to its hub and then out. Everything they are doing is taking fat out of the system at every joint. I was in India after the nuclear alert of 2002. I was interviewing Vivek Paul at Wipro shortly after he'd gotten an email from one of their big American clients saying. "We're now looking for an alternative to you. We don't want to be looking for an alternative to you. You don't *want* us to be looking for an alternative to you. Do something about this!" So I saw the effect that India's being part of this global supply chain had on the behavior of the Indian business community, which eventually filtered up to New Delhi.

**And that's how you went from your McDonald's Theory of Conflict Prevention—two countries that have a McDonald's will never go to war with each other—to the Dell Theory of Conflict Prevention.**

Yes. No two countries that are both part of a major global supply chain like Dell's will fight against each other as long as they are both part of that supply chain. When I'm managing your back room, when I'm managing your HR, when I'm doing your accounting—that's way beyond selling you burgers. We are intimately in bed with each other. And that has got to affect my behavior.

**In some sense, then, the world is a gigantic supply chain. And you don't want to be the one who brings the whole thing down.**
Absolutely.

**Unless your goal is to bring the whole thing down. Supply chains work for al Qaeda, too, don't they?**
Al Qaeda is nothing more than a mutant supply chain. They're playing off the same platform as Wal-Mart and Dell. They're just not restrained by it. What is al Qaeda? It's an open source religious political movement that works off the global supply chain. That's what we're up against in Iraq. We're up against a suicide supply chain. You take one bomber and deploy him in Baghdad, and another is manufactured in Riyadh the next day. It's exactly like when you take the toy off the shelf at Wal-Mart and another is made in Shen Zhen the next day.

**The book is almost dizzily optimistic about India and China, about what flattening will bring to these parts of the world.**
I firmly believe that the next great breakthrough in bioscience could come from a 15-year-old who downloads the human genome in Egypt. Bill Gates has a nice line: He says, 20 years ago, would you rather have been a B-student in Poughkeepsie or a genius in Shanghai? Twenty years ago you'd rather be a B-student in Poughkeepsie. Today?

**Not even close.**
Not even close. You'd much prefer to be the genius in Shanghai because you can now export your talents anywhere in the world.

**As optimistic as you are about that kid in Shanghai, you're not particularly optimistic about the US.**
I'm worried about my country. I love America. I think it's the best country in the world. But I also think we're not tending to our sauce. I believe that we are in what Shirley Ann Jackson [president of Rensselaer Polytechnic Institute] calls a "quiet crisis." If we don't change course now and buckle down in a flat world, the kind of competition our kids will face will be intense and the social implications of not repairing things will be enormous.

**You quote a CEO who says that Americans have grown addicted to their high salaries, and now they're going to have to earn them. Are Americans suffering from an undue sense of entitlement?**
Somebody said to me the other day that—I wish I had this for the book, but it's going to be in the paperback—the entitlement we need to get rid of is our sense of entitlement.

**Let's talk about the critics of globalization. You say that you don't want the antiglobalization movement to go away. Why?**

I've been a critic of the antiglobalization movement, and they've been a critic of me, but the one thing I respect about the movement is their authentic energy. These are not people who don't care about the world. But if you want to direct your energy toward helping the poor, I believe the best way is not throwing a stone through a McDonald's window or protesting World Bank meetings. It's through local governance. When you start to improve local governance, you improve education, women's rights, transportation.

**It's possible to go through your book and conclude it was written by a US senator who wants to run for president. There's a political agenda in this book.**

Yes, absolutely.

**You call for portable benefits, lifelong learning, free trade, greater investment in science, government funding for tertiary education, a *system of wage insurance. Uh, Mr. Friedman, are you running for president?***

[*Laughs loudly.*] No, I am not running for president!

**Would you accept the vice presidential nomination?**

I just want to get my Thursday column done!

**But you are outlining an explicit agenda.**

You can't be a citizen of this country and not be in a hair-pulling rage at the fact that we're at this inflection moment and nobody seems to be talking about the kind of policies we need to get through this flattening of the world, to get the most out of it and cushion the worst. We need to have as focused, as serious, as energetic, as sacrificing a strategy for dealing with flatism as we did for communism. This is the challenge of our day.

**Short of Washington fully embracing the Friedman doctrine, what should we be doing? For instance, what advice should we give to our kids?**

When I was growing up, my parents told me, "Finish your dinner. People in China and India are starving." I tell my daughters, "Finish your homework. People in India and China are starving for your job."

**Think about your own childhood for a moment. If a teenage Tommy Friedman could somehow have been transported to 2005, what do you think he would have found most surprising?**

That you could go to PGA.com and get the scores of your favorite golfer in real time. That would have been amazing.

## THE 10 GREAT LEVELERS

### 1. Fall of the Berlin Wall
The events of November 9, 1989, tilted the worldwide balance of power toward democracies and free markets.

### 2. Netscape IPO
The August 9, 1995, offering sparked massive investment in fiber-optic cables.

### 3. Work flow software
The rise of apps from PayPal to VPNs enabled faster, closer co-ordination among far-flung employees.

### 4. Open-sourcing
Self-organizing communities, à la Linux, launched a collaborative revolution.

### 5. Outsourcing
Migrating business functions to India saved money *and* a third world economy.

### 6. Offshoring
Contract manufacturing elevated China to economic prominence.

### 7. Supply-chaining
Robust networks of suppliers, retailers, and customers increased business efficiency. See Wal-Mart.

### 8. Insourcing
Logistics giants took control of customer supply chains, helping mom-and-pop shops go global. See UPS and FedEx.

### 9. In-forming
Power searching allowed everyone to use the Internet as a "personal supply chain of knowledge." See Google.

### 10. Wireless
Like "steroids," wireless technologies pumped up collaboration, making it mobile and personal.

# Top Ten Reasons to Oppose the World Trade Organization

## Global Exchange

*This flyer, created by the group Global Exchange, largely avoids the term glo-balization. Instead of opposing the historical process of globalization, which one might argue has been occurring for centuries, it targets the policies and actions of a specific organization. The World Trade Organization (WTO) is an international organization that negotiates the rules of trade between nations, fostering a process of globalization that many see as favoring the rights of corporations over all else. Read the following piece along with "Why the World Is Flat" (pp. 449–454) and its introduction.*

### 1. The WTO Is Fundamentally Undemocratic

The policies of the WTO impact all aspects of society and the planet, but it is not a democratic, transparent institution. The WTO's rules are written by and for corporations with inside access to the negotiations. For example, the U.S. Trade Representative gets heavy input for negotiations from 17 "Industry Sector Advisory Committees." Citizen input by consumer, environmental, human rights and labor organizations is consistently ignored. Even simple requests for information are denied, and the proceedings are held in secret. Who elected this secret global government?

### 2. The WTO Will Not Make Us Safer

The WTO would like you to believe that creating a world of "free trade" will promote global understanding and peace. On the contrary, the domination of international trade by rich coun-tries for the benefit of their individual interests fuels anger and resentment that make us less safe. To build real global security, we need international agreements that respect people's rights to democracy and trade systems that promote global justice.

### 3. The WTO Tramples Labor and Human Rights

WTO rules put the "rights" of corporations to profit over human and labor rights. The WTO encourages a "race to the bottom" in wages by pitting workers against each other rather than promoting internationally recognized labor standards. The WTO has ruled that it is illegal for a government to ban a product based on the way it is produced, such as goods produced with child labor. It has also ruled that governments cannot take into account "non commercial values" such as human rights, or the behavior of companies that do business with vicious dictatorships such as Burma when making purchasing decisions. The WTO has more power to punish countries that violate its rules than the United Nations has to sanction violators of international human rights standards.

### 4. The WTO Encourages Privatization of Essential Services

The WTO is seeking to force national governments to privatize essential public services such as education, health care, energy and water so that these sectors are open to multinational corporations. The WTO's General Agreement on Trade in Services, or GATS, includes a list of about 160 threatened services including elder and child care, sewage, garbage, park maintenance, telecommunications, construction, banking, insurance, transportation, shipping, postal services, and tourism, and is currently being expanded into new areas. When free trade and corporate globalization turn government supplied services over to private for-profit corporations, those least able to pay for vital services—working class communities and communities of color—are the ones who suffer the most.

### 5. The WTO is Destroying the Environment

The WTO is being used by corporations to dismantle hardwon local and national environmental protections, by attacking them as "barriers to trade." The very first WTO panel ruled that a provision of the U.S. Clean Air Act, requiring both domestic and foreign producers alike to produce cleaner gasoline, was WTO illegal. The WTO also declared illegal a provision of the Endangered Species Act requiring shrimp sold in the United States to be caught with an inexpensive device allowing endangered sea turtles to escape. The WTO is now attempting to deregulate service industries such as logging, fishing, water utilities, and energy distribution, leading to further exploitation of natural resources.

## 6. The WTO is Killing People

The WTO's fierce defense of "Trade Related Intellectual Property" rights (TRIPs)—patents, copyrights and trademarks—comes at the expense of health and human lives. The WTO has protected pharmaceutical companies' "right to profit" against governments seeking to protect their people's health by providing lifesaving medicines in countries in areas like sub-Saharan Africa, where thousands die every day from HIV/AIDS. Developing countries won an important victory in 2001 when they affirmed the right to produce generic drugs (or import them if they lacked production capacity), so that they could provide essential lifesaving medicines to their populations less expensively.

Unfortunately, in 2003, many new conditions were agreed to that will make it more difficult for countries to produce those drugs. Once again, the WTO demonstrates that it favors corporate profit over saving human lives.

## 7. The WTO is Increasing Inequality

Free trade is not working for the majority of the world. During the most recent period of rapid growth in global trade and investment (1960 to 1998) inequality worsened both internationally and within countries. The United Nations Development Program reports that the richest 20 percent of the world's population consume 86 percent of the world's resources while the poorest 80 percent consume just 14 percent. WTO rules have hastened these trends by opening up countries to foreign investment and thereby making it easier for production to go where the labor is cheapest and most easily exploited and environmental costs are low.

## 8. The WTO is Increasing Hunger

Farmers produce enough food in the world to feed everyone—yet because of corporate control of food distribution, as many as 800 million people worldwide suffer from chronic malnutrition. According to the Universal Declaration of Human Rights, food is a human right. In developing countries, as many as four out of every five people make their living from the land. But the leading principle in the WTO's Agreement on Agriculture is that market forces should control agricultural policies—rather than a national commitment to guarantee food security and maintain decent family farmer incomes. WTO policies have allowed dumping of heavily subsidized industrially produced food into poor countries, undermining local production and increasing hunger.

## 9. The WTO Hurts Poor, Small Countries in Favor of Rich Powerful Nations

The WTO supposedly operates on a consensus basis, with equal decision-making power for all. In reality, many important decisions get made in a process whereby poor countries' negotiators are not even invited to closed-door meetings—and then "agreements" are announced that poor countries didn't even know were being discussed. Many countries do not have enough trade personnel to participate in all the negotiations or to even have a permanent representative at the WTO. This severely disadvantages poor countries from representing their interests. Likewise, many countries are too poor to defend themselves from WTO challenges from the rich countries, and are forced to change their laws rather than pay for their own defense.

## 10. The WTO Undermines Local Level Decision-Making and National Sovereignty

The WTO's "most favored nation" provision requires all WTO member countries to treat each other equally and to treat all corporations from these countries equally regardless of their track record. Local policies aimed at rewarding companies who hire local residents, use domestic materials, or adopt environmentally sound practices are essentially illegal under the WTO. Developing countries are prohibited from creating local laws that developed countries once pursued, such as protecting new, domestic industries until they can be internationally competitive. California's former Governor Gray Davis vetoed a "Buy California" bill that would have granted a small preference to local businesses because it was WTO-illegal. When the WTO was created in 1995, entire sections of U.S. laws were rewritten. Many countries are even changing their laws and constitutions in anticipation of potential future WTO rulings and negotiations.

## 11. There are Alternatives to the WTO

Citizen organizations have developed alternatives to the corporate-dominated system of global economic governance. Together we can build the political space that nurtures a democratic global economy that promotes jobs, ensures that every person is guaranteed their human rights to food, water, education, and health care, promotes freedom and security, and preserves our shared environment for future generations. Check out the International Forum on Globalization's Alternatives to Economic Globalization: A Better World is Possible (available on the Global Exchange online store).

## 12. The Tide is Turning Against Free Trade and the WTO!

International opposition to the WTO is growing. Massive protests in Seattle of the 1999 WTO Ministerial brought over 50,000 people together to oppose the WTO—and succeeded in shutting the meeting down. When the WTO met in 2001, the trade negotiators were unable to meet their goals of expanding the WTO's reach. The WTO met in Cancún, Mexico in September of 2003, and met thousands of activists in protest. Developing countries in the negotiations refused to give in to the rich countries' agenda of WTO expansion and caused the talks to collapse! The next Ministerial meeting of the WTO will be in December of 2005 in Hong Kong, however, negotiations on many issues are ongoing. Find out how you can help Stop the WTO!

# Part 9

## THE CHANGING SHAPE
## OF AMERICAN SOCIETY

In his final State of the Union address in January 2000, at the beginning of a new millennium, President Bill Clinton spoke of building a bridge to the future. The 1990s were good times for America. The nation had rarely seemed stronger. And by the end of the decade, though the extraordinary economic growth of the 1990s had begun to slow, many Americans still believed in unlimited economic expansion. The nation was at peace, with no major enemy in sight. Poverty rates were declining, levels of health care coverage rising, homeownership at an all-time high. The bridge to the future was an inspiring metaphor.

The election of 2000, in which Clinton's vice president Al Gore confronted the son of previous president George H. W. Bush, was so extraordinarily close that it was decided by the Supreme Court. The divide in the electorate might suggest that Americans were divided about the future of their nation—but many voters, at the time, said they saw little difference between the two men or between the two political parties to which they belonged. That was a radical misunderstanding—at least in hindsight—but it made sense to people who expected no major changes, no major challenges, to their lives and to the nation's progress into a new century.

The attacks of September 11, 2001, seemed to destroy the optimism of the late twentieth century. They—and the events that followed—exposed the divisions among the American people. The divisions were not new, nor were many of the challenges America faced. But in a time of insecurity, people approached them with new seriousness.

As Democratic nominee John Kerry (see pp. 251–255) ran against George W. Bush in 2004, the nation was divided over the war in Iraq, over tax cuts for wealthier Americans and the future of such government

461

programs as Social Security, Medicare and Medicaid, over security and civil liberties, over environmental protection and government regulation, over the role of religion in public life, over abortion, even over the definition of marriage. In another very close election, George Bush prevailed. This time, however, no one talked about "Tweedledum and Tweedledee"—as Ralph Nader had characterized George Bush and Al Gore when he ran as a third-party candidate in the 2000 election. In 2004, the divisions among American voters were very much apparent.

The new shorthand for those divisions came from the electoral map on which states were allocated to one candidate or another. There were red states, whose electoral votes went to the Republican candidate, and blue states, whose votes went to the Democrat. The South was red, along with most of the heartland. Blue states hugged the coasts; a few of the old industrial Rust Belt states in the Midwest were blue splashes in the red expanse. In fact, the divides were not so simple. Moving beyond state electoral votes to voting patterns on the county level, larger urban centers tended to blue, rural areas to red. And if one mixed the percentage of Democratic votes (blue) with the percentage of Republican votes (red) on either a county or a state level, the nation was a study in magenta. Very few places fell into a recognizable "red" or "blue" color. But the shorthand remains powerful. Red states and blue states, now, are how we talk about the continuing "culture war" in America.

This final section of *A History of Our Time* turns from history to contemporary society. The readings here address the (primarily) domestic challenges that America faces in this new millennium. We begin with historian J. R. McNeill, who offers a global perspective on environmental change and human action, looking ahead to an uncertain and increasingly volatile future. Also addressing the relationship between the global and the domestic are charts and figures and statistics that demonstrate the impact of immigration on the United States in the years since 1965. The U.S. population is increasingly diverse. The rapidly increasing number of Latinos in the United States has made African Americans the third largest ethnic/racial group, and demographers predict that by the middle of the twenty-first century, whites will no longer make up the majority of the nation's population. In recent years, new scientific methods, including relatively inexpensive DNA testing, have combined uneasily with insights drawn from sociological and anthropological research to complicate our definitions of "race." Stephan Thernstrom, in an article written for the conservative *National Review,* critiques the assumptions about race underlying the 2000 census—and critiques their policy implications.

For years, historians had taught students that the 1920s Scopes trial was the triumph of scientific understandings over religious fundamentalism. In the past decade, however, in classrooms ranging from Pennsylvania to New Mexico to Texas to Kansas, the teaching of evolution has been challenged by Americans who want either biblical explanations of creation or the doctrine of intelligent design to have a place in the nation's classrooms. Here we include an article from the *American School Board Journal,* authored by evolutionary zoologist Robert George Sprackland, who argues that it is critically important to teach *only* science in science classrooms. Further complicating the cultural divide between those who call upon religious versus secular value systems, historian of the family Stephanie Coontz discusses (heterosexual) marriage and perceptions of its fragility in contemporary America. Finally, journalist Anne Kornblut takes on "red" and "blue." If you don't already know which you are, her culture-oriented quiz will help you figure it out. And if not, it's a bit of humor about a difficult subject.

*A History of Our Time* concludes with some general information—undigested pieces of evidence—about American society and culture today. These lists and charts and statistics might help you to think about the state of the nation and its possible futures.

In the first decade of the new millennium, the challenges facing America seem as perilous and difficult to resolve as at any time during the last five decades of the twentieth century. As complex as the issues of post–World War II America were, they may well pale beside those of the new millennium.

# Our Gigantic Experiment with Planet Earth

## J. R. McNeill

*In 1962, biologist Rachel Carson published the first of the articles that would become her best-selling book* Silent Spring, *in the* New Yorker. *Carson's work redefined popular understandings of environmentalism, shifting focus from the preservation of unspoiled "wilderness" to an awareness of "the intricate web of life whose interwoven strands lead from microbes to man." America's environmental movement grew throughout the 1960s, drawing new members to existing groups such as the Sierra Club and lending support to a whole series of environmental protection initiatives, including the creation of the Environmental Protection Agency (EPA) in 1970.*

*Increasingly in the latter part of the twentieth century, scientists and environmental activists attempted to draw Americans' attention to the global nature of environmental change and the global impact of our actions. Environmental policies have become key issues in recent elections, with Democratic candidates much more likely to support a range of environmental protections. The Clinton-Gore administration set aside large tracts of open land from development, adopted tough new standards for emissions and for air and water quality, and approached issues of environment and climate change as a global issue. George W. Bush began his administration, in contrast, by refusing to sign the Kyoto Protocols, a worldwide treaty aimed at reversing global warming by reducing the production of greenhouse gases, and by moving to open the Arctic National Wildlife Refuge to oil drilling.*

*In this excerpt from his influential book,* Something New under the Sun, *historian J. R. McNeill argues that the environmental changes brought about by humankind are ultimately more significant than any other aspect of twentieth-century history. Even more than the other authors in this section, McNeill focuses on the global challenges of the twenty-first century. In a "total system of global society and environment," what role can a single nation—even one as powerful as the United States—play? Can the United States's wealth insulate it from ecological catastrophe?*

Environmental change on earth is as old as the planet itself, about four billion years. Our genus, *Homo*, has altered earthly environments throughout our career, about four million years. But there has never been anything like the 20th century.

Asteroids and volcanoes, among other astronomical and geological forces, have probably produced more radical environmental changes than we have yet witnessed in our time. But humanity has not. This is the first time in human history that we have altered ecosystems with such intensity, on such scale and with such speed. It is one of the few times in the earth's history to see changes of this scope and pace. Albert Einstein famously refused to "believe that God plays dice with the world." But in the 20th century, humankind has begun to play dice with the planet, without knowing all the rules of the game.

The human race, without intending anything of the sort, has undertaken a gigantic uncontrolled experiment on the earth. In time, I think, this will appear as the most important aspect of 20th-century history, more so than World War II, the communist enterprise, the rise of mass literacy, the spread of democracy, or the growing emancipation of women. To see just how prodigal and peculiar this century was, it helps to adopt long perspectives of the deeper past.

In environmental history, the 20th century qualifies as a peculiar century because of the screeching acceleration of so many processes that bring ecological change. Most of these processes are not new; we have cut timber, mined ores, generated wastes, grown crops, and hunted animals for a long time. In modern times we have generally done more of these things than ever before, and since 1945, in most cases, far more. Although there are a few kinds of environmental change that are genuinely new in the 20th century, such as human-induced thinning of the ozone layer, for the most part the ecological peculiarity of the 20th century is a matter of scale and intensity.

Sometimes differences in quantity can become differences in quality. So it was with 20th-century environmental change. The scale and intensity of changes were so great that matters that for millennia were local concerns became global. One example is air pollution. Since people first harnessed fire half a million years ago, they have polluted air locally. Mediterranean lead smelting in Roman times even polluted air in the Arctic. But lately, air pollution has grown so comprehensive and large-scale that it affects the fundamentals of global atmospheric chemistry.

Beyond that, in natural systems as in human affairs, there are thresholds and so-called nonlinear effects. In the 1930s, Adolf Hitler's Germany acquired Austria, the Sudetenland, and the rest of Czechoslovakia without provoking much practical response. When in September 1939 Hitler tried to add Poland, he got a six-year war that ruined him, his movement, and (temporarily) Germany. Unknowingly—although he was aware of the risk—he crossed a threshold and provoked a nonlinear effect. Similarly, water temperature in the tropical Atlantic can grow warmer and warmer without generating any hurricanes. But once that water passes 26° Celsius, it begins to promote hurricanes; a threshold passed, a switch was thrown, simply by an incremental increase. The environmental history of the 20th century is different from that of time past not merely because ecological changes were greater and faster, but also because increased intensities threw some switches. For example, incremental increases in fishing effort brought total collapse in some oceanic fisheries. The cumulation of many increased intensities may throw some grand switches, producing very basic changes on the earth. No one knows, and no one will know until it starts to happen—if then. . . .

In 1930 the American physicist and Nobel Prize–winner Robert Millikan (1868–1953) said that there was no risk that humanity could do real harm to anything so gigantic as the earth. In the same year the American chemical engineer Thomas Midgley invented chlorofluorocarbons, the chemicals responsible for thinning the stratospheric ozone layer. Millikan, although certainly a man "of talents," did not understand what was brewing. What Machiavelli said of affairs of state is doubly true of affairs of global ecology and society. It is nearly impossible to see what is happening until it is inconveniently late to do much about it.

It is impossible to know whether humankind has entered a genuine ecological crisis. It is clear enough that our current ways are ecologically unsustainable, but we cannot know for how long we may yet sustain them, or what might happen if we do. In any case, human history since the dawn of agriculture is replete with unsustainable societies, some of which vanished but many of which changed their ways and survived. They changed not to sustainability but to some new and different kind of unsustainability. Perhaps we can, as it were, pile one unsustainable regime upon another indefinitely, making adjustments large and small but avoiding collapse, as China did during its "3,000 years of unsustainable development." Imperial China, for all its apparent conservatism, was ... adopting new food crops, new technologies, shifting its trade relations with its neighbors, constantly adapting—and surviving several crises. However, unsustainable society on the global scale may be another matter entirely, and what China did for millennia the whole world perhaps cannot do for long. If so, then collapse looms, as prophets of the ecological apocalypse so often warn. Perhaps the transition from our current unsustainable regime to another would be horribly wrenching and a fate to be avoided—or at least delayed—at all costs, as beneficiaries of the status quo so regularly claim. We cannot know for sure, and by the time we do know, it will be far too late to do much about it.

The future, even the fairly near future, is not merely unknowable; it is inherently uncertain. Some scenarios are more likely than others, no doubt, but nothing is fixed. Indeed, the future is more volatile than ever before: a greater number of radically different possibilities exist because technology has grown so influential, because ideas spread so rapidly, and because reproductive behavior—usually a variable that changes at a glacial pace—is in rapid flux. Moreover, all these variables are probably more tightly interactive than at most times in the past, so the total system of global society and environment is more uncertain, more chaotic, than ever.

All that said, the probability is that sharp adjustments will be required to avoid straitened circumstances. Many of the ecological buffers—open land, unused water, unpolluted spaces—that helped societies weather difficult times in the past are now gone. The most difficult passages will probably (or better put, least improbably) involve shortage of clean fresh water, the myriad effects of warmer climate, and of reduced bio-diversity.

While one cannot say with any confidence what forms an ecological crunch might take, when it might happen, or how severe it might be, it is easier to predict who will have the worst of it. The poor and powerless cannot shield themselves from ecological problems today, nor will they be able to in the future. The wealthy and powerful in the past have normally had the wherewithal to insulate themselves from the effects of pollution, soil erosion, or fishery collapse. Only in a very severe crunch are they likely to face heavy costs. Of course, just who is rich and who is poor is subject to change: consider South

Koreans, who in 1960 were on average poorer than Ghanaians, but by the 1990s were among the world's richer populations. This very fact inspires great efforts, individual and collective, to escape poverty and weakness, which efforts often aggravate ecological problems. South Koreans after 1960 paid dearly for their economic miracle, suffering from noxious urban air, toxic industrial effluent in the rivers, and many other disagreeable conditions. But now they are in a much better position than Ghanaians to weather serious ecological dislocations—because they are much richer.

If one accepts the notion that there is a significant chance that more serious ecological problems lie ahead, then, bearing Machiavelli in mind, it is prudent to address the prospect sooner rather than later. My interpretation of modern history suggests that the most sensible things to do are to hasten the arrival of a new, cleaner energy regime and to hasten the demographic transition toward lower mortality and fertility. The former implies concentrated scientific and engineering work, and probably interventions in the marketplace that encourage early retirement of existing energy infrastructures and faster diffusion of new ones. The latter implies furthering the formal education of girls and women in poor countries, because poor countries are where the demographic transition is incomplete, and because female education is the strongest determinant of fertility. There may be other desirable initiatives, such as converting the masses to some new creed of ecological restraint or coaxing rulers into considering time horizons longer than the next election or coup. These are more difficult and less practical, precisely because they are more fundamental.

# The New Immigration

## United States Census Bureau

"America is a nation of immigrants." It's a truism, and a fairly accurate one. But who those immigrants are—where they come from and why; how big a proportion of the U.S. population they represent; where they settle and what they do—all has changed dramatically over the course of U.S. history. In the late twentieth century, Ellis Island and the Statue of Liberty have been replaced by LAX (the Los Angeles airport) or by the U.S.–Mexico border as immigrants' first glimpse of their new land.

And despite the patriotic rhetoric describing America as a nation of immigrants—whether the metaphor employed is melting pot, stew pot, or salad bowl—immigration has been a difficult issue in American life since well before the Civil War. A strong anti-immigration party emerged in the 1850s, following a dramatic rise in the number of Irish immigrants during Ireland's great potato famine. In 1882, Congress passed the Chinese Exclusion Act in response to pressure from native-born workers who wanted to prevent competition for jobs from low-paid Chinese laborers. In the 1920s, Congress enacted a series of Immigration Acts meant to stem the flow of immigrants—the "barbarian horde," in the words of one congressman—and to establish quotas based on "national origins" that favored immigrants from northern and western Europe over those from eastern and southern Europe.

Though the 1924 Immigration Act was modified somewhat through the years (in 1943 the United States opened its borders to 105 Chinese immigrants per year), it was the 1965 Immigration and Nationality Act that fundamentally changed American immigration policy—and the face of America. In keeping with other legislation aimed at ending racial discrimination, the act replaced the national quotas with hemispheric "ceilings," emphasized family reunification, and gave professionals and skilled workers high priority. In the years following 1965, immigration from Latin America

From Bureau of the Census, http://www.census.gov.

*and Asia grew dramatically. And so did the number of immigrants to the United States and the proportion of immigrants in the U.S. population.*

*The following material is drawn from reports created by the U.S. Census Bureau. Using this evidence to think historically, what trends do you see developing? What are the possible implications of these trends? What possibilities do these trends offer, and what challenges might they pose? In retrospect, the 1965 Immigration Act may have changed the United States more than any other piece of Great Society legislation, with the exception of the Civil Rights Act. But it was scarcely debated, and was passed by Congress with little comment. Why did people at the time not understand its significance?*

National Quick Facts: 2002

- In 2002, 32 million (12 percent of the U.S. population) were foreign born.
- In 2002, 12 million (37 percent of the foreign born) were U.S. citizens through naturalization.
- 49 percent of the foreign born entered the U.S. between 1990 and 2002.

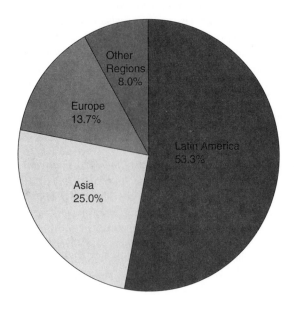

Percent Distribution of Foreign Born by World Region of Birth: 2003

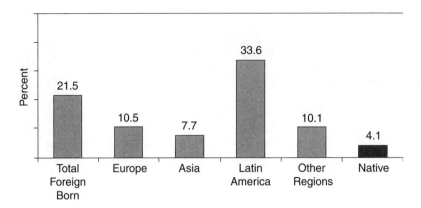

Percent of Population with Less Than 9th Grade Completed by World Region of Birth: 2003 (Population 25 Years and Over)

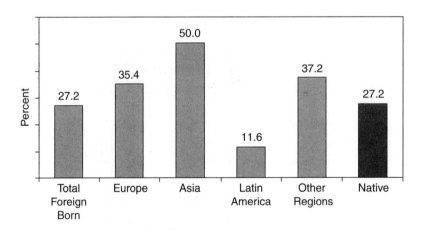

Percent of Population with a Bachelor's Degree or Higher by World Region of Birth: 2003 (Population 25 Years and Over)

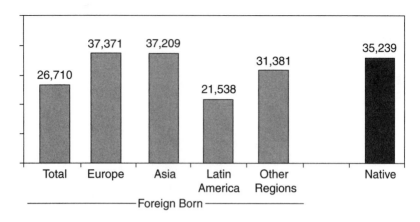

Median Earnings of Year-Round, Full-Time Foreign-Born Workers by Place of Birth: 2001 (Population 15 years and over with earnings) (in dollars)

**Language Spoken at Home for the Foreign Born: 2002 (Population 5 years and over)**

|  | *Percent* |
|---|---|
| Total Foreign Born | 100 |
| Speak only English | 17 |
| Speak a language other than English | 83 |
| Speak Spanish | 45 |
| Speak Asian or Pacific Island languages | 18 |
| Speak other Indo-European languages | 17 |
| Speak other languages | 3 |

Source: American Community Survey 2002.

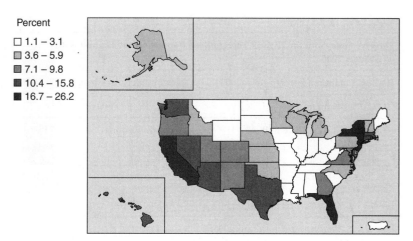

Percent Foreign Born Within Each State: 2000

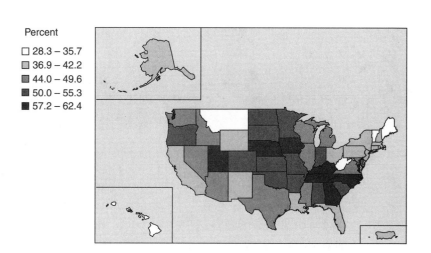

Percent of Foreign Born Who Entered 1990 to 2000 by State: 2000

**Top Five States with the Highest Foreign-Born Population and Highest Rate of Change: 2000**

| Highest Number of Foreign Born 2000 | | Highest Percent Change 1990–2000 | |
|---|---|---|---|
| | Number | | Percent |
| California | 9 million | North Carolina | 274% |
| New York | 4 million | Georgia | 233% |
| Texas | 3 million | Nevada | 202% |
| Florida | 3 million | Arkansas | 196% |
| Illinois | 2 million | Utah | 171% |

Source: U.S. Census Bureau, Census 2000.

# A Racialist's Census (2000)

## Stephan Thernstrom

*In the 2000 census, for the first time, Americans could identify themselves as belonging to more than one race. This change, while significant, was not the first time census racial categories had shifted: In the early part of the twentieth century, Americans were asked to select simply between "white" and "Negro and other races."*

*Much of the impetus for the 2000 census multiracial category came from the parents of multirace children. It is hard to chart the growth in the number of multiracial children in the United States, because the census did not gather that data. But fewer than half a million American children lived in "mixed-race" families in 1970. By 1990 almost two million (or about 4 percent of America's children) had parents drawn `from different racial groups. Many of these parents did not want their children counted as belonging to only one race.*

*New understandings of "race" supported this change, as well. As Stephan Thernstrom notes below, the nineteenth-century notion that humans are divided into distinct biological races has been thoroughly discredited, and the single-race designations seemed uncomfortably reminiscent of the old Jim Crow "one-drop-of-blood" definition of race.*

*What seems a reasonable response to changing demographic realities and social understandings, however, became quite controversial. Census data is not gathered only to provide a portrait of the nation; it is meant as hard data for government policy and planning. Many who were concerned with questions of social justice and economic equality feared that the new census categories would undercount America's racial minorities and thus lessen their political power. Caught in a bind, the Clinton administration created a compromise.*

*In the following article from the conservative* National Review, *historian and social commentator Stephan Thernstrom compares the attempts of civil rights organizations to maintain single-race categories to the Jim Crow laws of the early twentieth century. Thernstrom's argument is in part, a brief against affirmative action. But he raises some difficult questions about the meanings and uses of racial categories in the contemporary United States. How should one's race be determined? Is identity a matter of blood? Of culture? Will racial categories become more or less important in the future? Should we give up on the notion of race altogether and substitute "ethnicity" instead? What are the implications of Thernstrom's argument for government policies?*

"The United States is the only country in the world in which a white woman can give birth to a black baby but a black woman cannot give birth to a white baby." Not long ago, when the civil rights movement was unquestionably on the side of the angels, liberals were fond of pointing that out, with a mixture of dismay and smugness. How stupid! they said. You were deemed black if either of your parents was black. Indeed, you were deemed black even if your only black ancestor was one great-grandparent—the infamous "drop" rule made it so.

That rule was essential to the either-or logic of the Jim Crow system, in which being only part-black was as inconceivable as being part-pregnant. Nor was there room for people with other racial identities; those who were not white were thrown into the category of— as the Census Bureau traditionally termed it—"Negroes and other races." Under this system, if you recognized the remarkably mixed ancestry of a Tiger Woods, what public school would you assign him to? Where would you have him sit on the bus? Jim Crow is now dead, but its legacy lives on in current racial-classification practices. Ironically, though, it is now those on the left, who are pleased to call themselves liberals, who insist that we all belong in rigid, mutually exclusive, color-coded compartments. Their views, alas, are reflected in the decisions made recently about the Census of 2000, now in mailboxes throughout the country.

In the past, the Census Bureau was not totally oblivious to the reality of the American marital melting pot. To the question about "ancestry or ethnic origin" that appeared in both the 1980 and 1990 Censuses, it was allowable to give as many as three answers. You could report your ancestry as German, Italian, and Irish, or as Polish, Greek, and Swedish. But when it came to identifying yourself racially, no such latitude was given. The "races" of the United States were assumed to be mutually exclusive categories, and you could name only one.

This rigid rule came under growing criticism in the 1990s because of the spectacular surge in intermarriage between Americans of different "races." In some Asian groups—not so long ago categorized as "Orientals" and forbidden to marry non-Asians in some states—a majority of current marriages are to non-Asians, mostly whites. Fully half of all American Indians today are married to non-Indians. Even black/white intermarriages, once illegal in all southern states and taboo in all but the most cosmopolitan communities, are by now far from uncommon. More than one in eight African Americans who married in 1994 had white spouses, and that figure is doubtless higher by now. The rapid growth in the number of children born of racially mixed unions, and the resentment of their parents at being forced to put the child in just one racial box, forced the planners of the 2000 Census to recognize the new reality. It would now be possible, they announced, for racially mixed Americans to identify with more than one racial group when they fill out their forms.

In the infighting that led up to the decision, the battle to preserve the old, mutually exclusive conception of race was led, not by white dinosaurs, but by the major civil rights organizations. If a significant proportion of African Americans reported themselves as partly white, they worried, it could mean fewer affirmative action slots at colleges and universities, fewer jobs for black applicants, a smaller share of public contracts set aside for black-owned businesses, fewer safe black seats on city councils, in state legislatures, and in Congress. All of these programs take proportional representation as the goal, so a decline in the total numbers of a minority group means a reduced entitlement.

In a 1995 Vanderbilt Law Review article, an African American attorney pursued the implications of the new "civil rights" position on this issue to its appalling but logical conclusion. Since race was now being used to award societal benefits, and properly so, he argued, it was necessary to devise new legal tools to prevent "racial fraud." Whites would have a much better chance of getting into the school of their choice or of finding a desirable job if they claimed they were black. To prevent that, the author called for a stricter racial-classification system for all Americans, with "fines and immediate job or benefit termination" for those who "falsified their racial identity." What was needed was a new body of law that recognized the "permanent importance" of racial divisions.

Of course, many of our states had such laws before: these laws were essential to the Jim Crow system. For example, a 1924 Virginia statute required statewide racial registration and provided a year in jail as the penalty for making a "false" report of one's racial identity. Obviously, this was designed to discourage blacks from attempting to "pass" as white. One of the arguments advanced by the plaintiffs in *Plessy v. Ferguson* was that Homer Plessy was entitled to sit in the "white" railroad car because he was white, being only one-eighth black. But the Supreme Court was not impressed, declaring that it was up to the state of Louisiana to decide "the proportion of colored blood necessary to constitute a colored person." To be one-eighth black in Louisiana was to be black—that was that. It is breathtaking to find old ideas about "blood" now resuscitated in a respectable law review, and by an African American scholar. The fear now is that whites will try to "pass" as black. We have come a long, long way from the days of the *Brown* litigation, when Thurgood Marshall insisted that "classifications and distinctions based upon race or color have no moral or legal validity in our society."

Fortunately, the attempts of the civil rights organization to preserve "racial purity" were unsuccessful. The Census Bureau agreed to modify the instructions that accompanied the race question on the 2000 Census, and to indicate that it was possible to choose two or even more racial identities. Homer Plessy could say that he was both white and black, if he chose. Racially mixed Americans would be counted as they wished to be counted.

"Counted" in the simple sense that they may record their perceptions of their own racial identity. But what they report themselves to be, it has now become clear, will be of no practical import. The Office of Management and Budget has just issued guidelines governing how all federal agencies are to employ the racial and ethnic data gathered on the 2000 Census. Those guidelines reveal that the civil rights lobby lost the battle but won the war. When it comes to figuring out the racial composition of the population for purposes of "civil rights monitoring and enforcement" (i.e., to set quotas, goals, or targets in education, employment, and public contracting, and to determine whether racial minorities can claim that their right to political representation has been "diluted"), the complex identifications of racially mixed Americans will be ignored.

Though the Bureau will not tabulate data for every possible racial combination, it will keep track of a mind-boggling 63, so that we will have figures, for example, on the number of people who consider themselves part-white, part-black, and part-American Indian. But when the figures are to be used to determine whether civil rights laws have been violated, these distinctions will disappear. Citizens who say they are not only white but also a member of a "minority race" will be counted as belonging to the "minority race"—period. In other words, for these purposes, it is still the case that "a white woman can give birth to a black baby but a black woman cannot give birth to a white baby." If you have enough black or Asian "blood" to mention it on the census form at all, you will be put in the black or Asian column that the Equal Employment Opportunity Commission and similar agencies will be using to decide whether some company has "enough" employees of the right kind.

This decision means that civil rights groups need not fear that the number of their constituents will be reduced. Indeed, they will grow, if Americans of mixed race who reported themselves simply as white on past censuses now choose to mention that they have black ancestry as well. That mention will land them in the black column.

The most dramatic, indeed bizarre, effect will be on the enumeration of the American Indian population. A mere 2.1 million people checked the "American Indian, Eskimo, Aleut" box on the 1990 Census race question. That is the figure everyone uses for the Indian population in that year. But the separate question about "ancestry or ethnic origin" on the same Census, on which multiple choices were possible, yielded a staggering 8.7 million people who claimed to have some Indian ancestors. If all of the additional 6.6 million identify themselves as both Indian and something else on the 2000 Census race question, now that multiple race choices are possible, the Indian-population figures used for purposes of civil rights enforcement will suddenly quadruple. And most of these born-again Indians will be thoroughly assimilated Americans who have no contact or cultural connection to any Indian tribe today; but they will now count as if they had never left the reservation.

Some of us hoped that making it possible to give multiple answers to the race question would reveal a picture of such intricate complexity that it would call into question the very effort to divide us all into racial boxes. Sadly, our federal government today is attempting to prevent this fate, by retabulating the raw information in a manner that seems designed to ensure the "permanent importance"—as that Vanderbilt Law Review contributor put it—of race.

Deplorable though this is, it is too simple to say flatly that we should stop gathering any information at all about the racial and ethnic composition of the U.S. population. I have been strongly tempted to take the abolitionist position on this issue, and I respect Ward Connerly and others who do. I'm certainly disgusted to see that Americans who have been sent the Census short form—and they are five out of six of us—are asked to provide virtually no information except what racial box they belong in. Nevertheless, I have regretfully concluded that it is impractical and unwise to go to the extreme that many of my comrades in the anti-preference camp advocate.

Why? As early as the middle of the 19th century, the United States made its decennial census into something more than a simple head count of the population. The 1850 Census was the first to inquire into such matters as who had been born abroad and in what country, the occupations Americans were engaged in, and the school attendance of their children. Subsequent enumerations added questions about income and unemployment, housing, modes of travel to work, and dozens of other topics. All modern societies have felt compelled to compile such information, not least because businesses find such information extremely useful. The libertarian view that none of these matters is a proper concern of government is hopelessly utopian.

Even if all racial and ethnic questions were removed from the census, surely we would continue to hear complaints that blacks are far more likely than other Americans to live in poverty. Indeed, in the absence of authoritative data, the magnitude of such social problems would likely be even more exaggerated. Even with official statistics, a recent Gallup poll found that the American public thought that 32 percent of the population was black and 21 percent Hispanic (more than double the actual figures). Furthermore, it is only by gathering the facts that we are able to discern the close connection between black poverty, the remarkably high proportion of female-headed black families, and the huge racial gap in levels of literacy and numeracy. Surely we want to know if black third graders are far behind whites in reading and math competence, and the correlation between that difference and family structure or economic circumstances. It is at least possible that social-science knowledge will guide us toward solutions.

The problem, then, is not with the gathering of social and economic facts. The problem is what might be termed the "the privileging of race." The idea that mankind is divided into a very few, physically and cultural distinctive, racial groups is a thoroughly outmoded and discredited 19th-century notion. In setting out the officially recognized racial categories, the Office of Management and Budget cautions that "these classifications should not be interpreted as being scientific or anthropological in nature." That's for sure—but this admission only makes OMB's decision to use them more dubious. If these categories are not "scientific" or "anthropological," what are they? Why should the U.S. government distinguish some citizens from others on a basis that is not "scientific" or even "anthropological" (whatever that means) and use these distinctions in allocating public resources? "Race" is a bad idea whose time has come and gone. It does not belong in statistics that appear with the stamp of approval of the government of the United States.

Ethnicity (as distinct from crude, unidimensional race categories), however, is another matter. We cannot pretend that African Americans are not a distinctive group with an uniquely oppressive history they are still struggling to overcome, nor that Chinese Americans or Ukrainian Americans are like everyone else in every way. But we need not assume that Americans of Chinese origins are a separate "race," while classifying Ukrainians as "white." The census question on "ancestry or ethnic origin" is quite sufficient to identify subgroups of the population, and it will do the job nicely—with one important modification.

In the past, the Census Bureau has framed the instructions on the ancestry question in a manner that discourages the response "American." Despite that discouragement, 13 million people—5 percent of the population—said that their ancestry was "American" or "United States" on the 1990 Census, and another 27 million—11 percent of the population—said that they were unable or unwilling to specify any ancestry. If it were made clear that "American" is a perfectly acceptable response, those numbers might soar. And that would not be a bad thing at all.

# Why We Must Promote Proper Science in Science Classes (2005)

*Robert George Sprackland*

*For decades, when American historians taught about the Scopes trial of 1925, in which teacher John Scopes was convicted of breaking a Tennessee law that prohibited teaching the theory of evolution in public school classrooms, they often described this trial as the last gasp of (Christian) religious fundamentalism in the United States. Historians were wrong about the fate of Christian fundamentalism; while survey results vary (as do definitions of fundamentalism), up to 30 percent of Americans describe themselves as religious "fundamentalists." And questions about the role of religious beliefs in the science classroom are far from settled in the United States.*

*At stake is the question of whether the First Amendment to the U.S. Constitution allows states to ban the teaching of evolution because it is perceived to contradict religious beliefs about the creation of the universe. While most opponents initially proposed teaching the biblical version of creation along with—or instead of—the theory of evolution, more recent challenges have rested on the concept of "intelligent design." Proponents of intelligent design believe that features of the universe as a whole and of living things within it can only be explained by an "intelligent cause" and not by an "undirected process such as natural selection." Though the intelligent cause is not specified, many of those who believe in creationism find this explanation in congruence with their beliefs.*

*In state and local school boards across the nation, Americans are struggling over this issue. In 2005 U.S. District Court judge John E. Jones decided that the ruling of a local school board in Dover, Pennsylvania, that science teachers read a statement about intelligent design before discussing evolutionary theory in high school biology classes was unconstitutional. Jones concluded, following a six-week trial, that intelligent design is not a scientific theory, but a religious belief and thus cannot be taught, constitutionally, in public school classrooms.*

*In the following document, taken from the* American School Board Journal, *evolutionary zoologist Robert George Sprackland makes his case for the importance of teaching science in science classes.*

Ensuring that only science is taught in science courses is not a trivial matter. Science is an essential component of modern experience, and students who fail to understand it will find fewer job possibilities. Science provides the entry to technology and underlies ecology, medicine, and many other critical disciplines. In the 21st century, our nation depends more than ever on an educated populace that should be at the forefront of intellectual accomplishment. To achieve this, we must ensure that students learn about science in science classes.

When societies have perverted and redefined science, the result has been tragedy. "In Nazi Germany, relativity was considered 'Jewish science' and therefore unacceptable, while in the Soviet Union, modern genetics was rejected as un-Marxist in favor of the ravings of the chairman Lysenko," wrote anatomist Ejnar Fjerdingstad in July in *Science.* The Nazis also misinterpreted the science of genetics in their eugenics movement, while China's Chairman Mao ran the nation's agricultural practices with his own "science." More Soviet and Chinese citizens were to die of starvation from this disregard for science than from combat during the Second World War. Those who mold science to political, religious, or philosophical aims do so at great peril to the rest of us.

If the ID/creation movement comes to your district, you may use these valid reasons why the subject should not be taught in a science class:

- ID/creationism is not science. It is not derived from scientific methods, cannot be tested, and does not allow for its source material (Genesis) to be corrected in the presence of facts.
- There is no "debate" about the validity of evolution. Scientists consider evolution as fact and the explanation of how it occurs as theory, which in science means a well-supported body of ideas and explanations. The only debates about evolution in the scientific community deal with specifics of how evolution occurs.
- ID criticizes biology but offers no new scientific model to replace Darwinism. Having no scientific alternative theory disqualifies ID from being a science.

- Science is an intellectual activity that requires questioning, testing, and revising ideas in the face of new evidence; ID is dogmatic, untestable, and a first step toward converting the entire science curriculum into religious instruction. (Remember that fundamentalists find unacceptable several other topics, including the Big Bang, the age of the earth, dinosaurs existing long before humans, germs as causes of disease, and quantum mechanics, among others, affecting the sciences of cosmology, geology, paleontology, medicine, and physics.)

Schools have neither the obligation nor the time to discuss creation stories in a science class. There are too many creation stories, and none is scientific. Discussion of these stories would be appropriate in a comparative religion or philosophy class, but not in a science class.

Science gives us great and important insights into the nature of our past and present and helps us forge into the future. It can only do that if science is allowed to be science, whether or not we like what reality may show us. Educators and scientists may not be able to convince those whose agenda is as political as it is religious. But if we fail, there are many other nations ready and willing to assume our position as world leader in science innovation and application.

# Great Expectations (2004)

## Stephanie Coontz

*Much analysis of the 2004 presidential election focused on the role "values" voters played in distinguishing the "red" states whose electoral votes went to George Bush from the "blue" states whose votes went to John Kerry. Those who paid strict attention to the ways polls were conducted argued that the role of "values-motivated" voters was exaggerated, while Democrats asked why some strong beliefs (antiabortion, for example, or anti-same-sex marriage) were defined as moral values while others (alleviating poverty, for example) were not. Nonetheless, this discussion highlighted the ways in which concerns about "values" are often expressed as concerns about the shape of the nation's families.*

*The American family, statistically speaking, has changed dramatically over the past twenty-five years. The divorce rate has fallen since its height in the late twentieth century, but approximately two-fifths of first marriages end in divorce or separation within fifteen years. Nuclear families make up a falling percentage of American households—down from 39 percent in 1970 to 24 percent in 2000. The number of mother-only households rose 25 percent in the last decade of the twentieth century to 7 percent of all families, while the number of father-only households jumped 62 percent—though that number represents a bit less than 2 percent of all families. The number of unmarried partners living together grew 71 percent in the 1990s; that number includes same-sex couples, many of whom have actively sought the right to marry or form legal partnerships that carry the same legal rights as marriage. It is politically interesting that the state with the lowest divorce rate is Massachusetts, one of the "bluest" states, while the southern states that voted solidly Republican have divorce rates roughly 50 percent higher than the national average.*

*In the following editorial, which draws on the argument she makes in* Marriage, A History, *historian Stephanie Coontz examines the changing role of marriage in American society. What implications does her argument have for those who are concerned about the changing shape of the American family?*

*How might such an understanding affect the policy initiatives constructed by both conservative and liberal interest groups or politicians?*

The problem with modern marriage, according to conventional wisdom, is that today's couples don't make marriage their top priority and put their relationship above all else. As one of my students once wrote, "People nowadays don't respect the marriage vowels." Perhaps she meant IOU.

But my research on the history of marriage convinces me that people now place a higher value on marriage than ever before in history. In fact, that's a big part of the problem.

One reason marriage is fragile today is that we expect so much more of it than we used to, and many of our expectations are contradictory.

Most people recognize that marriage takes sacrifice, hard work and the ability to put up with the bad in your partner as well as the good.

But they also expect marriage to be the ultimate source of their happiness and the most fulfilling, passionate relationship in their lives.

When Arkansas Gov. Mike Huckabee "upgraded" his marriage vows on Valentine's Day before an audience of 5,000 enthusiastic marriage advocates, a banner reading "Passion Transformation Intimacy Oneness Covenant" summed up their case for marriage.

Unfortunately, people who expect to find passion, transformation, intimacy and oneness in their marriages often end up disappointed in their covenant, and the higher their expectations, the greater their disappointment.

Europeans and Americans used to view marriage as a work relationship in which passion took second place to practicality and intimacy never interfered with male authority. As that view of marriage has changed over the past 100 years, the divorce rate has risen steadily.

For most of history, people had modest expectations of marital happiness. The upper classes of Europe in the Middle Ages, who arranged their marriages for political and economic gain, believed that true love and passion could only exist outside marriage, in an adulterous affair.

In the 18th and 19th centuries, conventional wisdom among middle-class men was that the kind of woman you'd want for a wife was incapable of sexual passion. One marital advice expert even wrote that frigidity was a virtue to be cultivated in women. When wives wrote about their husbands in diaries, they were much less likely to describe intimate conversations than to record persistent feeling of loneliness. A successful marriage was more often based on resigned acceptance than on transformation.

In the early 20th century, people came to expect marriage to be based on love, sexual attraction and personal fulfillment. But women often settled for less because of their economic dependence on men.

As late as the 1960s, polls found that nearly three-fourths of college women said they would marry a man they didn't love if he met their other criteria. In the 1970s, the working-class women interviewed by psychologist Lillian Rubin defined a good husband in terms that had little to do with intimacy or passion. "He's a steady worker; he doesn't drink; he doesn't hit me. That's a lot more than my mother had."

Today, by contrast, the desire for a "soul mate" is nearly universal. Eighty percent of women say it's more important to have a husband they can confide in than one who earns a good living. And more than two-thirds of men say they want a more rounded relationship with their wife than their father had with their mother, one marked by passion, intellectual equality, intimacy and shared interests.

Recognizing the potential for disillusion in such high hopes, some people counsel couples to tamp down their expectations of personal fulfillment and happiness. Certainly, anyone who expects each day with his or her spouse to be filled with passion, joy and transcendent oneness will be disappointed a lot of the time.

But having spent many years researching the low-expectation marriages of the past, I don't think high expectations are such a bad thing. True, they raise the risk of disappointment and disillusionment when one or both partners refuse to work on problems in the relationship. But they also motivate many people to put more energy into their relationships than couples did in centuries past.

When a marriage works well today, it works better than anyone in the past ever dared to dream. When it doesn't work well, people have more options to leave. And when people have doubts about their future, they have the option not to marry at all.

We may not always approve of the choices that people make and the relations they aspire to. But in marriage, as in politics, that is the price of democracy. People have the right to change their minds. We cannot foreclose people's choices and tamp down their aspirations without losing most of the things that make modern marriage so rewarding.

# Red or Blue—Which Are You?

## (2004)

*Anne E. Kornblut*

*The terms* red states *and* blue states *became shorthand for the differences among American regions during the presidential election of 2004. Journalist Anne Kornblut created this humorous quiz for the on-line* Slate *magazine in the summer of 2004 to allow readers to determine their own red/blue identity. Scoring information follows the quiz: answers give you either "red points" or "blue points," and the ratio of your red and blue scores determines where you fall on the political and cultural range of "red" to "blue."*

Red and blue are states of mind, not actual states. Red and blue aren't absolute predictors of political leanings, either. There are plenty of blue cities in red states, red enclaves in blue states, red-leaning governors of blue states, people who vote Republican but are of a blue state of mind, and so on. It's not as simple as liberal vs. conservative, elite vs. populist, urban vs. rural, religious vs. nonreligious, educated vs. uneducated, rich vs. poor—if it were, the terms "red" and "blue" wouldn't have taken off as the best shorthand for a divided America.

Instead, it's an amorphous condition. To some extent, people are red and blue by choice and by self-definition. (GWB comes to mind.) But the background noise where you live plays a big role—the local news, what your neighbors talk about, how you get from one place to another, the kinds of culinary and artistic options available, what I like to think of as the "cultural soundtrack" that you can hum automatically because it's always on. If you're a blue-stater, you might happen to have learned how often Rush Limbaugh is on the air, but if you're a red-stater, chances are you know it off the top of your head.

Originally published in *Slate*, 14 July 2004. Reprinted with permission of author.

That instinctual knowledge is what this quiz intends to judge, not how smart you are about the other side. And there are many people who are purple—neither red nor blue, or both red and blue.

Put another way—Bush once said: "To you, it's sushi. To me, it's bait."

And to some people, it's just raw fish.

1. Is Lee Greenwood
   a. a celebrity chef
   b. a singer/songwriter
   c. the head of the Office of Management and Budget
   d. an evangelical preacher

2. The LIRR is the
   a. group that tracks right-wing and religious bias on TV
   b. fan club honoring Ronald Reagan
   c. magazine run by former *New York Times* restaurant critic Ruth Reichl
   d. railroad connecting Manhattan and Long Island

3. Dog owners: Do you pay someone else to walk your dog while you're at work during the week?
   a. yes
   b. no
   c. sometimes
   d. don't have a dog/not applicable

4. Which one of these is NOT part of the Big 12?
   a. Indiana State University
   b. Iowa State University
   c. Texas A&M
   d. Texas Tech

5. Jon Stewart is
   a. an editorial cartoonist
   b. the secretary of education
   c. a comedian
   d. a morning deejay

6. What does a bumper sticker or tattoo of a winged No. 3 represent?
   a. Dale Earnhardt
   b. Dale Earnhardt Jr.

    c. Richard Petty
    d. Tom Petty

7. Who sings the 1999 hit country single "How Do You Like Me Now?"
    a. The Dixie Chicks
    b. Toby Keith
    c. Lee Ann Womack
    d. Josh Bolten

8. In the aftermath of Sept. 11, it was appropriate to wear an American flag pin for how long?
    a. three to six months
    b. until the first anniversary of the attacks
    c. forever after
    d. not at all

9. Which are the Quad Cities?
    a. Peoria, Akron, Duluth, and Sioux City
    b. Rock Island, Moline, Davenport, and Bettendorf
    c. Dubuque, Galena, Prairie du Chien, and Spring Valley
    d. Ann Arbor, Detroit, Cleveland, and Toledo

10. Women should wear white pantyhose
    a. only with white or pastel business suits
    b. only between Memorial Day and Labor Day
    c. to weddings
    d. never

11. "Whole Foods" refers to
    a. the raw-food movement
    b. the trend of not cutting or dicing vegetables
    c. an upscale grocery chain known for organic products
    d. the famed vegan restaurant in Aspen

12. Do you eat
    a. lunch and dinner
    b. dinner and supper
    c. lunch and supper
    d. lunch and tea

13. Do you eat brisket with
    a. barbecue sauce
    b. carrots and pearl onions

    c. slices of white bread

    d. horseradish aioli

14. What does "the UP" refer to?

    a. Universal Press Syndicate

    b. the Upper Peninsula of Michigan

    c. slang for the direction toward the sky

    d. someone who is honest

15. Jed Bartlet is the name of

    a. President Bush's communications director

    b. the character Martin Sheen plays on *The West Wing* on NBC

    c. the character Nathan Lane plays in *Merry, Married, and Gay* on Broadway

    d. the editorial page editor of the *New York Times*

16. When you run most of your basic errands groceries, dry cleaning, drugstore, etc.) on weekends, do you

    a. walk

    b. drive and pay for parking

    c. drive and park for free

    d. take a taxi or public transportation

17. What does the Eighth Commandment prohibit?

    a. stealing

    b. coveting your neighbor's wife

    c. avarice

    d. committing adultery

18. What does Door County refer to?

    a. where Jim Morrison was born

    b. where Mackinac Island is

    c. a vacation destination in Wisconsin

    d. a discount furniture hub in North Carolina

19. The most appropriate earrings for a professional woman to wear to a job interview are

    a. pearl studs

    b. hoops

    c. anything

    d. none at all

20. Sam's Club is a subsidiary of which company?
    a. Kmart
    b. Sam Houston and Sons
    c. Sanford and Son
    d. Wal-Mart

21. Who is said to have written the Book of Revelation?
    a. Matthew
    b. Martin
    c. Joseph
    d. John

22. Larry Kramer is
    a. the gangly character on *Seinfeld*
    b. a film director
    c. the AIDS activist/writer
    d. the founder of Starbucks

23. Jim Caviezel is
    a. the former finalist on *American Idol*
    b. creator/producer of *The Sopranos* on HBO
    c. the actor who played Jesus in *The Passion of the Christ*
    d. the weekend host of *Fox and Friends*

24. Rush Limbaugh is on the air for
    a. two hours daily on weekdays
    b. three hours daily on weekdays
    c. two hours three times a week
    d. three hours two times a week

25. What is Avenue Q?
    a. the last stop on the New York City subway's No. 2 line
    b. a Broadway musical
    c. a famous gay/lesbian club in Philadelphia
    d. the nickname for the generation after Generation X

26. Jim Jarmusch is
    a. the former Kerry campaign manager
    b. a film director
    c. host of *Queer Eye for the Straight Guy*
    d. weekend anchor of NPR's *All Things Considered*

27. Who is Dr. Laura Schlessinger?
    a. activist wife of the famous historian
    b. political pundit made famous during the Clinton impeachment
    c. prominent actress *The Mothman Prophecies, Love Actually*)
    d. host of a morality-based call-in talk show

28. How close are you to the nearest Wal-Mart Supercenter NOT the regular Wal-Mart)?
    a. within a mile or so
    b. 2–30 miles
    c. more than 30 miles
    d. it's called Super Wal-Mart, not Wal-Mart Supercenter

29. The difference between a condo and a co-op apartment is:
    a. a condo is bigger
    b. "co-op" is the term for units in buildings built before World War II
    c. condo owners possess each individual unit; in co-ops, you own a share
    d. nothing; they are interchangeable

30. Have you ever eaten at the Ivy, either location?
    a. yes
    b. no
    c. don't know/never heard of it

31. Have you ever been to Branson, Mo., on vacation?
    a. yes
    b. no

32. Have you ever fired a gun?
    a. yes
    b. no

33. Have you ever lived for a length of time, post-college, without access to a car or other vehicle—i.e., relying solely on walking and public transportation to get to work?
    a. yes
    b. no

34. Would you purchase *Angels in America* for your home video collection?
    a. yes
    b. no
    c. never seen it/don't know

35. Would you purchase *We Were Soldiers Once ... and Young* for your home video collection?
    a. yes
    b. no
    c. never seen it/don't know

36. Would you purchase *Annie Hall* for your home video collection?
    a. yes
    b. no
    c. never seen it/don't know

37. Would you purchase *True Grit* for your home video collection?
    a. yes
    b. no
    c. never seen it/don't know

How the test is scored:

Each answer is assigned a 5- or 10-point value. Some answers score red points; some score blue.

The ratio of your red and blue scores determines where you fall on the red/blue scale.

1. A (+10 blue); B (+5 red); C (+10 blue); D (+10 blue)
2. A (+10 red); B (+10 red); C (+10 red); D (+10 blue)
3. A (+5 blue); B (+5 red); C (0); D (0)
4. A (+5 red); B (+5 blue); C (+5 blue); D (+5 blue)
5. A (+10 red); B (+10 red); C (+5 blue); D (+10 red)
6. A (+10 red); B (+5 red); C (0); D (+10 blue)
7. A (+5 blue); B (+10 red); C (+5 blue); D (+10 blue)
8. A (0); B (+5 red); C (+10 red); D (+10 blue)
9. A (+10 blue); B (+5 red); C (0); D (+10 blue)
10. A (+5 red); B (+5 red); C (0); D (+5 blue)
11. A (+5 red); B (+10 red); C (+5 blue); D (+5 red)
12. A (0); B (+5 red); C (0); D (+5 blue)

13. A (+5 red); B (+5 blue); C (+10 red); D (+10 blue)
14. A (+5 blue); B (+5 red); C (0); D (0)
15. A (+5 red); B (+5 blue); C (+10 red); D (+5 red)
16. A (+10 blue); B (+5 blue); C (+5 red); D (+10 blue)
17. A (+10 red); B (0); C (+10 blue); D (0)
18. A (+5 blue); B (0); C (+5 red); D (+5 blue)
19. A (+5 red); B (0); C (+5 blue); D (+5 blue)
20. A (0); b (+10 blue); C (+10 blue); D (+10 red)
21. A (0); B (+10 blue); C (+10 blue); D (+10 red)
22. A (+5 red); B (+5 red); C (+10 blue); D (+10 red)
23. A (+5 blue); B (+5 blue); C (+10 red); D (+10 blue)
24. A (+10 blue); B (+10 red); C (+10 blue); D (+10 blue)
25. A (+10 red); B (+10 blue); C (+10 red); D (+10 red)
26. A (0); B (+10 blue); C (+10 red); D (+10 red)
27. A (+10 blue); B (+10 blue); C (+10 blue); D (+10 red)
28. A (+10 red); B (+10 red); C (+5 blue); D (+10 blue)
29. A (+10 red); B (+10 red); C (+5 blue); D (+5 blue)
30. A (+5 blue); B (0); C (+10 red)
31. A (+5 red); B (0)
32. A (+5 red); B (0)
33. A (+5 blue); B (0)
34. A (+10 blue); B (0); C (0)
35. A (+5 red); B (+5 blue); C (0)
36. A (+5 blue); B (+5 red); C (0)
37. A (+10 red); B (0); C (0)

# The American People in the Early Twenty-first Century

*On the pages that follow are statistics about the American people and their culture—from how many miles Americans travel on the nation's highways each year to their favorite baby names to the median cost of a single-family house. All the information is in aggregate—statistical averages or medians—so it does not capture the full diversity of American experiences. Yet, at the end of a course on contemporary America, this information offers one way to take stock of the ways in which historical trends have shaped American society and the lives of the American people.*

- Population, January 31, 2006 (estimate): 298,008,172
- Population, February 2, 2006 (estimate): 298,025,216

- Frequency of births: one every 8 seconds
- Frequency of deaths: one every 12 seconds
- Frequency of immigration: one person (net gain) every 28 seconds
- Rate of population increase: one person every 28 seconds

- Fastest growing state: Nevada (for past 19 consecutive years)
- Number of 10 fastest growing U.S. counties (2000–2005) that are in Georgia: 4
- Most populous state: California
- Least populous state: Wyoming

- Percentage of U.S. citizens age 25 and older with high school degree: 83.9
- Percentage of U.S. citizens age 25 and older with Bachelor's degree or higher: 27%

- State with highest percentage of Bachelor's degrees: Massachusetts (33.2%)
- State with lowest percentage of Bachelor's degrees: West Virginia (14.8%)
- U.S. literacy rate (percentage people age 15 or older who can read and write): 97%

- Median age (total population): 36.27 years
- Median age (female): 37.6 years
- Median age (male): 34.94
- Sex ratio (age 16–64), male to female: 1 to 1
- Sex ratio (age 65 and above), male to female: .72 to 1
- State with highest percentage of population age 65 and over: Florida (17.6%)
- State with highest percentage of population under age 5: Utah (9.4%)

- Percentage of 26-year-olds living with parents, 1970: 11
- Percentage of 26-year-olds living with parents, 2006: 20

- Real median household income (2004): $44,389
- Median cost of single-family house (2005): $213,900
- Home ownership, by race/ethnicity: White (non-Hispanic) 76%; Black 49.1%; Hispanic 48.1%; Asian 59.8%
- Poverty rate (2004): 12.7%
- Percentage of population without health insurance (2004): 15.7%

- Median age at first marriage for men: 1960, 22.8; 1980, 24.7; 2000, 26.8
- Median age at first marriage for women: 1960, 20.3; 1980, 22; 2000, 25.1
- Interracial marriages, as percent of married couples: 1960, .36; 1980, 1.3; 2000, 2.5

- Divorce rate (per 1000 population): 1960, 2.2; 1980, 5.2; 2000, 4.1; 2004, 3.7
- Birth rate (per 1000 population): 1940, 19.4; 1960, 23.1; 1980, 15.9; 2000, 14.4
- Infant mortality rate in U.S. (per 1000 live births): 6.5
- Infant mortality rate in Sweden: 2.8
- Infant mortality rate in Angola: 191.2

| Most Popular Baby Names | | |
|---|---|---|
| **1960** | **1986** | **2004** |
| David and Mary | Michael and Jessica | Jacob and Emily |
| Michael and Susan | Christopher and Ashley | Michael and Emma |
| James and Linda | Matthew and Amanda | Joshua and Madison |
| John and Karen | Joshua and Jennifer | Matthew and Olivia |
| Robert and Donna | David and Sarah | Ethan and Hannah |

- Racial/Ethnic composition of U.S. population (2005): White (non-Hispanic) 69%; Hispanic 14.1%; Black 12.9%; Asian 4.2%; American Indian 1.4%; Native Hawaiian/Pacific Islander .2%

- Religious affiliations of Americans (2002): Protestant 52%; Roman Catholic 24%; Church of Latter Day Saints 2%; Jewish 1%; Muslim 1%; Other 10%; None 10%

- Percentage of driving-age population with licenses: 1950, 57; 2000, 88
- Number of people 70 years or older with driver's licenses: 1970, 8.8 million; 2000, 18.9 million
- Average age of automobiles in use: 1970, 5.6 years; 2000, 9.0 years
- Average miles per gallon for automobiles: 1970, 12.0; 2000, 16.9
- Annual miles traveled on U.S. highways: 1960, .69 trillion vehicle miles; 2000, 2.7 trillion

- Percentage of Americans who are obese, according to National Center for Health Statistics: 1960, 13; 2000, 31

- Number of iPods sold, by mid-2005: 22 million
- American adults who have never used internet (2005): 1 in 5
- Percentage of home internet uses with broadband connection: 53
- Percentage of teens (12–17) who use internet (2006): 87

| Most Frequent Google Searches | |
| --- | --- |
| **2004** | **2005** |
| Britney Spears | Janet Jackson |
| Paris Hilton | Hurricane Katrina |
| Christina Aguilera | tsunami |
| Pamela Anderson | xbox 360 |
| chat | Brad Pitt |
| games | Michael Jackson |
| Carmen Electra | American Idol |
| Orlando Bloom | Britney Spears |
| Harry Potter | Angelina Jolie |
| mp3 | Harry Potter |

# Suggestions for Further Reading

Literature on America's becoming a world power continues to expand and deepen. One of the best places to start is with the work of J. L. Gaddis, especially *The United States and the Origins of the Cold War* (1972); *Strategies of Containment* (1982); *The Long Peace* (1987); *Russia, the Soviet Union, and the United States* (2nd ed., 1990); *We Now Know: Rethinking Cold War History* (1997); and *The Cold War: A New History* (2006). For significantly different interpretations, see T. J. McCormick, *America's Half Century: United States Foreign Policy in the Cold War* (1992); W. LaFeber, *America, Russia and the Cold War* (6th ed., 1991); M. Leffler, *A Preponderance of Power* (1992); T. Patterson, *Meeting the Communist Threat: Truman to Reagan* (1988); and *On Every Front: The Making and Unmaking of the Cold War* (1992). See also W. Isaacson and E. Thomas, *The Wise Men: Six Friends and the World They Made* (1986); D.Yergin, *Shattered Peace: The Origins of the Cold War and the National Security State* (1977); and L. Gardner, *Architects of Illusion: Men and Ideas in American Foreign Policy, 1941–1949* (1970). On McCarthyism, see R. Fried, *Nightmare in Red: The McCarthy Era in Perspective* (1990); R. Griffith, *The Politics of Fear* (1970); D. Oshinsky, *A Conspiracy So Immense* (1983); and E. Schrecker, *No Ivory Tower: McCarthyism and the Universities* (1986). For evidence of communist infiltration of the American government, see J. E. Haynes and H. Klehr, *Venona: Decoding Soviet Espionage in America* (1999).

Some of the best works on the economic boom that swept America in the postwar years—and its social consequences—are the classics: J. K. Galbraith, *The Affluent Society* (1958); W. Whyte, *The Organization Man* (1956); C. W. Mills, *The Power Elite* (1956); P. Goodman, *Growing Up Absurd* (1960); D. Riesman et al., *The Lonely Crowd* (1950); and D. Bell, *The End of Ideology* (1950). More recent works include F. Levy, *Dollars and Dreams: The Changing American Income Distribution*

(1987), and D. Vogel, *Fluctuating Fortunes: The Political Power of Business in America* (1989). R. Fox and T. J. Lears, eds., *The Culture of Consumption* (1983), is a collection of trenchant essays, as is L. May, ed., *Recasting America: Culture and Politics in the Age of the Cold War* (1989). J. Patterson, *America's Struggle Against Poverty, 1900–1994* (1995), is an excellent overview of the persistence of poverty in the midst of affluence. See also F. F. Piven and R. Cloward, *Regulating the Poor* (1993), and W. J. Wilson, *The Truly Disadvantaged* (1987). On the domestic ideology of the postwar period, see E. T. May, *Homeward Bound: American Families in the Cold War Era* (1988). On affluent society media, see E. Barnouw, *Tube of Plenty: The Evolution of Modern Television* (1975); R. Sklar, *Prime-Time America: Life On and Behind the Television Screen* (1980); and P. Biskind, *Seeing Is Believing: How Hollywood Taught Us to Stop Worrying and Love the Fifties* (1983).

The literature on the African American freedom struggle is both broad and deep. For a comprehensive overview, see H. Sitkoff, *The Struggle for Black Equality* (1993); R. Wiesbrot, *Freedom Bound* (1991); and S. Lawson, *Running for Freedom* (1994). On the *Brown* decision, see R. Kluger's classic narrative, *Simple Justice* (1974), and J. Patterson's *Brown v. Board of Education* (2001). The life of Martin Luther King, Jr., is brilliantly portrayed in T. Branch's three-volume biography, *America in the King Years* (1988, 1995, 2005), and in D. Garrow's *Bearing the Cross* (1986). C. Payne's *I've Got the Light of Freedom* (1995) tells the story of the movement in Mississippi, as does J. Dittmer, *Local People* (1994). Community studies of the Civil Rights movement have received increasing attention. See W. H. Chafe, *Civilities and Civil Rights: Greensboro, North Carolina and the Black Struggle for Freedom* (1980), and R. Norrell, *Reaping the Whirlwind: The Civil Rights Movement in Tuskegee* (1985). On the role of the church and SCLC, see A. Morris, *The Origins of the Civil Rights Movement* (1984). On SNCC, see C. Carson, *In Struggle: SNCC and the Black Awakening of the 1960s* (1981). T. Tyson's *Radio Free Dixie* (1999) discusses the impact of Robert Williams, an early advocate of Black Power. K. Kruse's *White Flight* (2005), M. Lassiter's *The Silent Majority* (2005), and M. Countryman's *Up South* (2006) represent recent additions to the literature on race. On women in the movement, see M. King, *Freedom Song* (1987); K. Mills, *This Little Light of Mine: The Life of Fannie Lou Hamer* (1993); and B. Ransby, *Ella Baker* (2005). On the Chicano movement, see I. Garcia, *Chicanismo: The Forging of a Militant Ethos Among Mexican-Americans* (1997); R. Acuna, *Occupied America: A History of Chicanos*

(2000); C. Munoz, Youth, *Identity Power: The Chicano Movement* (1989); and B. Marquez, *LULAC* (1993).

An excellent way to begin exploring the women's movement of the 1960s and 1970s is through R. Rosen's *The World Split Open: How the Modern Women's Movement Changed America* (2000). On the origins of this movement, see S. Evan's now-classic *Personal Politics: The Roots of Women's Liberation in the Civil Rights Movement and the New Left* (1978), and D. Horowitz's *Betty Friedan and the Making of the Feminine Mystique: The American Left, the Cold War, and Modern Feminism*. A. Echols, *Daring to Be Bad: Radical Feminism in America, 1965–1975* (1989), and N. Caraway, *Segregated Sisterhood: Racism and the Politics of American Feminism* (1986), examine divisions within the larger movement. See also I. Blea, *La Chicana and the Intersection of Race, Class, and Gender* (1992), and E. DuBois and V. Ruiz, eds., *Unequal Sisters: A Multicultural Reader in Women's History* (1990). A. Kessler-Harris, *In Pursuit of Equity: Women, Men, and the Pursuit of Economic Citizenship in 20th-Century America* (2001), is essential reading. On conservative women, see D. Critchlow, *Phyllis Schlafly and Grassroots Conservatism: A Woman's Crusade* (2005), and L. McGirr, *Suburban Warriors: The Origins of the New American Right* (2001). *Roe v. Wade* is examined in D. Garrow, *Liberty and Sexuality: The Right to Privacy and the Making of Roe v. Wade*. On the sexual revolution, see B. Bailey, *Sex in the Heartland* (1999); J. D'Emilio and E. Freedman, *Intimate Matters: A History of Sexuality in America;* and J. Howard, *Men Like That: A Southern Queer History* (1999). On the gay rights movement, see D. Clendinen and A. Nagourney, *Out for Good: The Struggle to Build a Gay Rights Movement in America* (1999).

The writings on the Vietnam War are voluminous and show no signs of diminishing. The best comprehensive accounts include G. Herring, *America's Longest War: The United States and Vietnam, 1950–1975* (1986); J. Olson and R. Roberts, *Where the Domino Fell: America and Vietnam, 1945–1990* (1996); and M. B. Young, *The Vietnam Wars* (1991). Conflicting explanations of why the United.States became involved in the Vietnam War include L. Gardner, *Pay Any Price: Lyndon Johnson and the Wars for Vietnam* (1995); M. Hunt, *Lyndon Johnson's War: America's Cold War Crusade in Vietnam, 1945–1968* (1996); David Kaiser, *American Tragedy: Kennedy, Johnson, and the Origins of the Vietnam War* (2000); M. Lind, *Vietnam, the Necessary War: A Reinterpretation of America's Most Disastrous Military Conflict* (1999); F. Logevall, *Choosing War: The Lost Chance for Peace and the Escalation of the War in Vietnam*

(1999); and R. McNamara et al., *Argument without End: In Search of Answers to the Vietnam Tragedy* (1999). Opposition to the war is covered in M. S. Foley, *Confronting the War Machine: Draft Resistance during the Vietnam War* (2003); A. Hunt, *The Turning: A History of Vietnam Veterans against the War* (1999); R. Jeffreys-Jones, *Peace Now! American Society and the Ending of the Vietnam War* (1999); M. Small, *AntiWarriors: The Vietnam War and the Battle for America's Hearts and Minds* (2002); and T. Wells, *The War Within: America's Battles over Vietnam* (1994). Also see C. Appy, *Working-Class War: American Combat Soldiers in Vietnam* (1993); K. Beattie, *The Scar That Binds: American Culture and the Vietnam War* (1998); and J. Westheider, *Fighting on Two Fronts: African Americans and the Vietnam War* (1997).

Important overviews of the sixties include D. Farber, *The Age of Great Dreams* (1994), and M. Isserman and M. Kazin, *America Divided: The Civil War of the 1960s* (2000). On "the movement," see A. Bloom and W. Brienes, eds., *Takin' It to the Streets: A Sixties Reader* (1996): T. Anderson, *The Movement and the Sixties* (1995); and D. Rossinow, *The Politics of Authenticity: Liberalism, Christianity, and the New Left in America* (1998). Excellent works on the counterculture include P. Braunstein and M. Doyle, eds., *Imagine Nation: The American Counterculture of the 1960s and '70s* (2001); T. Miller, *The '60s Communes: Hippies and Beyond* (1999); J. Stevens, *Storming Heaven: LSD and the American Dream* (1987); and P. Coyote's memoir, *Sleeping Where I Fall: A Chronicle* (1999). On international aspects of sixties' movements and global politics, see J. Suri, *Power and Protest: Global Revolution and the Rise of Detente* (2003). M. Flam, *Law and Order: Street Crime, Civil Unrest, and the Crisis of Liberalism in the 1960s* (2005) analyzes domestic turmoil and political backlash in the sixties era. Overviews of the 1970s include B. Schulman, *The Seventies: The Great Shift in American Society, Culture, and Politics* (2002); E. Berkowitz, *Something Happened: A Political and Cultural Overview of the Seventies* (2005); and B. Bailey and D. Farber, eds., *The Seventies in America* (2004). On Watergate, see S. Kutler, *The Wars of Watergate: The Last Crisis of the Nixon Presidency* (1990). D. Farber analyzes the Iran hostage crisis in relation to the American 1970s in *Taken Hostage: The Iran Hostage Crisis and America's First Encounter with Radical Islam* (2004).

On conservatism, in addition to the important historical analyses excerpted in this section, see T. Frank, *What's the Matter with Kansas? How Conservatives Won the Heart of America* (2004); M. Jacobs, *Pocketbook Politics: Economic Citizenship in Twentieth-Century America* (2004); and

J. Schoenwald, *A Time for Choosing: The Rise of Modern American Conservatism* (2002). On the Right and American politics, see R. Mason, *Richard Nixon and the Quest for a New Majority* (2004); R. Perlstein, *Before the Storm: Barry Goldwater and the Unmaking of the American Consensus* (2001); and J. Reichley, *Conservatives in an Age of Change: The Nixon and Ford Administrations* (1981). On the South, see P. Applebome, *Dixie Rising: How the South Is Shaping American Values, Politics, and Culture* (1996), and D. Lublin, *The Republican South: Democratization and Partisan Change* (2004). For conservative intellectuals, see J. D. Hoeveler, Jr., *Watch on the Right: Conservative Intellectuals in the Reagan Era* (1991); J. Judis, *William F. Buckley, Jr., Patron Saint of the Conservatives* (1988); and J. E. Moser, *Right Turn: John T. Flynn and the Transformation of American Liberalism* (2005). For the religious Right see S. Bruce, *The Rise and Fall of the New Christian Right: Conservative Protestant Politics in America* (1990); J. D. Hunter, *Culture Wars: The Struggle to Define America* (1991); and W. Martin, *With God on Our Side: The Rise of the Religious Right in America* (1996). For students and conservatism, see J. A. Andrew, *The Other Side of the Sixties: The Young Americans for Freedom and the Rise of Conservative Politics* (1997), and G. Schneider, *Cadres for Conservatism: Young Americans for Freedom and the Rise of the Contemporary Right* (1999). Other studies worth consulting include E. Avila, *Popular Culture in the Age of White Flight: Fear and Fantasy in Suburban Los Angeles* (2005), and J. Zimmerman, *Whose America? Culture Wars in the Public Schools* (2002).

The end of the Cold War and 9/11, much less their aftermaths, are too recent to yet have the kind of analyses and narratives that constitute good history, but it is essential that we begin to understand what happened and why. Important contributions to the "first draft" of this history include M. J. Hogan, ed., *The End of the Cold War: Its Meaning and Implications* (1992); S. Hoffmann, *World Disorders: Troubled Peace in the Post–Cold War Era* (1998); R. Kagan, *Of Paradise and Power: America and Europe in the New World Order* (2003); and C. Prestowitz, *Rogue Nation: American Unilateralism and the Failure of Good Intentions* (2003). The National Commission on Terrorist Attacks Upon the United States, *The 9/11 Commission Report* (2004), is indispensable. So are D. Benjamin and S. Simon, *The Age of Sacred Terror* (2002); R. Clarke, *Against All Enemies: Inside America's War on Terror* (2004); S. Coll, *Ghost Wars: The Secret History of the CIA, Afghanistan, and Bin Laden from the Soviet Invasion to September 10, 2001* (2004); P. Heymann, *Terrorism, Freedom, and Security: Winning without War* (2003); B. Hoffman,

*Inside Terrorism* (1999); and G. Posner, *Why America Slept: The Failure to Prevent 9/11* (2003). On the Middle East and the war in Iraq, see T. S. Purdum, *A Time of Our Choosing: America's War in Iraq* (2004); W. Murray and R. H. Scales, Jr., *The Iraq War: A Military History* (2003); and M. Viorst, *In the Shadow of the Prophet: The Struggle for the Soul of Islam* (2001).

Strong arguments about human impact on the global environment are made by J. R. McNeill, *Something New Under the Sun: An Environmental History of the Twentieth-Century World* (2000), and A. Gore, *An Inconvenient Truth: The Planetary Emergence of Global Warming and What We Can Do About It* (2006). For an overview of American environmental history, see C. Merchant, *The Columbia Guide to American Environmental History* (2002), and H. Rothman, *The Greening of a Nation: Environmentalism in the United States Since 1945* (1998). For discussions of the significance of race in America, see G. Gerstle, *American Crucible: Race and Nation in the Twentieth Century* (2001), and J. Hochschild, *Facing Up to the American Dream: Race, Class, and the Soul of America*. On affirmative action, see T. Anderson, *The Pursuit of Fairness: A History of Affirmative Action* (2004), and H. D. Graham, *Collision Course: The Strange Convergence of Affirmative Action and Immigration Policy in America* (2002). On immigration, G. Gerstle and J. Mollenkopf, eds., *E Pluribus Unum? Contemporary and Historical Perspectives on Immigrant Political Incorporation*, is useful. Specific portraits appear in M. M. Suárez-Orozco and M. M. Páez, eds., *Latinos: Remaking America* (2002); R. Suro, *Strangers Among Us: How Latino Immigration Is Transforming America* (1998); F. H. We, *Yellow: Race in America Beyond Black and White* (2002); and H. Zia, *Asian American Dreams: The Emergence of an American People* (2002). Recent, revealing works on American society and culture include E. Klinenberg, *Heat Wave: A Social Autopsy of Disaster in Chicago* (2002); E. Schlosser, *Fast Food Nation: The Dark Side of the All-American Meal* (2001); and A. Stein, *The Stranger Next Door: The Story of a Small Community's Battle over Sex, Faith, and Civil Rights* (2001).